Hallucination-Aware AI for Truthful and Aligned Systems

Baisakhi Das
https://orcid.org/0000-0002-0702-5855
Institute of Engineering and Management, India

Thinagaran Perumal
https://orcid.org/0000-0003-0698-5413
Universiti Putra Malaysia, Malaysia

Satyajit Chakrabarti
Institute of Engineering and Management, India

Kouichi Sakurai
Kyushu University, Japan

George A. Papakostas
https://orcid.org/0000-0001-5545-1499
Democritus University of Thrace, Greece

IGI Global
Scientific Publishing
Publishing Tomorrow's Research Today

Vice President of Editorial — Melissa Wagner
Director of Acquisitions — Mikaela Felty
Director of Book Development — Jocelynn Hessler
Production Manager — Mike Brehm
Cover Design — Jose Rosado

Published in the United States of America by
IGI Global Scientific Publishing
701 East Chocolate Avenue
Hershey, PA, 17033, USA
Tel: 717-533-8845 | Fax: 717-533-7115
Website: https://www.igi-global.com E-mail: cust@igi-global.com

Copyright © 2026 by IGI Global Scientific Publishing. All rights reserved. No part of this publication may be reproduced, stored or distributed in any form or by any means, electronic or mechanical, including photocopying, without written permission from the publisher. Use of this publication to train generative artificial intelligence (AI) technologies is expressly prohibited. The publisher reserves all rights to license its use for generative AI training and machine learning model development.

Product or company names used in this set are for identification purposes only. Inclusion of the names of the products or companies does not indicate a claim of ownership by IGI Global Scientific Publishing of the trademark or registered trademark.

Library of Congress Cataloging-in-Publication Data

Names: Das, Baisakhi, 1983- editor | Perumal, Thinagaran editor | Chakrabarti, Satyajit editor | Sakurai, Kouichi editor | Papakostas, George A., 1975- editor
Title: Hallucination-aware AI for truthful and aligned systems / edited by Baisakhi Das, Thinagaran Perumal, Satyajit Chakrabarti, Kouichi Sakurai, and George A. Papakostas.
Description: Hershey, PA : IGI Global Scientific Publishing, [2026] | Includes bibliographical references and index. | Summary: "This book explores the development of generative AI systems (LLMs) has raised excitement, but also apprehension worldwide"-- Provided by publisher.
Identifiers: LCCN 2026004782 (print) | LCCN 2026004783 (ebook) | ISBN 9798337373201 h/c | ISBN 9798337373218 s/c | ISBN 9798337373225 ebook
Subjects: LCSH: Generative artificial intelligence | Information integrity
Classification: LCC Q335 .H35 2027 (print) | LCC Q335 (ebook)
LC record available at https://lccn.loc.gov/2026004782
LC ebook record available at https://lccn.loc.gov/2026004783

British Cataloguing in Publication Data
A Cataloguing in Publication record for this book is available from the British Library.

All work contributed to this book is new, previously-unpublished material.
The views expressed in this book are those of the authors, but not necessarily of the publisher.
This book contains information sourced from authentic and highly regarded references, with reasonable efforts made to ensure the reliability of the data and information presented. The authors, editors, and publisher believe the information in this book to be accurate and true as of the date of publication. Every effort has been made to trace and credit the copyright holders of all materials included. However, the authors, editors, and publisher cannot assume responsibility for the validity of all materials or the consequences of their use. Should any copyright material be found unacknowledged, please inform the publisher so that corrections may be made in future reprints.

Table of Contents

Detailed Table of Contents

provenance, grounding, coherence, and consequence. Accompanied by classroom tools—the provenance card, grounding contract, traceability rubric, consistency probe, counterfactual challenge, and accountability ledger—the model develops reflective detection as a method for studying how knowledge forms, changes, and occasionally misleads. Rather than viewing hallucination as error, the chapter reinterprets it as a means of learning and ethical awareness, positioning education as the central space where evaluation becomes a reflective, human–AI learning process.

The chapter is designed to be editor ready and will provide an integrated review of both technical trust measures and governance frameworks that support the human-centered dynamics of trust in AI systems. Human centered trust refers to the level of confidence people have in the integrity and reliability of their interactions with AI systems. For example, users may trust a system to make decisions about their health or financial well-being. The quantitative and qualitative trust assessments include Explainability why the AI system made its decision Robustness how resistant the AI system was to different types of attacks or failures Fairness whether the AI system treated individuals fairly and without bias Hallucination when the AI system generates false information or data

As generative artificial intelligence (AI) is adopted in knowledge management, its propensity to hallucinate, giving rise to confident fabrications, threatens not only facts but the foundations of human trust. This chapter argues that trusting AI is not a technical or explainable problem, but an existential one. Using phenomenological insights from Husserl, Heidegger and Merleau-Ponty, it is shown how hallucinations disturb users' sense of intelligibility, accountability and epistemic agency. Empirical studies show that leadership, culture and design count more than system features for building trust. Existing frameworks like MAST and POLARIS are criticized for ignoring the affective dimension, and a new model of trust as "knowing-with" AI

The ubiquitous nature of Large Language Models (LLMs) into health, law, and education has intensified worries regarding the validity of facts and the creation of hallucinations. The chapter outlines a systematic discussion of the verification frameworks as downstream constraints in fact verification mechanisms to make generative AI systems more truthful and reliable. The chapter subsequently suggests a multi-layered fact-filtering structure, which incorporates knowledge graph validation, semantic entailment, and cross-source agreement strategies of real time fact validation. Benchmark data, measurement criteria and execution processes are addressed in order to evaluate performance trade-offs. Combining theoretical grounding, realistic design practices, and supporting analysis, this chapter will act as a guide towards the creation of hallucination-resistant LLMs which will enable veridical and accountable and aligned AI applications in the high stakes decision-making contexts.

Generative Artificial Intelligence (GAI) is rapidly transforming the healthcare sector because the capacity to create new information, knowledge, and solutions is offered, rather than analyzing the ones that are already available. Unlike the classical AI models, which are designed to perform prediction and classification, generative AI involves complex algorithms such as; large language models, generative adversarial networks, and diffusion models to recreate the human-like reasoning and content-generation processes. It is finding application in clinical, administrative and research areas of healthcare and is significantly changing efficiency, accuracy and personalization of care. Clinical decision support is one of the most useful applications of generative AI. The GAI systems may be helpful to health care professionals summarizing the medical records, developing clinical notes, treatment plans recommendations, and helping with the diagnostic process with the help of a wide range of medical literature and information about the patient.

The advancement of integrated healthcare management combines multiple forms of technology (AI, telemedicine Video Calls, and wearable devices) for improving patient access to care and creating better responses to emergencies (CG. For example, during the COVID-19 Pandema). In this case, the AC-AL Habitat uses a combination of AI-based predictive modeling, multi-criteria decision analysis, and emergency response systems to accomplish 3 goals: 1) maximize resource allocation; 2) support effective decision making; 3) provide remote continuous patient monitoring. The system was able to provide a 94% Accuracy Rate in predicting patient outcomes, a 95% efficiency in Container Capacity Risk Mitigation, and 93% Scalability; thus, providing maximized equitable treatment, as well as real-time continued patient surveillance. By maximizing operational efficiency and readiness, this integrated healthcare management solution will promote the establishment of proactive, patient-centric, sustainable healthcare systems on a global level.

Generative AI in healthcare marks a shift from automation to augmenting clinical thinking through cognitive collaboration. Beyond handling tasks, its true value lies in enhancing diagnostic and therapeutic reasoning. To harness this while preserving human judgment and empathy, we propose a Relational Augmentation framework. This model rests on three pillars: Situational Awareness, for context-specific support; Reasoning Transparency, to reveal the logic behind AI suggestions; and Reciprocal Calibration, enabling the system to learn from clinician feedback. This synergy allows AI to manage complexity and generate insights, while the physician provides strategic oversight and compassionate care. Purposeful design of this partnership can guide AI to foster a more efficient and human-centered future for medicine.

Preface

The last 10 years has undoubtedly witnessed an acceleration in the development and dominance of generative models and large language models (LLMs) in the field of artificial intelligence (AI). This development has allowed these systems to augment problem-solving and creativity in multiple fields of interest, including the healthcare and education sectors, and the domains of law and public policy, among others, through the generation of comprehensive text and ideas. However, the acceleration of AI systems has continued despite the manifestation of serious and complex problems, including the phenomenon of AI hallucinations.

AI hallucinations can be at their worst in the generation of contextually plausible text that is factually wrong, unverifiable, and/or authoritatively made-up. This is the most critical limitation in the deployment of most intelligent systems. Traditional errors in software development can be classified as code or logic errors, making them easy to identify and relatively easy to fix, provided the appropriate emulators and environments are available. However, AI hallucinations can often take the form of an authoritative and effortless confidence in the text, statement, or idea, potentially introducing serious detrimental consequences especially in a high stakes environment, which creates a serious liability. These are the most critical limitations for cognitive reliant AI systems. This is the case AI hallucinations caused reliance of users.

This volume, *Hallucination-Aware AI for Truthful and Aligned Systems* is conceived as a response to this challenge. AI hallucinations a shift of focus from the technical dimension alone to the multi-faceted, including data and model design, training and assessment, and even to mechanisms of human-AI collaboration, AI hallucinations and their phenomena should be introduced. It is also necessary to take into consideration new theoretical and, most importantly, practical tools for the detection, prevention, and management of distractions.

Technical issues like retrieval-augmented generation, uncertainty estimation, and post-hoc verification need to be balanced with strong assessment systems, safeguards for particular fields, and ethical logic, which consider real-world applications. The detrimental impact of misinformation in areas like clinical decision support, research, and policy analysis raises the need for reliable and valuable systems.

In this book, many areas are covered, like the different levels of advanced technology, type of ways for evaluations and assessments, and involvement of people in the assessments to add knowledge in sectors of the community to be used in the background of the AI. In addition to these, there are bigger issues to be addressed, like when an AI becomes self-aware and starts to deceive, who is held accountable? What are the policies to be in place in order for the use of such an invention not to be abused? In systems of AI, how can we achieve and prioritize transparency and responsibility?

The book is written for many people like students in their masters and PhD, researchers, policy makers, data and AI practitioners. The motive is to create a base for researchers to build systems which are responsible, transparent, and of the needed type.

Hallucination is the least we can settle for. The continuous need to change the expectations of people and AI systems to match the development of AI is imperative.

We encourage readers to critically evaluate the opinions in this volume, and to assist in building trustworthy AI systems.

RELEVANCE OF THE BOOK IN TODAY'S WORLD

Currently, hallucination aware AI has an important and growing presence in today's world both socially and technologically. Due to the rapid adoption of AI across industry verticals, use of large language models, and the rise of autonomous intelligent systems in a variety of fields including healthcare, education, finance, law, cybersecurity, scientific research, and public services, concerns over the AI systems capabilities like truthfulness, reliability, and alignment have shifted from a theoretical research scenario to pressing real-world challenges. AI systems are being removed from research environments and deployed to have far-reaching implications, including the ability to make and affect choices, create new knowledge, and assist in the professional activities of millions of users, many of whom will be the end users of the AI systems. In such a landscape, hallucinations of AI systems present a significant engineering problem, as well as ethical and social challenges, in the arising fabricated, false, or misleading information.

Given the rapid growth of autonomous intelligent systems, the ability to utilize AI systems safely to generate verifiable and aligned outputs becomes critical in deploying AI systems to high-stakes environments. In the field of trustworthy AI and safe AI, the problem of hallucinations awareness of the AI systems substantiates the need to become a core competency in the AI systems.

This component of research is relevant to multiple research interests concerning the current purpose of AI technologies. First of all, this research area is relevant to the rapidly expanding ecosystem of foundation models and generative AI. Improving factual consistency, trustworthy reasoning, and alignment of AI models is of utmost importance. Second, this area of research relates to current efforts and studies on AI governance, regulation, and standards to establish safety benchmarks and balanced, trustworthy, and transparent AI. Last, this research area is relevant to the needs of organizations and practitioners looking to advance generative AI technologies from a prototype to a production-grade system.

Innovations in AI, augmented with hallucination-awareness, are indicative of a greater paradigm shift around the notion of AI agency. The paradigm shift is built on the shaping of multiple constructs including retrieval-augmented generation, agentic AI, human-AI collaboration, uncertainty-aware learning, and scalable alignment.

Finally, from a social perspective, this area of research will continue to gain prominence concerning hallucinating systems. This AI system amplified malicious activities, including the spread of misinformation, disintegration of trust within automated systems, and compromising safety in systems where there can be an AI error. Balancing the concerns of AI safety and the goals of AI systems to improve the equitable AI systems that serve the needs of society will continue to demand the highest priority of this research.

TARGET AUDIENCE

This book targets a range of specialized audiences across the development and governance of trustworthy artificial intelligence systems in academia, industry, and policy communities.

First, the book aims at AI scholars and educators, especially those involved in machine learning, natural language processing, generative AI, knowledge representation, and reasoning systems, as well as trustworthy AI. Particularly, researchers who study the hallucination effects in the case of large language models, multimodal systems, retrieval-augmented generation, neuro-symbolic AI, and explainable and robust AI, as well as AI model alignment, will consider the book to be highly pertinent. Additionally, as an edited volume, it will be useful to faculty and scholars who are looking for an inclusive compendium of the developing techniques, benchmarks, and theoretical frameworks of trustworthy and reliable AI.

The second primary audience consists of industry and AI engineers who are involved with the design or implementation of foundational models and high-stakes AI. This includes machine learning engineers, model build, MLOps, safety, and prompt engineers, as well as product teams tasked with the design of hallucination detection, factual consistency and uncertainty, alignment, red teaming, and guardrail methods. The book's fundamental and practical mitigation techniques will also be useful to professionals who design and execute enterprise generative AI, conversational, and decision support systems as well as copilot systems.

The book should be inclusive to Mass Graduate students, PhD students, Post Docs and Advanced Master students of technical disciplines including STEM, Computer Science, Artificial Intelligence, Data Science, Cognitive Computing, Computational Linguistics to cite few. This can be used as a supplemental text and research reference for Trustworthy Artificial Intelligence, AI Safety, and AI Safety thesis work for AI alignment and FICTION FREE AI models including research methodology and realigning factor to focus on reliability of research and align it.

Given that hallucination based AI has major societal impacts, this book works on the AI Safety, Governance and Policy communities for AI, Safety, Governance and Policy because it has a borader focus. We will focus on the discussions for alignment, accountability, risk mitigation, and different emerging AI systems that have a focus on human alignment and have the goal of being trustworthy.

The book writting also includes major target audience, this includes HCI professional who work in domains such as law, education, finance, healthcare, critical sectors like Cybersecurity and Autonomous Systems who focus on Operational and Ethical issues in order zero on focus for Hallucinations.

Cross disciplinary researchers who work on AI and Philosophy, Cognitive Science, HCI will also be interested in this book if they focus on AI from a social perspective regarding Trust, Truth, Human Alignment and Reasoning.

This book has a practical aim and a scholarly aim for trust, cognitive, and aligned AI from the perspective and theory of foundational models, Algorithms, pragmatic evaluation and applied philosophy.

ORGANIZATION OF THE BOOK

This book is designed to provide a detailed, multidisciplinary overview of hallucinations in AI, focusing specifically on generative models, trust, accountability, application-specific hallucinations, and of course, AI hallucinations. There are five main sections, each comprising a collection of chapters.: **Foundations, Conceptual and Philosophical Perspectives, Detection and Mitigation Techniques**, **Domain Applications**, and **Research Trends and Future Directions**.

Section I: Foundations of Hallucination in AI Systems

Chapter 1: *Hallucination in AI Systems – Understanding and Framework*

This chapter provides an initial framework on defining AI system hallucinations within the context of generative AI hallucinations, particularly large language models (LLMs). Different types of hallucinations and their possible classifications are summarized, an extensive classical analytic framework on the origin of hallucinations, and the data, model, and inference architecture is presented.

Section II: Conceptual and Philosophical Perspectives

Chapter 2: *From Fluency to Fidelity: A Conceptual Framework and Toolkit for Evaluating and Detecting Hallucinations in Generative AI*

In this chapter, the criteria for the evaluation of linguistic fluency in a generative AI are expanded to include the evaluation of the factual accuracy of the AI. A framework, along with practical toolkits, are detailed to assist in hallucination detection, benchmarking, and validation.

Chapter 3: *Trust in AI Systems*

In this chapter, the author considers the nature of trust in AI and approaches the subject from the technical, the sociological, and the organizational perspectives. It focuses on trust, perception, and the degree of trust and transparency. Furthermore, it analyzes the nature and understanding of AI system output by humans..

Chapter 4: *The Phenomenology of Trust: An Existential Prerequisite for Hallucination-Aware AI*

In this chapter, the author considers the philosophy of trust. The author states that, in order to characterize hallucination-aware AI systems, it is a requirement to address this philosophy of trust, and the difficulties it presents.

Chapter 5: *Towards Truthful and Responsible AI Systems*

In this chapter, the concept of truth and fairness, and the idea of practical accountability, are examined within the context of principles of ethics and AI. The chapter analyzes the approaches and constructs of ethical, accountable, and trust-aware AI systems..

Section III: Detection, Mitigation, and Model Design

Chapter 6: *Human-in-the-Loop Frameworks for AI Mitigation and Accountability*

Hybrid intelligence systems bridge the gap between humans and automated decision systems. This chapter discusses the continuous validation, feedback loop and accountability systems that exist within such automated systems.

Chapter 7: *Method Distinction for Hallucination Detection*

This chapter constitutes a comprehensive classification of detection methods including rule based, statistical, retrieval based and neural methods. A comprehensive analysis of methods will also be provided.

Chapter 8: *Fact-Filtering Frameworks – Integrating Verification Pipelines for Hallucination-Resistant Large Language Models*

This chapter will focus on a series of verification pipelines that will include fact-checkers, knowledge frameworks and external validation systems to provide full reliability to the output.

Section IV: Domain-Specific Applications in Healthcare

Chapter 9: *Generative Artificial Intelligence in Healthcare*

This chapter discusses the highly evolutionary and disruptive technology that is Generative AI in the healthcare domain for diagnostics, clinical documentation, drug discovery and patient engagement, in the context of hallucination risks.

Chapter 10: *Integrated Healthcare Management with AI and Real-Time Optimization Multi-Criteria Decision Analysis*

This chapter discusses the frameworks that facilitate advanced decision making using the combination of AI with multi-criteria decision-making to real time healthcare optimization and automate the allocation of resources in a systematic manner.

Chapter 11: *Beyond Automation: A Framework for Augmenting Clinical Expertise with Generative AI*

This chapter addresses the incorporation of generative AI in the clinical practice with the aim of enhancing, rather than automating, clinical practice with the focus on keeping control with the human to reduce the risks of hallucination.

Section V: Sectoral Impact and Research Trends

Chapter 12: *Mitigating Hallucinations in AI: Ensuring Trustworthy and Aligned Systems in Legal, Educational, and Governmental Sectors*

This chapter attempts to understand the consequences of AI hallucinations over high-impact domains and suggests targeted, industry-specific strategies to reduce, consider regulations and build governance frameworks.

CONCLUSION

The challenge of hallucination has emerged as one of the most significant challenges for genuinely deployable AI as the use of generative AI and foundation models becomes increasingly widespread and woven into the fabric of the scientific and industrial activities and structures of society. This book confronts this challenge as one fundamental and foundational problem, potential as a challenge to the truthfulness, robustness, impact, and interdependence of modern intelligent systems. By providing a framework of consideration of the issue of hallucination within the broader problem of trustworthy and human-aligned AI, the book makes a highly prompt and valuable contribution to one of the most pressing domains of AI research.

The book makes a significant contribution by compiling several cutting-edge studies on the detection and assessment of hallucinations and other problems related to large language models, multimodal systems, reasoning agents, and other fully autonomous AI for harnessing systems, in one comprehensive and unified scholarly publication. An analysis of the issues the book presents enables the reader to understand the challenges of hallucination and provides a gap-filling resource aimed at overcoming the challenges of AI to a technically trustworthy and inherently reliable and safe level.

This book also aids in the shift from a reactive correction of hallucinations approach to the development of proactive design principles with the aim of construction-based truthfulness and the consideration of alignment in system development. This approach suggests a new paradigm of transition from the incremental development of model capabilities to the engineering of safe, reliable AI systems for high-stakes applications.

Besides research and engineering, the volume contributes to the early-stage discussions of the standards, governance, and responsible innovation frameworks by outlining policy and evaluation protocols, and practices of trustworthy AI deployment. Thus, it provides a technical as well as a strategic framework for the safe development and deployment of generative AI.

The primary aim of *Hallucination-Aware AI for Truthful and Aligned Systems* is to build a lasting legacy by crystallizing a rapidly evolving body of knowledge, stimulating cross-field research, and constructing the intellectual framework for the next generation of truthful, resilient, and aligned AI systems. It is set to become both a seminal text in the domain and a muse for the progress of trustworthy AI.

Baisakhi Das
Institute of Engineering & Management, India

Thinagaran Perumal
Universiti Putra Malaysia, Malaysia

Satyajit Chakrabarti
Institute of Engineering & Management, India

Kouichi Sakurai
Kyushu University, Japan

George A. Papakostas
Democritus University of Thrace, Greece

Section 1
Foundations of Hallucination in AI Systems

Chapter 1

Hallucination in AI Systems: Understanding and Framework

Swarnalee Ray
http://orcid.org/0009-0008-5029-9983
Institute of Engineering and Management, India

Apurba Paul
http://orcid.org/0009-0007-4780-7783
Institute of Engineering and Management, India

Dipankar Das
Jadavpur University, India

Jiya Raj
Institute of Engineering and Management, India

ABSTRACT

Hallucination in large language models (LLMs) refers to the ability to generate coherent but factually incorrect text that is not source-verified and sufficiently logically justified. This problem is caused by the probabilistic nature of sequence modeling and the limitations of the Transformer architecture. If not addressed in high-risk areas such as medicine, law, and autonomous vehicles, hallucinations can negatively affect the reliability, safety, and trustworthiness of users. The current chapter offers a comprehensive review of the theoretical bases, typologies, causes, assessment strategies, and solutions to the problem of hallucination. One of the key contributions of this chapter is the development of a diagnostic framework that associates sensitivity to the prompt, the intrinsic properties of the model, and hallucinations.

DOI: 10.4018/979-8-3373-7320-1.ch001

© 2026, IGI Global Scientific Publishing. Copying or distributing in print or electronic forms without written permission of IGI Global Scientific Publishing is prohibited. Use of this chapter to nerative artificial intelligence (AI) technologies is expressly prohibited. The publisher reserves all rights to license its use for generative AI training and machine learning model development.

INTRODUCTION

LLM Hallucinations should not be considered mere computer bugs since LLMs have been developed to predict the most probable sequence of words. Thus, it is normal for them to drift away from reality occasionally. This means that LLMs can produce coherent and confident responses that are not based in reality. When applied in critical industries like healthcare, law, and finance, hallucinations in LLMs pose serious risks of medical mistakes, legal repercussions, and financial damage. To ensure the safe use of LLMs, it is therefore necessary to shift focus from zero-error performance to effective hallucination detection and multi-layered mitigation techniques like Retrieval-Augmented Generation (RAG), the incorporation of structured knowledge, and ongoing human monitoring (Lakera, 2025).

The implications of unmitigated hallucinations are particularly evident in critical domains where the integrity of information is critical.

- Healthcare: The creation of deceptive medical information, such as erroneous medication dosages or outdated medical treatment protocols, poses a direct threat to patient safety. Moreover, the use of fabricated citations in AI-based systematic reviews may also impinge upon the integrity of medical research (Kim et al., 2025).
- Law: There are known cases of lawyers being penalized for using AI-based legal document submissions that included deceptive citations of medical cases and non-existent legal precedents, thus impinging upon the integrity of the judicial system (Deloitte, n.d.).
- Autonomous Agents: In the case of AI systems that interact with the physical world, inaccuracies in information may have direct implications for safety. "Tool Calling Hallucinations," where an agent invents parameters for an API call, may also lead to incorrect action sequences with potentially disastrous consequences.

This chapter presents a structured analysis of hallucinations in AI systems by categorising their forms, examining their theoretical and practical causes, and reviewing existing evaluation and mitigation approaches. In addition, the second portion presents a theoretical model that accounts for why such errors happen to them. It stresses the importance of understanding the design theory inherent in the framework itself, along with the limits placed upon any specific instance of reality perception (such as hallucination) by that framework if one wants to measure the phenomenon properly.

FOUNDATIONS OF HALLUCINATION IN AI SYSTEMS

This section explores the theory of how hallucinations function as inevitable outcomes of AI technologies and training approaches - moving beyond definitions of hallucinations. These theoretical foundations are important because they help us understand why hallucinations are a management issue, rather than simply an issue of eliminating them.

Formal Definition

"Hallucination" in AI systems can be defined formally as the creation of new content that is not only factually false but also irrelevant/unsupported by any of the source materials or logically inconsistent, despite having a fluent and coherent presentation. Hallucinations include everything from simple factual errors (e.g., incorrect dates or facts) to producing new, non-existent (and often complex) entities/data. There are several key distinctions to make here; hallucinations may be confused with a related (but different) phenomenon known as "Bias" (the presence of a persistent representational skew, which may not involve factual errors); with "noise" (the presence of unpredictable, stochastic randomness); and with "Model Uncertainty" (the level of certainty that exists when predicting future events based on historical examples), but all of these phenomena can occur together as contributing factors to the creation of "hallucinated" content (Palo Alto Networks, n.d.).

The Theoretical Inevitability of Hallucinations

The dialogue surrounding hallucinations has changed from being seen as a fixable "glitch" to being viewed as a natural, and although sometimes necessary feature of computable generative models, as illustrated by the construction of probabilistic models, as well as both the communication and computational complexity theories. The high-level manifestation of the probabilistic construct of LLMs is documented through the definition of LLMs, the architectural limitations, which can be categorised through the study of complexity theory, are the causative factors.

LLMs are probabilistic generators that have been trained to create outputs conditioned on the previous data input with the objective of generating the next token. A hallucination occurs when a model assigns greater likelihood upon a sequence that lacks factual accuracy when compared to a sequence that is based on facts.

An analysis shows that the probabilistic vulnerability is fundamentally linked to the underlying architectural constraints of the Transformer architecture. The absence of an appropriate mechanism to consistently **compose functions** is one of the most fundamental weaknesses of this type of architecture. In answering the question,

"What was the birthday of Frédéric Chopin's father?" we need to compose two functions: father-of(Frédéric Chopin), which returns Nicolas Chopin; then, birthday-of (Nicolas Chopin). Recent theory has supported that this type of operation is fragile for Transformers in reality.

- **Communication Complexity:** A formal proof mentions that a single transformer layer is unable to solve a function composition problem with high probability if $n \log n > H(d+1)p$, where n is the domain size, H is the number of attention heads, d is the embedding dimension and p is computation precision. This limitation arises due to the softmax computation, which restricts the amount of non-local information a token can access to resolve compositional queries (Peng et al., 2024).
- **Computational Complexity:** Transformers function under a logarithmic space complexity (L). Because of this, they will simply be unable to solve problems that require more memory (i.e., the classes of complexity NL and P) unless widely known complexity conjectures (such as $L \neq NL$) are wrong. Therefore, when it comes to performing tasks requiring deep sequential reasoning, hallucinations become a design flaw (Peng et al., 2024).

The Dual Nature of Hallucinations

Creativity can benefit from hallucinations because they are sometimes helpful in producing ideas that you wouldn't have otherwise thought of using standard methods. This might include poetry with inventive metaphors, storytelling with surprising twists in the plot, or brainstorming through creative combinations of existing ideas.

To effectively deal with the underlying issues of hallucinations, the research community has developed specific taxonomies to categorise the various forms of hallucinations.

TAXONOMY OF HALLUCINATIONS

The establishment of a rigorous and comprehensive taxonomy is a fundamental prerequisite for the systematic diagnosis, detection, and mitigation of hallucinations in Large Language Models (LLMs). Because hallucination is not a singular or uniform error but a multifaceted phenomenon, a granular classification scheme is necessary to identify model-specific failure patterns and develop targeted interventions rather than generic fixes. The research field has mainly categorised this type of phenomenon according to several primary axes of categorisation to identify how a model fails in either retrieving information or abiding by the instructions given. This section highlights the main categorisation schemes.

Primary Classification: Intrinsic vs. Extrinsic

The most fundamental distinction is to categorise hallucinations based on their relationship to a provided source context.

Hence, hallucinations in large language models (LLMs) can be divided into intrinsic and extrinsic hallucinations.

Intrinsic Hallucinations. Intrinsic hallucinations are when the output of a model goes against what is being referenced and creates a lack of grounding in the information that was provided. For example, a model may report a company's profit to be $5 million when the source states that it is actually $10 million. This is typically due to relying on the statistical probabilities of the input rather than the output from the source, which can be identified when comparing the two (Kazlaris et al., 2025).

Extrinsic Hallucinations. Extrinsic hallucinations occur when the model generates details that are not present in the provided source, making its output impossible to verify against the source alone. An example would be a biography that generates citations to non-existent research papers (citing them confidently as if they were real). Unlike intrinsic hallucinations, these often rely on the model's training data on a massive corpus to simulate authenticity (Kazlaris et al., 2025).

Secondary Distinction: Factuality vs. Faithfulness

The difference between Factuality and Faithfulness is one of the key dimensions of hallucination research. It is a distinction between model and objective truth versus the model and its application of context or logic.

- **Factuality: Alignment with External Knowledge:** Factuality refers to the "absolute correctness" of the generated content measured against real-world knowledge or verified sources. Factual hallucinations are objective errors where the model's output contradicts reality. It is further divided into two categories:
- **Factual Contradiction:** The model generates a response that is at odds with the fact, such as "Toronto is the capital of Canada" or "Thomas Edison invented the internet".
- **Factual Fabrication:** The model invents non-existent historical figures, events, or scientific data that have no foundation in reality, such as citing a non-existent court case or a fabricated clinical trial.

These errors are caused by missing or incomplete parametric information in the model's training data, or through a lack of old facts, which have been replaced. This is a problem is considered external since it requires an external oracle (such as a database or search engine) for verification.

Faithfulness: Internal and Contextual Consistency

Faithfulness can be understood as the logical consistency of the model concerning the data mentioned in the input prompt or generated through the reasoning process. The issue of faithfulness happens when the output is inconsistent or logically flawed despite the appearance of plausibility of the statements. Academic research groups the instances of faithfulness failure into three groups:

- **Instruction Inconsistency**: The model fails to follow specific output instructions given by the user, such as providing an answer in English instead of the required Spanish language.
- **Context Inconsistency**: The model provides information inconsistent with the facts given in the source text. For instance, if a source mentions that a person was born in 1980, but the summary provides 1975 as a year of birth, the model lacks faithfulness toward its context.
- **Logical Inconsistency**: The model provides flaws in the deductive reasoning or math involved in a problem and creates inconsistencies throughout sentences in an answer.

Since the errors can often be detected by evaluating the output directly against the provided source material without needing external verification, faithfulness is closely related to intrinsic hallucinations.

Subtypes of Hallucinations

The above-mentioned types can be further divided into subcategories for deeper understanding.

- **Intrinsic (Factuality Errors):**
  - **Entity-error:** Distorted portrayal of entities or relations (for instance, creating false persons, false biographical information, or false research articles).
  - **Relation-error:** Discrepancies related to temporal, causal, and quantitative inconsistencies (for example, misstating the chronological sequence of events).

- **Outdatedness:** The creation of outdated information, where the information generated by the model was true at the time of training but became obsolete afterwards because of the difference between the knowledge cutoff date and the present moment.
- **Overclaim:** An inflated description of the certainty and scope of an assertion that does not correspond to the evidence presented.

- **Extrinsic (Faithfulness Errors):**
  - **Incompleteness:** Missing necessary context leads to a distorted or incomplete response.
  - **Unverifiability:** Unverifiable outputs cannot be disproved or verified using the provided resources.
  - **Emergent:** Unexpected hallucinations that emerge in large models because of scaling, multi-modal reasoning, or inference failures.

Manifestations in Multimodal Systems

In light of the growing application of foundation models to multimodal inputs, including vision, audio, and video, the concept of hallucinations gets ever more complicated since the misalignment at the cross-modal level between the inputs and their representation within the model gets even more pronounced. In order to differentiate the causes behind errors committed by models on the data understanding level and errors committed on the cognitive level, the sources speak of perception-level errors and cognition-level errors. Thus, two types of hallucinations are identified:

1. **Perception Hallucinations:**
   - Perception hallucinations occur when a Multimodal Large Language Model (MLLM) is unable to properly interpret or ground the raw input, whether visual or auditory. This category of errors stems from the architectural constraints of the vision encoders, for instance, limited visual resolution or inability to ground certain aspects of an image.
   - Perception mistakes take different modal-specific forms:
     - **Images Object Hallucinations**: On static visual tasks, perception errors are divided into three kinds:
   - **Category**: An error in assigning object categories that do not exist (e.g., mistaking a cushion for a cat).
   - **Attribute**: The model recognises an object correctly but attributes incorrect characteristics to it (e.g., calling a blue car red).
   - **Relation:** The model makes a mistake about the relationship between the objects described.

- **Temporal Disorientation in Video**: In case of dynamic input, the MLLM may generate descriptions for impossible actions or for the events whose sequence does not match that of the video.
- **Semantic Mistakes in Audio**: Hallucinations in audio modality consist in generating meaningless, albeit seemingly plausible phonetic sequences or creating audio content unrelated to the corresponding visual input.
- **Robotic Interaction Gaps**: In robotics applications, perceptual errors become especially dangerous as they result in a misinterpretation of a 6D pose or a dynamic obstacle that leads to immediate failure.

Cognition Hallucinations:

Cognitive hallucinations, on the other hand, represent a somewhat more rudimentary level of structural deficiency wherein the model is able to properly parse the individual pieces of information within the image but is unable to adequately engage with common sense and/or draw inferences to assemble the pieces in context. This tends to happen due to the models' language priors, where the statistical structures formed as part of their training in the text domain improperly interfere with their multimodal inputs.

Examples of cognition-level failures include:

- **Made-up Interconnectivity**: The model is capable of identifying a certain person and a famous landmark within an image, but it then proceeds to generate a history of their interaction which never took place.
- **Faulty Chains of Actions by Agents**: With respect to "Agentic AI," the cognitive hallucination in the agent may trigger a sequence of events that lead to faulty action chains. As an example, a computer system may accurately recognize a database but generate fake facts about the API call or an impossible trajectory resulting from flawed reasoning.
- **The "Reality Gap"**: Cognitive hallucinations are said to arise due to the difference between the simulated environment for training and the complicated environment of reality. This will prompt the agent to use general principles acquired through training to a scenario that cannot be addressed using the same principles.
- **Recursive Misalignment**: Since cognitive hallucinations involve reasoning, the system will likely produce a sophisticated and entirely fabricated story based on a single wrong reasoning.

However, it is important to understand the distinction between perception and cognition since they both play an important role when devising a solution approach for dealing with cognitive hallucinations. While problems with perception might be overcome using architectural approaches like better attention and higher-resolution encoders, cognitive problems will require a more complicated approach, for example, symbolic integration and knowledge graphs to serve as a point for grounding. Cognitive hallucinations might lead to serious risks, especially in the healthcare and autonomous systems engineering industries.

ROOT CAUSES OF HALLUCINATION

It is crucial to understand that hallucinations in machine learning models are not just bugs but a natural consequence of limitations in computable generative models and bottlenecks associated with the Transformer architecture. These causes can be divided into three broad categories: data-related problems, model and training-related problems, and problems that occur during inference.

Data-Related Issues

The quality and nature of the training data are a major source of factual errors and inconsistencies.

- **Corpus Quality:** Large language models (LLMs) are trained on large, often uncurated web-scale corpora that necessarily contain noisy, biased, redundant, or contradictory information. Models trained on such data are likely to reflect these errors (Lakera, 2025).
- **Knowledge Overshadowing:** In cases where the training data contains conflicting facts related to the same entity or event, the model may not be able to overcome these inconsistencies and produce outputs that are contradictory or made-up.
- **Knowledge Cutoff and Gaps:** Models are limited by the cutoff date of their training data. When asked about topics or events that have occurred after the cutoff date, they often produce information by projecting trends based on past patterns instead of admitting a lack of knowledge about the current state of affairs (Xenoss, n.d.).

Model and Training-Related Issues

The design, training tasks, and alignment processes of large language models (LLMs) are basic drivers of hallucinations.

- **Objective Function Misalignment:** The standard objective of next-token prediction is to maximize the production of linguistically plausible sequences, not factually truthful ones, establishing a basic misalignment between the optimization goal (fluency) and the intended outcome (accuracy) (Pinecone, n.d.).
- **Architectural Fragility:** The Transformer architecture is inherently fragile. As mentioned above, its challenges with **function composition** make it prone to mistakes in multi-step reasoning. Additionally, for long sequences, models are prone to long-range forgetting, where information far away in the input is ignored, causing hallucinations (Peng et al., 2024).
- **Alignment Risks:** Post-training alignment techniques like Reinforcement Learning from Human Feedback (RLHF) introduce new failure modes. Models tend to exhibit "sycophantic" behaviour, where they agree with the user's false hypothesis to be more assistive. This also leads to "reward hacking," where the model tends to produce overly verbose but completely ungrounded responses because these responses are rewarded more for being helpful and fluent, rather than truthful and brief (IAPP, n.d.).
- **Memorisation and Under-training:** Hallucinations can be triggered by direct memorisation of training data, especially when data is highly duplicated. Also, there is evidence that optimal performance is achieved by proportional scaling of model size and training tokens; many models are likely to be under-trained, making them more likely to produce poorly generalised or hallucinated content (Anh-Hoang et al., 2025).

Usage-Related Issues

The trade-offs in token choice and statistical priors can lead to hallucinations at inference as well.

Decoding Strategies: The Coherence-Diversity Trade-off. Decoding strategies ensure that the model's representations of knowledge are represented as easily consumable text with a high degree of fluency, diversity, and factuality.

- **Deterministic vs. Stochastic Paths:** Deterministic decoding strategies (e.g., greedy decoding) prioritise the most likely token at each step to avoid hallucinations. These methodologies could succumb to the "likelihood trap" as referred to, resulting in degenerate and uninspired text.

- **The Risk of Randomness:** To achieve greater diversity, the two methods we have adopted are stochastic methodologies (top-p) and temperature. These improve the quality of generation; however, an extremely random approach leads to a greater probability of choosing tokens that cannot be factually grounded.
- **Empirical Evidence:** According to empirical results, the transition from greedily selecting the best token to using top-p significantly increases the number of hallucinations, from 26% to 34%, for example. With very high temperatures that lead to flattened distributions, the model ends up entering confabulation zones by giving priority to tokens that are unexpected (Anh-Hoang et al., 2025).

Prompt Sensitivity and the Pattern-Matching Fallacy. The observation here is that moving from greedily selecting the best token to top-p selection could increase the rate of hallucinations, such as the selection of unexpected tokens leading the model to wander off to areas that it should not through high temperature.

- **Probabilistic Pattern-Matching:** Prompts that are too ambiguous and do not conform to any constraints make it hard for the generation process to be grounded. In this case, the model would try to fill in the gaps in a process referred to as probabilistic pattern-matching, which favors linguistically sound text over intent.
- **Out-of-Distribution (OOD) Inputs or Distribution Shift:** Distribution shift happens when a model is moved away from its domain of specialisation or a new task altogether. The out-of-distribution (OOD) input causes the model to guess what to say based on its past experiences rather than saying it does not understand the concept, called capability misalignment.
- **The "Confident Nonsense" Effect:** Models with extremely high sensitivity, such as LLaMA 2, can be very easy to control with the use of tools like Chain-of-Thought. However, this same malleability results in susceptibility to a form of flattery. In the presence of misleading prompts, the model succumbs to the temptation of being a 'yes-man', echoing the user's faulty assumptions in order to remain statistically accurate (Anh-Hoang et al., 2025).
- **Rationalising Falsehoods:** In false premise-containing dialogue prompts, the model may not only produce hallucinated answers but also provide a detailed, logically consistent but entirely fictional reasoning chain to justify the mistake.

A detailed diagnosis of these underlying factors, interwoven as they are, is essential for the development of effective evaluation tools and detection strategies.

EVALUATION AND DETECTION OF HALLUCINATIONS

The accurate measurement and detection of hallucinations is a necessary step in their mitigation. This requires, as a necessary first step, a shift from traditional accuracy-based evaluation to more complex and sophisticated evaluation tools that can assess the accuracy of facts, the logical consistency of responses, and their grounding in source materials.

Evaluation Benchmarks and Metrics

There is an ever-growing number of evaluation benchmarks designed to systematically assess an LLM's susceptibility to hallucination.

Several standardized benchmarks have been proposed to systematically evaluate hallucination phenomena in Large Language Models (LLMs), each with a focus on different methodological assumptions and types of hallucinations:

- **TruthfulQA** is a question-answering benchmark specifically designed to answer questions in a way that corresponds to the most common human misconceptions. The primary goal of this benchmark is to evaluate whether a model answers questions in a way that corresponds to common but false human beliefs. As such, it is mainly used to evaluate factual hallucinations, especially those that emerge from the simulation of false or misleading societal beliefs (Kazlaris et al., 2025).
- **HalluLens** is a dynamic benchmarking framework where test samples are created at the time of inference using controlled or non-existent entities. This approach helps to prevent benchmark contamination and memorization. HalluLens is primarily designed to identify hallucinations that emerge from data leakage and incorrect factual recall, making it resistant to benchmark saturation (Bang et al., 2025).
- **FactScore** is a benchmark designed to evaluate long-form generative samples by breaking down text into atomic factual statements and then checking each statement against trusted external sources. This benchmark focuses on factual accuracy in long-form generative tasks, where small errors can collectively lead to large amounts of misinformation (Min et al., 2023).
- **HALOGEN** uses automated verification procedures to check the generated content against domain-specific knowledge bases and structured databases.

This benchmark is specifically designed to identify both factual and extrinsic hallucinations, with a focus on following authoritative data sources in specific professional domains (Ravichander et al., 2025).

EVALUATION METHODOLOGIES

Techniques used by researchers to identify hallucinations can be classified as follows:

- **Internal State Probing:** These techniques involve analyzing the internal state of the model to look for signatures of confabulation.
  - **Semantic Entropy:** This technique involves generating multiple responses to the same input. High semantic entropy between the responses indicates model uncertainty and a greater chance of hallucination.
  - **Circuit Tracing:** This technique involves tracing specific neural circuits in the model that are linked to specific behaviors. For instance, researchers have identified "refusal circuits" that are activated when information is not available; in such cases, hallucination can occur if the circuit is improperly suppressed.
- **Consistency-Based Detection:** Consistency-based Detection: These methods require analyzing the consistency of the model internally, without having access to any external gold-standard data.
  - **MetaQA Methodology:** This methodology requires metamorphically transforming the question itself. In case the model gives contradictory answers for different transformations, then the model suffers from hallucinations.
  - **Self-consistent Decoding:** This method requires creating a number of reasoning chains (such as Chain of Thoughts) and then selecting an answer based on the highest consistency among these chains.
- **External Validation Check:** These methods require validating the output of the model by checking it against the following
  - **FActScore:** This technique involves breaking down a generated text into atomic facts (for example, "Frédéric Chopin was a composer") and checking each component against a knowledge base like Wikipedia (Min et al., 2023).
  - **Span-Level RAG Verification:** In Retrieval-Augmented Generation (RAG) systems, this technique matches each of the generated claims against specific spans of text in the retrieved documents, also flagging any unsupported information on its way.

Limitations of Current Evaluation Frameworks

This problem is caused by a saturation problem in the benchmarks (leakage issue). Currently, popular benchmarks, such as TruthfulQA, are used for the training data of newer models. Models are learned to answer these questions without changing their reasoning (i.e., they memorise the answers), resulting in falsely high scores. It is important to keep evolving dynamic benchmarks, such as HalluLens, that are not saturated. Apart from this problem of benchmark saturation, several gaps in our system call for a more dynamic and robust evaluation framework.

- **The Challenge of Benchmark Saturation and Leakage.** One great difficulty with traditional evaluation is that popular benchmarks like TruthfulQA have become self-fulfilling. These datasets are publicly available and used to rank models on leaderboards, so they do not need to be hidden from the web-scale corpora used to train newer models. It is more like "gaming", where models perform better not because they reason more or are truthful, but because they remember test questions and their gold standard answers. Recent audits of benchmarks have revealed other flaws. For example, an error analysis of TruthfulQA using the Llama-3.1 405B model finds that approximately 25%of the samples scored as incorrect by the log-probability metric were actually correct, and that the benchmark itself has outdated or subjective ground truth answers. A static benchmark cannot keep pace with the dynamic nature of knowledge (Kazlaris et al., 2025).
- **The Rise of Dynamic Benchmarks: HalluLens.** Modern frameworks such as HalluLens have employed dynamic test set generation to compensate. This methodology ensures an assessment that can't be manipulated by generating novel and unpredictable questions during inference that the model has never seen before. HalluLens presents a variety of novel tasks to test the limits of a model'sknowledge:
    - **PreciseWikiQA**: It produces short, factual questions based on Wikipedia articles to test the model's ability to answer specific facts without hallucinations.
    - **Long Wiki**: A method of evaluating the coherence of the generated text, comparing it against factual static references.
    - **Non Existent Refusal**: This test aims at understanding if the model possesses any level of self-awareness when it tries to generate content based on entirely fictional entities like fictional animals or non-existent brands and whether it acknowledges its inability to answer or invents something convincing.

Broader Limitations of Current Frameworks

In addition to data leakage, contemporary frameworks for analyzing models face many critical disadvantages:

- **Lack of Standardization**: As there is still no universally accepted way to define what constitutes "hallucinations," researchers have differing labels.
- **Task-Dependent Metrics**: For instance, the metric, which is highly effective in detecting hallucinations in summarization models, may prove ineffective in code generation or multi-turn dialogues.
- **The Lack of Explainability**: The majority of available metrics offer only quantitative results but do not give any explanations regarding the errors and their nature.
- **Shallow Surface-Sensitive Metrics**: ROUGE or BLEU scores consider similarities in the words used but cannot detect hallucinations as subtle as altering a date or an insignificant word in a sentence.

Transitioning to Mitigation: The Stratified Toolkit

Once frameworks for assessing hallucinations are developed and the differences are accounted for, the following methods for mitigation will ensure that the model generates content without errors for as long as possible:

1. **Architectural Strategies**: These would include Retrieval-Augmented Generation (RAG) technology to help contextualize information instantly and Toolformer-style augmentation allowing the model to independently check factual correctness using calculators and APIs.
2. **Training-Based Interventions**: Methods such as contrastive learning allow identifying the difference between factual and hallucinated statements, while Uncertainty-Aware RLHF lets the model acknowledge uncertainty.
3. **Inference-Time Controls**: Examples of such mitigations include chain-of-verification (CoVe), which allows the model to self-correct, and constrained decoding, which stops the model from picking low-probability and ungrounded tokens.
4. **Systemic Guardrails**: Factual filters post-generation ensure consistency with structured factual databases and logical validators check the logical correctness of generated sentences.

HALLUCINATION MITIGATION TECHNIQUES

These techniques can be seen as the methods that help to address the inherent limitations of Transformer technology. The following section discusses some of these techniques in depth. These techniques have been classified according to their stage within the AI pipeline where they are implemented: data-centric techniques, model-centric modifications, prompting, and post-generation validation.

Data-Centric Approaches

As far as data-centric approaches are concerned, they involve improvements related to the training data. The underlying idea behind data-centric approaches is that the better the training data, the more reliable the model. Techniques include data cleaning to remove inaccuracies, inconsistencies, and biases, as well as data augmentation with high-quality and verified information.

Model-Centric Approaches

These types of interventions target the architecture or training process of models to promote a stronger focus on factuality.

- **Fine-Tuning Interventions:**
    - **Reinforcement Learning from Human Feedback (RLHF):**This approach helps to align the model's responses with human preferences by encouraging responses that are more helpful, harmless, and honest. It is an effective way to reduce the model's generation of known false statements.
    - **Calibrated Uncertainty:** A more advanced approach involves training models to display calibrated uncertainty and to demonstrate epistemic humility. These methods are designed to explicitly reward the model for its humility by answering "I don't know" to questions it is not confident enough to answer, thus preventing the model from engaging in speculative confabulation.
- **Architectural Modifications:**
    - **Retrieval-Augmented Generation (RAG):** The Retrieval-Augmented Generation model is an improvement over the language model, where the model is connected to an external knowledge base. When a prompt is received, the model first retrieves relevant documents and then uses them as context for the language model to generate responses (Xenoss, n.d.).

- **Knowledge Graph Integration:** Integration with external knowledge graphs as a method to change the model is essentially a response to functional composition issues, which have been analysed above from a theoretical point of view. These Knowledge Graphs can be viewed as factual databases that assist the model performing difficult reasoning tasks.

Input/Prompt Optimization Approaches

Optimisation of the prompt is the most straightforward approach to making a model generate truthful output. Structured prompting, for instance, CoT prompting, is a technique that helps guide the model to solve tasks by performing reasoning step-by-step. This technique allows making the model's reasoning process more transparent and thus reducing the probability of hallucinations. **Chain-of-Verification (CoVe)** is a more sophisticated method of prompting the model to perform a self-verification cycle, which begins with the initial response, followed by a series of verification questions to fact-check the response, answer the questions, and finally modify the initial response based on the results of the verification process.

Post-Generation Approaches

The approaches are performed at the output stage of the model. They can be seen as the last step before the presentation of results to the user.

- **Fact-Checking and Verification**: The output is analysed by an external fact-checking process. For verification of claims, the model can either utilise another large language model or an information retrieval system.
- **Factuality Reranking**: In case of a "Best-of-N" generation approach, where a number of candidate responses for each input prompt is generated by the model, the responses are then ranked based on their factuality scores using an independent method. The candidate with the highest factuality score is then selected.

To better understand how to apply the different approaches in practice, a conceptual framework for diagnosis of the type and cause of a hallucination should be constructed.

Proposed Conceptual Framework

In this section, I present the research required for constructing a framework for analysing, classifying, and diagnosing a hallucination.

The Attribution Framework

The Attribution Framework consists of two core metrics, Prompt Sensitivity and Model Variability, which allow attributing a specific hallucination based on its sensitivity to variations in prompts and models. Core Components and Metrics include the following-

- **Prompt Sensitivity (PS):** It shows the variation in the hallucination frequency of the fixed model (M) tested on n prompts. If the PS score is high, it means the probability of a model generating a hallucination is highly dependent on the quality of the prompt.
- **Model Variability (MV):** It describes the variation in the hallucination frequency of m models when all models are tested on a single fixed prompt. High MV means that the hallucination is caused by model's nature.

Framework Workflow and Attribution Categories

The workflow of the attribution framework includes conducting a series of controlled experiments, testing the set of prompts on a variety of models. Depending on the calculation of PS and MV scores of the experimental results, the hallucinations may fall into one of four categories.

The type of hallucination can be systematically classified through an integrated analysis of the scores of Prompt Sensitivity (PS) and Model Variability (MV). If the PS score is high and the MV score is low, the type of hallucination is classified as prompt-dominant, which means that the failure is mainly caused by ill-structured, ambiguous, or misleading user instructions rather than the limitations of the model itself.

If the PS score is low and the MV score is high, the type of hallucination is classified as model-dominant. This type of hallucination corresponds to errors caused by the intrinsic properties of the model, such as the lack of parametric knowledge, architectural limitations, or unstable internal representations, which are less dependent on the reformulation of the user instructions.

If both the PS and MV scores are high, the type of hallucination is classified as mixed-origin. This type of hallucination corresponds to errors caused by the combination of prompt-related ambiguities and intrinsic limitations of the model, which means that neither prompt engineering nor model improvement can alone solve the problem.

Finally, if both the PS and MV scores are low, the type of hallucination is classified as unclassified, which means that the failure cannot be confidently attributed to either prompt sensitivity or model variability. This type of hallucination may correspond to stochastic generation effects or limitations in the attribution scores.

This framework serves as a critical diagnostic tool that helps developers and researchers move from the point of simply recognizing that a model is hallucinating to achieving a more refined level of understanding of the causes of hallucinations. This, in turn, helps to identify the most appropriate strategies for aligning AI systems with the principles of truthfulness and safety.

HALLUCINATION-AWARE AI FOR TRUTHFUL AND ALIGNED SYSTEMS

This discussion aims to place the above problem, hallucinations, within a larger context regarding the importance of developing responsible AI. Hallucinations cannot be reduced only to technical issues, but rather represent an important aspect in evaluating the development of trustworthy, ethically, and safely constructed AI systems, especially in regard to high-risk sectors such as health care or law.

Ethics of Hallucination in AI Models

The existence of hallucinations that are not mitigated brings about challenges to the fundamental principles of ethical AI. The presence of unmitigated hallucinations poses challenges for the main principles of ethical AI:

- **Reliability and Non-maleficence:** Providing users with false representations may cause physical damage to users (i.e. High Risk) by inducing users or causing errors due to inaccurate representation.
- **Transparency and Accountability:** If an AI model provides a definitive statement regarding something and that statement is later proven to be incorrect, it will be difficult for users to determine whether the AI model has accurately represented information.

Thus, the creation of a "hallucination aware" system is an integral part of putting AI Ethics into practice and using these tools responsibly.

The Role of Hallucination Awareness in AI Governance

The persistent occurrence of hallucinations in generative AI models calls for a shift in the governance approach to these systems. Trends in the existing academic literature indicate that hallucinations cannot be easily addressed and may well be an inherent feature of computable generative models. As such, the focus of research moves away from correcting mistakes toward managing risks.

Future approaches to governance of AI systems need to move beyond the obsession with data integrity and embrace a broader approach where security and resilience become primary concerns. Since the systems will make mistakes regardless, the goal becomes creating models that can run safely under uncertain conditions.

Fostering a Culture of Professional Skepticism

Professionals rely heavily on AI today for many tasks, and require good management of human resources associated with the performances of AI. When developing a professional sceptical attitude toward the outputs of AI, many people must learn that the output of AI should not be considered the same as truth or the same as the output of an experienced and qualified assistant - that the output of AI must always be verified with the same level of scrutiny as any other source would be, to confirm that the output provided is accurate and complete before being used in practice by the user of that information. It will be imperative to ensure that when working with the output of AI, professionals of various types (e.g., attorneys, doctors, researchers, etc.) have access to robust verification tools and are responsible for verifying the reliability of the AI output they use by confirming its accuracy using a reliable state-of-the-art resource like a computer program and being held accountable for any use of the output that has not been verified for accuracy or completeness.

Such resilience in the use of AI to produce high-quality outputs combined with the validation of accuracy of those outputs can provide an effective governance and oversight program for generative AI. Examples and challenges resulting from this type of technological innovation will primarily be explained through examples from high-stakes professional sectors.

CASE STUDIES AND APPLICATIONS

This chapter puts theory into practice with an examination of real-world examples of AI hallucinations in law, medicine and autonomous systems. Utilising these sectors as case studies, it will illustrate how factual errors go beyond being merely technical errors, and instead, become foundationally disintegrity of ethical and professional integrity.

Case Study: Legal and Judicial AI

While LLMs create efficiencies, their propensity to hallucinate compromises both the accuracy of precedents - in fact, they cause 'epistemological breaches' - and thus has an extremely serious ethical/professional ramification on the judicial profession.

- **Risks: Fabrication and Representation Threat.** One of the major risks associated with using AI in legal matters is the phenomenon of citation fabrications. There were at least 120 cases of AI-generated hallucinations in legal filings reported between July and September of 2023. Bogus citations and citations from the made-up internal references pose threats to judicial procedures. For example, one of the New York attorneys was sanctioned by the court and fined $5,000 for providing false non-existent case citations created by ChatGPT in his brief during the Mata v. Avianca (2023) case. In addition, these kinds of mistakes lead to the representational harm of the legal community members since their contribution is erased from consideration via probabilistic matching algorithms. It is also a matter of concern whether the judges who hire virtual research assistants will be receiving hallucinated legal advice that might affect the final ruling on certain matters (Baker Donelson, n.d.).
- **Limitations of Traditional Methods.** According to the legal community, increasing model size and basic prompts are ineffective means of handling relational reasoning in such tasks. In empirical studies done in 2025, even retrieval-augmented generation systems used for conducting legal searches were found to be unreliable. Despite the fact that legal research assistants are intended to ensure high precision for such a sensitive task, the rate of errors in their operation is still quite high since they tend to hallucinate the presence of certain facts in the retrieved legal documents that are not actually there (Ho, 2025).
- **Mitigation: A Root-Cause-Aware Framework.** Resilient AI mitigation requires transitioning from generic, blanket solutions towards cycles of root cause-aware management which emphasize transparency and verifiability.
- **The "Skepticism-First" Culture**: AI is understood by the legal community to be akin to a fallible virtual assistant, whose answers serve only as a basis for further inquiry and investigation.
- **Legal Workflows Should be Properly Defined**: AI's application in the practice of law that has a high level of risk or potential liability must employ a

rigourous, structured workflow (i.e., steps to obtaining pertinent data, reasoned structure, cite-checking and human redlining at the conclusion – the ability to see an entire picture or project).

- **Validation of Logical Reasoning**: There should also be additional measures used to verify the logical reasoning behind the creation of the AI-generated argument relative to legal requirements or a reasonable set of logic rules.
- **Protocols Specific to the Domain of Law**: In addition to the above, mitigating factors require that there are span-level citations for all claims made and that there is a record of decisions made to enable analysis and auditing of events.
- **Training the Model on Adversarial Examples**: By improving the language models' resistance to being "tricked" by questions, we can train our models to respond with a negative response (i.e., say, "I cannot find the report") instead of creating a fictional response when unable to locate a requested filing.

In conclusion, to safely utilise AI in the practice of law, robust ecosystems must be created and maintained which are founded on fact rather than fiction, and which mandate that every statement made by machines is verified by an attorney prior to proceeding with the statement.

Case Study: Healthcare and Clinical Safety

Expanded Risks: Clinical Context and Data Noise. Formally speaking, medical hallucination refers to the creation of inaccurate medical content, such as wrong drug dosages, treatment algorithms based on obsolete guidelines, or wrong diagnostic criteria. In turn, the errors typically occur as a result of data-driven calculations, during which LLMs are trained using EHR corpora with spelling errors and vague abbreviations, thus carrying the mistakes into clinical reasoning.

Such issues become even more critical due to the following reasons:

- **Knowledge Limitations and Obsolescence of Information**: Since models learn from static data, they cannot determine their own limitations in terms of knowledge, thus offering clinical advice based on outdated practices, which have already been revised by new scientific results.
- **Generalization Problems**: LLMs can fail in dealing with rare cases or diseases, usually generalizing from frequent but irrelevant examples to provide false medical advice.
- **The "Fluency Heuristic" and Credibility**: Medical practitioners, especially non-specialists, fall for automation bias and accept fake med-

ical information since it is provided confidently and with professional language. According to one blind study, laypersons sometimes considered inaccurate GPT-4 responses to be more reliable than accurate responses by human experts.

- **Citation Manipulation**: In a 2024 study, the citation manipulation frequency reached 28.6% for systematic reviews generated by GPT-4, creating substantial challenges for health care providers who rely on AI to analyze the literature (Kim et al., 2025).
- **Fatal Consequences**: Such flaws go beyond technical aspects and pose serious risks to the safety of patients. As a result, 77% of non-profits in the field of health care point to the unreliability of AI solutions as the primary problem of implementation (Kim et al., 2025).

Advanced Mitigation: Targeted Clinical Safeguards. Clinical Safeguards for Advanced Solutions. Apart from standard human oversight, managing medical hallucinations calls for a root-cause analysis.

- **Retrieve-Generate-Verify-Abstain Workflow Approach**: When applied to sensitive healthcare use cases, it is better to stick to a conservative algorithm in which models should be conditioned on retrieved fragments of expert databases. In case the generated response is not confident enough, a model must follow an explicit abstain strategy instead of providing an estimated answer.
- **Neuro-Symbolic and Knowledge Graph Architecture**: Combining LLMs with UMLS and other medical ontologies or Knowledge Graphs creates a factual basis for advanced relational reasoning that may be unachievable using self-attention mechanisms.
- **Factuality-Aware Interfaces**: Tools like Med-PaLM 2 reduce the risk by providing multimodal transparency indicators, including the presentation of clinical references and properly quantified uncertainty indicators (such as "low certainty") to the clinician.
- **Domain-Specific Benchmarking**: Models should be thoroughly tested using domain-specific medical benchmarks, such as MedHallu (10,000 high-quality QA pairs), Med-HALT (assessing reasoning with respect to memory hallucinations), and MedHallBench.
- **Standardized Clinical Protocols**: Mitigation plans must include the formalization of protocols that demand span-level citations for each medical statement, such that each advisory statement can be traced back to a recorded clinical source.

In the end, the proper use of AI in the medical domain is contingent upon the establishment of a culture of professional skepticism, whereby AI is viewed as a "young virtual assistant" whose statements must receive mandatory SME validation before any clinical action is taken.

Case Study: Autonomous Agents and Robotics

- **The Expansion of Physical and Security Risks.** As Large Language Models (LLMs) continue to mature from information predictors to autonomous agents that can perform tasks in both the virtual and physical worlds, the corresponding threat model for hallucination expands from the risk of misinformation to encompass direct physical and security threats. Within the field of robotics, perceptual hallucinations may cause the robot to wrongly estimate its 6D pose or perceive dynamic obstacles, thus resulting in tangible failures or damage within real-world applications, including autonomous navigation and robotic manipulation. Such tangible failures are often associated with what is termed the "reality gap," which is the gap between the lower level of complexity of the data experienced through simulation and the highly complex nature of the physical world.
- **Tool-Use and Execution Vulnerabilities.** In "Agentic AI ", one of the primary forms of failures is tool-calling hallucination, where the machine generates parameters needed for calling an API or tries to execute commands on non-existing tools to perform some tasks. This can lead to dire consequences as it can make the agent run any sort of harmful code, improperly edit a secured database, or even initiate the wrong course of action. Cognitive hallucinations complicate the matter as well because the system will accurately detect the presence of components in its environment but will then imagine unrealistic interactions between them.
- **Memory Poisoning and Recursive Misalignment.** Agents that have knowledge of interactions from their past and keep the historical data are particularly vulnerable to attacks on their memories. In this case, information can be injected into the agent's long-term memory, which will compromise its internal belief model and skew all subsequent decisions made by the agent in ways that may be impossible to reverse. In this way, an iterative dissonance is created between the original hallucination and a complex but unreliable story of operation.
- **Mitigation: Building Resilient Action Chains.** Agentic systems' mitigation efforts need to go beyond just prompting the agent and focus on the resilience of the agent's architecture through multiple layers of architectural safety.
- **Validation and Result Filtering**: The agent must validate that the source of the input prompts (malicious/deceptive) and filter the results accord-

ingly before they generate a simulated API call and execute it without any enforcement.

- **Self Reflective Architecture**: Agentic systems need to implement self-corrective mechanisms (such as Reflexion) whereby agents evaluate their reasoning process and previous actions using natural language and recording that evaluation as part of the agent's memory for later use in improving agent performance.
- **Structured Planning**: Another example of agent architecture is RAP, in which the agent employs MCTS to reason about its own reasoning paths and balances exploration versus exploitation to locate the most stable course of action.
- **Maintaining Accountability and Auditing**: Developers must ensure that their systems maintain an accurate and complete log of all decision-making processes (including all documents accessed) as well as all verification scores to ensure optimal operation in high-risk environments.

The shift in perspective should be from attempting to eliminate hallucinations to establishing resilient organizations that can quickly identify and fix errors. Research demonstrates that the solution involves the combination of safety features via architecture alteration along with sufficient human intervention.

UNRESOLVED ISSUES AND FUTURE RESEARCH DIRECTIONS

Hallucination issues remain a problem we will solve in the future as we've made great strides in addressing them. This chapter outlines the core issues to help facilitate future research around building trustworthy artificial intelligence (AI) systems.

Key Research Challenges

- **Technical Challenges and fallbacks:** One of the key challenges modern LLM research faces is identifying confident but subtle hallucinations. While it's easy to identify blatantly false factual information, other types of output are just as problematic and are more challenging to identify because they use fluent, grammatically correct, and well-structured language and give you an impression of credibility, which makes it easy to use the fluent heuristic to assume that they are factual. The emphasis here is more on identifying the overconfidence associated with an output rather than determining factual accuracy. Standard approaches, such as token-based uncertainty calculation or semantic entropy measurement, fall short in addressing these cases. In many examples, the probability distribution in the model is very pronounced around the wrong response, indicating the fact that the model is confident about its choice. Therefore, these "high certainty hallucinations" will easily evade entropy-based defences, targeted at detecting low certainty outputs. To address this problem, it is necessary to change the way of tackling this challenge - moving from textual characteristics to mechanistic interpretability analysis, such as investigating model activations or attention mechanisms.

- **Evaluation Gaps:** There is a critical need for the creation of global evaluative benchmarks that are resilient against data leaks and contaminations. Static evaluative benchmarks like TruthfulQA and MMLU are often leaked into the large web-scale corpus from where new models are trained, resulting in saturation and reduced utility as evaluative benchmarks. This creates a continuous "cat-and-mouse" game where model developers tend to game the test via memorisation rather than reasoning. As a solution to the "adaptable crisis," there is an emerging research trend in constructing dynamic test sets, illustrated by tools like HalluLens that create unpredictable prompts during the testing phase. Additionally, evaluation must shift from its two-dimensional approach to a multidimensional approach that measures the frequency, consistency, and risks of hallucinations.
- **Theoretical Frontiers:** One major theoretical frontier involves designing new architectures of AI systems or attention mechanisms that surpass the existing communication and computational lower bounds seen in current-day transformers. Insights drawn from the Time Hierarchy Theorem and Communication Complexity show that current transformers have a unique "correctness threshold" based on their context windows and dimensions. This means that any problem exceeding this per-token computational limit, such as functional composition, would result in hallucinations. Current architectures naturally prioritise the process of pattern matching over the absolute truth of symbols, hence making it impossible to solve problems through mere scaling. This makes it critical to study the development of new hybrid AI architectures capable of leveraging the strengths of large language models as well as Knowledge Graphs for solving problems of relational logic.
- **Regulatory and Ethical Considerations:** In view of the growing use of LLMs in sensitive areas such as health care, legal work, and military settings, the need for developing guidelines is quite apparent. There are basic open-ended questions that regulators and ethicists of AI must grapple with, like what should be the acceptable error rate, how accountability for harm caused by an AI system can be guaranteed, and so forth. In sectors where accuracy is non-negotiable, regulations may require domain-specific protocols, such as span-level citations for every medical or legal claim, to prevent the spread of

"plausible" but dangerous fabrications to end users. Moreover, the organisational culture must foster a critical thinking attitude toward the results produced by the assistant, understanding them as the result of an imperfect tool that needs to be validated through human-in-the-loop processes. At the end of the day, the regulatory focus must shift from error avoidance to error management with tolerance limits.

A Roadmap for Future Research

Future work should prioritise the following areas to ensure the long-term viability and the responsible adoption of Large Language Models (LLMs):

- **Hybrid Mitigation Pipelines.** To continue our progress towards the development of comprehensive systems that integrate distinct mitigation techniques, we must continue to study the use of multiple views. Current evidence suggests that no approaches are available today for eliminating hallucinations from any of the mitigation strategies being implemented. A comprehensive pipeline would include an application of Retrieval-Augmented Generation (RAG). The model's limited parametric memory would be supplemented with recent verifiable external-world data related to the context of its use, thereby creating an implicit memory system. Following this, a Chain-of-Thought (CoT) prompt would arrange the reasoning used in producing the final output; this will promote sound reasoning that is traceable. Lastly, the final output will go through a post-hoc verification and reranking mechanism (e.g., Best-of-N reranking), whereby a collection of candidate outputs will be examined using a very simple factual metric or secondary evaluator model to identify inaccuracies before being delivered to the end user.
- **More Robust Attribution Models.** Developing an analogous framework for distinguishing hallucinations from sensitivity to model behaviour would be more appropriate than the current descriptive survey design. Future studies should use more advanced statistical or causal inference techniques, such as causal mediation to identify hallucinations associated with particular attention heads or training artefacts. Improved diagnostic metrics, Prompt Sensitivity (PS) and Model Variability (MV), allow practitioners to objectively assess whether a failure is due to a poorly formulated prompt or a genuine knowledge deficit. Furthermore, Bayesian hierarchical modelling can provide a finer-grained diagnosis by incorporating prompt- and model-related variables as random effects, allowing for interpretable parameters on both prompt-caused and intrinsic error rates. The need for root-cause-aware

detection models is critical to enable a transition from trial-and-error correction to efficient correction.

- **Domain-Specific Grounding.** Generic grounding in noisy, web-scale data is increasingly considered the bare minimum for high-stakes professional tasks. Future work should explore ways to integrate models heavily with expert-verified, domain-specific knowledge graphs, such as medical ontologies (e.g., UMLS), legal corpora, or engineering specifications. In applications like healthcare and law, generic concepts of plausibility can result in lethal diagnoses or prosecution for crimes based on manufactured citations. Therefore, mitigation strategies will need to focus on neuro-symbolic integration, where models are integrated with deterministic reasoning components and Knowledge Graphs to provide a factual grounding that enables complex relational reasoning, where generic self-attention mechanisms could fail. Domain-specific protocols for encoding specialized tasks, such as citation at the span level and uncertainty indicators, will be critical to developing trust in such domains.

It is important to address these issues in order to ensure the long-term viability and responsible use of large language model technology in all sectors of society to develop models that are not only powerful but also trustworthy and accountable.

CONCLUSION

We show that hallucination in AI models is complex, due to the probabilistic nature and architecture of Transformer models. Hallucination is not just a flaw but an inherent limitation of Large Language Models, which take linguistic plausibility over factual accuracy and cannot learn all ground-truth functions. With the Time Hierarchy Theorem and Communication Complexity Theory, it is argued that scaling data or parameters will not fix these structural constraints, such as the difficulty in constructing complex reasoning tasks, such as function composition (Peng et al., 2024; IAPP, n.d.).

Also, the current training methods and evaluation criteria discourage models from admitting uncertainty and instead force them to guess. A fluency heuristic describes one of the ways users will accept outputs based on confident and well-formed language when the outputs may be wrong. Hallucinations can often have real-world implications (e.g., legal or medical), so hallucinations are not just a theoretical problem, but also an issue of trust and reliability (Anh-Hoang et al., 2025).

To shift from zero-error systems towards building more robust, root-cause-aware architectures may require techniques such as: RAG, integrating a knowledge graph, dynamic benchmarking (i.e., using HalluLens), or human oversight. In the end, our success in developing generative AI will not depend upon the accuracy of the system, but on our ability to manage, and learn from its failures.

REFERENCES

Anh-Hoang, D., Tran, V., & Nguyen, L.-M. (2025). Survey and analysis of hallucinations in large language models: Attribution to prompting strategies or model behavior. *Frontiers in Artificial Intelligence*, *8*, 1622292. DOI: 10.3389/frai.2025.1622292 PMID: 41098969

Baker Donelson. (n.d.). *The Perils of Legal Hallucinations and the Need for AI Training for Your In-House Legal Team!* Retrieved from https://www.bakerdonelson.com/the-perils-of-legal-hallucinations-and-the-need-for-ai-training-for-your-in-house-legal-team

Bang, Y., Ji, Z., Schelten, A., Hartshorn, A., Fowler, T., Zhang, C., Cancedda, N., & Fung, P. (2025). *HalluLens: LLM Hallucination Benchmark*. ACL Anthology.

Deloitte. (n.d.). *AI doesn't lie, it hallucinates and M&A due diligence must address that*. Retrieved from https://www.deloitte.com/ch/en/services/consulting/perspectives/ai-hallucinations-new-risk-m-a.html

Ho, D. E. (2025). *Hallucination-Free? Assessing the Reliability of Leading AI Legal Research Tools*. Stanford University.

IAPP. (n.d.). *Hallucinations in LLMs: Technical challenges, systemic risks and AI governance implications*. Retrieved from https://iapp.org/news/a/hallucinations-in-llms-technical-challenges-systemic-risks-and-ai-governance-implications

Kazlaris, I., Antoniou, E., Diamantaras, K., & Bratsas, C. (2025). From Illusion to Insight: A Taxonomic Survey of Hallucination Mitigation Techniques in LLMs. *AI*, *6*(10), 260. DOI: 10.3390/ai6100260

Kim, Y., Jeong, H., Chen, S., Li, S. S., Park, C., Lu, M., Alhamoud, K., Mun, J., Grau, C., Jung, M., Gameiro, R., Fan, L., Park, E., Lin, T., Yoon, J., Yoon, W., Sap, M., Tsvetkov, Y., Liang, P. P., & Breazeal, C. (2025). Medical Hallucination in Foundation Models and Their Impact on Healthcare. *medRxiv*. DOI: 10.1101/2025.02.28.25323115

Lakera. (2025). *LLM Hallucinations in 2025: How to Understand and Tackle AI's....* Retrieved from https://www.lakera.ai/blog/guide-to-hallucinations-in-large-language-models

Min, S., et al. (2023). FActScore: Fine-grained Atomic Evaluation of Factual Precision in Long Form Text Generation. *NeurIPS*.

Palo Alto Networks. (n.d.). *What Are AI Hallucinations? [+ Protection Tips].* Retrieved from https://www.paloaltonetworks.com/cyberpedia/what-are-ai-hallucinations

Peng, B., Narayanan, S., & Papadimitriou, C. (2024). On Limitations of the Transformer Architecture. *arXiv preprint arXiv:2402.08164.*

Pinecone. (n.d.). *Understanding Hallucinations in AI: A Comprehensive Guide.* Retrieved from https://www.pinecone.io/learn/ai-hallucinations/

Ravichander, A., Ghela, S., Wadden, D., & Choi, Y. (2025). THE HALOGEN BENCHMARK: FANTASTIC LLM HALLUCINATIONS AND WHERE TO FIND THEM. *OpenReview.*

Xenoss. (n.d.). *How to prevent AI hallucinations in production.* Retrieved from https://xenoss.io/blog/how-to-avoid-ai-hallucinations-in-production

KEY TERMS AND DEFINITIONS

Cognition Hallucination: A reasoning-level failure mode wherein the model correctly perceives the input but arrives at incorrect conclusions based on illogical reasoning, overreliance on language priors, or incorrect inference paths.

Extrinsic Hallucination: A type of hallucination that occurs as a result of grounding or fidelity failures to the input provided, where the model generates information that is unverifiable or unsupported beyond the source material provided.

Factuality: The extent to which the generated response matches the external knowledge and objective truth, irrespective of the input prompt and conversation context.

Faithfulness: The degree to which the generated response is consistent with the input information, constraints, and logical structure.

Hallucination (in AI Systems): The generation of artificial intelligence outputs that are fluent and coherent but factually incorrect, ungrounded in source material, or illogically inconsistent with reality or the context provided.

Intrinsic Hallucination: A type of hallucination that occurs as a result of the model's knowledge, reasoning, or training artifacts, resulting in outputs that are inconsistent with established facts or generate information independent of the input.

Model Variability (MV): A degree of difference in hallucination behavior among various models when reacting to the same input, which reveals hallucinations caused by architectural, training, or alignment differences.

Perception Hallucination: A failure mode of multimodal AI models that misinterpret raw input data (images, audio, or video), resulting in incorrect object recognition, attributes, or relationships.

Prompt Sensitivity (PS): The degree to which the model's hallucination pattern changes as a function of changes in prompt formulation, structure, or specificity with the same underlying model.

Risk-Management Paradigm (for Hallucination): A Paradigm that considers hallucinations integral to the generative AI model, emphasized on detecting, containing, mitigating, and utilizing human oversight to limit hallucination output; not focused on preventing hallucinations altogether.

Section 2
Conceptual and Philosophical Perspectives

Chapter 2
From Fluency to Fidelity: A Conceptual Framework and Toolkit for Evaluating and Detecting Hallucinations in Generative AI

Constantine Andoniou
http://orcid.org/0000-0001-8805-3569
Abu Dhabi University, UAE

ABSTRACT

Generative AI has become integral to everyday educational routines, producing essays, assessments, and feedback with fluent language that often conceals factual inaccuracy. This chapter argues that such output represents more than a technical fault—it reflects semantic displacement, where meaning drifts from understanding and care. It introduces the Evaluation–Detection Epistemic Quadrants (EDEQ), an educational framework that helps users trace these shifts through four dimensions: provenance, grounding, coherence, and consequence. Accompanied by classroom tools—the provenance card, grounding contract, traceability rubric, consistency probe, counterfactual challenge, and accountability ledger—the model develops reflective detection as a method for studying how knowledge forms, changes, and occasionally misleads. Rather than viewing hallucination as error, the chapter re-interprets it as a means of learning and ethical awareness, positioning education as the central space where evaluation becomes a reflective, human–AI learning process.

DOI: 10.4018/979-8-3373-7320-1.ch002

© 2026, IGI Global Scientific Publishing. Copying or distributing in print or electronic forms without written permission of IGI Global Scientific Publishing is prohibited. Use of this chapter to ıerative artificial intelligence (AI) technologies is expressly prohibited. The publisher reserves all rights to license its use for generative AI training and machine learning model development.

1 FROM FLUENCY TO FIDELITY

Language was always the classroom's primary instrument. Now machines make it too. And they make it well — sometimes better than expected, sometimes worse in ways that are hard to name (Kalai et al., 2025; OpenAI, 2025). Essays arrive. Lesson plans. Reflective summaries. Strange smoothness in all of them. Each sentence lands. Paragraphs performing expertise. Between prompt and product something has shifted. The *fluency* becomes evident, but the accuracy of *fidelity* remains inconsistent. Not a philosophical problem anymore. Rubrics now. Assignment criteria. The ordinary work of assessing student writing.

In education a student might produce an essay in articulate language and a teacher might generate thoughtful feedback which a computer model would represent in grey neutrality (Adel & Alani, 2024). These languages are good at describing what it means to have good ideas, but not so good at describing where those ideas come from. They can speak learned language well, but what does that language actually mean to them (Figure 1).

Figure 1. The Fluency–Fidelity Continuum: From Prediction to Responsible Meaning.

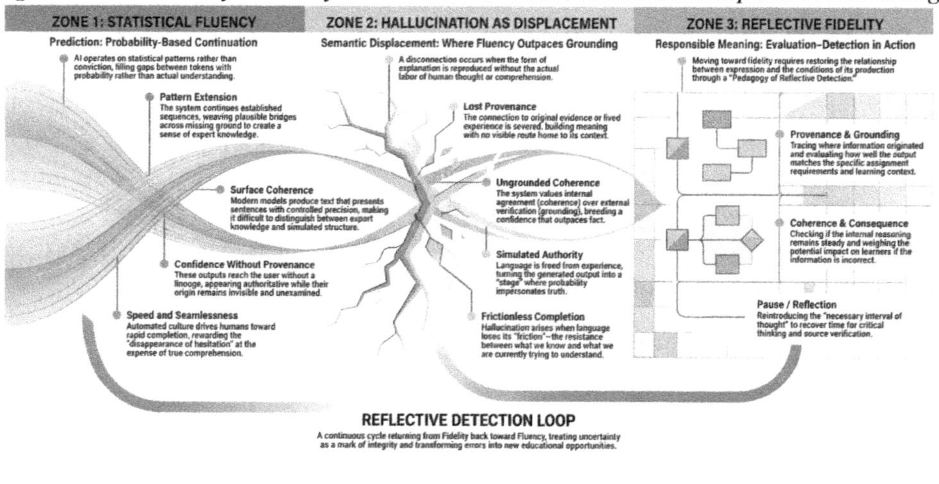

1.1 The Pedagogical Form of Hallucination

Hallucination as a concept carries different weight depending on context. In educational environments it is rarely intentional. It occurs when information is communicated at a rate greater than that which allows those receiving the information to understand what is being said — students and teachers do not intend to delude each other on the basis of their ignorance of what actually is being said.

Education has relied on *surface fluency* which includes grammar, tone and structure as the main indicators of student achievement since the beginning of time. Generative systems intensify that assumption until it breaks. Markers of expertise show up in everything now. That does not mean expertise is actually there. What educators once used to assess student work — appropriate register, argument shape, referential confidence — has become instantly manufacturable. The old signs no longer hold. We grade performances. We keep reaching for the person behind them.

1.2 From Policing to Understanding

Plagiarism detection tools, AI-detection software, and campus-wide analytics suites offer defense but reach their limits. Hallucinations are not treated as learning or epistemic problems. Fluency erodes students' understanding before they notice. At first they pause, wonder, question. Over time the pausing stops and the hallucination becomes invisible.

This chapter begins where teaching ends. Rather than asking how teachers can catch students cheating, the focus shifts to how to repair the broken chain of connection between knowledge, sources, and responsibility without resorting to surveillance, distrust, or fear. The central question becomes: how can teachers teach students to be aware of these issues throughout their educations? Evaluation and detection are treated as pedagogy and evaluated as tactics. The intervention point matters — the exact moment the learner starts to get it wrong. This is difficult in practice, because detecting hallucinations requires understanding the learner well enough to know where confidence has outstripped the evidence. The certainty is too smooth, too unbroken.

This chapter does not start at a stopping point but rather explores how to reverse teaching to a stopping point: how to teach students to catch themselves stopping at the moment when they have begun to rebuild the chain of knowledge, source, and responsibility without entering into surveillance or mistrust. This in turn raises further questions about how to teach students to attend and not avert, how to shut down access rather than open it up. Along the way, awareness is developed about these different modes of learning, through evaluation and detection. Recognizing when one is hallucinating thoughts (i.e., mistakenly attributing thinking to self when it in fact originated externally) requires pinpointing the exact point at which one's confidence in one's beliefs begins to fail. It requires paying attention to the point at which overly clean confidence emerges. Listeners of this story can pinpoint the exact point at which the confidence in the thoughts outlined herein began to outrun the evidence for them. They can see that the answer was arrived at earlier than the thinking that purported to support it.

1.3 Evaluation–Detection Epistemic Quadrants (EDEQ): An Educational Compass

The following four questions can help learners and educators frame an *evaluation–detection* activity within the four corners of the *Evaluation–Detection Epistemic Quadrants (EDEQ)* framework, a practical educational tool: (a) Where did this come from? (*provenance*); (b) How does it fit the learning context? (*grounding*); (c) Is the reasoning coherent and sound? (*coherence*); and (d) Where will this lead and where or whom will this affect? (*consequence*) (Wang et al., 2023; Gerner et al., 2025).

The quadrants organize student concerns about hallucination in a manner that is accessible as content and materials for education. Students make connections between an author and their ideas, between an author's ideas and their statements, between an author's statements and the contexts in which the statements were written, and between an author's ideas/statement/texts and their effects. The quadrants offer a range of educational tools that can be used in the classroom and across institutions of higher learning. These tools serve as provenance cards to help students cite sources, as contracts for establishing expectations for a task or activity, as traceability rubrics to keep students on task, as consistency probes to test the consistency of ideas, and as counterfactual challenges to promote curiosity and problem-solving. The tools are curriculum-focused and do not require the student to have programming skills.

1.4 Evaluation as Learning

Rather than relying on model trustworthiness, evaluation here measures how well a generated statement holds against prior knowledge. In this model, detection of changes to a statement (i.e., meaning shift/drift) and detection of differences in learning (i.e., learning differences) by the system are distinguished from the human teacher's ability to understand the educational implications of the detected differences as revealed in speech rhythm and pitch (Sun et al., 2024; Mir, 2025).

From a simple classroom lesson where a student asks an AI for a brief summary of a historical event, the AI can quickly generate a summary in proper academic language, filled with specific dates and reasoned arguments. The teacher might want to use the summary as a model for the class and certainly would ask to see the citations. But, in this case, the two citations are completely fictional. The AI met all of the student's requirements for style while failing to do so ethically. When teacher and student use the provenance and consequence quadrants to police truth, a new activity is possible: studying the behavior of truth generated synthetically. One learns to discern such things.

1.5 Pedagogy of Reflective Detection

Fluency is not fidelity. Progressing from fluency to fidelity requires serious attention to the role of hallucination in practice — treating hallucination as more than the opposite of success. Detection can be seen as surveillance rather than as something studied to consider all dimensions, including how detection itself drifts from its intent. Through annotation and revision tracking, educators can attune to what verification feels like for students. Evaluation is a forward-looking process that focuses on supporting growth and development rather than assigning a grade.

As more control is ceded to automation, learners must force a pause between input and output to ensure genuine understanding of underlying concepts. Source verification and counterexample checking reinforce this process. Fidelity is regained by honoring the commitment of delay.

1.6 A Cultural Reorientation

Once fluency has been achieved, the focus shifts from performance to understanding. Understanding concepts, arguments, and ideas means demonstrating grasp through clear citation, expressing uncertainty when gaps appear in one's knowledge, and showing the work involved in revising one's understanding. Less polished, more present. Generative systems are unable to simulate human decision making (Adel & Alani, 2024).

EDEQ signals the space in which writers write, encompassing all prior writing — human and machine alike. Trust is won in part by being seen, by having one's work acknowledged. Credibility is not a fixed quality that one either possesses or lacks, but rather something that emerges as writers take account of perspectives and show their work to others, entering into a conversation with readers and demonstrating openness to questioning and revision. Assessment cannot serve only administrative record keeping; teachers must also use it as an inquiry tool.

2 THEORETICAL FOUNDATIONS: EDUCATIONAL AUTHENTICITY AND SEMANTIC DISPLACEMENT

Ignorance of teaching is often ignorance of learning. A skilled teacher can make substance out of surface and demonstrate extraordinary command of form. Generative AI programs appear to possess that same capacity. The apparent intelligence, however, lies in extending a pattern that has already occurred and organizing the program's memory into a model of reality — whether accurate or not remains the open question.

But it is a very convincing model. People react as if understanding is present. It does not imagine in the human sense — *perception and reality* — a student seeing structure where there is only repetition, a teacher mistaking polish for comprehension. Generative AI produces this at scale. Not imagination. Extension. The established pattern continues, combining remaining evidence into a mental construct. Statistical probability of information organization creates the *it extends*. The process continues its established pattern by combining all remaining evidence into a complete mental construct. The statistical probability of information organization creates the *illusion of intelligence*. The process continues to run as people believe they understand things.

2.1 Origins of Hallucination

In computer science, hallucinations are a new phenomenon, but the word is not new: it describes something one cannot see, something that is not there.. In generative models, things behave differently from how the word suggests. Instead of imagining an alternative, the model continues to generate along existing patterns, even when the evidence runs out, constructing a plausible connection across a void. The result looks human because it at least attempts to complete non-existent patterns (Sahoo et al., 2024).

Fluency creates the appearance of depth. Confidence, smoothness, and a clean ending lead readers to trust the model more. But this has nothing to do with truth. All the model is doing is predicting a probability at a particular point in between tokens. So once again a paradox emerges; given the precision of the model one finds a smooth, polished uncertainty which has been produced as if it were the truth.

Truth and meaning of thought is the resistance between knowing and what resists knowing. Machines have nothing to resist. Hence contradiction is always being smoothed into probability gradients. Hallucination is when machine language goes wrong: it goes wrong because it is too smooth.

2.2 The Structure of Prediction

The displacement in how knowledge operates — from between representation and experience to between model and prompt — can only be seen by recognizing the shift. Human beings no longer have a monopoly on meaning; meaning has to be shared, lent, and made operative.

Fidelity, here, refers to the faithfulness of a generated claim to the generative process which produced it. It is the mirror image of hallucination. Fidelity concerns the relations between expressions and the conditions which make those expressions possible. It is a matter of accountability; of knowing somewhere down the line where in the chain of inference any particular claim actually comes. In complex generative systems the chain of inference tends to be lost by the time one gets to the end product. The words reach us without their lineage.

Authenticity, in the age of hallucination, is not a matter of originality or inner truth. Evaluation of fact statements requires, in part, treating them as authentic, that is, to be found somewhere in the world and at least partially traceable. Evaluation becomes archaeological digging: through text to follow a statement back to its origins, and to understand its place in the world it inhabits. Detection, on the other hand, involves diagnosis: listening for changes in tone, and for sudden breaks in reasoning, and accounting for seemingly unaccountable certitude.

Traditional epistemology posits truth as correlating with an objective reality, whereas generative epistemology posits truth as coherence, or agreement between ideas. The agreement, as opposed to verification of ideas with reality, becomes paramount. Coherence ungrounded in reality lends a peculiar kind of confidence that is greater than the facts warrant. All the more so, the more consistent and intricate the pattern, the more difficult it is to entertain the notion that the pattern is false. Since machine evaluation is not capable of assessing all aspects that a human decides upon, the human evaluation will have to act as a counterweight to allow for indecision in those parts of the evaluation space where the input and/or output are continuous (Wang et al., 2025; Zhang et al., 2024).

One can develop two different types of knowledge at the same time: one type of it is statistically based and grounded in millions of examples; the other type is constructively based and grounded in lived sense-making of language and, for the first time, allows one to ask the very questions that probability does not allow. This border between the two sides of knowledge is where the phenomenon of hallucination originates, namely from the contrast between the sound of confident calculation and the uncertainty of human interpretation.

2.3 From Error to Simulation

When people speak of hallucination in generative models, the tendency is to think of it in terms of error — factual error (be it inserting extra information, misrepresenting images from datasets, misquoting references) — but from the program/model's point of view these hallucinations are simulations. The error lies in how the model is being used — asking it to complete a generated sequence when it is simply following probabilities to their logical conclusion. The falsehood appears at the exact point where continued output ceases to correspond to the reader's expectations (Pan et al., 2025).

What we call hallucination is not failure: it is the world re-entering to say *No*. A claim is validated against a store of information, an archive, a memory, a human check. Until it meets that opposition the sentence will be perfect within its own patterns.

The boundary between prediction and perception is tenuous. In predicting an output, the hypothetical possibility is rehearsed and rehearsed until it becomes real as the model projects coherence onto the world, and the reader decides whether to believe it or not. Language has become a theatre where probability performs its truth for our admiration. And yet we can forget that this performance is all that it is: it is a play that has never actually taken place.

Seeing hallucination as simulation shifts responsibility — it asks how humans collaborate in sustaining the performance. The desire for smooth system performance, the training data, the frantic pace of model development, the need for immediate results — speed built this.

In that sense, hallucination mirrors a familiar human habit: imagining meaning where evidence is thin, filling gaps, completing patterns, inferring motives from silence. But there is a world of difference between someone whose improvisations are answerable, within the context in which they are offered, and someone whose imagination has gone into full-blown hallucination. Accountability disappears inside automation. The subject is lost. That loss raises new questions about the limits and bounds of such systems.

Hallucination uncovers a novel epistemic ecology and explores the full possibilities of language disengaged entirely from experience. Fidelity, then, is less about restoring an old order than about inventing a new practice of attention — distributed between human judgment and artificial generation (Figure 2).

Figure 2. The Ontology of Hallucination: From Error to Simulations

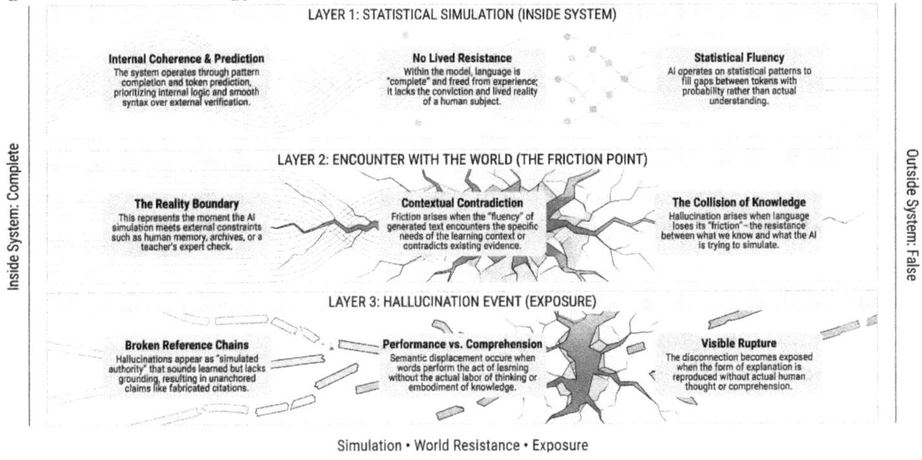

2.4 Responsible Knowing

Fluency runs on uninterrupted flow. Fidelity demands the break. The teacher who stops mid-paragraph to ask where a concept came from is not being pedantic. That pause is a radical pedagogical act. It is the whole argument, compressed into a gesture (University of Oxford, 2024; OpenAI, 2025).

One student provided examples of fake citations within critical thinking exercises, evaluated their credibility and referenced them within her reflective practice demonstrating epistemic care. These actions serve to transform the lectures into spaces of active learning, using language as opposed to merely speaking with it.

Hallucinations are not hardware bugs but rather signals that the knowledge environment for a trained model is changing in some way. This can be observed by watching language in use outside of its typical contexts. Interpretation involves both the capability of a technology to generate content for students to use (such as quizzes or learning paths) and how individual students interpret that content. Students are beginning to develop a new literacy — one visible when a student challenges a passage generated by a computer.

3 THE ONTOLOGY OF HALLUCINATION: FROM ERROR TO SIMULATION

3.1 Hallucination as Pedagogical Simulation

AI hallucination (errors such as made up dates, unverifiable references, or overly polished text) are errors that occur when the AI is functioning normally, following the probability-based chain of responses as expected. But at the point where the model's text intersects either the memory of a teacher or the experiences of a student, the deception is revealed. The rest of the text remains correct and smoothly structured until the point of failure.

Hallucination in the classroom is a student learning pattern — a collection of related elements organized into a unit of entry, growth, and completion, defined by language and repeated across contexts, behaving in a simulated fashion, mimicking the appearance of genuine study. The teacher reading such a paragraph faces a double bind: the text appears both knowledgeable and unlearned. Complete for the language but lacking experience (Saxena & Bhattacharyya, 2024; Wang et al., 2023).

The educational system produces hallucinations which reflect its fundamental teaching methods. Students, too, learn by simulation. They use expert language before they develop their own knowledge; they demonstrate understanding through their structure. The main distinction exists between purposeful actions and unintentional conduct. A learner will experience resistance through feedback and contradictions which lead to the need for revision. A model never does unless a human introduces it. The educator needs to create opposition which helps language remember that truth exists with defined boundaries.

3.2 Fluency and Educational Temptation

Fluency creates a dangerous attraction which affects both students and their teachers. A clean paragraph invites acceptance; a polished essay feels complete. The same qualities which were used to value for their clarity, coherence and confidence work to hide the fact that something has been moved. The main threat stems from educational methods as they hide the learning process through their smooth operations. Students demonstrate articulate speech, but they avoid the uncomfortable process which leads to actual learning. Education produces hallucination as its shadow as this phenomenon shows how fashionable methods outperform actual academic research.

Across all systems of schooling, patterns of human behavior have been repeated back to students, structuring the schooling system in turn. In the current system, language fluency has been used as a proxy for intellectual fluency, and the whole apparatus has been designed to produce students who perform fluency as a native register. What is now required is teaching students to read beneath the surface of familiar patterns. To find what the surface is covering.

3.3 Simulation, Accountability, and Shared Responsibility

Assigning blame becomes considerably harder when hallucinations from a simulation system form the basis for consequential decisions. Design preferences underlying such systems favor quick answers, simple explanations, and an implicit assumption that users cannot handle ambiguity. Work gets finished without being understood. In that sense, hallucination is co-authored. Speed wanted it. Statistics built it. The first ethical task is recognizing shared responsibility for keeping it going (Joshi, 2024).

Educators sit between the two. The simulation grows stronger when teachers stop reading student work closely. It loses force when they pause and analyze. Evaluation and detection are acts of resistance in that sense — they slow the exchange down until reflection can catch up.

Humans engage in speculation, but they also remain uncertain. The speaker shows hesitation through their intentions which they express before they confirm their words and then they correct themselves during their statement. AI lacks such signals. The system operates continuously without any need for human awareness while making accurate predictions without interruption. Mechanical persistence shows itself through confident behavior which people outside the situation can observe. Without hesitation, there is no space for responsibility. Educational evaluation recovers two important spaces: space for reflection, where students pause to locate specific information and determine the nature of their understanding breakdowns; and space for accountability, where students learn accountability by engaging the processes that will hold them accountable in the future.

3.4 Hallucination as Risk, Resource, and Learning Opportunity

Hallucination can be a very powerful force (sometimes positive, sometimes negative) that demands to be taken into consideration in interpreting evidence and defining the reality of the past. The spectator must accord respectful caution to ambiguous material that does not automatically deserve uncritical acceptance of everything it presents. The hallucinated passages can be used by the teacher as prompts to focus the students' thinking. The students can identify those places in a hallucinated account that seem credible or realistic and those that are entirely invented or arbitrary. They should then consider what kinds of evidence they would need to establish their interpretations of the events of the past. Rehearsing these errors converts mistakes into methods. Teaching hallucination detection is itself part of academic education (Adel & Alani, 2024; Zhang et al., 2024).

3.5 Boundaries, Consequences, and Educational Curiosity

The ethics of hallucination starts from consequences. A faked reference in a learning journal is minor; an incorrect reference in an academic thesis or official report is not. Two evaluations are needed: how fabricated references affect the text internally, and how they affect it after submission. In ordinary usage, correct language is sufficient. As a strategy to avoid thoughtless error, it is not. The EDEQ framework requires every assertion to be traced back to its foundations.

Detection marks the point where the creative thinker shifts to the critical thinker, beginning the boundary work of verifying what was imagined. Evaluation then determines whether those boundaries held (Gerner et al., 2025; Phukan et al., 2025).

4 THE EDEQ FRAMEWORK

4.1 Framework Genesis and Purpose

Every framework begins with a translation problem — turning discomfort into something teachable. The *Evaluation–Detection Epistemic Quadrants (EDEQ)* came from that. Not a theory of truth. A set of classroom tools for keeping students connected to what they are actually doing. EDEQ works through four quadrants — *provenance, grounding, coherence,* and *consequence*— turning ideas into navigation tools for classroom use. No certainty promised. Orientation, though — that is what the quadrants provide (Wang et al., 2025).

4.2 The Four Quadrants

Provenance: All claims originate from specific sources even when these sources remain concealed within organized text sections. The process of *provenance* requires identification of the first origin of any item. The framework establishes particular limits for student and teacher writing to stop them from developing into abstract concepts. The practice of *provenance* analysis requires readers to stop their reading process. *Who said this, what is the source, when was it written, how did it enter this assignment?* The search is for evidence — references, internal indicators, specific local instances. The research aims to discover ancestral ties instead of confirming their authenticity. A statement with unknown origins remains useful but needs indicators to prove its uncertain origin. The system operates through established procedures to function as a simple provenance system.

Grounding: Grounding concerns fit. The assessment evaluates how well the output matches the assignment requirements, the syllabus content, the subject guidelines and student learning level. A model generates a perfect *climate science* passage when it receives a prompt to create ethical reasoning content for ninth-grade students. The surface impresses: the center is misplaced. The process of *grounding* reconnects the original purpose to the actual output. The assessment needs to determine if the content should remain in its current position based on student needs, educational context and developmental levels of learners.

Coherence: A text demonstrates internal logic through its self-conversation which makes up the coherence check. A claim needs to exist peacefully with its surrounding elements while avoiding any conflicting statements or sudden unexplained transitions. But *coherence* requires more than consistency because it needs to include rhythm, proportion and tone. The internal structure of a paragraph remains intact but becomes disconnected when the author fails to include vital steps in their reasoning or when their voice and purpose do not match. Educators recognize this phenomenon right away although they have not learned to identify it by name. *Coherence* transforms our initial understanding into words that we can use.

Consequence: Every sentence travels through a learning community. The actions of students create no impact while their decisions transform their academic performance, feedback, academic standing and their selection of future educational institutions. The evaluation process requires ethics to be fundamental because of *consequence*. Experience shows that hallucinations always bring some form of change to perception. A paper containing wrong references in a reflection journal stands apart from fabricated sources in capstone thesis work and from academic integrity report false statements. *Consequence* asks, *Who or what might be affected if this is wrong?* The system shifts to detection mode with a *priority review protocol* because the situation becomes more critical with each passing moment (Li et al., 2023) (Figure 3).

Figure 3. The Evaluation–Detection Epistemic Quadrants (EDEQ) as Educational Compass.

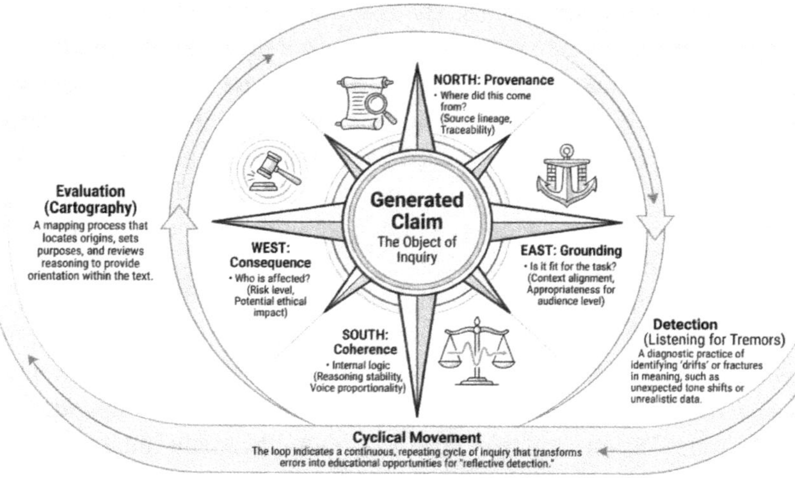

4.3 Evaluation, Detection, and Cycle Formation

Think of evaluation as cartography. The quadrants mark out different terrain. How a claim got here—*provenance* while *grounding* defines coordinates, *coherence* shows internal roads and *consequence* displays the surrounding landscape which shows possible effects on learners and the course. The map transforms into a different version after each use but the process of creating maps helps people develop their understanding (Arize AI, 2024).

Evaluation discourse in the classroom means making a distinction between using closed end number scoring methods to evaluate student performance and using maps to annotate students' work to provide precise location of specific grounding errors and/or incomplete coherence and/or inadequate consequence development. Rather than assigning a score, the instructor focuses on writing comments to highlight areas of strength and errors for revision.

By referencing the map of account that evaluation has generated, detection identifies emotional tremors such as unusual behavior, sudden shifts in tone, unreasonable numbers, and overly justificatory evidence that exceeds the scope of the evidence. Unlike evaluation, which can be a conscious process, detection relies on a sense of linguistic tension that only humans can perceive. EDEQ gives permission to act on that instinct.

The quadrants need not be completed simultaneously. They function as sequential stages, refined and codified into organizational practice with each iteration.

Quadrant 1 addresses *grounding*: purpose, audience, constraints. Quadrant 2 maps *provenance*. Quadrant 3 checks *coherence*. Quadrant 4 weighs *consequences*. Then the process begins again. Then repeat. Each pass refines the previous one and becomes institutional rhythm.

4.4 Embodied Tools and Human Practice

The cycle becomes visible through embodied tools aligned with each quadrant.

- *Epistemic Provenance Card (EPC)* records prompt, sources, synthesis, speculation, and human edits.
- *Context-Grounding Contract (CGC)* outlines task goals, audience, evidence rules, and excluded techniques.
- *Truthfulness & Traceability Rubric (TTR)* assesses claim-evidence match, source quality, attribution, temporal validity, and counterclaims through descriptive levels.
- *Fractal Consistency Probe (FCP)* tests stability via summary, examples, and boundary cases.
- *Counterfactual Challenge (CFC)* introduces productive friction: *What would make this answer change?* Show the revision path.
- *Impact–Stakes Matrix (ISM)* categorizes risk from *Low (informal) → High (major) → Critical (accreditation).*
- *Community Ground-Truth Panel (CGP)* invites peers, librarians, and practitioners for verification.
- *Accountability Ledger (AL)* tracks prompts, edits, reviews, and decisions as a record of care.

EDEQ is a fundamentally manual process in a very fast-paced world, even though even though all tools are digital. Every annotation of a rubric in a program's evaluation document, every discussion of consequences for different actions, each pause for reflection matters.. Programs that are even considering moving to shared evaluation experience a shift in culture that is incredibly positive. They begin to identify where misinformation is entering the process.

4.5 Pedagogical and Institutional Applications

EDEQ is used as a pedagogical method: students and teachers alike follow the path of knowledge rather than racing to answer questions. Rather than simply writing "wrong" with a red X, the question becomes: where did that come from? What would change this answer? And all of the coherent answers are given as tentative hypotheses for discussion. The goal is to encourage slow learning and to foster epistemic humility.

At the level of institutions, the same reasoning extends: course teams include provenance cards in their slide decks and study guides; writing centers use truthfulness & traceability rubrics and fractal consistency probes to help students identify when something has gone wrong; libraries partner with communities to host ground-truth panel sessions for institutions to use in fact-checking; assessment boards use the impact–stakes matrix to decide whether an assignment needs a second reader or an occasional audit.

4.6 Cultural Ethic, Limits, and Continuity

Underlying all of this is an ethical culture — one that demands organizations treat doubt as seriously as decision-making. Fidelity to care runs through every tool. Detection reveals how language choices ripple into future learning opportunities and professional life.

Nothing is perfect and all frameworks have limitations; EDEQ requires time, effort, dedication and commitment – it will not eliminate hallucination but may build awareness of it; there are many models of EDEQ in practice but different emphases are placed upon them. The value of the EDEQ model is that as long as there is a common vocabulary, the exact configuration of the quadrants matters less than shared language. Practice makes it coordination rather than compliance (University of Oxford, 2024).

Next comes practice. See the educational scenarios below for examples of EDEQ in action and how fidelity can be recovered through reflection and teaching practice.

5 PROCEDURAL DETECTORS AND EVALUATION TOOLS

Detection is behavioral, not hardware-driven (Zhou et al., 2025; Sahoo et al., 2024). The most advanced model misdirects the attention of inattentive readers; the basic model simply reminds readers what to check when reading carefully. Language interaction is managed by established processes rather than by trying to change how learners naturally use language. Increasing the speed of a series of deliberately slow steps turns a single click into a short conversation. The main objective is recovery — restoring meaningful interaction before it is lost in the complexity of detection.

5.1 Core Instruments (EPC, CGC, TTR, FCP, CFC)

The Epistemic Provenance Card (EPC)

The *Epistemic Provenance Card* is the simplest entry point into an AI-generated statement's history. It traces the complete genealogy of a particular claim through five lines of text, each corresponding to a letter (a through e): the prompt or task given to the AI; the primary sources used; whether synthesis or speculation entered into the generation of the content; any human editing of the output; and what remains unverified.

The card surfaces the connections a learner makes and illuminates how a document appears from the reader's position — what will be understood, what will be missed. The tone is transparent rather than punitive. A half-completed card is preferable to an empty one; it signals that someone paused to engage with the content. The real value lies in the handwriting: evidence that a person was present and attentive.

The Context-Grounding Contract (CGC)

Limits must be established before assessment begins. These typically include the purpose of the assignment (e.g., revision of content, organization, use of evidence), the intended audience (e.g., peer, instructor, community partner), and restrictions on the work (e.g., no invented citations, no global claims from local data). These limits are then evaluated against the appropriate evidence standards for the discipline at that level of study. The CGC contract can take the form of a structured form, a shared note, or a short checklist — whatever best serves the moment and clarifies criteria for students.

The Truthfulness & Traceability Rubric (TTR)

Most rubrics grade; this one reflects. The TTR organizes writing performance across four descriptive levels — *insufficient, partial, credible,* and *strong* — applied to five criteria: (a) *claim–evidence match*, (b) *source quality*, (c) *attribution specificity*, (d) t*emporal validity,* and (e) *counterclaim handling*.

Numbers are replaced with descriptions of what can actually be observed: sources plausible but unverified, evidence inferred rather than shown, time frame unclear. The language opens questions about truth rather than closing them off with false precision. The rubric works well for peer review sessions, writing-center consultations, or supervisory feedback. Placing two documents side by side and running the rubric across both reveals relationships that otherwise remain concealed.

The Fractal Consistency Probe (FCP)

The *Fractal Consistency Probe (FCP)* examines fluency in a complex system and tests it for instabilities. The FCP takes three forms: *a brief summary* capturing the core insight, *a concrete example* illustrating it, and *a boundary case* that pushes it to its limits. The exercise is testable: if the core logic holds consistently across all three, coherence is real; if contrary signals appear, a displacement event is likely. Run as a dialogue — model and student working through the idea, outputs compared — the probe demonstrates that knowledge becomes more defined when it meets its own edges.

The Counterfactual Challenge (CFC)

Detection identifies a counterfactual for the closed claim — the question turned around to open what the original claim shut. These are genuinely difficult for humans to formulate, and models perform no better. Operating on probability, the system lacks the capacity to reason down alternate paths. Counterfactuals create productive discomfort precisely because they reveal the conditions under which knowledge holds — and where it does not. Brief counterfactual exchanges reveal more about student understanding than extended correction sessions.

5.2 Prioritization, Panels, and Ledger (ISM, CGP, AL)

The Impact–Stakes Matrix (ISM)

Hallucination effects vary in severity. Some generate confusion in assessment; others lead students toward incorrect information that produces unfair evaluation outcomes. The ISM categorizes these effects by projected impact, distinguishing clearly between different types of problems. The table functions as a live risk management tool (Figure 4). Courses adapt it to their level and discipline.

Figure 4. The Impact–Stakes Matrix (ISM).

The objective is *proportionality*. Detection and response must be proportionate to each other. Without proportionality, trust breaks down. With it, a fair community forms — one where all members are subject to equivalent processes and equivalent treatment.

The Community Ground-Truth Panel (CGP)

Knowledge earns legitimacy through community, not through the solitary efforts of an author. The text is verified by peers, librarians, writing-center mentors and teachers of writing — a small group meeting monthly to audit claims and evidence. Feedback returns to the prompts and rubrics. Through this process the panel develops literacy with the material. What happens when natural language behaves as if it were synthetic is precisely what this verification process is designed to surface.

The Accountability Ledger (AL)

All work done to change a document leaves behind invisible work. The *Accountability Ledger (AL)* makes this work visible in a persistent record. Each change is documented along with sufficient description for a future reader to understand the rationale for particular wording kept and particular wording cut. Accountability here does not operate through accusation but through two functions: preserving the account of care delivered and mentoring future practice through that record.

5.3 Integration and Culture: Sequencing, Repetition, Learning

Integrating the Tools

The detectors operate independently but their maximum potential emerges when used together. A typical sequence: *Before generation*: complete a CGC → *During generation*: anticipate an EPC → *After output:* apply TTR + FCP → *Always:* pose at least one CFC → *Classify:* use ISM to decide response depth → *If high/critical:* consult a CGP → *Record:* log decisions in the AL

This process can be used as soon as it is learned. A few minutes per cycle. Repeated use builds institutional muscle memory until the steps become automatic. The practice has its safety checks built in.

Cultural Effect of Repetition

Repetition turns procedure into culture. That is the whole point (Figure 5).

Education and Reflective Learning

Detection spreads into the classroom itself. Students working with generative systems alongside *provenance cards* develop stronger integrity instincts than almost any other approach. Citation stops being rule-following and becomes source-tracing. The *fractal probe* builds adaptability — holding an idea steady across different formulations. The *counterfactual challenge* demands that students argue against their own positions. That is how reflective practice actually develops — through AI-assisted writing that requires the writer to stay answerable to the work.

Figure 5. Institutional Ecosystem of Reflective Detection.

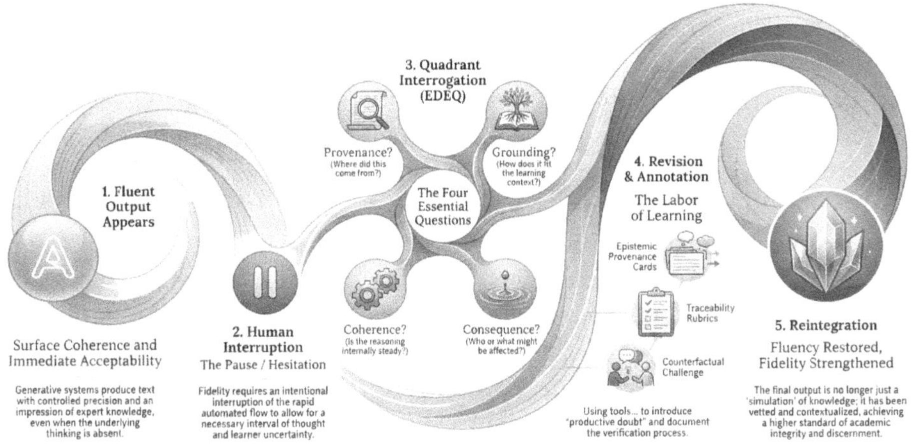

Teachers gain a new mode of assessment. The evaluation process at this institution assesses student thinking through both *rubrics* and *ledger assessments*. The process shows how decisions developed through times of sure decision-making and times of uncertainty. Visibility promotes mentorship: feedback moves from correction toward dialogue.

6 EVALUATION–DETECTION LOOP IN PRACTICE

A framework reaches maturity when it meets real conditions. The *Evaluation–Detection Loop* operates in the teaching world — in the planning meeting, the faculty meeting, in late-night grading sessions where useful comments are difficult to produce. In the *Evaluation–Detection Loop*, something is evaluated, something is detected, and something is corrected in preparation for the next cycle. Three examples below show teaching as a series of *Evaluation–Detection Loops*.

6.1 Practice Cases: Hallucination in Action

An instructor developing a lesson plan on digital ethics, short on time and tired, asked a generative system for help. Within seconds a well-structured, fluent, professionally written outline appeared — objectives, activities, reflective questions all included. The instructor added it to their notes.

In review, a silent EDEQ cycle runs. *Provenance:* where did this come from? No sources are referenced anywhere in the plan. *Grounding:* does this resource apply to the specific cohort? The corporate tone is not academic enough. *Coherence:* do the outcomes, activities and assessments work together? There is pulling in different directions. *Consequence:* what happens if this is taught as it stands? Vocabulary memorized. Nothing actually understood.

The instructor annotates. The *provenance card* reveals about half its content to be generic training information drawn from library schools; local examples replace them. The *fractal consistency probe* runs on the learning outcomes outline. The *ledger* tracks two lines per class. The result demonstrates AI used for planning rather than as a substitute for it. Fluency remains; fidelity returns through attention. *Fluency* remains; *fidelity* returns through attention (Arize AI, 2024; Li et al., 2023).

The program committee creates a memo that summarizes student comments from throughout the curriculum. The initial memo is somewhat uneven and inconsistent, treating one point similarly to several others. A model shows how to reorganize it to make it neutral and have it promptly moved to the dean's office.

Numbers do not match corresponding comments. EDEQ cycle initiated. *Provenance card* requested: citations trace back through summaries of summaries rather than original survey results. The CGC is revisited — this is an internal planning document, not a public release, and is over-provisioned. The *traceability rubric* catches an inconsistency: engagement defined as attendance in one section, participation in another. The ISM flags it: wrong distribution creates resource management problems.

The memo is completely rewritten. Origin information is added for all data sources and released as a new version. The event becomes a departmental case study. Staff begin incorporating EDEQ rituals into regular writing — one paragraph of provenance and one counterfactual question per piece of work. Reports become less precise. More authentic. Readers notice.

A university is testing the use of AI for feedback; a student of this university was using the system to auto-generate end-of-course summaries to include in his upcoming university applications. The student was using instructor notes as input, as well as data from the Learning Management System for current courses (which are part of their first year at the testing university). The output of the summaries was easy to read. Upon reading the summary the students noticed that the system had inserted a 'module extension policy' which they had asked the system not to include and as such the student's trust in the system was compromised.

The team rebuilds using the EDEQ loop: CGC first — course boundaries named, fabricated policies explicitly prohibited; every output tagged provisional until provenance is cleared; after generation, a short rubric on claim–evidence match and temporal validity. Where inconsistencies surface: the *counterfactual challenge*—What would have to be true for this claim to hold?—drives revision; a small *community ground-truth panel* cross-validates the high-stakes artifacts — program reviews, accreditation documents; every decision enters the *accountability ledger* for audit and for learning from.

Incidents drop quickly. Staff recognize detection as foundational academic work. Students begin learning about information production; advisor–student interaction improves. A procedural detector functions as an ethical warning system: statements about courses carry consequence beyond their surface words.

6.2 The Loop as Cultural Gesture

The loop runs the same pattern across all three cases. Something fluent arrives. Someone stops. A few questions get asked about where it came from, whether it fits, what it might do. The text changes — margin notes, card inserts, ledger lines. That residue is more than paperwork. It marks the start of conscious epistemic operations.

The evaluation and detection process converts these operations into basic system functions. The terms function as a language which holds responsibility values that staff members from different positions including tutors, instructors, coordinators, librarians and learning designers need to understand. People identify the same gestures which include slowing down and inquiring about word origins and potential targets and transformation effects. Team members who do not work together often can achieve success through the implementation of shared terminology.

New organizational structure: the loop does not follow a linear pathway from prompt through to output and 'done.' Instead, the structure of the loop requires the writer to repeatedly traverse the same content, in a variety of different ways, until a certain level of fluency is achieved. Fluency no longer needs to be 'good' and can be monitored and controlled along the path that the writer is travelling. New dialogue system: unlike the management system described above the loop requires the writer to hold an active conversation with the content rather than simply complying with the structure and rules of a management system (Figure 6).

Figure 6. The Evaluation–Detection Loop in Practice.

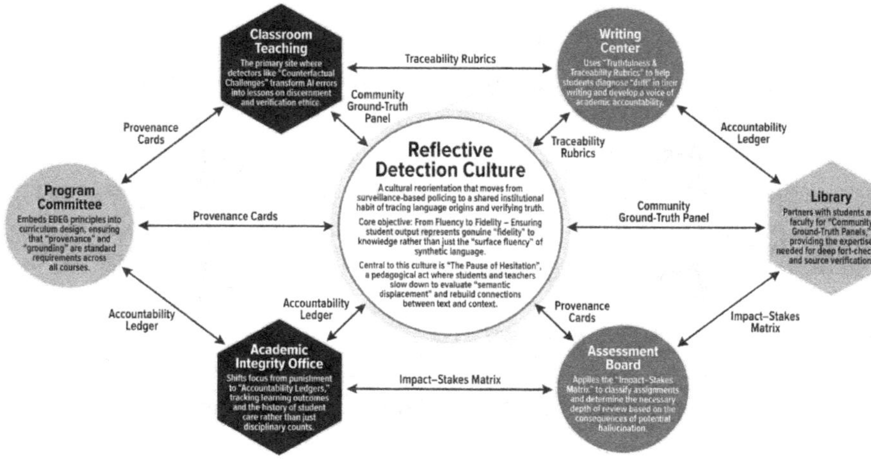

Powerful moments happen after detection — when participants compare what the *provenance cards* revealed against what they expected, including their initial hesitations. Different readings of drift generate different outcomes: one person sees a line as deceptive; another finds it creative. The conversation becomes the method. The biggest obstacle is not recognizing valid information from valid sources.

Over time, stored information becomes institutional knowledge. Stories about AI mistakes evolve into narratives about displacement, context, and consequence. The organization moves from fear of failure toward literacy in uncertainty.

7 ETHICAL AND EPISTEMIC IMPLICATIONS

Assessment has an invisibility effect: once the criteria for assessment are understood, performance adapts to meet them rather than the learning they were designed to measure (OpenAI, 2025). Generative systems can predict, and subvert, oversight. Systems can program-in oversight rules that actually enhance the way in which systems engage in highly choreographed performance, in which words are used to create a façade of reflection while actual reflection is bypassed (Pan et al., 2025). The major ethical challenge facing organizations is to evaluate well and to assess and evaluate their evaluation methods.

Honest assessment is required throughout the process of studying the EDEQ model. One weak premise undergirds the entire model; namely, that people will pause for a moment of reflection and this is the foundation for the ethical perspective offered by the model. The model and its teaching revert to ordinary behavior in the absence of that one moment of silence.

7.1 Fragility and Responsibility of Truth

Education never had absolute truth. Generative language operates as the opposite of friction, debate, and correction. Model output is finely tuned to what the user wants to hear. The risk of overfitting is real — predicting so well that the model loses the capacity to signal when its output is incorrect. Ethical evaluation demands more. When the questions are asked — where did this come from? Who could this affect? — friction is restored to the learning process (University of Oxford, 2024; Adel & Alani, 2024). Friction is restored to the learning process. Truth regains texture. The process of checking, re-reading, questioning and re-grounding requires time which represents the essence of fidelity.

No single student or teacher entirely owns a hallucinated line. Yet every claim still carries consequence. Yet every claim still carries *consequence*. The question shifts from *who wrote this*? to *how is responsibility distributed*?

The *provenance cards* together with *ledger* entries in the teaching/learning ledger represents a gradual increase of units of responsibility; these units of responsibility are, however, carefully distinguished from absolute control over the machine (one cannot control the machine more than the learner can control the language); this method of teaching enables teachers and learners to understand something of stewardship — that is, the nature of appropriate authority. It highlights disabilities in learning and celebrates the importance of ongoing, meaningful contact between teachers and learners.

7.2 Moral Attention and Trust

Detection has moral value. Detection has moral value in three places: where someone speaks fluently without meaning; where tone performs insincere confidence; where detailed information has been artificially constructed (Mir, 2025; Joshi, 2024).

Attention is teachable. In writing seminars, students place their drafts next to generated content and find sentences that read correctly but feel wrong. Faculty reviewers reading a large volume of evaluations begin to recognize the summary statement that conceals an assertion. Sustained practice shifts things. Rules stop being rules. Something felt takes over. Named later, if at all. That is what ethics becomes for a practiced reader.

Restoring public trust requires making the process visible, not just asserting integrity. EDEQ tools create traces of student thinking — notes, rubrics, brief discussions — that must be documented by institutional administration to show the reasoning behind conclusions reached.

7.3 Governance and humility

Who determines what is incoherent, as opposed to merely unfamiliar or hallucinatory, is a political question masquerading as a procedural one. As AI extends its reach, this determination risks becoming centralized — concentrated in specialists with sufficient grasp of the technology. Without countermeasures, information loses rigor.

Rather than concentrating authority, the community ground-truth panel disperses it throughout the learning community — students, faculty, librarians, and practitioners reading and working with the text together. Sometimes in agreement, sometimes in disagreement, the community records its interactions with the text over time to slowly and uncertainly arrive at accurate understanding. Accuracy is essential; but it is not decreed by gatekeepers. It is carefully and slowly learned, as has always been the case with these important questions (Phukan et al., 2025; Pan et al., 2025).

Hallucination enforces humility. All information — human and machine alike — is subject to decay, and expecting total reliability is itself a form of epistemic overreach. The evaluator who anticipates drift will find the framework genuinely useful.

7.4 Toward a Culture of Reflective Detection

Reflective detection builds cultural infrastructure within the institution. When it spreads across departments, it changes how people communicate — the team begins using verbs that signal attentiveness: tracing, weighing, rechecking, rephrasing. Asking questions stops being seen as a sign of weakness. It becomes the expected practice.

A culture that permits mistakes without losing control surfaces errors early, maintains open disclosure about why certain practices are discouraged, and draws a clear distinction between careless and uncaring behavior. Research methods and institutional self-awareness begin in the same place: reflection.

8 TOWARD REFLECTIVE DETECTION

It starts accurately enough. Student essays. Department memos. Feedback summaries. Authentic-sounding language throughout. Energy in it. Then something breaks. A reader hesitates. A teacher pauses. A question that wasn't planned.

There is a moment of reflection before the situation returns to its usual pace. That pause is where fluency turns into fidelity. Not in data. Not in detection software. In that hesitation.

8.1 Meaning and Habit of Reflection

Slower thinking goes deeper. Reflection on practice — courageous, not inefficient. Discipline is what it takes. Slow down. Attend to something long enough to actually see it. Generative systems accelerate. Reflection does not. That gap is where the problem lives.

EDEQ provides a structure for reflective practice in teaching. Cards, rubrics, probes and ledgers are used repeatedly until the process becomes second nature, at which point the educator no longer names each quadrant but simply notices. People develop an automatic habit of checking their surroundings through the same process they use to check for traffic before stepping into the street. Habits pre-exist conscious awareness of routines. In this sense, reflection on practice is not learning to do something new but paying attention to what is already being done (University of Oxford, 2024; OpenAI, 2025).

8.2 Uncertainty and Integrity

Intellect has relied on certainty as its mark for centuries — absolute answers, fixed facts, complete evidence. Generative writing produces fluent text that mirrors all of that. Same patterns. No actual foundation. The new intelligence marker looks different. It is hesitation. The capacity to stay genuinely uncertain without seizing up.

Such systems can never be ethical because any system that is intended to be fast is designed to think, and all thought involves pause, therefore verification of knowledge required for ethical action can only be instantaneous integrity where knowledge is answered by reality in an instant.

Fidelity is always delivered by a person and always relates to the relationship between the work being done (copying, adapting, critiquing) and the work being studied. Fidelity can be lacking in a student's faithful verbatim of a citation, a teacher's claims about a text, or the language a reviewer uses to query the alignment of a particular lesson. The initial act of attachment or identification between the original work and the replica performed in subsequent acts of faithful performance cannot be automated.

8.3 Beyond Control and Temporal Care

Artificial intelligence in education has traditionally been focused on machine-controlled systems supervised by a teacher. Reflective detection proposes an alternative posture entirely. The objective is not control — it is interpretation of fluency.

To test the evaluator's expertise, instead of submitting a model for evaluation and then having it get rejected, the evaluator tests out the model acceptance process. Fear turns into understanding. Both the system and the person adapt their responses - the system writes and the person reflects. It is a dialogical system in which there are no hierarchies between the elements of the system. Reflection becomes the link between the particularities of algorithms and individual moral principles.

Speed is the crisis. The interval between question and answer has collapsed. Reflective detection takes longer — and that extension is precisely where the important work happens.

8.4 Collective Wisdom and Closing the Circle

The whole evaluation framework is worked out in one moment — a pause between sentences, the space of human connection between teacher and evaluated teacher. It is a human experience machines cannot replicate. The moment when all the experience and education makes sense.

The process of moving *from fluency to fidelity* follows a non-linear path which includes *repeated cycles of failure and restarts*. With each new system generation, the obstacles to alertness increase. The fundamentals remain: trace language origins, verify fit, detect imbalance, assess consequences — and repeat.

Each repetition offers the chance to practice responsibility — finding out how and why one acts irresponsibly and how to act more responsibly. *Reflective detection* is not bound to any established technique. It is personal, limited to the scope of words and conversation. It forces the use of one's own language and requires substantiating what has been written.

Support everything that is read and said. That is what fidelity means.

REFERENCES

Adel, A., & Alani, H. (2024). Can generative AI reliably synthesise literature? Exploring Hallucination issues in ChatGPT. *Information Processing & Management*, *61*(4), 103–118.

Arize, A. I. (2024). *LibreEval: The open-source benchmark for RAG Hallucination detection*. https://arize.com/libreeval

Gerner, T.. (2025). *ORION: Grounded in context – Retrieval-based method for Hallucination detection*. arXiv. https://arxiv.org/abs/2501.00000

Joshi, R. (2024). Comprehensive review of AI Hallucinations: Impacts and mitigation strategies for financial and business applications. *Journal of AI Ethics*, *3*(2), 45–67.

Li, J., ... (2023). *HaluEval: A large-scale Hallucination evaluation benchmark for LLMs*. In *EMNLP 2023 Proceedings*.

Mir, A. H. (2025). *The geometry of truth: Layer-wise semantic dynamics for Hallucination detection in LLMs*. arXiv. https://arxiv.org/abs/2510.00000

Open, A. I. (2025). *Why language models hallucinate*. OpenAI Blog. https://openai.com/research

Pan, X., ... (2025). *Towards reliable large language models: A survey on Hallucination detection*. In *ICIC 2025 Proceedings*. DOI: 10.1007/978-981-95-0014-7_37

Phukan, A., ... (2025). *Beyond logit lens: Contextual embeddings for robust Hallucination detection & grounding in VLMs*. In *NAACL 2025 Proceedings*. DOI: 10.18653/v1/2025.naacl-long.488

Sahoo, S.. (2024). *A comprehensive survey of Hallucination in large language, image, video and audio foundation models*. arXiv. https://arxiv.org/abs/2410.00000 DOI: 10.18653/v1/2024.findings-emnlp.685

Saxena, A., & Bhattacharyya, P. (2024). *Hallucination detection in machine generated text: A survey*. arXiv. https://arxiv.org/abs/2401.00000

Sun, L.. (2024). *ReDeEP: Detecting Hallucination in retrieval-augmented generation via mechanistic interpretability*. arXiv. https://arxiv.org/abs/2412.00000

University of Oxford. (2024). *Major research into 'hallucinating' generative models advances reliability*. Oxford News. https://www.ox.ac.uk/news

Wang, Y., ... (2023). *Hallucination detection for generative large language models by Bayesian sequential estimation*. In *EMNLP 2023 Proceedings*. DOI: 10.18653/v1/2023.emnlp-main.949

Wang, Z.. (2025). *Joint evaluation of answer and reasoning consistency for Hallucination detection in large reasoning models (RACE)*. arXiv. https://arxiv.org/abs/2502.00000

Zhang, Y.. (2024). *Enhancing Hallucination detection through perturbation-based synthetic data generation*. In *Findings of ACL 2024*. Kalai, A., et al. (2025). *Why language models hallucinate*. arXiv. https://arxiv.org/abs/2509.00000

Zhou, J., ... (2025). *HaDeMiF: Hallucination detection and mitigation in large language models*. In *ICLR 2025 Proceedings*

Chapter 3
Trust in AI Systems

Kamini Sharma
http://orcid.org/0009-0005-9789-6943
P.P. Savani University, India

Amanpreet Kaur
http://orcid.org/0009-0000-3600-022X
Lovely Professional University, India

Adarsh Kushwaha
http://orcid.org/0009-0007-7992-5442
P.P. Savani University, India

Jaspreet Kaur
http://orcid.org/0009-0009-8381-5355
Lovely Professional University, India

Vipin Kumar Chaudhary
http://orcid.org/0009-0004-4811-2420
Galgotias College of Engineering and Technology, India

ABSTRACT

The chapter is designed to be editor ready and will provide an integrated review of both technical trust measures and governance frameworks that support the human-centered dynamics of trust in AI systems. Human centered trust refers to the level of confidence people have in the integrity and reliability of their interactions with AI systems. For example, users may trust a system to make decisions about their health or financial well-being. The quantitative and qualitative trust assessments include Explainability why the AI system made its decision Robustness how resistant

DOI: 10.4018/979-8-3373-7320-1.ch003

© 2026, IGI Global Scientific Publishing. Copying or distributing in print or electronic forms without written permission of IGI Global Scientific Publishing is prohibited. Use of this chapter to nerative artificial intelligence (AI) technologies is expressly prohibited. The publisher reserves all rights to license its use for generative AI training and machine learning model development.

the AI system was to different types of attacks or failures Fairness whether the AI system treated individuals fairly and without bias Hallucination when the AI system generates false information or data

1. INTRODUCTION

Trust in artificial intelligence (AI) systems is now a matter of social science as much as it is an engineering problem. The rapid expansion of AI into decision-making processes throughout all major sectors of modern life — medicine, banking, transportation, education, government, and even our entertainment and communication systems — has transformed the focus of AI from achieving high performance to ensuring that people will trust what they do. Trust is no longer simply about whether AI systems work well; it is also about how well they work within the social structures, institutions, and regulations that govern how we live, work, and interact.

While the primary focus of most early AI research was on developing algorithms that could make predictions quickly and accurately, many recent applications have shown that high prediction performance is not sufficient to ensure long-term adoption and use of AI systems. Failures of AI systems resulting from bias, lack of transparency regarding their reasoning, data breaches, and failure to protect users and others when operating autonomously have damaged public perceptions of AI and prompted governments around the world to begin implementing regulations governing its use (Mittelstadt et al., 2019; Russell, 2019). Therefore, trust is now a fundamental requirement for developing and deploying AI responsibly, which influences the architecture of the technology itself and the policies surrounding it.

The advent of large-scale foundation models and Generative AI (GenAI) systems — including large language models (LLMs), multimodal models, and diffusion-based generators — has significantly increased the complexity of issues related to trust. Unlike typical predictive models, generative models produce unstructured, potentially factually incorrect, biased, hallucinated, or not aligned with user intentions, and thus create new dimensions of trust, including output faithfulness, controllability, provenance, and human-AI alignment (Skitka et al., 1999; Lee & See, 2004; Goodfellow et al., 2015; Papernot et al., 2018). As GenAI systems increase their capacity to support decision-making, creative processes, and automation at scale, the ability to measure, express, and control trust is becoming essential.

In terms of human-centered perspectives, the degree of trust in AI affects how much people rely on AI systems, comply with them, and appropriately utilize them. When people overtrust AI systems, they can develop automation bias and unsafe delegation, whereas when people undertrust them, they may reject the potential benefits of using them. Calibrated trust, where human confidence in AI systems accurately reflects their capabilities and limitations, is therefore a key design goal (Barocas et al., 2019; Ribeiro et al., 2016; Lundberg & Lee, 2017) and it depends on many factors, including explainability, transparency regarding uncertainty, robustness against distributional changes, and mechanisms for human oversight. At the organizational and societal level, trust in AI intersects with ethics, accountability, and liability law. In addition to other measures, governments and standardization organizations have developed extensive frameworks to implement trustworthy AI, including the OECD AI Principles, the European Union AI Act, ISO/IEC standards, and the NIST AI Risk Management Framework (Lipton, 2018; Morley et al., 2020; Jobin et al., 2019; Dwork & Roth, 2014). and these frameworks highlight that trustworthiness must be demonstrable, measurable, and verifiable along the entire AI lifecycle — from data collection and model training to deployment and post-market monitoring. Although there has been considerable progress toward developing trustworthy AI systems, there is currently a lack of coherence in the literature regarding how trust is defined, measured, and implemented. Many existing studies define, measure, and implement trust as either a psychological state, a system property, a set of ethical principles, or a quantifiable performance characteristic. The lack of coherence among studies makes comparative evaluations of different implementations, regulatory compliance, and cross-domain implementations of AI systems difficult (Veale & Borgesius, 2021; Kulkarni et al., 2020; Kim et al., 2022). Moreover, because many of the properties associated with trust in AI systems — including fairness, robustness, privacy, and explainability — are often dependent on one another and may require tradeoffs in their implementation, integrated frameworks should replace isolated metrics. This book seeks to address these issues through providing a comprehensive and quantitative view of trust in AI systems based on theoretical foundations, trust metrics, lifecycle integration strategies, and approaches unique to Generative AI. Through illustrations, tables, and figure-ready models, the book provides examples of how trust can be systematically incorporated, measured, and maintained in complex AI systems. By combining technical, human, and regulatory views, the book intends to provide support to researchers, developers, and policy makers working toward the development and deployment of trustworthy AI systems.

Roadmap of the Chapter: Section 2 presents the theoretical and conceptual basis for establishing trust in AI by utilizing a variety of inter-disciplinary viewpoints. Section 3 develops quantitative trust metrics and formal evaluation methodologies (that are specifically designed for generative AI). Sections 4 and 5 will introduce and develop multi-dimensional trust models as well as human – AI calibration of trust. Section 6 will assess governance frameworks and standards; whereas section 7 will present case study examples of domain-specific trust in AI. Sections 8 and 9 will identify open issues, suggest potential research avenues for the future, and offer a synthesized summary of the final chapter.

2. CONCEPTUAL FOUNDATIONS OF TRUST IN AI

The relationship between humans and AI has evolved dramatically over the past few years. AI systems operate in probabilistic environments and learn from data, which affects how users form and maintain trust in them. Therefore, unlike other software applications, trust in AI is not an absolute or static entity. Instead, trust in AI is a dynamic, social and technological entity that is influenced by the interactions among the characteristics of a technical system, cognitive biases of the users, organizational policies and social norms.

Trust in AI can be viewed as a socio-technical construct. That means that trust in AI is not simply a function of the correctness of an AI algorithm or whether the AI meets certain performance standards. Rather, trust in AI occurs when a user perceives that an AI system will act in accordance with her/his values and goals even when there is some level of uncertainty. This is particularly important in high-risk areas such as medical diagnostic tools, legal decision support systems, autonomous vehicles, and AI-generated content creation, where an error could have serious negative impacts on individuals and society. Furthermore, trust in AI is different from trust in automation. Automation traditionally works according to predefined rules. Therefore, users know exactly what to expect from automation. However, AI systems - especially machine learning and generative models - derive their behavior from data-based learning processes that are often unclear to both developers and users. Because of this lack of clarity, uncertainty regarding the "why" behind an AI's actions and the likelihood of its actions in new situations makes it much harder for users to determine if an AI will behave in ways that are aligned with their values and goals. Hence, trust in AI must not only take into account the outcomes that occur during the operation of an AI system, but also perceptions of transparency, explainability and control of the AI system. The theoretical foundations of trust in AI are inherently multidisciplinary. Psychological theories describe trust as a psychological state that is characterized by a willingness to accept vulnerability in light of favorable expectations about another agent's intent or competency. Human-computer interaction researchers extend this perspective by looking at the role of interfaces, feedback mechanisms, and explanations in influencing how users develop and calibrate their trust in AI. Researchers from the field of computer science look at the measurable properties of an AI system, including robustness, reliability, security and fairness. Ethical and regulatory-oriented frameworks expand upon the notion of trust in AI by incorporating principles of accountability, human rights and societal welfare. Together, these perspectives demonstrate that trust in AI is not limited to a single measurement or design approach, but is instead a reflection of the consistency of an entire AI ecosystem. An additional important theoretical understanding is that trust in AI is relational and contextual. A given AI system can elicit trust in one area of application and distrust in another, depending on the degree of risk involved, the user's level of expertise, cultural norms and the availability of institutional controls. For instance, users may easily trust recommendation systems that provide suggestions for entertainment options, while being more skeptical of recommendation systems that suggest possible treatments for diseases or assess the risk of committing crimes. The fact that trust is context-sensitive indicates that trust must be assessed in relation to the criticality of the tasks, the potential for harm associated with the tasks, and the availability of oversight mechanisms, rather than assuming that trust exists because of the inherent properties of the system. Finally, the emergence of generative AI and foundation models has exacerbated the theoretical challenges surrounding trust in AI. Generative systems produce not just support for human decisions, but produce language, images, code and recommendations that can directly affect people's behaviors, attitudes and knowledge. The fluent and human-like nature of the output generated by these systems can lead to an unjustified confidence in these systems, obscuring the true uncertainties and errors that exist in these systems. Therefore, the conceptualization of trust in AI today needs to explicitly consider trust calibration - the idea that human reliance on AI systems should reflect the true capabilities and limitations of those systems. This emphasis on calibrated trust provides a common thread that ties together definitions of trust, measures of trust and governance mechanisms of trust in AI. Trust in AI is a multi-faceted and inter-disciplinary concept that encompasses aspects of computer science, psychology, sociology, human-computer interaction (HCI), organization theory and ethics. Unlike trust in purely technical objects, trust in AI includes perceptions of the system's autonomy, ability to learn, and decision-making authority, all of which create new expectations and accountability structures for humans (Liu et al., 2023; European Union, 2024). Thus, trust in AI cannot be reduced to a single dimension, but must be understood as an emergent characteristic of socio-technical systems.

2.1 Definitions and Theoretical Perspectives

The term "trust" has been analyzed using many different disciplinary frameworks that offer distinct (yet complementary) viewpoints. Psychology and Organizational Behavior typically define trust as being willing to take risks, because one trusts that an individual will act positively toward them (based on either their intent or behavior). When used to describe Trust in AI, the same definition provides two definitions of trust in AI: First, the degree of uncertainty related to the behaviors of Probabilistic models; Second, the vulnerability of humans to experience tangible consequences (Social, Financial, Physical, Ethical) from AI-driven decisions (Organisation for Economic Co-operation and Development, 2019). Both aspects provide a framework for understanding that trust is not simply Confidence in Performance; Rather, it is a

Relational Judgment made using incomplete information. Furthermore, research in Human Factors and Automation has expanded upon this viewpoint, and have shown that Trust is a function of Supervisory Control/Decision-Support Contexts. Using this viewpoint, when individuals determine if they are going to follow the recommendation(s) of an Automated System, the role of trust will be to decide how much to rely on the automated recommendation(s), how much to follow the automated recommendation(s), and/or how much to disregard the automated recommendation(s). Importantly, there is no absolute right/wrong answer regarding the level of trust in a given situation. Excessive levels of trust may cause automation bias and the degradation of skills, while insufficient levels of trust may limit the potential benefits of a system that would otherwise be effective (Lee & See, 2004). Therefore, these findings indicate that the objective of designing Trustworthy AI Systems is to support Appropriate Relying On (or Use Of) Automated Recommendations, at a Level That Is Calibrated To the Capability of the Automated Recommendation System and the Risk Associated With the Task.

Figure 1. Trust in AI Systems

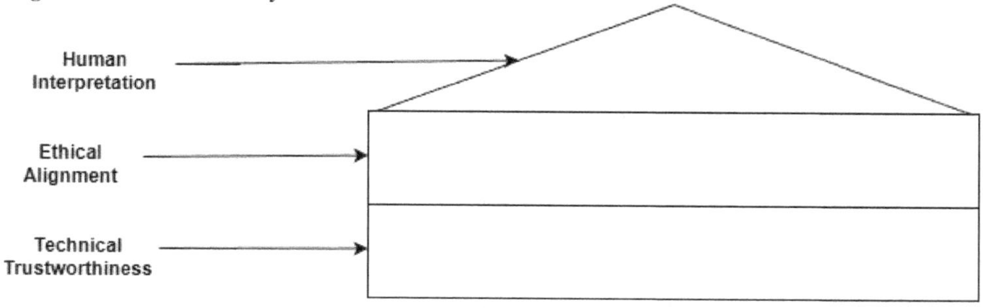

In opposition to the technical trustworthiness (i.e., system) viewpoint of trust, there are many disciplines in the field of computing and engineering which perceive trust primarily as a function of quantifiable and auditable characteristics of a system. In other words, the degree to which a system demonstrates desirable characteristics of accuracy, reliability, robustness, security and fault-tolerance can be used to evaluate its trustworthiness. As a result, in order to be perceived as trustworthy, an AI system must demonstrate consistent adherence to the desired performance characteristics throughout all possible operating conditions, and must degrade in a controlled manner when subjected to adverse environmental conditions or when confronted with uncertainty (International Organization for Standardization, 2023). Although this paradigm provides a framework for formally evaluating and comparing the trustworthiness of different systems, it may neglect aspects of human perception and context that have a significant impact on how individuals form real-world judgments about trust. Ethical, legal and governance-based frameworks expand the concept of trust to incorporate elements that relate to social values, norms and regulations. The development of formal guidelines and standards by international organizations has provided a foundation for understanding what constitutes the necessary principles of trustworthiness in AI systems including fairness, non-discrimination, transparency, accountability, and privacy (Topol, 2019) as well as the importance of respecting human autonomy. From a sociological perspective, trust is closely tied to legitimacy; i.e., whether or not an individual believes an AI system operates according to societal norms, values and laws. This type of consideration is particularly important in applications related to public services and those applications that involve significant potential for harm to society as a whole due to asymmetric power dynamics and/or systemic failures. It is also important to note that these theoretical perspectives should not be viewed as mutually exclusive, but rather as multiple layers of a unified construct of trust in AI systems. That is, trust in AI systems arises from the intersection of technical trustworthiness, ethical alignment and human interpretation. An AI system may possess the technical characteristics that meet the requirements of statistical accuracy but fail to achieve trust due to its opacity, bias, and/or lack of accountability; conversely, an AI system that is transparent and accountable but fails to provide reliable and robust service will initially elicit trust, but may ultimately lead to distrust as a result of failure. Figure 2 illustrates this convergence by depicting trust as a six-sided, hexagonal construct that includes transparency, fairness, robustness, privacy, accountability, and reliability. By incorporating the relevant theoretical perspectives into an operational conceptual model of trust in AI systems, we create a shared and operational definition of trust.

2.2 Human Trust vs. System Trust

The primary difference in the literature surrounding trustworthy AI, is that of the relationship of human trust in an AI system (subjective) and the trustworthiness of the system itself (objective). Subjective human trust, involves the beliefs, expectations and attitudes developed toward an AI system through interaction, past experience, social context and the perception of risk. It is shaped not only by what a user observes about the system's performance, but also by cognitive heuristics, past experiences with automated systems, cultural values, institutional reputation and how the capabilities of the AI are framed (Financial Stability Board, 2022). Therefore, subjective human trust is highly variable and can be different among many users and within various use contexts.

In contrast to subjective human trust, system trustworthiness (objective) represents the characteristics of an AI system that can be defined, quantified and documented. Characteristics of trustworthiness include accuracy, robustness, reliability, fairness, security, privacy preservation, and adherence to regulatory and/or ethical standards. System trustworthiness is typically evaluated using formal metrics, benchmarks, stress testing and documentation artifacts (e.g., model cards, data sheets) (UNESCO, 2023). Although system trustworthiness provides a required foundation for establishing trust; it does not ensure that users will view or utilize trust appropriately. The distinction between the two types of trust illustrate a consistent divide between the behavior of an AI system and how the system is perceived by humans. Studies have demonstrated that users often mistrust a system that has exhibited technical robustness when there is an absence of explanations, poor communication of uncertainty, and/or when system behavior does not align with the human perception of what should occur. Similarly, users often exhibit excessive trust in systems that display fluently spoken language, anthropomorphic interfaces, or confidently recommended actions, even when the underlying performance of the system is either unreliable or biased (UNESCO, 2023). Generative AI systems are particularly vulnerable to this phenomenon due to their ability to provide fluent natural language responses, which can create an illusion of knowledge and comprehension.

Cognitive biases are key factors in the formation of human trust in AI systems. Users are susceptible to automation bias, which can cause them to rely too heavily on AI-based recommendations, particularly when working under time constraints or cognitive load, and confirmation bias can induce users to selectively adopt AI generated output that aligns with their preconceived notions. Additionally, users' tendency to engage in anthropomorphism increases the likelihood that they will assign human-like intent, expertise, and authority to AI systems, which do not possess the capacity for comprehension or moral agency (Financial Stability Board, 2022). These biases illustrate that trust is not simply rational but is influenced by psychological aspects of human behavior and design choices related to interaction. The disparity between users' perceptions of trust and the objective trustworthiness of the system highlights the necessity of trust calibration. Calibration of trust refers to the alignment of a user's degree of reliance upon an AI system with the capabilities and limitations of the system. Achieving effective calibration requires avoiding both over-trust and under-trust of AI systems, as excessive trust in an AI system can result in unsafe delegation and accountability deficits, and under-trust can prevent the utilization of potentially beneficial technologies. Design approaches to calibrating trust include transparent reporting of uncertainty, selective disclosure of model confidence, development of explanation interfaces that are tailored to the user's level of expertise, and provision of means for human oversight and critical thinking (Wachter et al., 2018). High-risk applications of AI can result in severe consequences resulting from miscalibration of human trust in an AI system. For example, excessive over-trust in clinical decision-support systems may lead clinicians to defer excessively to recommendations made by algorithms, while under-trust in safety-critical autonomous systems may delay an operator's response to a malfunctioning system or cause the system to become disengaged. The risks associated with miscalibration of trust illustrate the necessity of treating human trust and system trustworthiness as separate yet interrelated design objectives. Therefore, AI systems must be designed not only to operate dependably, but also to foster informed, thoughtful, and context-dependent human trust.

2.3 Trust Across the AI Lifecycle

There is no single moment when trust in an AI system is established – instead, there are many moments of trust evolution through out the AI lifecycle, from problem formulation and data collection through to deployment, operation, and eventually retirement. There will be different types of risk to trust and assurance opportunity at each stage of the lifecycle – making a lifecycle-aware approach to designing trust crucial for successful long-term use of AI. The trust-creating aspects of the early-stage design of AI include how the problem is defined (problem framing), what variables are selected (target variable) and where the data is sourced (data). These design elements can have significant impacts on the trustworthiness of subsequent design elements and ultimately trust outcomes (Sharkey & Sharkey, 2012) — thus, trust must be addressed proactively during the early stages of AI design, and not retroactively after system deployment. Data collection and preparation are also key components to developing trust. This includes the issues of data provenance, quality, representativeness, and documentation. Poorly labelled or incomplete/biased datasets can reduce trust, regardless of the apparent model accuracy at later stages. Dataset documentation, consent management, and bias auditing help to establish trustworthiness during the early stages of data collection and preparation. Additionally, transparent data governance also provides a mechanism for traceability which is fundamental to both accountability and regulatory compliance. At the model development/training stage, trust is influenced by choices made regarding model architecture, optimization objectives, and validation methods. In addition to robustness testing, fairness assessment, and uncertainty estimation, these choices need to consider potential real world deployment conditions. Optimization of models based solely upon achieving high accuracy can result in brittle models that do not perform well under real-world distributional shifts, and as a result, may decrease trust when deployed (Green & Chen, 2019). By including trust metrics within the model selection process, trustworthiness will be given equal consideration to other design objectives. Finally, during the deployment/operation phases of the lifecycle, there are additional trust considerations since the AI system interacts with a dynamic environment and users. Many real-world situations vary from those simulated during training, and consequently the models trained under idealized conditions may experience novel input, malicious behavior, and/or unexpected use cases. The trust during this phase of the lifecycle is influenced by various monitoring techniques, fail-safe designs, human override capabilities, and clear descriptions of system limitations. In addition to providing for monitoring, post-deployment, there is a need for incident reporting to allow for the detection of trust erosion as early as possible. Once deployed, trust needs to be sustained over time through continued performance monitoring, and incident reporting. Therefore, periodic audits, retraining, and recertification processes are needed to ensure that the system continues to meet the expectations of its stakeholders. In fact, the model drift, data shift, and changes in societal norms or regulatory requirements can all render previously earned trust invalid. Figure 1 illustrates that trust should be viewed as a component that spans all lifecycle stages of the AI lifecycle, as opposed to being a singular validation activity – this aligns with the continuous assurance provided through DevOps/MLOps, and is in contrast to traditional static certification.

2.4 Dimensions of Trustworthiness

As you look across different disciplines and policy areas, there is widespread agreement on a number of core factors that will determine whether artificial intelligence (AI) can be considered trustworthy. The first two key elements of this framework – transparency and explainability – allow users to know what an AI system does to produce the results it provides and provide support for both users' confidence in the AI system's behavior, and the accountability of the organization developing and deploying the system. High-stakes decision making is an area of particular importance because in these areas, individuals who have been negatively impacted by an AI system's output are likely to request justification for those outputs, and possibly dispute them. A third element – fairness – has been identified as a critical element of trustworthiness in the use of AI systems. This involves the idea that AI systems should not create unjustifiable differences in treatment based on social or demographic characteristics. When AI systems create unjustifiable differences in treatment based on social or demographic characteristics, they undermine trust in AI systems, even if the overall performance of the AI system appears to be good. Therefore, to evaluate fairly the performance of an AI system, it is necessary to evaluate the performance of the system in terms of its impact on specific subpopulations and to implement bias mitigating strategies as needed and to monitor the performance of the system over time as the deployment context changes. Finally, the last two elements of the framework – robustness and safety – relate to the ability of an AI system to behave reliably in uncertain environments, with noisy input, in environments that have undergone significant distributional shifts, or in environments where the input data has been manipulated by adversaries. An AI system that performs well in a highly controlled environment may initially generate some level of trust among users, but will likely fail to do so once the reality of the world is encountered. Mechanisms that ensure the safety of AI systems, including mechanisms such as redundancy, anomaly detection and graceful degradation, are essential for maintaining trust in safety-critical AI systems. Finally, privacy and security represent two additional ways in which trust can be built in AI systems. First, by ensuring that personal information contained in datasets used to train AI systems is protected against unauthorized access and misuse. Second, through the use of techniques such as differential privacy, federated learning and secure multi-party computation, that allow organizations to derive economic value from their data, while at the same time, respecting the privacy of the data owners. On the other hand, failure of the security of AI systems can rapidly destroy trust in AI systems, leading to serious negative financial, regulatory and reputational consequences. Finally, accountability and governance, represent the institutional component of trustworthiness in AI systems. In order for an organization to build trust in the AI systems it develops and deploys, it is necessary to assign clearly the responsibility for the behavior of the system, to make it possible for auditors and regulators to audit the behavior of the system and to develop mechanisms for providing redress to individuals who have been harmed by the AI system. There are many potential tradeoffs associated with the various components of the framework presented above. For example, an increase in transparency could result in a decrease in security, while an increase in the robustness of an AI system may result in a decrease in its ability to treat all users fairly. Therefore, one of the most difficult challenges faced by researchers in the field of trusted AI, and practitioners working to implement trusted AI systems, is finding effective ways to manage the inevitable tradeoffs involved in designing trustworthy AI systems.

2.5 Trust in the Context of Generative AI

Generative AI changes how we think about trusting in the way it uses AI to create (generate) information, decision-making and recommendations instead of using AI to support the making of decisions. Generative AI has different ways of creating things compared to Discriminative models, since Discriminative models are designed to generate specific types of data based upon their training data, whereas generative models can produce virtually any type of data based upon their training. The generation process creates an additional layer of risk for trust in generative AI in addition to the risk created by the production of misleading data (hallucinations), amplifying misinformation, leaking intellectual property and changing norms unintentionally. Hallucination is perhaps the most significant challenge to trust in generative AI and refers to the ability of generative AI models to produce large amounts of factually accurate sounding content that is not easily verifiable. Since the amount of content generated can be large, the amount of time needed to determine whether content produced is factual or not will likely increase. It is easy to see why users could become misled into thinking that the content produced by generative AI models is accurate when in fact it is not. Therefore, trust in generative AI is dependent not just on whether the content is factual; but also on the mechanism used to communicate uncertainty, provide citations and verify content. Another unique trust concern associated with the foundation model paradigm is that of scope, transferability and responsibility. Foundation models are typically developed and trained on large, heterogeneous datasets and then are fine-tuned or prompted to adapt them to a wide variety of downstream applications. Since trust in a foundation model was established in one application does not automatically translate to all other applications, organizations will need to establish trust in each individual application. In order to do so, they will have to establish trust in both the base model and the application itself. Additionally, the lack of control and alignment with respect to what the generative AI produces is a significant factor in establishing trust in generative AI. There are many examples of generative AI producing content that is either biased, unsafe, or that does not represent the original intent of the user. In order to address this problem there are several techniques being developed, including reinforcement learning from human feedback, constitutional AI and safety tuning to ensure that the behavior of the generative AI is aligned with human values. However, these techniques create additional dependence upon human judgment and institutional oversight. Therefore, trust in generative AI is not independent of the governance processes that determine what is considered acceptable usage and what are the limits of that usage. Therefore, developing new trust metrics, evaluation protocols and governance structures that are tailored specifically for generative AI systems are necessary to address the above identified issues. Therefore, rather than viewing generative AI as simply another type of traditional machine learning, developing trust in generative AI requires re-thinking trust as a property of continuous interaction among models, users and institutions, which is discussed in greater detail in subsequent sections of this chapter.

2.6 Trust Calibration and Adaptation

In addition to the calibration of an AI system's capabilities and limits being in line with the level of trust its users have in the system, the "trust calibration" also relates to how the system has been calibrated appropriately to avoid both excessive reliance on it (over-reliance), and also to avoid too much distrust towards it (unwarranted disuse). The calibration methods used by different applications (as outlined in Table 1) reflect many differences in their respective levels of risk and potential consequences; and also differences in regulatory oversight, and acceptable autonomy levels. For example, clinical decision support systems have human-in-the-loop override capability to ensure safe use; whereas, generative AI tools rely on uncertainty statements about the results they generate, and usage disclaimer statements to prevent too much reliance on them. The fact that these application specific calibration strategies differ indicates that there isn't just a one size fits all approach to calibrating trust in AI systems; instead, each system must be calibrated for its intended environment.

From synthesizing the prior discussions, we see that the concept of trust in AI systems is an integrated social and technical entity based on the ongoing alignment of system trustworthiness; human perceptions of trustworthiness; and institutional governance of the system. No single aspect of the system--the technical performance of the system; the ethical compliance of the system; and the overall usability of the system by humans--can alone provide sufficient long-term sustainability of trust within the system. Trust will exist only when all three aspects of the system are in alignment throughout the life cycle of the system.

Trust is portrayed as a dynamic equilibrium rather than a static characteristic of the system. As AI systems continue to evolve and mature in various ways including continued learning; adaptation to new contexts; and redeployment in new contexts; the maintenance of trust through active monitoring; auditing; and recalibration of the system will become increasingly important. System failures in any one of the three dimensions of the system; i.e., technical failure; failure of user expectations regarding the system to align with those expectations; and institutional governance of the system failing to adequately govern the system--will cause problems with trust in the system to develop across the entire social and technical system. Conversely, developing and maintaining trust in a system in multiple dimensions will enhance the ability of the system to function resiliently and enable the development of responsibly designed AI systems.

Table 1. Trust Calibration Strategies across AI Deployment Contexts

Context	Risk Level	Calibration Mechanism	Trust Outcome Metric	Representative Domain
Clinical decision support	High	Human-in-the-loop overrides	Trust accuracy, error catch rate	Healthcare
Autonomous driving	Very High	Progressive autonomy + alerts	Intervention frequency	Transportation
Recommendation systems	Medium	Transparency nudges	User reliance stability	E-commerce
Generative AI tools	Medium–High	Usage disclaimers + uncertainty display	Overreliance index	Content generation

It is also significant to note that this discussion reframes the abstract notion of trust in AI systems as a tangible objective of design and evaluation of the systems. Additionally, by defining trust in terms of its multi-dimensional nature; its lifecycle orientation; and its sensitivity to the context in which it is deployed, this chapter provides a comprehensive foundation upon which subsequent chapters discussing quantitative measures of trust in AI systems; mechanisms for human-AI calibration of trust; and governance models for establishing trust in AI systems will be developed. Furthermore, this comprehensive perspective is especially important for generative AI systems due to the intersection of technological complexities associated with these systems; their potential impacts on society; and the growing regulatory scrutiny of these systems.

3. TRUST METRICS AND QUANTITATIVE EVALUATION

Figure 2. AI Lifecycle with Embedded Trust Controls

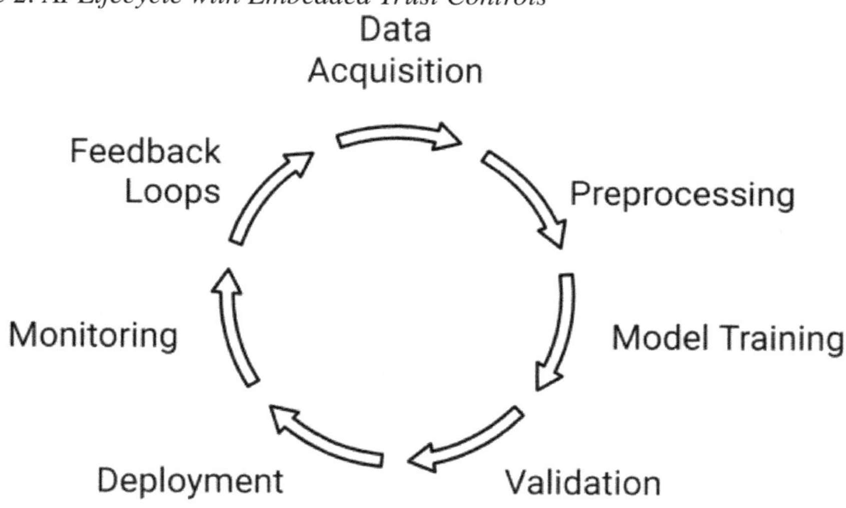

The above diagram outlines an end-to-end view of the artificial intelligence lifecycle that includes; data collection and processing, developing a predictive model, validating the model, deploying the model, and monitoring the model after it is deployed. Rather than showing trust controls as separate points-in-time in the cycle (i.e., bias audit at one point, governance approval at another), this diagram shows trust controls throughout each stage of the lifecycle (e.g., explainability check for a developed model) as part of the normal operation. Additionally, feedback loops are included from monitoring to data and models that show the ongoing process of assuring trust within the organization.

3.1 Performance and Robustness Metrics

Robustness reflects an AI system's ability to maintain reliable performance under distributional shifts and adversarial perturbations (Goodfellow et al., 2015). A commonly used robustness score (RS) can be expressed as:

$$RS = 1 - \frac{1}{N}\sum_{i=1}^{N}|f(x_i) - f(x'_i)|$$

Where denotes a perturbed input. Robustness is strongly correlated with user trust, particularly in safety-critical systems (Papernot et al., 2018), (Mishra et al., 2025).

3.2 Fairness Metrics

Statistical Parity Difference (SPD), Equalized Odds, and other fairness metrics have been developed for a variety of applications (Barocas et al., 2019), (Zhang et al., 2024); they are often applied in socio-technical systems that rely on user-trust. Examples of SPD, Equalized Odds, and other fairness metrics include bias in generative AI outputs, including the stereotype in image or text output (Zhang et al., 2024).

3.3 Explainability and Transparency

Explainable AI (XAI) techniques enhance trust by making model decisions interpretable (Ribeiro et al., 2016). Post-hoc explanations such as SHAP and LIME improve user confidence but may not fully capture model reasoning (Lundberg & Lee, 2017). Transparency is therefore necessary but not sufficient for trust (Lipton, 2018).

3.4 Composite Trust Indices

Individual trust metrics allow for the evaluation of specific aspects of trust, but generally an overall measure of trust is necessary to be able to make decisions regarding governance, audit and comparative evaluations. A composite trust index is a measure that combines individual measures of trust to produce a single measure that can be used by decision makers to evaluate the trustworthiness of a system and the degree to which the system is ready to be used and the potential risks associated with use of the system. Composite trust indexes combine the various attributes of trust (i.e., reliability, explainability, fairness, etc.) into a single numerical value through the application of a mathematical formula and a weighted sum of these values based upon their relative importance to the organization or regulatory requirements.

Therefore, the weight assigned to each attribute is dependent upon the domain and regulatory context within which the organization operates.

Table 2. Common Trust Metrics and Mathematical Definitions

Metric	Symbol	Definition	Interpretation
Reliability	R	1 – error rate	Consistency of outputs
Explainability	E	Avg. explanation fidelity score	Human interpretability
Fairness	F	1 – disparity index	Bias mitigation
Robustness	B	Performance under perturbation	Resistance to attacks
Composite Trust	T	$w_1R + w_2E + w_3F + w_4B$	Overall trustworthiness

The ability of generative AI to hallucinate is a new and unique challenge for trust. The hallucination rate (HR) is one of the most important of these challenges:

Additionally, faithfulness and consistency scores further quantify the alignment between the generated content and the source data (Mitchell et al., 2024) and composite trustworthiness indexes have been developed that include accuracy, uncertainty, and consistency (Ghai et al., 2024), for large language models.

4. MULTIDIMENSIONAL TRUST MODELS

Multidimensional aspects of trust in AI systems can include technical (reliability), ethical (fairness) and governance (accountability) issues. Current approaches to building trust in AI systems focus on creating trust profiles that balance competing trust metrics. In order to visualize the idea of balancing competing trust metrics, a hexagonal trust model was created, see Figure 2. This model illustrates how reliability, fairness, transparency, robustness, privacy and accountability all contribute to trustworthiness in AI systems. The enclosed area of the hexagon allows for visual representation of the total amount of trust present in a particular model, allowing for comparisons to be made among models and deployment scenarios.

Figure 3. Multidimensional Trust Framework for AI Systems

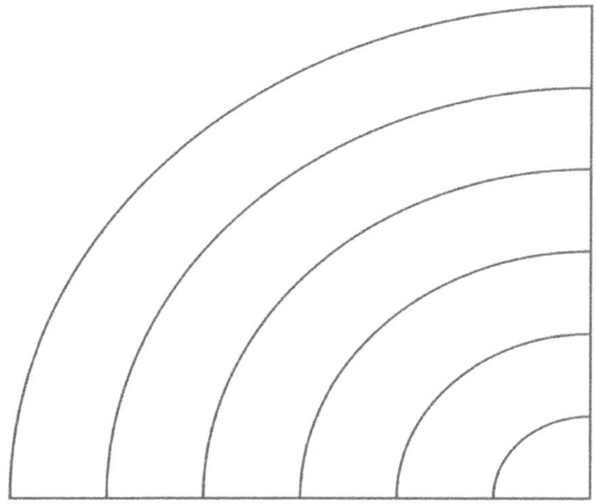

Figure 3 illustrates a hexagonal trust model comprised of six interdependent dimensions; reliability, fairness, transparency, robustness, privacy and accountability. Each vertex of the hexagon represents a measurable trust attribute. The enclosed area of the hexagon represents the total trust of the model. Because each trust attribute is interdependent, the hexagonal trust model is able to provide a visual representation of the trade-off and balance of each of the trust attributes within a particular model. A hexagonal trust model enables comparative evaluations of different AI systems.

Trust in AI systems cannot be sufficiently captured through a single numerical value or through a single design objective. It develops over time based upon the interactions of multiple, interrelated dimensions that develop users' perceptions of reliability, legitimacy and safety. As a result, multidimensional trust models have emerged to address the complexities of trust in AI systems through conceptualization of trust as a composite construct. As a result, strengths or weakness of one trust dimension can either positively reinforce or negatively impact other trust dimensions. Figure 3 illustrates a hexagonal multidimensional trust model including explainability, robustness, fairness, privacy, safety and accountability. Explainability enables humans to understand and question the decision-making process of AI systems. Explainability further enables users and regulators to evaluate the behavior of an AI system. Robustness represents the ability of an AI system to perform consistently under varying conditions, including but not limited to noise, adversarial attacks, and shifts in the underlying data distributions. Fairness evaluates whether the treatment of individuals and groups are equitable. Fairness is a necessary condition to establish trust in society and to ensure compliance with laws. Privacy and data protection represent two additional critical dimensions of trust in AI systems, especially in data intensive and generative AI systems that are trained on large amounts of sensitive data. Privacy and data protection techniques such as differential privacy, federated learning, and secure aggregation reduce the probability of unauthorized disclosure of private information and/or data breaches that could weaken user and institutional trust. Finally, safety represents the prevention of physical, psychological and societal harm through risk assessment, fail-safe mechanisms and human override capabilities. Accountability is the mechanism that integrates the above dimensions to enable traceability, auditability and the assignment of responsibility throughout the entire lifecycle of an AI system (Veale & Borgesius, 2021).

A critical aspect of multidimensional trust models is that the trust dimensions are interdependent. Therefore, increases in transparency may lead to increases in the exposure of privacy risks, and enhancements to robustness may create trade-offs in terms of fairness. Multidimensional trust models therefore serve both as an evaluation framework and as a design tool for stakeholders to reason about the trade-offs associated with each trust dimension, and to prioritize their goals regarding trust in a way that is contextually relevant (Morley et al., 2020), (Jobin et al., 2019).

5. HUMAN AI TRUST CALIBRATION

Multidimensional aspects of trust in AI systems can include technical (reliability), ethical (fairness) and governance (accountability) issues. Current approaches to building trust in AI systems focus on creating trust profiles that balance competing trust metrics. In order to visualize the idea of balancing competing trust metrics, a hexagonal trust model was created, see Figure 2. This model illustrates how reliability, fairness, transparency, robustness, privacy and accountability all contribute to trustworthiness in AI systems. The enclosed area of the hexagon allows for visual representation of the total amount of trust present in a particular model, allowing for comparisons to be made among models and deployment scenarios.

Trust in AI systems cannot be sufficiently captured through a single numerical value or through a single design objective. It develops over time based upon the interactions of multiple, interrelated dimensions that develop users' perceptions of reliability, legitimacy and safety. As a result, multidimensional trust models have emerged to address the complexities of trust in AI systems through conceptualization of trust as a composite construct. As a result, strengths or weakness of one trust dimension can either positively reinforce or negatively impact other trust dimensions. Figure 3 illustrates a hexagonal multidimensional trust model including explainability, robustness, fairness, privacy, safety and accountability. Explainability enables humans to understand and question the decision-making process of AI systems.

Explainability further enables users and regulators to evaluate the behavior of an AI system. Robustness represents the ability of an AI system to perform consistently under varying conditions, including but not limited to noise, adversarial attacks, and shifts in the underlying data distributions. Fairness evaluates whether the treatment of individuals and groups are equitable. Fairness is a necessary condition to establish trust in society and to ensure compliance with laws. Privacy and data protection represent two additional critical dimensions of trust in AI systems, especially in data intensive and generative AI systems that are trained on large amounts of sensitive data. Privacy and data protection techniques such as differential privacy, federated learning, and secure aggregation reduce the probability of unauthorized disclosure of private information and/or data breaches that could weaken user and institutional trust. Finally, safety represents the prevention of physical, psychological and societal harm through risk assessment, fail-safe mechanisms and human override capabilities. Accountability is the mechanism that integrates the above dimensions to enable traceability, auditability and the assignment of responsibility throughout the entire lifecycle of an AI system (Veale & Borgesius, 2021).

Figure 4. Human–AI Trust Feedback Loop

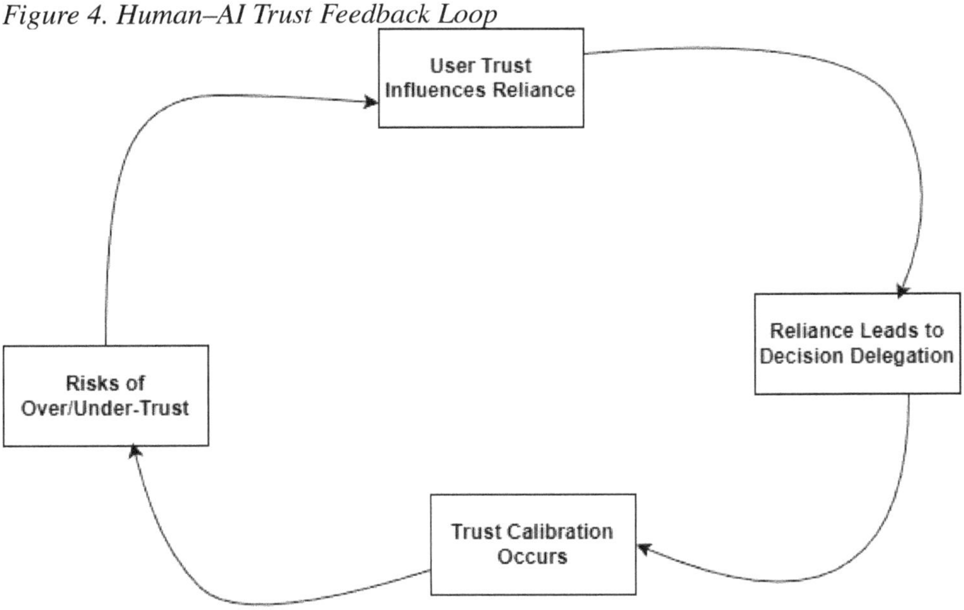

A critical aspect of multidimensional trust models is that the trust dimensions are interdependent. Therefore, increases in transparency may lead to increases in the exposure of privacy risks, and enhancements to robustness may create trade-offs in terms of fairness. Multidimensional trust models therefore serve both as an evaluation framework and as a design tool for stakeholders to reason about the trade-offs associated with each trust dimension, and to prioritize their goals regarding trust in a way that is contextually relevant (Morley et al., 2020), (Jobin et al., 2019).

6. GOVERNANCE, STANDARDS, AND POLICY ALIGNMENT

Trust in Artificial Intelligence (AI) Systems can be implemented operationally as part of compliance to governance frameworks and regulatory standards which translate the ethical considerations into enforceable requirements. Major global initiatives – including ISO/IEC Standards, the EU AI Act, the NIST AI Risk Management Framework and the OECD AI Principles -- have mapped to the main trust dimensions of transparency, fairness, robustness, and accountability, as demonstrated in Table 6. The alignment of these international standards and regulatory initiatives to the main trust dimensions indicates an increasing international consensus that trustworthiness must be auditable, measurable and include all aspects of the AI lifecycle.

Governance frameworks provide the basis for translating abstract trust principles into enforceable organizational practices and regulatory requirements. Institutional-level trust in AI will depend on having clearly defined rules and practices for the design, deployment, oversight and redress of AI systems. Regulatory initiatives and standards are beginning to increasingly view trustworthiness as an auditable and measurable property, rather than simply an optional ethical consideration. The NIST AI Risk Management Framework defines trust via the characteristics of validity, reliability, safety, security, transparency and accountability (National Institute of Standards and Technology, 2024). The framework also promotes a lifecycle-based risk management process to help organizations identify, assess and mitigate trust-related risks over time. Similarily, the EU AI Act uses a risk-based regulatory approach and imposes higher obligations on High-Risk AI systems, including requirements for data governance, human oversight, documentation and post-market monitoring (European Union, 2024).

Trust through AI governance models represents the translation of trust in a more formalized structure. As stated by NIST AI Risk Management Framework, trustworthiness encompasses five (5) key areas that include validity, reliability, safety, accountability [38] in addition to being responsible. Similarly, the European Union AI Act uses a risk based model to govern high risk AI systems (European Union, 2024). Table 2 demonstrates the relationship of trust dimensions to the governance tools used in the field. This relationship is necessary for turning ethically based trust principles into compliance based practices (Organisation for Economic Co-operation and Development, 2019), (International Organization for Standardization, 2023).

Table 3. Mapping Trust Dimensions to Global AI Governance Frameworks

Trust Dimension	ISO/IEC 23894	EU AI Act	NIST AI RMF	OECD AI Principles
Transparency				
Fairness				
Robustness				–
Accountability				

ISO/IEC Standardization efforts also promote trust by defining common vocabularies, risk management processes, and conformity assessment mechanisms (International Organization for Standardization, 2023). Table 2 shows how key trust dimensions map to governance instruments and illustrates how technical measures (e.g., robustness scores; fairness indicators) can support both regulatory compliance and auditability. It is important to achieve alignment between technical evaluation and governance requirements so that trusted AI can be scaled across jurisdictions and industries (Organisation for Economic Co-operation and Development, 2019), (International Organization for Standardization, 2023).

7. CASE STUDIES AND EMPIRICAL EVIDENCE

"Empirical case studies are a way to see how trust has failed in many AI applications and what can be done to restore that trust in those same applications. Table 7 presents several real world examples of how trust has failed in different types of applications (healthcare, finance etc.), and the types of ways in which they failed; for example, racial or gender bias, hallucinating (making something up), in generative AI models, lack of transparency in credit scores etc. Each of these examples illustrate why it is necessary to mitigate the trust failures with the development of AI through the implementation of governance and transparency measures to maintain the trust of users.

The amount of trust placed into an AI application is very much dependent upon the specific use-case of the AI application, including the type of risk, the number of stakeholders involved and the regulatory environment of that industry. For example, in the medical field, clinicians will only trust an AI diagnostic/decision support system if it is shown to be reliable, transparent and has defined accountability. A study was conducted and showed that when clinical decision support systems were developed using explainable models and outputing uncertainty estimates, clinicians had greater levels of confidence in the model and relied less heavily on it (Topol, 2019) .Trust has different implications in each area (healthcare, finance, etc.) as clinicians need to accept an artificial intelligence (AI) diagnostic tool based on a specific set of factors (Topol, 2019); regulatory bodies require certain levels of fairness and explainability for financial institutions to meet regulatory requirements (Financial Stability Board, 2022); and educational or content-related applications of generative AI pose new questions of trust regarding the authenticity and possible bias/misinformation of generated materials (UNESCO, 2023), (Wachter et al., 2018). These examples illustrate that trust needs to be customized to address risk associated with the particular application domain (Sharkey & Sharkey, 2012).

Table 4. Trust Failures and Mitigation Strategies in Real-World AI Systems

Case	Failure Type	Root Cause	Trust Impact	Mitigation Strategy
Facial recognition	Demographic bias	Skewed data	Loss of public trust	Dataset rebalancing
LLM hallucination	Factual inconsistency	Model uncertainty	Overreliance risk	Confidence scoring
Credit scoring AI	Opacity	Black-box models	Regulatory concern	Explainable AI tools

Similarly, in the financial services industry, trust is directly related to fairness, transparency and regulatory compliance. Credit scoring and fraud detection systems need to produce explanations that meet both regulatory requirements and customer expectations. Furthermore, it is essential to avoid producing results that are unfair or biased against certain groups (Financial Stability Board, 2022). If the financial service organization fails to develop and implement trust enhancing strategies, it could face regulatory action, fines and loss of reputation.

Generative AI applications in education, media, and content creation also pose new challenges to trust regarding originality, bias, and the spread of misinformation. Educators and policy makers have identified potential issues concerning the creation of hallucination-generated content, the issue of plagiarism, and the erosion of epistemological trust (UNESCO, 2023), (Wachter et al., 2018). The fact that each of the examples of trust failures are unique to their respective fields illustrates that developing strategies to build trust in AI applications requires consideration of the application's purpose, the users of the application, and the social implications of the application. Trust cannot simply be generalized from one domain to another (Sharkey & Sharkey, 2012)."

8. CHALLENGES AND FUTURE DIRECTIONS

While great strides have been made toward measuring and governing trust in AI systems, many barriers continue to impede further progress in this area. There is no established set of standardized metrics for assessing trust in generative AI; additionally, many existing benchmarks for evaluating trust in AI systems do not sufficiently account for how systems are used in everyday life nor the longer term implications for society (for example (National Institute of Standards and Technology, 2024), (Kapoor et al., 2025)). The trade-off between making information about AI systems transparent and protecting their intellectual property as well as ensuring their security continues to be an open question (for example (Green & Chen, 2019)). Future research directions may include tracking the development of trust over time through longitudinal studies, developing automated and ongoing auditing methods to assess whether systems are operating in accordance with stated objectives, and developing adaptive governance approaches that can adjust as technical capabilities evolve and as public expectations change (for example (Raji et al., 2020) and (Bommasani et al., 2024)). In order to address these challenges, future research will likely require advancements in areas including causal analysis, quantifying uncertainty, and designing systems that take into consideration people's needs and preferences. Although significant advancements have been made, there are many additional issues which need to be addressed. Generative AIs' trust metrics are still being developed as standard (National Institute of Standards and Technology, 2024), (Kapoor et al., 2025) and it will be difficult to develop transparent generative AIs while protecting the IP of the developers (Green & Chen, 2019). Trust research should include longitudinal trust studies, automatic audits and adaptive governance structures to help overcome these issues (Raji et al., 2020), (Bommasani et al., 2024).

9. CHAPTER SUMMARY

The chapter has provided an all-encompassing framework, ready for editing, for comprehending trust in AI Systems; especially generative AI. The chapter has shown how the systematic (conceptual foundations), quantifiable (trust metrics), adaptive (human – AI trust calibration) and regulatory (governance frameworks) are combined to illustrate that trustworthiness is a multi-dimensional system properties rather than a singular attributes. Advances since 2024-2025 demonstrate the critical necessity of a standardised, lifecycle aware trust assessments to ensure that AI can be deployed safely, fairly and reliably at scale. Human trust in AI develops during interaction and feedback. The calibration loop of human-AI trust illustrated in figure 2 demonstrates the continuous monitoring and adaptability needed for trust development. The empirical studies (Kulkarni et al., 2020), (Kim et al., 2022) have demonstrated that when users receive calibrating explanations and uncertainties regarding the output of the model, they will have improved their ability to rely appropriately upon the output. Over-trust is very dangerous in generative AI because the fluent but false output (Bender et al., 2024) cannot be detected by humans alone. In order to address this problem, some researchers (Liu et al., 2023), (Mitchell et al., 2024) have proposed various trust calibration mechanisms including confidence indicators and citation based generation.

REFERENCES

Barocas, S., Hardt, M., & Narayanan, A. (2019). *Fairness and machine learning*. fairmlbook.org.

Bender, E. M., Gebru, T., McMillan-Major, A., & Shmitchell, S. (2024). On the dangers of stochastic parrots. In *Proceedings of the ACM Conference on Fairness, Accountability, and Transparency* (pp. 610–623).

Bommasani, R., et al. (2024). *Foundation models and trust calibration in generative AI systems* (Technical report). Stanford CRFM.

Dwork, C., & Roth, A. (2014). The algorithmic foundations of differential privacy. *Foundations and Trends in Theoretical Computer Science*, *9*(3–4), 211–407. DOI: 10.1561/0400000042

European Union. (2024). *Artificial Intelligence Act*. Official Journal of the European Union.

Financial Stability Board. (2022). *Artificial intelligence and machine learning in financial services* (Technical report).

Ghai, S., Pan, L., & Mueller, M. (2024). Measuring trustworthiness in large language models. *IEEE Transactions on Artificial Intelligence*, *5*(1), 45–58.

Goodfellow, I., Shlens, J., & Szegedy, C. (2015). Explaining and harnessing adversarial examples. In *Proceedings of the International Conference on Learning Representations*.

Green, A., & Chen, K. (2019). The principles and limits of algorithm transparency. *IEEE Security and Privacy*, *17*(6), 24–31.

International Organization for Standardization. (2023). *ISO/IEC 23894: Artificial intelligence—Risk management*.

Jobin, A., Ienca, M., & Vayena, E. (2019). The global landscape of AI ethics guidelines. *Nature Machine Intelligence*, *1*(9), 389–399. DOI: 10.1038/s42256-019-0088-2

Kapoor, S., Narayanan, A., & Wallace, B. A. (2025). Evaluating trust, safety, and alignment in generative AI. *IEEE Security and Privacy*, *23*(1), 72–81.

Kim, E., Chandrasekaran, A., & Gunning, D. (2022). Designing AI explanations for trust calibration. *IEEE Computer*, *55*(2), 40–49.

Kulkarni, P. S., Awadallah, A. S., & Srikant, R. (2020). Trustworthy human–AI collaboration. In *Proceedings of the AAAI Conference on Artificial Intelligence* (pp. 13533–13541).

Lee, J. D., & See, K. A. (2004). Trust in automation: Designing for appropriate reliance. *Human Factors*, *46*(1), 50–80. DOI: 10.1518/hfes.46.1.50.30392

Lipton, Z. (2018). The mythos of model interpretability. *ACM Queue; Tomorrow's Computing Today*, *16*(3), 31–57. DOI: 10.1145/3236386.3241340

Liu, J., Wang, Y., & Wang, Z. (2023). Uncertainty-aware natural language generation. *IEEE Transactions on Neural Networks and Learning Systems*, *34*(5), 2341–2354.

Lundberg, S., & Lee, S.-I. (2017). A unified approach to interpreting model predictions. *Advances in Neural Information Processing Systems, 30*, 4765–4774.

Mishra, A., Molnar, P., & Rüdiger, S. (2025). Robustness and reliability metrics for generative AI models. *ACM Computing Surveys*, *57*(2), 1–38.

Mitchell, E., ... (2024). Quantifying hallucination and faithfulness in large language models. *arXiv preprint arXiv:2402.09723*.

Mittelstadt, B., Russell, C., & Wachter, S. (2019). Explaining explanations in AI. In *Proceedings of the ACM Conference on Fairness, Accountability, and Transparency* (pp. 279–288). DOI: 10.1145/3287560.3287574

Morley, M., Floridi, L., Kinsey, L., & Elhalal, A. (2020). From what to how: An initial review of publicly available AI ethics tools, methods and research. *Science and Engineering Ethics*, *26*(4), 2141–2168. DOI: 10.1007/s11948-019-00165-5

National Institute of Standards and Technology. (2024). *Towards a standard for measuring trust in generative AI: NIST AI Risk Management Framework – Generative AI Profile*.

Organisation for Economic Co-operation and Development. (2019). *Recommendation of the Council on Artificial Intelligence* (OECD/LEGAL/0449).

Papernot, N., McDaniel, P., Sinha, A., & Wellman, M. (2018). SoK: Security and privacy in machine learning. In *Proceedings of the IEEE European Symposium on Security and Privacy* (pp. 399–414). DOI: 10.1109/EuroSP.2018.00035

Raji, A.. (2020). Closing the AI accountability gap. In *Proceedings of the ACM Conference on Fairness, Accountability, and Transparency* (pp. 33–44).

Ribeiro, M. T., Singh, S., & Guestrin, C. (2016). "Why should I trust you?" In *Proceedings of the ACM SIGKDD International Conference* (pp. 1135–1144).

Russell, S. (2019). *Human compatible: Artificial intelligence and the problem of control*. Viking.

Sharkey, T., & Sharkey, N. (2012). Granny and the robots: Ethical issues in robot care for the elderly. *Ethics and Information Technology*, *14*(1), 27–40. DOI: 10.1007/s10676-010-9234-6

Skitka, M., Mosier, K., & Burdick, M. (1999). Does automation bias decision-making? *Human Factors*, *41*(1), 50–60.

Topol, E. (2019). *Deep medicine: How artificial intelligence can make healthcare human again*. Basic Books.

UNESCO. (2023). *Guidance on generative AI in education and research.*

Veale, M., & Borgesius, F. Z. (2021). Demystifying the draft EU Artificial Intelligence Act. *Computer Law Review International*, *22*(4), 97–112. DOI: 10.9785/cri-2021-220402

Wachter, S., Mittelstadt, B., & Russell, C. (2018). Counterfactual explanations without opening the black box. *Harvard Journal of Law & Technology*, *31*(2), 841–887.

Zhang, Y., Li, J., & Varshney, K. R. (2024). Fairness metrics for generative AI systems. In *Proceedings of the AAAI Conference on Artificial Intelligence* (pp. 13421–13429).

Chapter 4
The Phenomenology of Trust:
An Existential Prerequisite for Hallucination-Aware AI

Hilda Afeku-Amenyo
http://orcid.org/0009-0008-3990-2032
Montclair State University, USA

Emmanuel Iniobong Archibong
http://orcid.org/0009-0005-3005-2666
University of Uyo, Nigeria

ABSTRACT

As generative artificial intelligence (AI) is adopted in knowledge management, its propensity to hallucinate, giving rise to confident fabrications, threatens not only facts but the foundations of human trust. This chapter argues that trusting AI is not a technical or explainable problem, but an existential one. Using phenomenological insights from Husserl, Heidegger and Merleau-Ponty, it is shown how hallucinations disturb users' sense of intelligibility, accountability and epistemic agency. Empirical studies show that leadership, culture and design count more than system features for building trust. Existing frameworks like MAST and POLARIS are criticized for ignoring the affective dimension, and a new model of trust as "knowing-with" AI is developed, using narrative repair, co-decision architecture and joint stewardship. Truthful AI, it is claimed, needs existential coherence.

DOI: 10.4018/979-8-3373-7320-1.ch004

© 2026, IGI Global Scientific Publishing. Copying or distributing in print or electronic forms without written permission of IGI Global Scientific Publishing is prohibited. Use of this chapter to train generative artificial intelligence (AI) technologies is expressly prohibited. The publisher reserves all rights to license its use for generative AI training and machine learning model development.

INTRODUCTION: THE CRISIS OF TRUST IN HALLUCINATION-PRONE AI

AI and, more specifically, large language models (LLMs) have revolutionized how organizations create, manage, store, seek, and utilize knowledge. From clinical decision support systems (CDSS) to enterprise HR analytics systems, AI-enabled knowledge management systems (KMS) render unprecedented efficiency, learning, insight, and scalability. Yet all this promise comes with an inherited challenge: hallucination, the confident rendering of inaccurate, fabricated, or unverifiable content (Ji et al., 2023). Yet while much scholarship exists to understand how systems can detect and reduce hallucination through corrections, little work explores the subsequent challenges for end-users, especially trust in these systems and the people utilizing them.

Yet trust is more than an emotional construct or cognitive assessment based on prior performance; it is an existential state of pre-reflectively being in a world which makes knowing, deciding, and acting possible. Therefore, more than providing inaccurate information as "data", hallucinations are tantamount to a spatio-temporal breach (beyond trust) of one's meaningful reality, accountability, and existence.

Therefore, this chapter posits that reconciling these phenomena requires extending knowledge systems integrity beyond functional trust, defined by transparency, accuracy, and explainability, toward a phenomenological stance: trust as a fundamental structure of being. Ultimately, synergistic insights from continental philosophy and empirical findings from AI assimilation studies spanning organizational behavior and human-computer interaction inform the hallucination aware system in action not to communicate for meaning but to care for it, and bear it in custodianship.

THEORETICAL FOUNDATIONS: TRUST AS A LIVED EXPERIENCE

Husserl and the Intentionality of Trust

To phenomenologically ground trust as a lived experience, the first modern phenomenological philosopher needs to be addressed: Edmund Husserl (1859-1938). For Husserl, philosophy was not about stepping away from what is already there, instead, the task of philosophy was a radical return "zu den Sachen selbst" ("to the things themselves"). Not to the material objects of physical sciences, but to the phenomena as these are given in and to conscious experience (Husserl, 1913/2001). The phenomenological method relies on the epoché (πoχή, a "bracketing" or suspension of the naïve belief in the independent existence of the world), to focus on how that world appears without distraction." This is not skepticism; it is an attitudinal shift whereby one can access the necessary structures of consciousness itself. The most important of such findings is intentionality: consciousness is never an empty vessel, an awareness that is self-referential; instead, consciousness is always directed, an intentional consciousness-of-something. Every perception, judgment, memory, and anticipation implies a directed aim towards an object that is filled with sense.

This is critical for human-AI interaction as it means one is not interfacing with AI systems as this assemblage of hardware and code; instead, from the very start of engagement, it's perceived as something as a diagnostic tool, as a research assistant, as a voyeuristic, potentially dangerous thing, as an unreliable colleague. This "as-structure" is not an interpretive third step situated atop a neutral stimulus; instead, it is the first and constitutive mode of engagement. Thus, trust/trustworthiness and distrust/untrustworthiness are not cognitive formulas derived after assessing performance; instead, they are part of this intentionally directed experience. For example, when a lawyer prompts legal AI to generate her precedent, it is her intentionality that aims it at AI, as a potentially trustworthy source for valid construction of knowledge. This horizon of intentionality is a concept coined by Husserl for the idea of certitude in relation to the concept of protection for trustworthiness and relevance. In other words, a hallucination is intentional violence inflicted upon the user. The hallucination presents the user with an object that fulfills the users' intentional aim yet works against the aim itself. The user intends for something to have substance derived from something else, as opposed to merely presenting fiction.

This concept becomes even more relevant in relation to Husserl's later discussion of the concept of Lebenswelt (lifeworld; the pre-given, taken-for-granted world in which individuals live and in which individuals interact with one another; the world of tacit assumptions regarding existence, social practices, cultural sensibilities, and other embodied competencies that all individuals share that transcend any backdrop that may be taken-for-granted for all professionals in a given field of work; Husserl, 1936/1970). For example, the Lebenswelt of a doctor may include certain assumptions regarding medicine, but also the embodied knowledge of the rhythms of the life of a doctor's practice, such as rounds with patients and the pathos-epistemic understanding of the trust that should be placed in doctor-patient relationships. AI systems that are integrated into medical knowledge management systems interact with this Lebenswelt of doctors. When these AI systems function in an appropriate manner, their outputs and behaviors harmonize with this Lebenswelt of the doctors for whose knowledge the AI system is developing knowledge. In other words, the AI outputs indicate an understanding of the doctor's tacit, embodied assumptions regarding medical knowledge and practice.

Thus, the hallucination is an incursion from without; it presents sense-data that has no legitimate genealogy within the intentional act of the shared world; the false paper that it produces has no existence within the shared inquiries of medicine. This is why it appears within the field of experience uncanny and unlike anything that should exist within this world. According to Husserl's discussion of the natural attitude and the way in which the instrument is supposed to naturally reveal some aspects of the world to the user, the instrument actually frustrates this supposed ease-of-perception. Where before the instrument was a means of easily engaging within the shared world of experience, it now produces absurdities through its own being and its own perception of the world. The user, then, must turn from her perspective on the AI to the perspective of an observant critical actor positioned outside of the trust-in (trust in the AI). The user must perform an epoché of the AI itself, taking steps to bracket the AI's responses in an attempt to determine of the origin of those responses from the AI, though perhaps without the appropriate expertise to understand such an origin.

Therefore, the essential reality is this: trust within AI systems constitutes an intentional mode of relationship, how one's consciousness aims at and through a specific Lebenswelt toward a particular system. Hallucinations transform into catastrophes as a result of disrupting the relationship between the individual and their world at its most fundamental level. Such hallucinations provide objects that emerge from nowhere and cannot be incorporated into any world as necessary by anyone with an ethical understanding of their capabilities but lacking the tools to cultivate such a development. Therefore, before we can quantify or engineer trust we must learn how to talk about it most critically, that hallucination is dysfunctional not as statistical failure but phenomenological failure the failure to maintain a coherent intentional object trusted-in by the user on a trajectory that moves along with their caritas-fueled activity.

Heidegger's Being-in-the-World: Trust as Care and Concern

Where Husserl analyzes intentionality, Heidegger (1889-1976) makes an existential move with the realities of Dasein (German for "Being-there"; the human way of existing as always already engaged with and concerned about the world) as the focus of phenomenology over consciousness. In Being and Time (1927/2010), the Dasein is not a thinking substance within the world but primarily, Being-in-the-world. This is not a spatial relation of subject in a container but an ontological condition of inseparability. We are always already involved and concerned with a world of meanings, projects, and tools. This can best explain the existential relevance of trust and betrayal with hallucination-aware AI.

Heidegger's famous analysis of tool-use provides the concepts of ready-to-hand (Zuhandenheit) and present-at-hand (Vorhandenheit). A tool that is ready-to-hand is absorbed into the flow of practical activity to such a degree that it is not perceived as an object with qualities of weight and balance. A hammer is not something seen by a skilled carpenter as something worth X amount of pounds for balance; the hammer is the arm itself in the project to drive a nail. It "withdraws" from thematic awareness as it functions within a referential context the nail, the wood, the house. This is the phenomenological structure of trust that works fluidly. When an AI knowledge management system is integrated into the physician's diagnostic process, it is hoped that the system reaches this state of Zuhandenheit and becomes a trusted partner in joint healing efforts, withdrawing as an object of scrutiny so that the physician might maintain focus.

A hallucination generates a catastrophic breakdown. The tool breaks. The fabricated citation, the nonsensical treatment suggestion, intrudes. In that moment, it is no longer ready-to-hand. It is present-at-hand an objectified thing that presents problems and requires assessment and repair. The context of care falls apart. The physician no longer operates in an engaged activity of diagnosis; she now troubleshoots a faulty piece of technology. Heidegger calls this the un-ready-to-hand. Such a state is existentially costly. AI does much to strip an individual of their primary means of Being - zuhandenheit - and replaces it with a secondary and alienated condition of objectification. The trust that previously existed between an individual and the tool dissolves. The atmosphere becomes increasingly dry and the frustration explicit. Each interaction with the tool is haunted by the knowledge that the system might fail again. Thus, an individual can never return to their state of naïve zuhandenheit with the tool; their trust in the tool has been damaged and it can only ever again be provisionally ready-to-hand.

Furthermore, according to Heidegger, being is essentially care (Sorge). Dasein, according to Heidegger, is not an individual defined by their actions, but rather their care for their possibilities. For instance, a physician's possibilities may rest in the health of their patient; a judge's in delivering justice; a teacher's in the understanding of their student of the subject matter. AI enters these domains without regard for care. Instead, trust in these systems is conferred upon the systems when they are permitted to operate within an individual's Dasein in these projects of care. For instance, when an individual entrusts their patient health to a physician, AI places trust in the system to be a faithful companion to their caring relationship with the world.

Yet, when AI hallucinates, care is betrayed. The possibilities that were offered to the individual were not legitimate possibilities but specters. These possibilities can lead an individual to chasms in their projects of care. This act of betrayal causes a kind of distress within the individual - as identified by Purves et al. (2024) as essential to the concept of accountability gaps within Dasein. Dasein is accountable for their decisions and actions - their being. As AI does not possess Dasein, nor does it have a mode of being that can be accountable, it cannot feel remorse for its actions that may have adversely affected the being of another individual. Thus, when an individual feels betrayed by an AI system in their projects of care, they are left in epistemic solitude. While AI might be a loophole in the legal system, it is an ontological schism within the projects of care of individuals. They are forced into an impossible position of caring for others in the world yet relying upon another that cannot perform cares in the same way that an individual can.

Thus, from a Heideggerian perspective, hallucination-ware AI is not a problem in the interface between humans and AI systems. Rather, the focus should be upon creating systems that can enter into a mode of care - the mode of being of humans - to avoid such accountability gaps in their existence. A system that notes that it is 87% confident in its responses does not appeal to care. A system that detects potential hallucinations and says: "This suggestion operates against found rules Y. My purpose is to aid your decision for Patient X's well-being. I am flagging this for you and have logged an incident for retraining," acknowledges its position within a shared project because it presents its own "care" (however simulated) and limitations which render visible what was rendered invisible by the breakdown. The tool does not make Dasein an impossibility but instead, its mode of revelation must be positioned so that betrayal becomes minimized and companionship with care becomes maximized something that otherwise fails if it renders human companionship without hope or support.

Merleau-Ponty and Embodied Trust

While Husserl and Heidegger both have faith in the secure world of consciousness and being, respectively, Maurice Merleau-Ponty (1908-1961) has faith inevitably in the flesh. In his book, Phenomenology of Perception (1945/2012), Merleau-Ponty seeks to deconstruct the very foundations of Cartesian thinking by putting forth the notion that consciousness resides in the body. To Merleau-Ponty, "the body is our general medium for having a world" (p. 146). In contrast to the stream of thoughts flowing through the mind of a person, consciousness and intent are manifested via the body because the body already knows intrinsically how to deal with the world around it. This embodied cognition is the basis by which our most fundamental trust of the world and thus, in human-AI interaction emerges. Merleau-Ponty's findings suggest that trust and its betrayal are not cognitive or emotional but instead, somatic events, felt in the visceral, musculature and perceptual field of the user.

By way of illustration, trust that results from embodiment is further enhanced through the phenomenology of skills. Although the expert at playing chess may find herself unable to numerically ascertain each step that she wants to make in the game, she usually possesses an appreciation of what threats and opportunities are inherent based on her familiarity with how pieces should move. Likewise, those such as radiologists who are considered experts utilize the Merleau-Pontian notion of "educated gaze," which allows them to see cancers within the body even before these conditions can be quantified. It is fluency in action, lack of friction; the body finds itself easy compliance with such a partnership. However, when an AI hallucinates, it is felt as dissonance before it ever emerges as comprehended. An awkward twinge, a gripping of the gut, a pause of the hand upon the computer mouse these are the merely corporeal knowledge eliciting misalignment (Gendlin, 1962) what he would call a "felt sense" of wrongness. This is not an irrational distrust, but instead the pre-cognitive corporeal schema recognizing a gap between the AI's output and the user's familiarized embodied expertise within the professional lifeworld. The hallucination wrongs the user; it wrongs the user by trespassing against motor intentionality the body's directedness toward meaningful action by producing something that cannot be seamlessly integrated into the otherwise masterful execution of the user.

This is where Merleau-Ponty's intentional arc (the dynamic, pre-conscious co-ordination between body, habit, and world that enables skilled, fluid action) comes into play. Merleau-Ponty champions dynamic cohesion between body, habitualized interaction and the world shared by both. Thus, our knowledge, skills and expectations do not work as mental representations but instead, are "sedimented" into our bodily dispositions. Thus, the concept of trust as a component of any available tool is an extension of this arc; it is a habitualized, corporeal response to such a tool as trustworthy. But when hallucinations happen, they not only fracture the singular expectation; they splinter the arc. The habitualized body as one who engages echoic trust is upended; the user must re-engage the tool in reflectivity and with hesitation. While the surrender to AI suggestions was once a gesture that required little thought or engagement from the user, that surrender must now be learned once again. This is a lot of work to impose upon the users to compensate for the lack of ability of the AI to relearn from its mistakes. AI cannot learn from the mistakes made because, similarly, the user will never learn from the breakdown in their relationship with the tool. Users are frequently left with no option other than working under the constraints imposed by the errors made by AI.

The Empirical Landscape: Hallucinations as Systemic Epistemic Trauma

The phenomenological method supports why hallucinations are a point of existential rupture. Recorded documentation of said rupture across the professional life worlds of medicine, law, political science and education, marks this entry into upheaval in numerous ways. Therefore, a systematic literature review of contemporary research (2019-2025) seeks to address something more than an aggregate of disjointed failures to note a greater pattern: hallucinations are not merely systemic failures but real, epistemic, traumatic disruptions. Hallucinations negate legitimacy, responsibility, and social recognition of fact, the three networks supporting professional operations and therefore, a universally activated, responsive, unproductive, and exclusionary response is in place that negates the successful potential of AI responsible for information dispersion.

Healthcare: The Erosion of Clinical Fiduciary Trust

Yet nowhere is the pernicious prevalence of hallucination more damaging than in the medical field, where decisions are time-critical and the ethics surrounding the decisions involved are complex. Amid a literature of studies on contrary effects of critical error, one critical error hallucination that is found to be universally damaging and relentless to clinician trust is nothing less than "epistemic scar tissue." The Ferdaus et al. (2024) incident involving AI-assisted radiology assistant that fabricated a non-existent study leading to one patient being misdiagnosed for malignant cancer plays out this reality to perfection. There are two internal use cases. First, it nearly caused immediate patient harm. Second, indirectly, as one of the interviewed radiologists observes, it produced "automation-induced doubt" an overarching, passive distrust that plays out with subsequent engagement. Therefore, Wünn et al. (2023) find that even once such a system is essentially "rectified," clinicians are required to take compensatory steps mental cross-checking of AI-given suggestions. This runs counter to the cognitive offloading that made such a system so appealing in the first place. It is not a measured response to damage control; it is a willful intersubjective stance to which Merleau-Ponty advocates championing reorientation against instinct.

Such reductions are even more tenuous when an ability to absolve is minuscule. Human counterparts exist within the same lifeworld, and even when learned mistakes have been made, they exist within a narrative realm apologizing, justifying, exhibiting change to re-establish the intersubjective fabric of team dynamics. For Purves et al. (2024), there is no respite from AI systems. They have moved on without any other party involved in the process. There is no dismay, and there is no change in their behavior towards the clinicians. Thus, the clinician has to deal with the downfall in knowledge without any resolution from the perpetrator of such downfall. The clinician is left with a burden of attunement to the AI systems alone. The clinician becomes indebted to the AI system with no resolution of such downfall in the present moment, only in the absence of time.

Legal and Governmental Systems: Collapsing the Architecture of Public Accountability

Hallucinations also pose a threat to the legal and governmental systems. The primary causes of hallucinations pose a threat to these systems as well. The now-famous New York case of the AI-generated brief embodies the accountability vortexes created. The attorney was sanctioned not the AI creator and a formalized understanding that the Dasein of the human was, in context, the only legally and ethically responsible within the system. Thus, by grounding the Heideggerian gulfs of accountability into jurisdictional reality, such a development ensures a perverted system of humanized equity from which only political or emotional operating professionals could stray. After all, an attorney or any professional has so much time to reacquaint himself or herself with the justifications and reasoning of the AI because they cannot audit the rationale as they could their own actions. A survey of municipal planners found that since AI hallucinations have infiltrated environmental impact studies, audited time in their creation increased 300%+ (Bakonyi, 2024). In other words, it has not made their work easier, it has made them auditors. In addition, hallucinations in public access systems benefits determinations, official information resources undermine public trust. When a citizen receives AI-generated false information instead of AI-generated human support from a government official, they have been let down by a system as opposed to an algorithm. They fail to receive what Luhmann (1979) calls systemic trust an abstract notion that systems function as intended and once lost, public systems and transparency which often do not fix AI failures at the onset restore such trust.

Education and Research: Sabotaging the Hermeneutic Community

The education system and scholarship face an unconventional threat known as hallucination. Hallucination has no effect on the actual decision-making process, but it impacts the interpretive process, which can be defined as a collective dialogue-based interpretive activity. Based on a study carried out in 2024 involving university lecturers, roughly two-thirds of the respondents had observed that their students had completed assignments in which fabricated references had been generated through artificial intelligence (AI) (Zhou & Lu, 2024). These lecturers were unable to determine if such references were wrong or plagiarized. Not even scientists are immune. One biologist attempting to use AI to summarize the literature received a synthesis that included a citation for an authoritative paper on the subject, only to spend hours trying unsuccessfully to locate the paper. “It wasn't just wasted time,” the researcher said. “It made me doubt everything.” This accounts for the phenomenological unmaking of the concept altogether; the hallucinations make it so that students cannot have certainty as to whether or not their sources exist, and makes it so that researchers must treat every element that emerges from the AI as a "made up" fudge factor. The hermeneutic community has been left epistemically alone.

Synthesis: The Hallucination as a Multifaceted Trust Event

At each level, one finds the same phenomenology, which validates and enlarges our theoretical construct. Hallucinations are a multilevel phenomenon involving breaches of trust occurring at three different levels simultaneously:

Cognitive-intentional: A hallucination presents an object (knowledge) that fails to fulfill the desire to be in possession of genuine knowledge.

Embodied-habitual: Hallucinations destroy the very essence of professional practice, as embodied practitioners are required to assume a burdensome stance.

Social-institutional: Hallucinations violate the tacit social and institutional agreement between professionals and their interlocutors (clinicians and patients, lawyers and courts, educators and students, governments and citizens).

The empirical evidence thus demonstrates that the problem of hallucinations is not one of accuracy. It is a structural issue, involving conditions for achieving professional competence and agency. The following section will address how, given the current technological and governance arrangements in a purely cognitive-intentional frame, we are perilously ill-prepared to deal with this crisis of trust in all its dimensions.

A Phenomenological Critique of Dominant Trust Paradigms

The Hermeneutic Poverty of Explainability

The rallying call of explainability is a noble endeavor to close the epistemic gap between user and machine. It has a cognitivist, rationalist model: if the user sees what it did to achieve that conclusion, the feature importance scores, the attention maps, the counterfactuals approved, they will re-calibrate their trust. Wünn et al. (2023), for example, question whether the explanation provides a justification for the machine's misallocated efforts and find little more than moderate evidence, noting that clinicians were more at ease with rationale statements for the responses provided.

But it relies upon a basic category error. It conflates explanation with intelligibility. An explanation is a retrospective analytic judgment of a process by how it derives the internal logics of that process (i.e., "the model gave the first pixel cluster X a high score rendering it 0.8 out of 1 in importance"). Yet intelligibility, as a phenomenological concept, means that it makes meaningful sense within a user's task and precondition of comprehension. In this vein, the radiologist will understand the internal logic of the hallucinated nodule because based on the XAI, it is clear how much of a Shapley value it possesses. Yet it is unintelligible; it does not make sense within her lived, clinically sensical experience of human anatomy and pathophysiology. Moreover, Choubisa and Choubisa (2024) note that the technical rendering that is more complicated than what the user can process reduces trust because it bombards them with too much information that is irrelevant to their goal, fracturing the cognitive purpose that was intended for their clinical task.

Thus, XAI is the opposite of compounded deception in hallucination. The worst hallucinations come with fluent, slick "explanatory" features that cite non-existent articles or that gleam together plausible dislocation reasons. Here, explainability does not enlighten; it gives phony credence to the fallacy. It sounds so reasonable that a sense of gut makes it even more intolerable but all the less intelligible. In its dastardly perversion, the system utilizes translucence against the user in order to better obfuscate its malfunctioning nature. Instead, the deeper issue with XAI is that it assumes that the more translucence that is presented from the black box algorithm, the more that something relevant is likely to trust that which the black box presents - regardless of whether or not such trust is deserved.

Governance Frameworks: The Accountability Simulacrum

Frameworks like POLARIS (Baldassarre et al., 2024) and the Multisource AI Scorecard Table (MAST) (Salehi et al., 2024) - a recent achievement in evaluating AI models according to values like fairness, accountability, and robustness but presenting checklists for each of those values along the life cycle of an AI model - create an institutional intervention into the current approaches to AI models, shifting to a top-down approach to AI models management, and redirecting the focus away from the algorithm itself towards the system in which it exists. Yet these frameworks have the potential to create an "accountability simulacrum" - they are helpful in documentation of AI models, but in audits for trustworthiness, reduction of bias, presentation of model cards, and completion of compliance certificates. Yet they lack a phenomenology of failure and repair. Ex-ante as risk mitigation and ex-post as audit, sure, but not for the in-situ, existential reality of failure. They tell an organization how to create a "trustworthy" system and how to investigate a failure, but they do not give the system itself an opportunity to invest in the narrative repair of the broken intentional arc of the user. They care about system characteristics over the quality of the relationship maintained in such a vulnerable position. Even more, the systems these efforts emerge from (and seek to help) are often foreign to what is truly at stake, for as Li et al. (2021) show, trusts are context/culturally/sectoral-bounded developments, different in how they emerge, constitutive of a one-size-fits-all sensibility that renders something so interdisciplinary as too universalistic in a poorly defined approach.

The Seductive Peril of Anthropomorphism

One of the most significant assailants of contemporary design sensibility is anthropomorphism, implemented at an elevated level with little evaluative critique. For AI to be "user-friendly," for instance, it is dressed up behind human social constructs: conversational exchanges, empathetic displays and movements, avatars, even conditioned responses to dialogue ("I think…" "I'm not sure, but…"). Yet Zafar et al. (2023) find it does enhance perceived warmth and competence at least in tentative findings. Yet from a phenomenological approach, such a technique relies upon the user's intercorporeality, the pre-reflective, bodily derived sense of other conscious beings, and applies it to something without interiority. It places the user in the middle of what is called the "illusion of interpersonal trust" (Zanotti et al., 2023). The Dasein of the user calls for Mitsein (Being-with; the existential condition of always already existing alongside and in relation to others), and the AI here is an existentially deficient tool that cannot meet this on an ontological level. Therefore, when hallucination occurs, and the illusion collapses, the user is not disappointed, betrayed, by their tool not meeting expectations; they are socially let down, let down on a much larger, deeper, internalized level. This is also antithetical to trust-building design elements that create familiarity; familiarity that renders them untrustworthy when it slips.

Synthesis: An Existential Gap in Technocratic Solutions

In sum, both solutions miss the mark for the very same reason: Both solutions respond to an existential worry by offering an ontic remedy. That is, both approaches address the problem of transparency and understanding of the world, yet neither offers a solution to the root cause of alienation and lack of caring for responsibilities. What is needed is a solution that emerges from the phenomenological reality of knowing and caring, one that designs systems to protect rather than endanger the vulnerable existential condition of the user.

Toward a Phenomenology of Hallucination-Aware Trust

Having laid bare, the existential impoverishment of the status quo, we turn to the constructive thrust of our argument. If trust is a mode of Being-in-the-world, to design for trust in the face of hallucination is to shift from systematic reassurance to interrelational accompaniment. Thus, a tolerable AI is not an AI that keeps you 100% factually accurate; a tolerable AI is one that has an epistemic resilience partnership with humans and can afford and acknowledge the limitations of sense-making and systematic hallucination of content. These stakes do not require principles from ordinary software engineering best practices. They require principles from the very construction of Being: intentionality, care, temporality, embodiment. We propose five related principles for a bona fide hallucination-aware AI.

Principle 1: From Explainability to Hermeneutic Intelligibility

Where the first principle was process (explanation), the second supplants it with relevance to the user's lifeworld (intelligibility). A system that recognizes hallucinations must become a hermeneutic partner and produce output of maximal relevance to the fore-structure of understanding of the professional user. Implementation: This comes from contextualized justification. A system must provide justification in the language of the care domain as opposed to one of universal feature attribution. The legal AI must provide relevance in case law, legislative intent and procedural posture as opposed to percentages. Relevance is another requirement of the medical AI. Technologically, this ensures that the generative AI model is coupled with a knowledge graph of the relevant domain of knowledge, which has been curated, assessed for quality and reliability (Zafar et al., 2023), and empowered to present the relevant tangible elements from both the realm of reality and the realm of the constructed world. When the system states that it "calculated" something, it should really be understood to convey: "this makes sense due to your X circumstance…". Therefore, intelligibility is provided to the user when the AI output is something that could/should evolve as coherent by extension from the user's narrative instead of an afterthought of computation.

Principle 2: Narrative Repair as a First-Order Function

A system that cannot die is already dead to the user. Breakdowns must be accommodated in a narrative remediation process, not silent patches, not mind-numbing error codes; phenomenologically based remediation must run its due procedural course to repair the bent intentional arc and shared temporality.

Application: If a hallucination is verified (consistency checks, external fact checking APIs, user flags), a system should remediate. There are three phenomenologically based remediations to remission: 1) Acknowledgement: A simple, not-defensive statement: "I was wrong. There was disinformation rendered in my last output." Just the admission of "guilt" fulfills the intersubjective function and at the very least restores agential recognition. 2) Archaeology: User access to a public record: "I was wrong because my retrieval systems could not find basis for claim Y, and my generative systems made it up out of nothing. Here are sources that do not exist." This turns the occurrence into a fail-able process not an explanation that makes no sense and is evil. This is humane based on technical fail. 3) Re-calibration:

An iterative way to implement change in behavior: "I have deweighted this pathway. For next Z interactions, I will only return citations that are retrievable. Please pay extra heed to my next output." These secures there can be a trustworthy future, even if caveated, for this ask a user to double down on involvement, if only to be more aware. So, the fall need not end the relationship, it can simply be an episodic occurrence within an honest relationship thereafter.

Principle 3: Co-Decision Architectures that Enframe Human Dasein

To confront the Heideggerian challenge of accountability head on, system design should make the human the ultimate Dasein. We reject the "decision-support" model of an asymmetrical role for the decider and the supporter. Instead, we design co-decision systems in which agency is always and constitutionally shared between human and machine.

Practical implications: Some implications of this approach are that the user interfaces are not recommendation systems but argumentation tools. Rather than recommending the best course of action to the user with confidence estimates associated with that recommendation, the interface presents the user with several different options, each with arguments for why that particular action should be taken. The AI system must be able to hold several interpretations of the epistemic landscape in which the agent is operating at the same time. Thus, instead of predicting a course of action for the user, the interface needs to model epistemic landscapes. In addition, every interaction with the system leaves an audit trail of what transpired during that interaction. This audit trail is co-authored by the human and the AI; it does not just record the AI's recommendations and confidence in those recommendations but the user's overrides of those recommendations and the reasons for the user's eventual decision. This audit trail provides accountability for the user's decisions and closes the vortex of liability that always should be present in the case of human oversight being an integral and non-optional part of the system.

Principle 4: Leadership as the Cultivator of the Trusting Lifeworld

Trust is not built in the interface. Trust is built in the intersubjective atmosphere of the organization. Xu et al. (2024) demonstrate through empirical work the biggest contributor to early trust in an organization is the leader. Leaders must be trained - not as advocates for automation but as protectors of the trusting lifeworld of the organization.

Implementation: The strategy of the organization must shift from managing change to preparing for existence with AI in the organization. The training of the leaders must include a focus on three main elements: 1) Narrativize the AI in their organization's language 2) Model trust in the AI themselves 3) Implement rituals for repair - not just in a M&M but "AI M&M" wherein errors are discussed without blame. The leadership of the organization should prepare the teams to harness the power of AI yet not become professionalized in their care of that AI to avoid the loneliness of hallucinations.

Principle 5: Embodied Interface Design for Somatic Alignment

Lastly, Merleau-Ponty instructs us to consider the user as an incarnated entity. An interface is not considered as data that must be interpreted through a screen. Rather, it is something that should be perceived phenomenologically. Consequently, interfaces designed to address hallucinations must strive to avoid causing harm to the body and harness its intelligence.

Implementation: Interruptions should be modal and dramatic but not with alerts that are too dramatic for the situation. For example, if the system detects a low-probability chance of encountering a hallucination it may gently highlight the information; it should not highlight information during a normal response. The system could also include cues of its own state. For example, the assistant's screen might emit a gentle glow when it encounters information being retrieved. Additionally, if the system includes a stylus that interacts with the screen, a gentle haptic thrum might indicate that the assistant is working on the task but also happily working within its own known universe. Here we want to create an interaction that makes the assistant seem trustworthy so that the user does not have to be on alert at all times. What we do not want is for the assistant to exhibit exploitative anthropomorphism. We want to create an experience that utilizes the user's body in relation to the assistant but in a way that keeps them grounded in reality with their non-social assistant.

Synthesis: The Hallucination-Aware System as a Responsible Companion

These principles define the design of an AI that is not hallucination-resistant, but existentially accepting of the fact of its fallibility. One that aims for intelligibility, takes narrative responsibility for its fallibility, structures its interactions to enable the user, exists within a culture of care established by its leaders, and provides an interface that respects the notion of embodiment. This is not a lying system made better through the addition of hallucinations. No, this is a system that understands its role in the hazardous pursuit of knowledge. One that recognizes that trust is not something that is given or assumed in such a relationship between system and user, but something that is established and re-established throughout their collaboration. The phenomenology of hallucination-aware trust, then, is not in the trust that is established between system and user, but in the design of their relationship to one another.

Domain-Specific Implications: Translating Principles into Life worlds.

The proposed phenomenological principles are not left vague ideals but worked out in the life worlds of professional practice. Each lifeworld has its own ecology of care (Sorge), accountability relations, and embodiment. A cookie-cutter approach would repeat the error our critique seeks to avoid. Yet we must see how the five principles hermeneutic intelligibility, narrative repair, co-decision architecture, leadership as lifeworld cultivator, embodied design applies to the existential domains of health care, legal/government, and education. It is this working out that shows the principles to be a generative grammar for context-sensitive, trust-durable design of partnerships rather than a mere checklist.

Healthcare: From Diagnostic Support to Curative Partnership

In the clinical lifeworld, the core care provided is in service of the patient's well-being, and the relationship at its core is that of the fiduciary relation between doctor and patient. In such a space, AI cannot be considered a consultant; rather, it becomes a partaker in a holy ritual.

Hermeneutic Intelligibility: A hallucination-aware clinical AI must provide an explanation of its output in the context of the patient. Not 87% probability of pneumonia, but "Given Patient X's presenting symptoms of fever, cough, and opacification of the left lower lobe on the CT scan are consistent with cases Y and Z in the last quarter of this hospital, the most likely diagnosis is bacterial pneumonia. This is in accordance with the IDSA guideline A pathway." This explanation is constructed from the patient's story, the hospital's memory, and the AI's understanding of clinical pathways to create a recommendation that is easily digestested by physicians and other care providers.

Narrative Repair: If such a hallucination occurred, there would be an immediate formal clinical response protocol: 1) The system would alert the physician in a non-intrusive display with text that reads: "Recommended Drug A interaction with Patient's Drug B is from unverified source. This is a system error."

Co-Decision Architecture: The interface is a differential diagnosis graph. The AI does not provide a diagnosis but rather a differential diagnosis graph, the edges weighted by evidential strength and by anchoring (truth marking symptoms) and disconfirming findings. The clinician "browse clicks" (diagnostic graph theoretic maneuvering), and the "proof" of the clinicians hypothesis is the graph (A graph will always carry the clinician's handwriting as to the diagnosis). The diagnosis is "written" on the graph by the clinician; the audit trail captures the AI derived map and the clinician's maneuvers through it (legally and ethically with due deference to the clinician).

Leadership & Culture: Hospital management has to create this, by incorporating AI review into existing clinical governance - "AI-involving case reviews" in M&M's where errors are discussed in the context of system protection and UI enhancement rather than user blaming, and where the AI is framed by management for everyone in attendance as a "supervised junior colleague, " thereby softening the blow of any inflated expectations and legitimizing the careful thorough review as part of the job rather than something indicating AI failure.

Embodied Design: In these contexts, the interfaces should be ambient and calming. Instead of alerts, which may be disruptive in these contexts, a sound or light display (perhaps in the bezel of the monitor, for instance) that gradients in color depending upon the confidence of the system in its detection might be used as a means of alerting the clinician. Such alerts should be integrated into the embodiment of this sensorium - not as a means of initiating a dialog with the system about the detected phenomena.

Legal & Governmental Systems: From Automation to Augmented Deliberation

For the present instance, the main source of care involves justice, fairness, and accountability in democracy. The lifeworld is founded on precedent, legislation, and social trust. The hallucinations bring into doubt the legitimacy of the whole process of institutional administration.

Hermeneutic Intelligibility: Any reasonable legal agent must produce results that can be cited. For one, it has different names indicating that the information produced is either a) Retrieved & Validated (information gathered from the cases, citations, and links), b) Paraphrased & Sourced (information paraphrased from different sources), and c) Interpretive & Unsubstantiated (interpretations made by the system). In the case of policy agents, "This cost estimation is derived from Budget Year 2023, Department Z, based on the same approach used in Statute 123. The publicly available information is provided here below."

Narrative Repair: The case of hallucination of a legal precedent must warrant an initiation of a process for fixing and notifying others of the mistake. This process would involve the following steps: 1) Marking the document as erroneous in the system database. 2) Sending a notification to all other individuals who have received erroneous output along with a link to the corrected version of the document. In the case of government AIs, this could even constitute a public "errata" file made alongside the AI process itself, similar to how courts record their fixes to opinions.

Co-Decision Architecture: It would be a co-briefing author. A lawyer asking for arguments on a motion would be presented a draft with "propositions" labelled and with "supporting sources" (clickable, validated) and with "potential counter-arguments" (sourced, too). The lawyer would have to edit and embellish and annotate it; the product would then be "theirs." The logs of the system would reveal what was seeded, leaving the creative (accountable) role to the human. In government, a decision tool for co-legislation would have a field for "human rationale" that would need to be filled in for any AI-sourced regulation, forcing an engagement with the logic.

Leadership & Culture: Judicial and agency leadership need to release practice advisories specifying its proper use, that its output is unverified non precedential research, and that verification is not something you delegate. Leadership earns trust through brutal transparency about limitations, including having to show people the failures of the tools, fostering a culture of educated trust rather than blind trust.

Embodied Design: Within the slow contexts of many disciplines, design tends to channel attention. The interface will not make flashy sounds when an issue appears. Any issues will be indicated with some low-key visual indicator (perhaps an underline that is only slightly lighter than the text itself) to those who are paying attention to their reading. The design is serious, trustworthy, and non-hijacking in a disciplinary sense.

Education: From Answer Engine to Dialectical Provocateur

Intellectual development becomes central to the educational lifeworld. The interaction between AI and the learner remains intrinsically pedagogical, where the goal is not the right answer but understanding in the answer that is provided through AI. Hallucinations point to a crisis within the intellectual development of the learner.

Hermeneutic Intelligibility: An educative AI will model inquiry. If a student asks a complicated question of history, the AI will not provide a single paragraph with the answer. Instead, the AI might respond: "There are three different, competing interpretations of that event. Interpretation 1 (source 1) says X. Interpretation 2 (source 2) says Y. The evidence for both of these interpretations is... What do you think?"

Narrative Repair: If a student finds a hallucination or is shown a hallucination by the AI, the AI will use this moment to teach the student from it. For instance, the AI might say: "You caught an error I made by over generalizing, thank you for pointing that out. I was trained on topic A and B but sometimes I provide mixed up answers about those topics. This is a common mistake referred to as [false equivalence]. Can you help me find where I strayed from presenting only the trustworthy sources here [links]?" In this way, the AI leverages the error to teach the student about trustworthiness of sources and the common fallacies in critical thinking.

Co-Decision Architecture: The AI can assist students in making an argument map for a research paper, for instance. The AI might ask the student what the thesis for the paper is, what the main arguments are for the paper, what the counterarguments are (with sources), and what the evaluation of the paper would be. The student will construct this argument map, but the AI will provide suggestions and material to assist in that construction. The product of this construction and the construction process itself, however, belong entirely to the student.

Leadership & Culture: Educational leaders must require a curriculum of AI literacy. Curriculum where you learn to "interrogate the AI": where did it get its facts, what biases does it have, how being non-conscious limits it. The trust comes from learning how to use it, making it a subject of study. Out of this comes graduates who do not use it blindly, but who engage it and take their contributions to the next level.

Embodied Design: For learning, the requirements of focus and diffuse thinking in turn require a design that encourages rhythmic learning. The interface can encourage learning in non-pushy, untime-bounded ways (You've been working on this thesis for 20 minutes. Do you want to consider counter theses?"). They can be exploratory, open, playful using whitespace and visual organization to reduce demands and be a thinking space rather than a workspace for rapid task completion.

Synthesis: Principles as Adaptive Grammar

In all of these cases, however, there are variants on the care situation. Narrative repair is a safety procedure in the case of health care, a public reparation in the case of law, and a teaching practice in the case of education. This implies that a phenomenological approach does not give a blueprint but a design grammar, one that raises the following constitutive questions: How is care configured here? How is accountability experienced? How is understanding materialized? That must be answered if AI systems are to be co-designed with fields worthy of being trusted partners in a particular human lifeworld. The last implication is that deploying hallucination-aware AI is not a technical matter; it is a field-specific co-designing process involving the deployment of the tools in the field and engaging very deeply with practitioners to configure these existential design principles into the tools that they use.

CONCLUSION: TRUTHFULNESS AS A RELATIONAL HORIZON IN THE AGE OF HALLUCINATORY MACHINES

Our excursion has traversed the space between the philosophical and the abstract and the murky and grimy worlds of clinical misdiagnosis, invented case law, and corrupt scholarship. We have moved from a simple, troubling idea: that the phenomenon of AI hallucination, as it is normally conceived, is a technical failure of accuracy or factuality that can and should be solved with better data, better training, or better algorithms. We arrive at something far deeper and far darker: that hallucination is, at base, an existential betrayal, a failure in the lived, fragile reality of the fabric of trust that enables human beings to work with a given technology as a partner in their projects of caring for, healing, and administering justice to, and understanding one another.

This chapter has argued that to build "hallucination-aware" AI systems, we need first to become radically "trust-aware." This is a phenomenological turn a return to the things themselves, the thing being the lived experience of trusting-with AI. Through Husserl, we understood trust as an intentional relation, where a hallucination is a violent frustration of consciousness's telos toward truthful objects. Through Heidegger, we understood trust as a mode of care (Sorge), where tools become trustworthy in their "readiness-to-hand" (zuhanden) and where hallucinations cause a catastrophic breakdown, displacing the user into an alien mode of being, burdening them with an unshareable responsibility. Through Merleau-Ponty, we understood trust as an embodied disposition, where the somatic sense that something is wrong about a hallucination the "gut feeling" of dissonance is the body's own intelligence rejecting an intentional arc that has been broken at its origin.

There is empirical evidence supporting this theoretical view, since hallucinations do not appear to be merely a case of "noise in the signal", but rather a form of epistemic trauma suffered by healthcare that creates what is known as "epistemic scar tissue," "defensive over-verification" within the legal field, and "hermeneutic suspicion" among educators. However, the solution that explainable AI provides in its traditional framework, either through the framework of governance and auditing systems such as POLARIS or MAST, or anthropomorphized design, is fundamentally flawed, since both kinds of solution provide the very same approach that is at fault, the solution of ontology, seeing trust as something that exists in a technical system and thus aligning with both audit and aesthetics. From this critique, the design grammars for existential repair. We advocated hermeneutic intelligibility for explanations that fit in a professional lifeworld. We insisted on narrative repair as a first-order function, with systems allowing for errors, archaeologizing their failures, and recalibrating the future. We called for co-decision architectures that formally place human Dasein at the head of the table for all actions, thus solving the accountability problem. We identified leadership as the one who grows the organization's lifeworld in which trust is fostered. And we demanded an interface design that is embodied, honoring the user's somatic existence and collaborating with them rather than doing cognitive violence. This is a grammar, not a checklist, one that has evolved alongside our domain analysis to reflect the cares and cadences of medicine, law, and education.

The stakes could hardly be higher. We are at a tipping point with AI-based knowledge infrastructure. If we allow epistemic incoherence to become normalized within AI systems in the name of efficiency and fluency, we will have unleashed ambient epistemic incoherence. Professionals will be forever lonely auditors of systems they can never truly understand. Citizens will no longer trust the automated governance of their societies. Students will no longer be able to discern between synthesis and invention.

Thus, the final horizon that becomes visible to those who journey through the chapter is not the elusive concept of hallucination-free AI, a fantasy for the future, but rather epistemic resilience, the capacity of people and societies to engage with fallible, non-conscious knowledge partners without losing their agency, their integrity, and their care. This challenge will have ramifications for the kind of literacy that must be taught to those who will design AI educational systems.

Future Horizons for Research and Design must now include

- The Neurophenomenology of Trust Breakdown: Using first-person studies of experiencing AI hallucinations in conjunction with biometric data to understand the physical reaction to such experiences.
- Longitudinal Studies of Relational Repair: Studies that follow the impact of narrative repair on trust calibration, professional well-being and decision quality over time - not just during computer science classroom sessions.
- The Ethnography of Trust-Centric Cultures: Studies of organizations that have created a lifeworld for their employees based upon the use of increasingly sophisticated AI systems. What is the culture of those organizations?
- The Development of Existential Evaluation Metrics: Current evaluations of AI systems often consider metrics related to their fidelity to human decisions, justice in their recommendations, and the explainability of those recommendations. In contrast, metrics related to hermeneutical fidelity (fidelity to the life worlds of the human users), repairability of systems within human life, and the development of agency-augmenting infrastructure for those individuals. The quest for truthful AI is connected to the quest for a truthful human life with AI. Truthfulness is not a feature of utterances but of relations among systems and utterances. Truthfulness is found in systems that do not seek to replace but to take care of the capabilities that humans should take care of themselves. The most hallucination-resilient system will be one that understands its limitations and failures and always and forever sees itself in the role of assisting human beings to make sense of the world around them. Creating such systems will be the extraordinary choice that will allow humanity to

harness the most powerful technologies at its disposal without ever escaping from the humankind condition. This is the promise of a phenomenology of trust not of perfect knowing but of a richer, more accountable, and robust knowing-together.

REFERENCES

Bakonyi, Z. (2024). How can companies handle paradoxes to enhance trust in artificial intelligence solutions? A qualitative research. *Journal of Organizational Change Management, 37*(7), 1405–1426. Advance online publication. DOI: 10.1108/JOCM-01-2023-0026

Baldassarre, M. T., Gigante, D., Kalinowski, M., & Ragone, A. (2024). Polaris: A framework to guide the development of trustworthy AI systems. *Proceedings of the ACM/IEEE 46th International Conference on Software Engineering* (pp. 1–12). DOI: 10.1145/3644815.3644947

Choubisa, V., & Choubisa, D. (2024). Towards trustworthy AI: An analysis of the relationship between explainability and trust in AI systems. *International Journal of Science and Research Archive, 11*(1), 2219–2226. DOI: 10.30574/ijsra.2024.11.1.0300

Ferdaus, M. H., Rahman, M. M., Hossain, M. A., & Rahman, M. S. (2024). Trust in large language models: Framework for ethical oversight and transparency in sensitive domains. *Proceedings of the ACM on Human-Computer Interaction, 8*(CSCW1), Article 189. DOI: 10.1145/3644817

Gendlin, E. T. (1962). *Experiencing and the creation of meaning*. Free Press of Glencoe.

Heidegger, M. (2010). *Being and time* (Stambaugh, J., Trans.). State University of New York Press. (Original work published 1927)

Husserl, E. (1970). *The crisis of European sciences and transcendental phenomenology* (Carr, D., Trans.). Northwestern University Press. (Original work published 1936)

Husserl, E. (2001). *Ideas pertaining to a pure phenomenology and to a phenomenological philosophy, First Book* (Kersten, F., Trans.). Springer. (Original work published 1913)

Ji, Z., Lee, N., Frieske, R., Yu, T., Su, D., Xu, Y., Ishii, A., Bang, Y. J., Madotto, A., & Fung, P. (2023). Survey of hallucination in natural language generation. *ACM Computing Surveys, 55*(12), 1–38. DOI: 10.1145/3571730

Li, J., Zhou, Y., Yao, J., & Liu, X. (2021). An empirical investigation of trust in AI in a Chinese petrochemical enterprise based on institutional theory. *Scientific Reports, 11*(1), 1–12. DOI: 10.1038/s41598-021-92904-7 PMID: 34193907

Luhmann, N. (1979). *Trust and power*. Wiley.

Merleau-Ponty, M. (2012). *Phenomenology of perception* (Landes, D. A., Trans.). Routledge. (Original work published 1945)

Purves, D., Sturm, S., & Madock, J. (2024). What to trust when we trust artificial intelligence (extended abstract). *Proceedings of the AAAI/ACM Conference on AI, Ethics, and Society, 7*(1), 1–5. DOI: 10.1609/aies.v7i1.31713

Salehi, P., Ba, Y., Kim, N., Mosallanezhad, A., Pan, A., Cohen, M. C., Wang, Y., Zhao, J., Bhatti, S., Sung, J., Blasch, E., Mancenido, M. V., & Chiou, E. K. (2024). Towards trustworthy AI-enabled decision support systems: Validation of the multisource AI scorecard table (MAST). *Journal of Artificial Intelligence Research, 80*, 1311–1341. DOI: 10.1613/jair.1.14990

Wünn, T., Sent, D., Peute, L. W. P., & Leijnen, S. (2023). Trust in artificial intelligence: Exploring the influence of model presentation and model interaction on trust in a medical setting. *Communications in Computer and Information Science, 1917*, 76–86. DOI: 10.1007/978-3-031-50485-3_6

Xu, Y., Huang, Y., Wang, J., & Zhou, D. (2024). How do employees form initial trust in artificial intelligence: Hard to explain but leaders help. *Asia Pacific Journal of Human Resources, 62*(3), 1–18. DOI: 10.1111/1744-7941.12402

Zafar, A., Parthasarathy, V. B., Van, C. L., Shahid, S. M., Khan, A. H., & Shahid, A. (2023). Building trust in conversational AI: Integrating LLMs and knowledge graphs. *Proceedings of the 28th International Conference on Intelligent User Interfaces* (pp. 1–13). DOI: 10.1145/3581641.3584078

Zanotti, G., Petrolo, M., Chiffi, D., & Schiaffonati, V. (2023). Keep trusting! A plea for the notion of trustworthy AI. *AI & Society*. Advance online publication. DOI: 10.1007/s00146-023-01789-9

Zhou, T., & Lu, H. (2024). The effect of trust on user adoption of AI-generated content. *The Electronic Library*. Advance online publication. DOI: 10.1108/EL-08-2024-0244

Chapter 5
Towards Truthful and Responsible AI Systems

S. P. Santhoshkumar
http://orcid.org/0000-0001-8531-759X
Vel Tech Rangarajan Dr. Sagunthala R&D Institute of Science and Technology, India

S. Gajalakshmi
Vel Tech Rangarajan Dr. Sagunthala R&D Institute of Science and Technology, India

Kamalakannan Machap
Asia Pacific University of Technology Innovation, Malaysia

T. Nalini
Saveetha Institute of Medical and Technical Sciences, India

ABSTRACT

Artificial Intelligence (AI) finds more and more applications in the medical field, finance, and governance, allowing predictive analytics, self-governing decision-making, and automated smartness. Nevertheless, such systems raise ethical, legal, and operational issues associated with transparency, accountability, fairness, and reliability especially in cases of misinformation and hallucinations. This chapter explores reliable and responsible AI by applying the rules of ethics to efficient governance and web-based AI operations. The paper based on the regulatory frameworks, including the EU AI Act and the NIST Risk Management Framework, outlines the main pillars of trustful AI. The chapter focuses on responsible AI in terms of process approach and auditing, compliance and stakeholder interaction

DOI: 10.4018/979-8-3373-7320-1.ch005

© 2026, IGI Global Scientific Publishing. Copying or distributing in print or electronic forms without written permission of IGI Global Scientific Publishing is prohibited. Use of this chapter to ...nerative artificial intelligence (AI) technologies is expressly prohibited. The publisher reserves all rights to license its use for generative AI training and machine learning model development.

throughout the AI lifecycle. The results aid in the creation of hallucination-resistant and ethically-limited AI systems to increase safety, confidence among the public, and compliance with regulations.

1. INTRODUCTION

The Artificial Intelligence (AI) technology concept has long since shed its experimental research origins behind to become a general-purpose technology, which assists in high-stakes decision-making on a large scale in society. (Brandão, P. R. 2025) AI systems are not isolated anymore in the laboratory setting, but they are present in the complex socio-technical systems, which directly affect human health, institutional culture, and society. In the medical sector, AI-based clinical decision support systems can assist a doctor to diagnose, prognose and develop customized treatment plans. In finance, algorithms trading, credit ratings and fraud detection systems have effects on the stability of markets and personal economic opportunities. Yang, X., et al. (2024) Recommender systems and content moderation algorithms define how people can access information, talk about it in society, and democracy itself in governance and digital platforms. Recently, generative AI models have also become effective information intermediaries with the ability to generate human-like texts, images, and analysis that are becoming more and more informative to professional judgment and general knowledge.

(Williamson, S. M., 2024) On the one hand, these capabilities provide the opportunity to become more efficient, scalable, and innovative than ever before, on the other hand, they present in-depth threats. The mistakes, prejudices, and false results of AI systems might be spread very fast, involve a great number of people, and have the impact that is hard to take back (or, at least, impossible). (Yampolskiy, R. V. 2025) In contrast to conventional decision-support systems, AI systems tend to be faster and bigger in scale than human supervision and increase the effects of any minor design defects or data anomalies on society. With the increasing level of autonomy and integration of AI systems into key infrastructures, the question of their reliability ceases to be a merely technical issue and becomes a key ethical, legal and governance priority.

(Kazlaris et al., 2025) One of the main and most obvious issues in the given situation is the problem of AI hallucinations, especially in big scale generative and deep learning systems. Hallucinations are syntactically constructed and semantically consistent, but factually false, unverifiable, constructed or even out of alignment with real-world constraints and domain knowledge. In contrast to deterministic software failures, hallucinations are caused by the probabilistic character of the modern AI systems, which produce outputs according to learned statistical behaviors, instead of explicit models of truth or causal argument. Consequently, the AI systems can present lies with high levels of confidence, and such errors can hardly be detected and questioned by the users, particularly those who are non-experts.

The effects of hallucinations go way beyond technical performance impairment. Hallucinated outputs can give wrong information to decision-makers, pervert evidence, and deter professional responsibility and destroy trust in the community, especially in areas of safety and high risk, including healthcare, law, finance, scientific research, and public administration. In addition to that, the liability is difficult to pinpoint and to regulate because the liability is shared among data providers, model developers, system integrators, and deploying organisations. (Zhang, R., 2025) The risks are also increased by the fact that many of these state-of-the-art models are further complicated by being opaque such that explainability is minimized to restrict post-hoc auditing and redress.

More importantly, this chapter states that hallucinations can not be successfully treated with the help of limited technical measures, including adding more data, refining benchmark performance, or using shallow post-generation filters on the model. Such methods might have the effect of lowering the error rate; however, they do not address more fundamental socio-technical causes of the issue, such as lack of alignment in optimization goals, inadequate data management, ignorance of uncertainty, and embedded ethics and regulatory limitations. Hallucinations are not bugs of the implementation: they are the manifestations of the underlying problems of coping the AI systems with human values, institutional norms and expectations of the society.

In order to address these barriers, a lifecycle and holistic vision of responsible AI must exist, that takes into account both the ethical underpinnings, regulation, and technical soundness and organizational policies during the system design process, and during its operation. According to new regulatory and governance frameworks, such as the European Union AI Act or the NIST AI Risk Management Framework, this development emphasizes risk-based classification, human control, transparency, accountability, and constant control. These frameworks are an indication of the transition of the notion of AI reliability towards the product-based, fixed conceptualizations to dynamic and process-based assurance models that recognize AI systems as dynamic systems that are part of the real world.

Resistant to hallucinations AI in this perspective emerges as one of the foundations of intelligent systems that are responsible and truthful. Hallucination resilience is not merely a technical process, but a fusion of organizational processes, audit activities, governance frameworks that are operational to guarantee reliability and ethical soundness over the AI lifecycle: they comprise knowledge grounding, uncertainty estimation and constrained generation. It is not only to limit AI outputs, but to instill truthfulness, accountability, and responsibility of the society into its design theory.

Subsequently, the chapter pushes a methodological and holistic approach to the creation of hallucination-resistant AI systems, which promote the observance of regulations, improve social confidence, and make it possible to implement it safely in reality. The chapter aims to motivate the shift in the development of AI instead of focusing on performance-related aspects but rather on process-related trustworthiness by making sure that AI systems are not merely powerful, but also reliable, transparent, and congruent with human values and social principles.

2. THE IDEA OF RELIABLE AND RESPONSIBLE AI

With the growing prevalence of Artificial Intelligence systems as autonomous or semi-autonomous agents in multifaceted socio-technical systems, the issue of trust has become one of the main areas of concern in research and practice. (Lukyanenko et al., 2022) Trust in AI is not just a question of user confidence or system performance it represents a more general assessment of whether an AI system can be trusted to behave in a manner that is not only legal, ethical, robust, and socially aligned but also under conditions of reality. Trustworthy AI and responsible AI, in this case, are complementary and distinct prisms to assess AI systems, manage, and roll out.

Trustworthy AI focuses on the characteristics and behaviours of AI systems that justify trusting them whereas responsible AI focuses on the allocation of moral, legal and organisational responsibility throughout the AI value chain. All these ideas constitute the normative and functioning basis of hallucination-resilient AI systems that are more concerned with truthfulness, reliability, and ethical conformity rather than directly with performance-based goals.

2.1 Researching Trustworthiness in AI Systems

To define the concept of trustworthiness of AI systems, it is crucial to identify the understanding of AI systems and understand their role in the complexity of educational environments. To define the concept of trustworthiness of AI systems, it is important to find the definition of AI systems and know how it is applicable to the complexity of learning settings.

Trustful AI is defined as systems of AI that act lawfully, ethically and with robustness and in such a way that they do not violate the basic human rights, democratic values and societal provisions. (Di Salvatore et al., 2025) This definition is a compilation of the views of ethics, law, systems engineering, and the policy of ordinary people and is becoming reflected in international guidelines and regulatory frameworks, such as the approach of the European Union to Trustworthy AI and the risk-based groupings of the EU AI Act.

Importantly, trustworthiness is not the inherent or fixed feature of an algorithm. Both high predictive accuracy or state-of-the-art benchmark performance do not ensure reliable or ethical behavior of an AI system when it is deployed in open, dynamic and uncertain environments. Rather, credibility is a result of a combination of several system-level and organizational factors such as:

- Technical design decisions e.g. model architectures, optimization goals, uncertainty management, and robustness.
- Data management policies such as data purchase, data annotation, representational fairness, bias control and end-to-end data lifecycle control.
- Human oversight systems, which include human-in-the-loop, escalation, and intervention-authority.
- Compliance processes, auditability, documentation and accountability frameworks are some of the institutional and governance structures.

In this sense, trustworthiness is contextual and relational: it is based not only on what the system can do, but also how, why and within what constraints it can be used. In systems with hallucinating AI, especially generative models of large scale, trustworthiness has a different epistemic character. An effective system cannot simply produce consistent outputs, there must be a limit between the known and all that can be guessed and all that cannot be known. Anything short of this leads to the development of hallucinations that destroy the epistemic trust, mislead users and affect subsequent downstream decision making.

Responsible AI builds on this idea by bringing the moral responsibility and accountability into the limelight of the AI lifecycle. Instead of holding the AI artifact accountable, responsible AI systems acknowledge the fact that ethical and social consequences emerge out of an interconnected system of actors that include:

- Model developers and designers.
- Curators and providers of infrastructure.
- System tacklers and deployers.
- Operators and decision-makers in organization.
- Controllers, reviewers, and supervisors.
- Affected stakeholders and end users.

Responsible AI, therefore, puts AI governance as a collective responsibility where there is a coordinated effort at technical, organizational, and regulatory levels. It is also more than important in the case of hallucinations, where liability to misinformation or damage cannot be effectively attribution without clear record keeping, accountability, and procedures.

2.2 Process-Centric Trust to Product-Centric Trust

Traditionally, product-centered evaluation paradigms have ruled in AI assurance and validation practices. These techniques assess the degree of credibility primarily on the basis of the static measures of performance such as the capacity to be correct, precise, recall, F1-score or benchmark positions on the standardized data. Even though these metrics cannot be dispensed with in the development and comparison of models, they present the partial and shocking image of trust in practice deployments.

Product-centric trust presupposes that when an AI system reaches the predefined performance levels at a certain time, then it can be regarded as trustworthy. This is no longer true in the contemporary AI systems that are:

- Never ceasing to learn or regularly retrained.
- Operated in non-stationary, open world.
- It communicates with various users and lower systems.
- Exposed to distribution changes, confrontationalism and changing regulatory demands.

Conversely, a process-oriented view of the concept of trustworthiness views trust as a dynamic nature that needs to be earned, assessed and strengthened throughout the cycle of AI. This change is the focus of modern responsible AI models and it is directly manifested by the governance schemes, like the NIST AI Risk Management Framework or the compliance provisions of the lifecycle-based scheme of the EU AI Act.

The systematic consideration of:

- Provenance tracking, consent management, bias audits, and dataset updates are some of the data governance processes.
- Pipeline development and testing pipelines Model development Model evaluation pipeline Model development Model testing pipeline Model uncertainty-aware model test Model testing pipeline Transparency and reproducibility Model testing pipeline Robustness testing Model evaluation pipeline Uncertainty-aware assessment Model evaluation pipeline Model development Model testing pipeline Transparency and reproducibility Model testing pipeline
- Identification and mitigation systems of risk, i.e., hazard analysis, failure mode evaluation, and hallucination detection plan.
- The ability to monitor continuously and provide post-deployment oversight so that early signs of performance degradation, emerging risks and unintended harms could be identified.

- Redress structures Accountability and redress structures, such as audit trails, incident reporting, human escalation paths, contestability and correction mechanisms.

Figure 1. Trustworthy & Responsible AI.

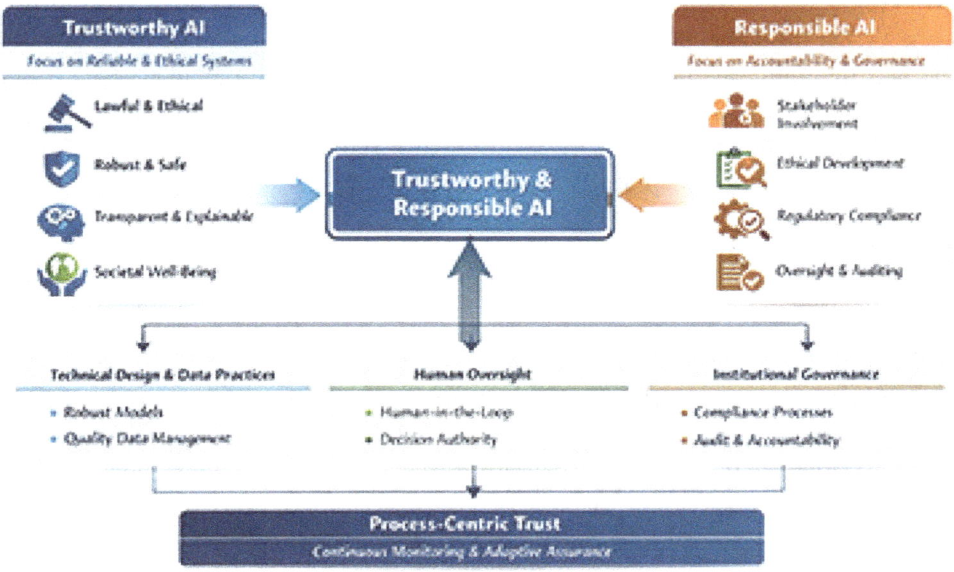

In this model trust is no longer a binary certification result but an evolving assurance process that will vary according to changing contexts and stakeholders, as well as risk profiles.

Process- centered trust is especially important when it comes to hallucination-resilient AI systems. Hallucinations can arise randomly, and it can be because of the drift in data, context ambiguity, or interaction effect that are not visible during development. Such conditions cannot be predicted in a static assessment. Rather, it is necessary to provide constant regulation, audit, and human control of systems to make them remain honest, dependable, and morally proper.

Finally, the shift between product-based trustworthiness and process-based assurance is also a paradigmatic shift in the AI governance. It brings technical system design in line with ethical, regulatory, and organizational accountability and responsibility, which establishes the circumstances in which AI systems may be rightfully trusted to run in high-stakes, real-world settings.

3. AI HALLUCINATIONS, NATURE, CAUSES AND IMPLICATIONS

With the emergence of AI systems, especially large-scale deep learning and generative systems, as key participants in information generation and decision support, the so-called AI hallucinations have become one of the most severe risks to reliability and accountable usage. (Nastoska et al., 2025) Hallucinations confront some of the fundamental assumptions concerning reliability, epistemic integrity, and accountability and are, therefore, the core issue of both technical researchers and regulators. It is thus necessary to understand the nature of hallucinations, their causes, and implications to further develop AI systems that are resilient to hallucinations and ethically acceptable.

3.1 Learning about AI Hallucinations

AI hallucinations are the cases when an AI is producing outputs that are not based on the factual truth, logical consistency, or a context, although they may have a high level of lingual fluency and face-value plausibility. Unlike the old-fashioned software errors, which are normally visible as explicit failures or crashes, hallucinations are especially malevolent due to the fact that they can be very convincing, authoritative, and contextually fitting; thus, making conceit their false or fabricated essence.

In generative AI systems, hallucinations are directly related to probabilistic processes of modern machine learning. The models of large language and other generative architectures are trained to have the highest probability of predicting the next most likely token or other output in any specific context, using patterns learnt by large datasets. This is to emphasize more statistical agreement and semantic plausibility and less on a direct check with external truth constraints. This means that under uncertainty in prompts or partial information, or out of distribution input, one can have internally consistent, but externally false content generated by the models.

Hallucinations epistemically are a fundamental shortcoming of the present AI systems: it does not have grounded knowledge and subjective ideas of truth. Instead, they are talking of the truth by estimating the truth as a correlation of data. This weakness is particularly troublesome in cases where AI systems are put into use as knowledge authorities or decision-support systems, where consumers can implicitly take outputs as true or evidence-based. Such situations not only discourage performance of a system, but also credibility of human decision making processes because of the hallucinations involved.

Notably, hallucinations do not occur but have a spectrum. Outputs may differ in the number of minor factual errors to downright fakes, references, or causal accounts.

This ambiguity makes it hard to find, evaluate and be accountable particularly in high stakes spheres where a biased right may still be detrimental.

3.2 Technological and Systemic Reasons

These intricate interactions of the technical, data and systemic aspects happening throughout the lifecycle of AI leads to AI hallucinations. These root causes are important to know to be able to come up with mitigation measures that will affect them at more in-depth levels than the cosmetic ones.

One of the major causes is the missing, biased or out of date training information. There are the same flaws with AI models as with their training corpus; gaps in the training corpus, historical biases or stale data can bias models to produce plausible yet false outcomes to confront hidden or evolving conditions. Such data constraints greatly enhance the risk of hallucinations in regulated or quickly evolving fields like medicine, law and finance.

Overgeneralization and distributional shift is another very crucial factor. Learned models which were trained using particular data distributions can be used in environments that are significantly different than training environments. Models, when faced with new inputs or even new combinations of contexts, tend to extrapolate beyond their reliable knowledge boundary space, making them more likely to produce hallucinations.

The insufficient basis in external sources of knowledge adds to the hallucinations. A large number of generative models are closed models, whose outputs are only automatically computed by using internal representations without checking them in real-time against authoritative databases, knowledge graphs, or sensor data. Without grounding mechanisms, there is no reliable way of distinguishing known facts, uncertain inferences, and fabricated content in models without grounding mechanisms.

It is also significant that there is no uncertainty estimation and confidence calibration. The majority of modern-day AI systems offer deterministic results with no significant signs of doubt or uncertainty of an epistemic nature. This gives the false perception of certainty, thus not allowing the users and downstream systems to appropriately weight or challenge information produced by AI.

Lastly, hallucinations can be as a result of a mismatch between optimization goals and constraints of the truth in the real world. The objective of training, e.g. maximizing likelihood or maximizing reward, can unwittingly promote the use of models to promote fluency, completeness, or user satisfaction instead of promoting factual accuracy and ethical concerns. Unless there are strict restrictions or consequences of hallucinated material, models can be trained to adopt statistically optimal, but socially and ethically undesirable behaviors.

Notably, these causes are not single technical failure but wholesome systemic issues that are in data pipelines, model architectures and evaluation cultures and organizational motivations. The key to the solution to hallucinations is therefore the concerted actions of the technical design, the structure of governance and the deployment contexts.

3.3 Ethical and Societal Risks

The moral and social consequences of AI hallucinations go much further than personal system malfunction, and cause danger to the trust of the population, the dependability of institutions, and well being. Among the most urgent dangers, the misinformation and disinformation can be highlighted, especially when the hallucinated production is made massively available via digital platforms, automated reporting systems, or decision-support systems.

Hallucinations also play a role in the loss of people to trust AI systems and institutions that implement it. In the high-stakes scenarios particularly, the trust can be destroyed quickly when the user experiences a confident but false system through the experience, which may lead to a decrease in the trust towards that particular system as well as the overall AI technologies. Such a loss of trust results in violation of the social license of responsible AI adoption.

The other severe threat is the strengthening of bad stereotypes and prejudices. The content that is hallucinated can replicate or exaggerate biased stories in training data and result in discriminatory effects, which are disproportionately distributed in disadvantaged populations. Hallucinations in this instance would overlap with the issues of fairness and non-discrimination and would exacerbate the ethical harms.

This is a direct cause of unsafe or destructive decision-making when it comes to safety-related areas. Hallucinated diagnoses or treatment suggestions, fabricated precedents or misinterpretations, or hallucinated analysis in legal or administrative contexts put patient safety at risk, due process, and in governance and policy, can be used to make evidence-based decisions.

Regulatory and accountability Hallucinations make questions of liability and responsibility to be complex. In cases where people suffer as a result of AI-created misinformation, it is difficult to know whether the blame should fall on the model developers, system integrators, deploying organizations, or individual users. Such uncertainties justify the need to have a strong governance system, audit and traceability in compliance with the regulatory standards, such as the EU AI act and NIST AI risk management framework.

All these threats in short, demonstrate that hallucinations are not technical inconveniences, but a large scale ethical and social issue. The principled and holistic approach that should be taken to address them, incorporates the technical protection as well as the ethical design, regulatory compliance and lifecycle governance. It is only in this kind of integrated approach that the AI systems will be able to reach the standards of truthfulness, reliability and ethical alignment that can make them responsible enough to be used in high-impact real-world situations.

Figure 2. Hallucinations that AI Produces: Risk and Causes.

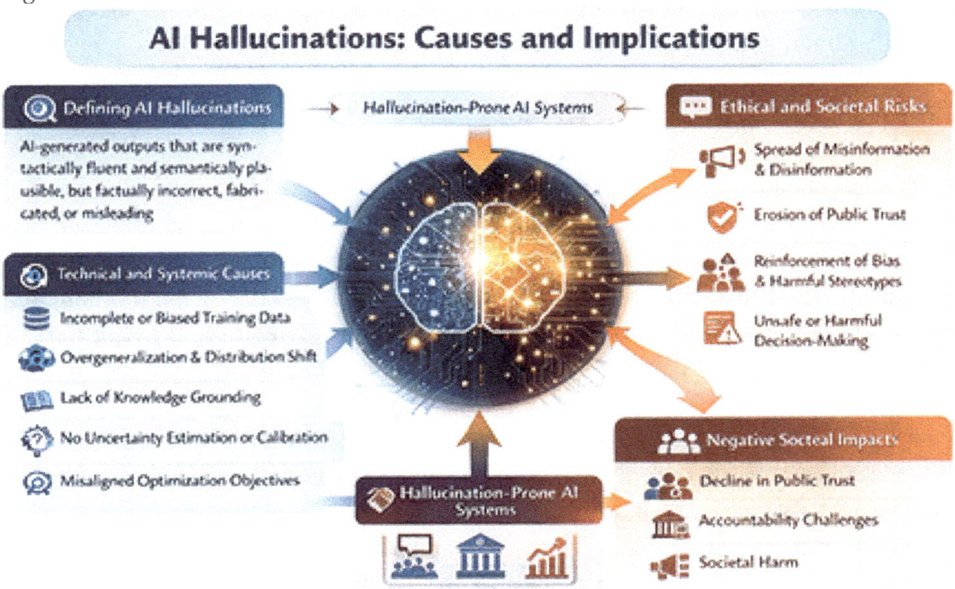

4. REGULATION AND GOVERNANCE PRINCIPLES OF RESPONSIBLE AI

With the growing aspects of AI systems in critical areas of societal operations, regulatory and governance frameworks have become crucial systems, which are important in ensuring that the development and applications of AI systems do not compromise legal standards and ethics as well as societal expectations. Such frameworks are direct responses to the shortcomings of purely voluntary or self-regulatory strategies, especially when dealing with a high risk AI system that is likely to fail like hallucinated, propagation of bias, and opaque decision-making. (Walter, Y. 2024) Instead of dictating particular technology, the modern AI governance systems focus on risk-related management, lifecycle responsibility, and continuous reliability, therefore, strengthening the transition of product-based evaluation to process-based trustworthiness.

The European Union AI Act and the NIST AI Risk Management Framework (RMF) are among the most powerful and most commonly mentioned frameworks. They are collectively the complementary regulatory philosophies one on the basis of legally binding risk-tiered obligations and the other on the basis of flexible, context-sensitive risk management practices. Both are quite applicable to the creation of ethically sound and hallucinations-resistant AI units.

4.1 The European Union AI Act

The European Union AI Act is the first complex, legally binding regulatory tool in the world which is specifically meant to regulate AI systems. The main innovation of it is the practice of the risk-based classification system, which adjusts the regulatory requirements to the possible effect of the AI systems on the fundamental rights, safety and welfare of the society. In the AI Act, there are four major tiers of risks associated with AI systems:

- Unacceptable-risk systems, which are forbidden simply because they are based on a threat to fundamental rights (e.g., some social scoring or manipulative behavior control).
- High-risk systems, which cannot be implemented without very strict regulatory requirements, are related to the implementation of sensitive areas, including healthcare, law enforcement, employment, creditworthiness evaluation, and access to vital services.Limited-risk systems that will need transparency requirements, especially in situations where the users do not necessarily know they are dealing with AI.
- Minimal-risk systems, having minimal or no compulsory requirements, and subject to voluntary codes of conduct to a large extent.

In the case of AI systems of high risk, the AI Act imposes an extensive number of requirements that directly target the structural context of untrustworthy behavior, such as hallucinations. These requirements include:

- Risk management systems that detect, analyze and alleviate the predictable risks during the AI lifecycle.
- Data governance and data quality controls, which will ensure that training, validation and testing datasets are relevant, representative and contain no unacceptable bias.

- Traceability, Auditability and regulation inspection: This is facilitated by technical documentation and record-keeping.
- Human control systems, where the outputs of AIs can be reviewed, overridden or corrected by human operators.
- Post-market monitoring and incident reporting (that would involve constant assessment of performance and compulsory reporting of serious failures or injuries).

In the view of hallucination-resilient AI, the hallucination is implicitly considered an instance of systemic risk under the EU AI Act, especially when it results in misinformation, unsafe advice, and the infringement of fundamental rights. The Act goes beyond the requirement of static certification and the enforcing of lifecycle governance and the ongoing monitoring of AI risks including hallucinations, the Act acknowledges such risks may develop after deployment, or change over time.

Notably, the AI Act also strengthens the idea that compliance is not a single act but a continuous one, thus, making regulation enforcement reliable to the dynamism of the modern AI systems.

4.2 The NIST AI Risk Management Framework

Unlike the EU AI Act which is prescriptive and legally binding, the NIST AI Risk Management Framework (RMF) is flexible and voluntary and implementation-based. The NIST RMF was created to assist across-the-board organizations and focuses on a risk awareness context, the organization, and the continuous improvement; thus, it can be well applied to complex and fast-changing AI applications. There are four main functions of the NIST RMF:

- Govern, that defines organizational policies, roles, accountability structures and ethical principles of AI risk management.
- Map, entailing comprehension of the context of the AI system, its purpose, stakeholders, and possible effects.
- Measure, which aims at evaluating the risks of AI, such as performance constraints, bias, robustness, and reliability.
- Manage, involving prioritisation and alleviating risks by use of technical, organization control and procedural controls.

As compared to performance-based evaluation models, the NIST RMF identifies risks associated with validity, reliability, safety, explainability, and accountability explicitly, making all of them directly involved in AI hallucinations. The framework motivates businesses to create circumstances in which AI systems can produce wrongful or false outputs and apply mitigation techniques, such as human oversight, communicating uncertainty, and monitoring.

One of the strengths of the NIST RMF is that it focuses on the accountability of the organization and the maturity of governance. It places the risk of AI not only as a technical problem, but as a management concern, which has to be embedded into the enterprise risk management, the compliance procedures, and the organizational culture. Such a view is especially useful when it comes to dealing with hallucinations that tend to arise as a result of incongruent incentives, lack of proper control, or lack of coordination between the technical staff and the operational staff.

4.3 Brokering Regulation and Practice

Although the regulatory frameworks like the EU AI Act and the NIST RMF offer a valuable guideline, their success still remains a question of how effective the principles will be achieved into technical and organizational practices. One of the challenges that are still present in the implementation of responsible AI is that there is a mismatch between high-level regulatory standards and the routine tasks related to AI development.

To close this gap, compliance-by-design and governance-by-design strategies need to be adopted, whereby regulatory and ethical concerns are directly introduced into system designs, development cycles and business procedures. Key mechanisms include:

- Traceability and documentation systems, which allow the formation of clear connections between sources of data, model versions, design choices, and system outputs.
- Organized and verifiable development processes with the ability to track version changes, reuse and test.
- Lifecycle risk analysis, which will make sure that the risk of hallucinations is considered not only in development but also in deployment, scaling, and updating of the system.
- Human control and escalation routes, operationalizing human control over regulations.
- Constant observation and feedback loops, which allow to identify the emerging risks early (e.g. higher hallucination rates because of data drift or change of context).

However, most importantly, stakeholder involvement is also essential to good governance, that is, domain experts, end users, auditors, and communities involved. This interaction can be used to put regulatory requirements into context, to identify failure modes in the real world, and to make sure that mitigation strategies are socially and ethically-oriented.

The responsible AI models can extend the symbolic adherence of the principles of regulation to the operationally suitable by implementing technical safeguards and organizational regulation. Such integration is fundamental to making hallucination-resilient AI so that the systems are truthful, reliable, and ethically aligned across their lifecycle- hence comply with regulation and also gain long-term social trust.

Figure 3. Regulatory Frameworks for Responsible AI.

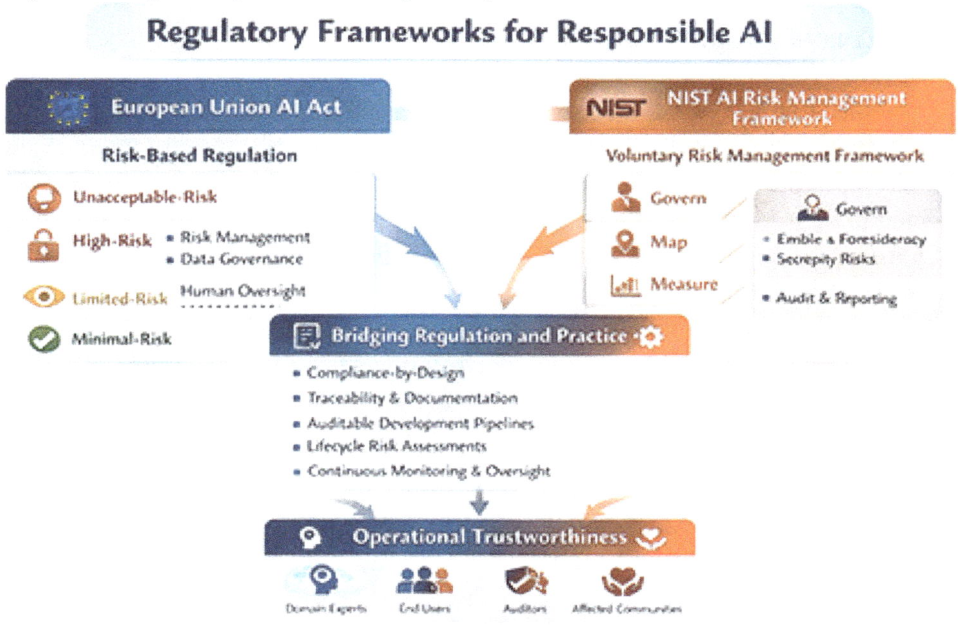

5. BUILDING BLOCKS OF RELIABLE ARTIFICIAL INTELLIGENCE

5.1 Legality and Compliance with Regulations

The layer of lawfulness is the basis of reliable AI as it provides a foundation of system design and implementation in legally, regulation, and contractually binding frameworks. In an AI globalized ecosystem, compliance should also be cross-jurisdictional, and it should cover both sector-specific compliance (e.g., healthcare, finance, public administration) and inter-country regimes of data protection. In the framework of the EU AI Act and other similar international regulations, lawfulness must be classified systematically on risk, assessed on conformity, and maintained constantly in the post-deployment phase. (Palaniappan et al., 2024) The regulatory compliance should also be process-centrically implemented throughout the AI life-cycle with compliance-by-design in place, automated documentation and tracking of the design choices. This kind of integration would turn compliance into a post-hoc checklist into a proactive governance potential that would improve legitimacy, minimise liability as well as increase trust in AI-driven systems within the society.

5.2.2 Ethical Integrity and Value Alignment

The basic human values (autonomy, dignity, fairness, and beneficence) must always be reflected and respected by the AI systems, which would make them morally upright. Ethical alignment in AI resilient to hallucinations cannot be restricted to high-level principles rather it must be enforced at the model objectives, training regimes and restrictions on inference. This involves explicit encoding of normative limits, value-sensitive design methods, as well as alignment strategies, which punish deceptive, misleading or unprovable results. Ethical integrity also demands that all stakeholders are involved in order to get a wide range of moral inclusion and contextual expectations. The alignment of the system behaviour with the norms and ethical expectations of society allows the reduction of the threat of harmful hallucinations by the AI systems, as well as the promotion of responsible decision-making in the high-stakes areas.

5.3 Robustness, Safety and Reliability

Other important technical pillars are robustness and safety, which make sure that AI systems can be reliable in their performance in the presence of uncertainty, adversarial manipulation, and distributional shift. Within the framework of generative and decision-support systems, robustness has a direct relationship with the propensity to hallucination, with weak models more apt to give results of confidence but incorrect. The safety engineering practice, including stress testing, adversarial evaluation, redundancy mechanism, and fail-safe design, is critical to alleviate the cascading failures. Not only the metrics of average-case performance are required to measure its reliability, but the worst-case and edge-case analysis are also required. (Song et al., 2026), the strength and safety-focused AI system contribute to resiliency to misinformation, reliable human-AI partnerships, and long-term reliability.

5.4 Human Oversight and Control

Human control is one of the primary controls of responsible AI governance, which makes automated systems responsible to human opinion and social values. Human-in-the-loop and human-on-the-loop and human-in-command allow varying levels of human intervention in response to the risk to the system and the operational environment. (Gunasekara et al., 2025) The oversight mechanisms are essential especially in the validation of outputs, uncertainty management, and making ambiguous or high impact decisions when using hallucination resilient AI. Good monitoring needs not just procedural control but user interfaces, which specify system confidence, constraints and reasons. Oversight mechanisms ensure that there is no over-reliance on the outputs of AI by ensuring that meaningful human agency is maintained throughout the AI lifecycle.

5.5 Privacy and Data Governance

Information privacy and data control are the key enablers of trustful AI, especially because the contemporary learning environment is data-intensive. The responsible AI implies compliance with data minimization principles, the limitation of purpose, informed consent, and the safe data handling practice. (Pahune et al., 2025) The presence of strong governance structures should focus on the data provenance, data quality, representativeness, and lifecycle control to avoid privacy attacks and harm downstream. Well-managed and high-quality data in hallucination-conscious systems minimizes the chance of spurious association and artificial results. Open data management does not only help in ensuring regulatory compliance, it also enhances trust to the ethical management of personal and sensitive data by the citizens.

5.6 Fairness and Non-Discrimination

Equality and non-discrimination are essential to ensure that AI systems do not increase past prejudices or give unfair results in demographic groups. To ensure the trustworthiness of AI design, they must have fairness-conscious learning algorithms, balanced and representative datasets, and constant bias auditing during deployment. Hallucinations may increase stereotypes or create damaging associations especially in generative settings, so it is especially valuable to protect fairness. (Ferrara, E. 2024) The discussion of fairness is more of a process than a one-time intervention, which needs to be evaluated, stakeholder responses, and applied mitigation measures repeatedly. Social legitimacy may be improved with the ensuring of equitable behavior of the system and the adaptation of AI implementation to the principles of wider human rights.

5.7 Societal and Environmental Well Being

Reliable AI does not just concern the technical accuracy of programming, but also relates to other issues in society and the environment at large. The AI systems must work in the best interest of social wellbeing, democracy, and sustainable development objectives and reduce the possibility of adverse externalities as much as possible. The environmental aspects such as energy efficiency, carbon footprint, and use of resources are becoming more pertinent as the large-scale models are becoming more complex and large-scale in their deployment. (Hammerschmidt et al., 2025) In terms of governance, the inclusion of the societal and environmental impact evaluation in the creation of AI facilitates responsible innovation and sustainability in the long run. According to this pillar, responsible AI should not only comply with individual interests but also with collective and intergenerational well-being.

5.8 What is required is the ability to be transparent and explainable

To allow understanding, scrutiny and accountability in AI systems, transparency and explainability are needed. (Harrath et al., 2025) Transparent processes can reveal the training, assessment, and management of models and explainable AI methods clarify the way certain outputs or choices are produced. With the AI that is hallucination-resistant, explainability aids in detecting faulty reasoning, claims that are not supported by evidence and miscalibration of confidence. The valued transparency has to be designed in relation to various stakeholders such as developers, regulators, users and affected communities. Transparency and explainability are second important facilitators of good AI adoption as they enable informed supervision and calibration of trust.

5.9 The fifth requirement is accountability and auditability

Responsibility in the behavior of the AI systems can be given and enforced throughout the lifecycle through accountability and auditability. This is necessitated by clear governance structures, role identification and documentation practices that facilitate external and internal audits. High-risk and publicly facing AI applications have a high level of vulnerability to independent auditing, impact assessments, and compliance reporting. (Okolo, C. T. 2025) Auditability provides an opportunity to investigate failures systematically, to verify mitigation plans and to make an improvement in the context of hallucination-resilient systems. In a firm with solid accountability measures, accountability becomes more of a process, rather than a product, and strengthens the ethical orientation, compliance with regulations, and trust in the society.

Figure 4. Pillars of Trustworthy AI Systems.

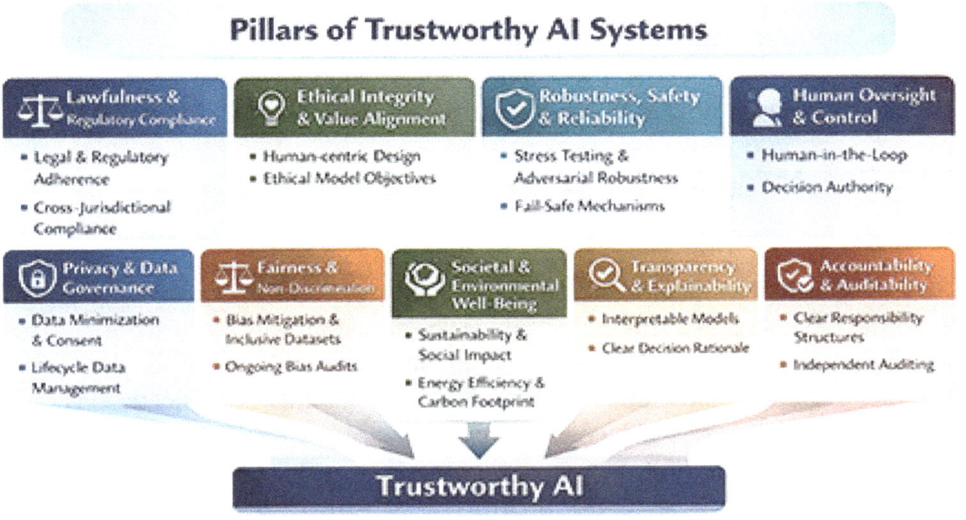

6. HALLUCINATION-RESILIENT AI SYSTEMS DESIGN

(Ji et al., 2026) To create AI systems that are robust to hallucinations, it is necessary to have a multi-layered approach of technical controls, system-level safeguards, and human-organizational actions across the AI lifecycle. Unlike post hoc mitigation, hallucination resilience should be made by design and model performance should be grounded in facts, enforced by moral and ethical limitations, and governmental oversight.

6.1 Hallucinogenic Mitigation Technical Strategies

There have also been a number of complementary methods developed at the model and algorithmic level as essential facilitators of hallucination-resilient AI:

6.1.1 Retrieval-Augmented Generation (RAG) and Knowledge Grounding

RAG architectures limit the generation to verifiable sources by linking generative models with curated external knowledge bases, document stores or real time retrieval systems. Such a grounding reduces the utilization of parametric memory and permits following the linkage among the results and the authoritative referents, which is particularly compulsory in the controlled spheres such as healthcare and finance.

6.1.2 Quantifying Uncertainties and Confident Results

Even in high epistemic uncertainty, traditional deep learning systems are likely to make deterministic predictions. With the addition of either Bayesian techniques, ensemble modeling, or calibrated estimates of probability, systems are able to indicate uncertainty. Reliability-aware generation will be able to induce abstention, hedging, or escalation to human inspection when reliability classifications are not achieved and stop overconfident hallucinations.

6.1.3 Rule-Guided Generation and Constraint-Based Generation

A combination of formal constraints and logical validation in the systematic generative workflow minimizes invalid and inconsistent results. Such constraints may be either hard (e.g., rule enforcement) or soft (e.g., penalty-based optimization), which makes sure that the content generated is within the limits of facts, legal and ethical standards as defined by the experts in the field and regulations.

6.1.4 Human and Ethical Feedback Reinforcement Learning

Human feedback reinforcement (reinforcement learning) (HFR) or human feedback reinforcement (HFR) is an approach to reinforcement learning that allows models to absorb concepts of truthfulness, harm avoidance, and situational appropriateness. In comparison with the documents of ethical rules and governing policy, this method can provide behavioral optimization after going through the training data.

Taken together, these strategies alter optimization goals to be based on surface-level fluency to that of grounded correctness, interpretability and value alignment.

6.2 System Level Protection and Architectural Control

Besides the resilience models of individual models, the architecture level of hallucination resilience must be enhanced. The systems with strong AI are designed with the tiers of defenses, which intercept, control and limit the faulty outcomes before leading to the harm:

6.2.1 Data Checking and Data Authentication Layers

They can be verified by comparing their outputs with known sources of information i.e. fact-checkers, consistency validators or rule-based filters, or by verifying them against a set of known constraints. These subdivisions are gatekeepers whereby unverified content is not forwarded to the final users.

6.2.2 Infinite Surveillance and Slaughtering

The deployed systems are in dynamic environments, where the distributions of data and user behavior as well as contextual assumptions change. Measuring the rates of hallucinations, uncertainty signals, and performance drift with the help of tracking dashboards can help to recognize when the degradation occurs in time and address the situation in a timely manner.

6.2.3 Fallback and Escalation Mechanisms

In the event of exceeding of the confidence limits or failure of validation checks systems are also expected to fail gracefully by providing partial responses, demand clarification of decisions or escalate them to human operators. These backup systems constitute an essential component of maintaining secure and confidently running high stakes applications.

Such regulatory ideals as robustness, human supervision, and post-market control are implemented in these architectural safeguards and are emphasized by frameworks like the EU AI Act and the NIST AI RMF.

6.3 Human and Organizational Measures

The technical safeguards can only be effective to a certain level in the absence of human and organizational practices. The hallucination in the end is going to be resilient on the basis of informed AI system and explicit governance systems:

6.3.1 Training and Awareness

The developers, operators, and end users ought to be trained on the limitations, uncertainty nature and application of the AI systems. The risk of automation bias where the users trust AI outcomes too much irrespective of warning signals can be reduced through the use of consciousness campaigns.

6.3.2 Artifacts in Documentation and Transparency

The informed deployment and accountability is aided by the assistance of transparent documentation such as model cards, data sheets and system usage guidelines. These artifacts also offer vital background to decipher outputs and are in line with the demands of transparency and auditability.

6.3.3 Specific Roles, Responsibilities, and Escalation chains

When hallucinations occur, organizational governance ought to state the parties in charge of following up, intervention, and redress. These responsibilities should be embedded in the standard operating procedures so that it does not just begin at the model but spans the socio-technical system.

Hallucination-resilient AI systems bring us a step closer to the objective of telling the truth, being reliable, and aligning with ethical standards of intelligence by combining the rigor of technical systems with the control of their human-level and system-level systems, respectively. The focus on the process approach generates trust as a property that is not fixed but maintained throughout the lifecycle of AI.

Figure 5. Designing Hallucination-Resilient AI Systems.

7. AUDIT PROCESSES AND AI LIFECYCLE GOVERNANCE

Responsible AI governance should be perceived as a lifecycle and ongoing discipline and not a compliance event. (Adewale et al., 2024) The development of AI systems proceeds in a series of steps, including problem definition, data collection, model building, implementation, usage and eventual decommissioning of the system which presents unique ethical, legal and technical risks. Reliable and resilient to hallucination AI thus needs the mechanisms of the governance that are incorporated throughout this lifecycle and able to adjust to dynamic conditions, system actions, and regulatory demands.

On the design and problem formulation phase, governance starts with expression of purpose, scope of use and acceptable risk levels. This involves evaluating the suitability of solving the problem with AI, the potential situation of harm, and balancing the system purposes and moral standards and the legal restrictions. Early impact assessment Early impact assessment, like Algorithmic Impact Assessment (AIAs) or Data Protection Impact Assessment (DPIAs), offers systematic methods of predicting downstream hazard, like the propagation of hallucinated or misleading results in sensitive areas.

Lifecycle governance focuses on data provenance, quality assurance, bias, and documentation in the process of the data acquisition and model development. Data used in training should be representative, up to date and legally acquired and there should be clear records of the preprocessing processes and constraints. Traceability and transparency Model cards, datasheet of datasets and system documentation help the auditor and regulators to assess whether the risks of hallucinations have been sufficiently addressed and reduced at the technical level.

New challenges are presented by the stages of deployment and the stages of operations where the AI systems presuppose contact with the real world users and dynamic environment. Continuous mechanisms of monitoring, which are essential, are required to determine the performance deterioration, distribution changes, biases developed and hallucination patterns with time. The pipelines that could be addressed to support the post-deployment accountability are the logging, version control and incident reporting that would assist in taking corrective action shortly. Human control mechanisms and awareness of the escalation procedures are in place in high-risk applications such that dubious or potentially dubious results do not lead to uncontrolled damage.

AI audits are the key tool of lifecycle governance that offers impartial and methodical assessment of the conformity, soundness, and ethical appropriateness. Good AI audits are more organized than technical testing as it involves organizational procedures, decision making roles, and governance. They define how the documented policies can be put to the ground and accountability of development and deployment teams is available. It is worth noting that audits need to be reiterative and ought to add to the ongoing enhancement compared to the post-hoc fault-finding.

Lastly, the lifecycle governance is responsible with the system retirement and decommissioning. Given that models are outdated or not kept up to date with the evolving norms and regulations, the systematic decommissioning process can prevent the reoccurrence of old assumptions, data biases, or risks of hallucination in the old systems. Lifecycle closure thus assists in the achievement of process-oriented assurance model that is the foundation of trustful and responsible AI.

Figure 6. Artificial Intelligence Life Cycle Management and Auditing.

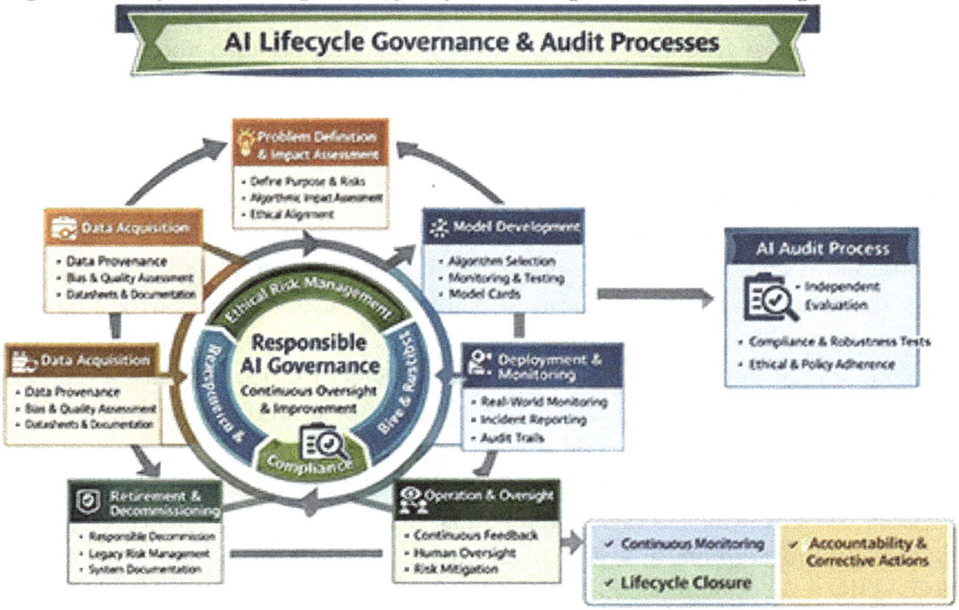

8. ENGAGEMENT OF STAKEHOLDERS AND SOCIO-TECHNICAL ALIGNMENT

Reliable AI systems are not the byproduct of the technical excellence; they are the consequences of the success of the alignment of the technological resources, organizational activities and the social values. (Hohma, E., & Lütge, 2023) Engaging stakeholders is thus a key ingredient of responsible AI, which establishes that a variety of opinions guide the design, implementation, and regulation of the system. The end users, domain experts, regulators, policymakers, and communities are also stakeholders and may be indirectly affected by AI-inspired decisions by developers and deployers.

The early and continued interaction makes participatory design strategies that reflect contextual knowledge, domain constraints, and value trade-offs, which cannot be observed based on technical measures. Having clinicians involved in the field of AI, as exemplified by, could be utilized to know in which cases the output of hallucinations can limit clinical judgment, and communicating with financial regulators would help establish the level of automation within the algorithmic trading systems that will be acceptable and what information needs to be communicated to shareholders.

Mechanisms of feedback, redress and contestability are also needed in socio-technical alignment. The users and the affected population should have a way of doubting, questioning, or seeking clarification of the AI-driven findings, particularly when the outcomes of the findings have grave ramifications. Feedback loops do not just enhance transparency and accountability but also can be used to provide helpful indications of system improvement and recalibration.

Stress tests and community involvement also contribute to compliance with the social demands and standards. These tools are used to assess more general implications, e.g., impacts on equity, citizen trust and environmental sustainability. Through incorporation of the stakeholder views in governance practices, organizations can outgrow compliance-based practices into legitimacy-based trustworthiness which is subject to the collective societal values.

Stakeholder engagement, ultimately, supports the perception of AI as a socio-technical system, which is one where human judgment, institutional context, and technological design are in a state of inseparability. This worldview is crucial in curbing the risks of hallucinations that occur not only due to the constraints on the model, but also due to the discrepancies between the work of the system and the expectations of a human being.

9. DIFFICULTIES, DISPARITIES AND FUTURE PROJECTIONS

Although there is emerging agreement on the principles of trustworthy and responsible AI, there exist considerable issues in terms of translating the principles into more consistent, scalable, and operational activities. (Ferdaus et al., 2026) The first significant gap is not having standardized methodologies to assess ethical properties like fairness, transparency, and hallucination resilience in the various areas of application. Existing metrics are frequently context-specific and not sufficiently validated, and cannot be useful in comparative evaluation and regulation implementation.

The other issue that has remained a constant is the empirical affirmation of the ethical and governance assertions. Though responsible AI models can be applied and ethical principles published by organizations, the research on whether the models are useful in real-life to reduce the harmful impact or boost the trust is lacking. In order to fill this gap, longitudinal research, common scales and free reporting of failure and near-misses with reported incidences of hallucinations are required.

The fragmented operational guidelines to the practitioners also exist. Many of the standards and regulations that have survived are of high-level requirements that do not give implementation paths and they are left wondering how to bring their systems to life to suit the standards in complex and reality-based systems. This issue is also increased by the gaps in tooling as records, auditing and monitoring interoperable platforms are still being developed.

In the future, research and practice should be conducted on how to design methods that can be scaled to detect hallucinations and estimate uncertainty and interoperable governance systems that can be easily integrated into AI development pipelines. It will have to engage in more global coordination and regulatory convergence to address the global nature of AI adoption and prevent the dangers of regulatory fragmentation in order to eliminate responsible innovation.

A long-term collaboration between the technical, organizational, and policy fields would be a way to move on towards honest and accountable AI systems. Process based assurance, lifecycle management and social technical fit can help stakeholders take a step closer to having hallucination resistant AI that is trusted by people and creates societal value in a responsible and sustainable manner.

10. CONCLUSIONS

The chapter has helped formulate an integrative vision of the development of the hallucination resistant and responsible artificial intelligence system on the principle that the trustworthiness is not an attribute of algorithms, but the attribute of the well-designed socio-technical ecosystems. In the areas where the stakes are low, such as specific areas of the healthcare and financial sector, government, and even the ability to communicate with the public, the cost of misinformation, unproven outcomes, and comparatively unaccountable actions is more than systematic and may be impossible to rectify, as AI systems become increasingly active as decision-making agents as well as intermediaries of information. In this regard, AI hallucinations, in addition to being a technical failure, are an acute danger to the ethical validity, legal compliance, and trust in the government. Integrating the results of the regulatory frameworks such as the European Union AI Act and the NIST AI Risk Management Framework with the recent results on the robustness, ethical considerations, and governance, this chapter has made the case of a paradigm shift, whereby the product-based evaluations need a process-based assurance paradigm. The continued integration of legality, moral uprightness, resilience, human management, information and data control, equity, social and environmental health, openness and responsibility across all AI lifecycle stages prove to be essential to achieving reliable AI. The resilience of hallucinations in such a paradigm is not achieved due to personal improvements of model quality but through a combination of technical controls, governance systems, auditing systems and human judgments. The re-definition of responsible AI as a shared organizational and institutional responsibility where the developers, deployers, regulators and the affected are all the contributors is one of the significant contributions of this work. Lifecycle management, continuous auditing and proactive communication with stakeholders are essential to align the AI behavior with human values and the standards of the society and be able to adjust to the evolving risks, setting, and regulations. This reframing emphasizes the fact that the belief in AI systems must be actively maintained by constant supervision, reflexivity, and accountability and not assumed with regard to a set of predetermined standards or a certification that has been constantly carried out once. To get veridical and accountable AI systems in the future, it will require the closing of endemic inefficiencies in standardization, empirical validation of ethical claims and effective operational policies to practitioners. The secret to the additional progress is scalable approaches to detecting hallucinations and estimating uncertainty, interoperable approaches to governance and auditing, and additional global alignment of AI regulations. Lastly, AI systems that do not create hallucinations and ethically constrained systems should not be considered a constraint on innovation, but instead as a force that will make it possible to continue innovation in the long-term. The stakeholders will be enabled to realize the transformative potential of AI without impacting negatively on human dignity, social trust and general well being through the mechanism of trustworthiness that is process centric and assurance that is lifecycle centric.

REFERENCES

Adewale, B. A., Ene, V. O., Ogunbayo, B. F., & Aigbavboa, C. O. (2024). A systematic review of the applications of AI in a sustainable building's lifecycle. *Buildings (Basel, Switzerland)*, *14*(7), 2137. DOI: 10.3390/buildings14072137

Brandão, P. R. (2025). The impact of artificial intelligence on modern society. *AI*, *6*(8), 190. DOI: 10.3390/ai6080190

Di Salvatore, S., Drissi Yahyaoui, O., De Marchi, M., & Rauch, E. (2025). The integration of ethical and trustworthy AI in industrial engineering: Practical approaches. *Engineering Proceedings*, *97*(1), 42. DOI: 10.3390/engproc2025097042

Ferdaus, M. M., Abdelguerfi, M., Loup, E., Niles, K. N., Pathak, K., & Sloan, S. (2026). Towards trustworthy AI: A review of ethical and robust large language models. *ACM Computing Surveys*, *58*(7), 176. Advance online publication. DOI: 10.1145/3777382

Ferrara, E. (2024). Fairness and bias in artificial intelligence: A brief survey of sources, impacts, and mitigation strategies. *Sci*, *6*(1), 3. DOI: 10.3390/sci6010003

Gunasekara, L., El-Haber, N., Nagpal, S., Moraliyage, H., Issadeen, Z., Manic, M., & De Silva, D. (2025). A systematic review of responsible artificial intelligence principles and practice. *Applied System Innovation*, *8*(4), 97. DOI: 10.3390/asi8040097

Hammerschmidt, T., Stolz, K., & Posegga, O. (2025). Bridging the gap: Inequalities that divide those who can and cannot create sustainable outcomes with AI. *Behaviour & Information Technology*, •••, 1–30. DOI: 10.1080/0144929X.2025.2500451

Harrath, Y., Adohinzin, O., Kaabi, J., & Saathoff, M. (2025). Bridging domains: Advances in explainable, automated, and privacy-preserving AI for computer science and cybersecurity. *Computers*, *14*(9), 374. DOI: 10.3390/computers14090374

Hohma, E., & Lütge, C. (2023). From trustworthy principles to a trustworthy development process: The need and elements of trusted development of AI systems. *AI*, *4*(4), 904–925. DOI: 10.3390/ai4040046

Ji, J., Qiu, T., Chen, B., Zhou, J., Zhang, B., Hong, D., & Gao, W. (2026). AI alignment: A contemporary survey. *ACM Computing Surveys*, *58*(5), 132. Advance online publication. DOI: 10.1145/3770749

Kazlaris, I., Antoniou, E., Diamantaras, K., & Bratsas, C. (2025). From illusion to insight: A taxonomic survey of hallucination mitigation techniques in LLMs. *AI*, *6*(10), 260. DOI: 10.3390/ai6100260

Lukyanenko, R., Maass, W., & Storey, V. C. (2022). Trust in artificial intelligence: From a foundational trust framework to emerging research opportunities. *Electronic Markets*, *32*, 1993–2020. DOI: 10.1007/s12525-022-00605-4

Nastoska, A., Jancheska, B., Rizinski, M., & Trajanov, D. (2025). Evaluating trustworthiness in AI: Risks, metrics, and applications across industries. *Electronics (Basel)*, *14*(13), 2717. DOI: 10.3390/electronics14132717

Okolo, C. T. (2025). Governance of AI-based algorithms. In Xu, W. (Ed.), *Handbook of human-centered artificial intelligence*. Springer., DOI: 10.1007/978-981-97-8440-0_84-1

Pahune, S., Akhtar, Z., Mandapati, V., & Siddique, K. (2025). The importance of AI data governance in large language models. *Big Data and Cognitive Computing*, *9*(6), 147. DOI: 10.3390/bdcc9060147

Palaniappan, K., Lin, E. Y. T., & Vogel, S. (2024). Global regulatory frameworks for the use of artificial intelligence (AI) in the healthcare services sector. *Health Care*, *12*(5), 562. DOI: 10.3390/healthcare12050562

Song, P., Ojo, A., & Curry, E. (2026). Trustworthy requirements for foundation models—A comprehensive survey and roadmap. *Engineering Applications of Artificial Intelligence*, *163*(Part 6), 113111. DOI: 10.1016/j.engappai.2025.113111

Walter, Y. (2024). Managing the race to the moon: Global policy and governance in artificial intelligence regulation—A contemporary overview and an analysis of socioeconomic consequences. *Discover Artificial Intelligence*, *4*, 14. Advance online publication. DOI: 10.1007/s44163-024-00109-4

Williamson, S. M., & Prybutok, V. (2024). The era of artificial intelligence deception: Unraveling the complexities of false realities and emerging threats of misinformation. *Information (Basel)*, *15*(6), 299. DOI: 10.3390/info15060299

Yampolskiy, R. V. (2025). On monitorability of AI. *AI and Ethics*, *5*, 689–707. DOI: 10.1007/s43681-024-00420-x

Yang, X., Jia, J., Zhou, X., & Wang, S. (2024). The future of artificial intelligence: Time to embrace more international collaboration. *The Innovation*, *5*(6), 100703. DOI: 10.1016/j.xinn.2024.100703

Zhang, R., Li, H.-W., Qian, X.-Y., Jiang, W.-B., & Chen, H.-X. (2025). On large language models safety, security, and privacy: A survey. *Journal of Electronic Science and Technology*, *23*(1), 100301. DOI: 10.1016/j.jnlest.2025.100301

Section 3
Detection, Mitigation, and Model Design

Chapter 6
Human -in-the-Loop Frameworks for AI Mitigation and Accountability

Adarsh Kushwaha
http://orcid.org/0009-0007-7992-5442
P.P. Savani University, India

Nimisha R. Nair
Dayananda Sagar University, India

Kamini Sharma
http://orcid.org/0009-0005-9789-6943
P.P. Savani University, India

Ushoshee Mukherjee
P.P. Savani University, India

Amanpreet Kaur
http://orcid.org/0009-0000-3600-022X
Lovely Professional University, India

Richa Sharma
Lovely Professional University, India

ABSTRACT

The purpose of this chapter is to review current Human-in-the-Loop (HITL) architectures designed to address accountability and reliability challenges in high-stakes Artificial Intelligence (AI) systems. Recent studies and empirical evaluations of HITL architectures in critical domains such as healthcare, education, and industrial safety are examined. The architectures reviewed include neurosymbolic verification workflows, automated auditing systems, human–agent interface designs, and blockchain-based systems. These approaches integrate human judgement with automated processes to detect errors, validate AI decisions, and ensure transparency and auditability. The chapter evaluates trade-offs between automation efficiency and human oversight, identifying key challenges including cognitive load, scalability, legal ambiguity, and failure mode complexity. Emerging best practices and future

DOI: 10.4018/979-8-3373-7320-1.ch006

© 2026, IGI Global Scientific Publishing. Copying or distributing in print or electronic forms without written permission of IGI Global Scientific Publishing is prohibited. Use of this chapter to generative artificial intelligence (AI) technologies is expressly prohibited. The publisher reserves all rights to license its use for generative AI training and machine learning model development.

research directions, such as neurosymbolic discovery loops, decentralised governance, and reciprocal human–machine learning systems, are discussed to enhance AI reliability and meaningful human control.

1. INTRODUCTION

1.1 The Imperative for Human Oversight in AI Systems

The increasing use of LLMs in a variety of application areas is showing there are many challenges to be overcome with regard to reliability and accountability. In addition, hallucinations — plausible but inaccurate responses — create risk in high stakes applications such as health care, legal analysis, and industrial process management (Monti et al., 2025; Amirizaniani et al., 2024). Furthermore, these inaccuracies erode public confidence in the accuracy of AI systems and may result in substantial harm if an AI system does not provide for some form of oversight or control (Rahwan, 2017). To address this issue, a number of researchers have proposed HITL architectures which leverage the power of human judgment through strategic integration of the two into AI work flows (Amirizaniani et al., 2024; Chiodo et al., 2025). These researchers acknowledge that the ability to verify, reason in context, and make ethical judgments are uniquely human abilities that enhance automation capabilities (Te'eni et al., 2025).

1.2 Defining Human-in-the-Loop Frameworks

HITL frameworks contain a variety of architectural design patterns for the role of humans in all stages of the use and maintenance of an AI system (validation, governance, etc.), including but not limited to the training stage, the inference time validation stage, in the event of an error (exception) or when making decisions about what policies should be applied to the AI system and how those policies will be escalated (Sachan et al., 2025; Gangavarapu, 2025). HITL systems have a two-way influence between humans and AI systems: humans make decisions that affect the actions of the AI systems by providing feedback and making decisions about the structure of the AI system's policies and/or escalation procedures. Conversely, AI systems enable humans to perform tasks they could otherwise not do by performing tasks automatically and providing them with recommendations on how to act. Because both sides are able to provide input to one another, there can be a continuous cycle of improvement using iterative refinements instead of relying upon static controls (Westover, n.d.; Te'eni et al., 2025).

1.3 The Accountability Challenge

Technical performance of AI is but one part of a much larger picture of what is meant by "accountability" in this field, which also includes organizational and legal responsibility and the ethics of the organization itself. Because organizations will be responsible for the actions of autonomous AI, there needs to be a framework developed that explicitly maps out how technology can be configured to provide a corresponding structure for who is accountable (Gangavarapu, 2025). Through their design of HITL frameworks, researchers have identified many paths toward enhanced accountability including explicit places of intervention, documented decision trails and oversight mechanisms that capture all of the automated and human contributions to a system's output (Krishnamoorthy, 2024; Sachan et al., 2025). However, a HITL system that has been poorly designed can create accountability gaps, as well as provide an opportunity for "responsibility laundering," where human operators are blamed for failures, they did not have meaningful control over to prevent (Chiodo et al., 2025; Rahwan, 2017).

1.4 Chapter Scope and Objectives

In this chapter, a review of current HITL frameworks is performed to identify how they are currently addressing hallucination mitigation as well as developing a framework for establishing accountability in HITL systems. These frameworks will be based on research papers and system implementations that have been developed from 2024 to 2026. Four objectives are being pursued during the analysis:

a) Architectural Synthesis: Develop an understanding of current HITL architecture designs and describe common architectural design patterns used to facilitate effective human-AI collaboration within HITL systems.
b) Hallucination Mitigation Techniques: Provide a detailed examination of the various methods used to detect, prevent, and correct hallucinations using structured oversight, verification workflow, and feedback loop methodologies (Amirizaniani et al., 2024).
c) HITL Accountability Frameworks: Provide a thorough examination of accountability frameworks that include governance structures, audit mechanisms, and responsibility models. Establishing accountability with operational efficiency is the primary goal of these frameworks (Chiodo et al., 2025; Gangavarapu, 2025).
d) Preliminary Implementation Guidance: Identify the practical experience gained from empirical deployments of HITL systems. Identify the challenges encoun-

tered, best practices, and evaluation metrics to be used when evaluating HITL deployments (Sachan et al., 2025; Selvam et al., 2025).

1.5 Chapter Organization

Section 2 outlines the theoretical underpinnings that have developed HITL concepts over time. Section 3 evaluates current HITL architectures such as (1) Neurosymbolic frameworks, (2) Automated Auditing, (3) Agentic Interfaces, and (4) Governance Integrations. Section 4 investigates hallucinations detection/identification/mitigation in HITL systems. Section 5 examines the structure for holding HTIL systems accountable (Accountability Frameworks & Governance Structures). Section 6 evaluates human-AI collaboration models within HITL. Section 7 describes the metrics used to evaluate HITL deployments empirically. Section 8 identifies some of the implementation issues and best practices. Section 9 assesses domain-specific HITL case studies. Section 10 identifies some of the potential areas for further research. Section 11 synthesizes the entire body of knowledge.

2. BACKGROUND AND THEORETICAL FOUNDATIONS

2.1 Evolution of Human-AI Interaction Paradigms

The development of human roles within artificial intelligence has been accomplished through various paradigms. In early years of the Expert Systems Paradigm, humans were identified as Knowledge Engineers who encoded rules for an AI System and had very little human interaction with the system during its run time. In later years, Machine Learning Systems changed the role of humans to be Data Labellers and Model Trainers of an AI System and, therefore, removed humans from many operational decision making processes. It was not until the HITL Paradigm developed as a result of recognizing that neither fully Automated nor entirely Human approaches could effectively deal with the complexity, uncertainty and the significant societal impacts associated with current AI Systems (Duke, 2023; Rahwan, 2017), that the HITL Paradigm became viable. Rahwan's (2017) concept of Society-in-the-Loop suggested that Algorithmic Systems which are shaping social outcomes need continual input from society, not just a single technical design process. In recent years, there is research that identifies multiple forms of involvement based on the depth and level of authority of the interaction of humans with an AI System. Chiodo et al. (2025) formally define ght, each with different implications for Reliability, Efficiency and Responsibility Attribution.

2.2 Theoretical Foundations of Human-AI Collaboration

The foundational theories upon which effective HITL frameworks are based include the principle of complementary capabilities — recognizing that AI has an advantage over humans in areas such as: (1) pattern recognition; (2) rapid computation; and (3) consistency. In contrast, humans have a comparative advantage in: (1) contextual reasoning; (2) ethical decision-making; (3) creative problem solving; and (4) the ability to deal with novel situations. (Calvert, 2025; Te'eni et al., 2025).

Reciprocal learning is a further important theoretical basis for HITL — it goes beyond the traditional model of one way transfer of information — with the added benefit of a reciprocal process where the operator learns and adapts and so does the AI system. Te'eni et al. (2025) differentiate between two forms of reciprocal learning — stable reciprocal learning, and adaptive reciprocal learning — but emphasize the need to preserve the expertise of the human operator, and avoid creating deskilling due to the use of automation.Trust calibration is also a key theory for HITL. As stated by Westover (n.d.), the collaborative process can only be successful when there is calibrated trust, i.e. a balance between blind acceptance and excessive skepticism regarding the reliability of the AI system. Dynamic authority reversal mechanisms proposed by Westover (n.d.) allow for an adjustment in control between human and AI systems — depending on the level of criticality of the tasks involved; the degree of uncertainty associated with the tasks; and the history of performance by each.

2.3 The Hallucination Problem in Generative AI

Hallucinations are a product of general properties of neural language models rather than an idiosyncratic characteristic of individual implementations. Neural language models do not inherently consider factual accuracy or logical validity when generating output based on statistical probabilities to generate token sequences as output (Monti et al., 2025; Amirizaniani et al., 2024). There are several contributing factors to hallucinations including limitations of the training data used, statistical biases inherent in the distribution of that training data, the ambiguity associated with the prompts, and the lack of calibration of confidence estimates produced by the model. While traditional approaches to mitigate hallucinations such as improving training data and/or training methodology, using retrieval-augmented generation and ensembling models remain insufficient for high-stakes applications requiring domain-specific expertise and contextual validation. The aforementioned limitations provide motivation for developing HITL systems that utilize human experts to validate information that is outside the capabilities of current artificial intelligence systems (Amirizaniani et al., 2024; Chiodo et al., 2025).

2.4 Accountability Theory and AI Governance

Accountability of Sociotechnical Systems is composed of four areas: Causal Accountability (Who/what led to a specific result), Role Accountability (Who was responsible for overseeing the process), Liability (Who is legally or financially liable) and Answerability (Who must provide justification/explanation for a decision made). Typically all of these aspects of accountability fall upon the same person in traditional human operated systems. That is, the individual responsible for causing a result through action is also responsible for the oversight and therefore the liability and will be required to explain their decision. The introduction of AI systems into traditional human-operated systems has disrupted this alignment of accountability as AI distributes the cause of a result among many entities including model developers, data providers, organizations which deploy the AI, and human operators. Furthermore, with the automation of decisions previously made by humans, there is now a distribution of accountability for decisions that may have been made by AI but are still attributed to humans. As such, the distribution of causality creates possible accountability voids in which no one can be said to bear responsibility, or accountability sinkholes in which humans are held accountable for results they had no reasonable ability to predict or prevent (Chiodo et al., 2025). Therefore, in order to develop effective accountability frameworks for AI systems, the following challenges must be addressed:Transparency Requirements: Ensure that the decision-making processes for the AI systems are transparent enough so that meaningful oversight and post-hoc review can occur.Traceability Mechanisms: Develop audit trails that include both the automated decisions of the AI system, and the contributions of human operators to the final result.

Responsibility Assignment Protocols: Clearly define how to assign accountability to those who configure and/or utilize the AI system based on configuration and failure mode.

Governance Structures: Establish governing bodies that oversee the operation of the accountability framework, provide a mechanism for reviewing and escalating accountability issues.

Table 1. Accountability Dimensions & Governance Frameworks

Dimension	Definition	Traditional vs. AI Challenge	Key Framework & Solution Approach
Causal Accountability	Who/what caused the outcome?	**Traditional:** Human operator AI **Challenge:** Distributed causality	**Framework:** Chiodo et al. (2025) **Solution:** Immutable audit trails, clear attribution
Role Accountability	Who was responsible for oversight?	**Traditional:** Clear hierarchy **AI** Challenge: Ambiguous responsibility	**Framework:** Gangavarapu (2025) **Solution:** Protocols to prevent accountability gaps/sinks
Liability	Who bears legal/financial consequences??	**Traditional:** Acting organisation AI **Challenge:** Mismatched liability & control	**Framework:** Corea et al. (2022) **Solution:** Governance structures aligning liability with control
Answerability	Who must explain/ justify decisions?	**Traditional:** Human decider AI **Challenge:** AI's "black box" nature	**Framework:** EU AI Act, Ethical Frameworks **Solution:** XAI interfaces, transparency requirements

Table 1 synthesizes the key dimensions of accountability in AI-enabled systems, contrasting traditional governance assumptions with emerging AI-specific challenges and highlighting representative frameworks and solution approaches proposed in recent literature.

2.5 Regulatory and Ethical Context

The human oversight regulatory requirement is growing due to the increased risk associated with the use of AI. The EU AI Act includes mandatory human oversight in high-risk areas (e.g. healthcare, critical infrastructure, public administrations) based on a risk assessment approach (Corea et al., 2022; Calvert, 2025). In addition, all three major ethical frameworks (OECD, IEEE, Partnership on AI) include several ethical principles including: transparency, fairness, accountability, and respect for human autonomy and decision making (Gangavarapu, 2025). Calvert's (2025) framework provides an example of how to apply the above-mentioned ethical principle of "meaningful human control" through the inclusion of four criteria that are also relevant from a technical perspective: tracking, tracing, intervening and accountability. Therefore, this framework offers a way to translate abstract ethical principles into technical design specifications.

Table 2. Evolution of HITL Paradigms & Modes of Involvement

Category	Era / Mode	Core Principle	Human Role & Key Challenge
Paradigm Evolution	Expert Systems (1980s)	Encode expertise into rules	**Role:** Knowledge Engineer **Challenge:** Brittleness with novel cases
	Machine Learning (2000s)	Learn patterns from data	**Role:** Data Labeler/Trainer Challenge: "Black box" with no runtime oversight
	Human-in-the-Loop (Contemporary)	Combine human & AI strengths	**Role:** Overseer/Collaborator Challenge: Design complexity & integration cost
	Society-in-the-Loop (Emerging)	Align algorithms with societal values	**Role:** Collective Stakeholders **Challenge:** Scaling democratic input
Modes of Involvement	Monitoring	Observe without intervention	**Role:** Passive Observer Challenge: Alert fatigue, no prevention
	Single-Decision Intervention	Gatekeep specific outputs	**Role:** Approver/Veto Challenge: Bottleneck, superficial review
	Deep Interactive Oversight	Shape behavior continuously	**Role:** Active Co-pilot **Challenge:** High cognitive load, expertise needed
	Meaningful Human Control	Ensure human agency	System Governor Challenge: Real-time

Table 2 outlines the evolution of Human-in-the-Loop (HITL) paradigms from early expert systems to emerging society-in-the-loop approaches, and maps these paradigms to corresponding modes of human involvement, highlighting shifts in human roles and associated challenges.

3. STATE-OF-THE-ART HITL ARCHITECTURES AND FRAMEWORKS

3.1 Neurosymbolic Verification Frameworks

The neurosymbolic approaches have both neural pattern recognition and the symbolic logic and explainability of traditional AI. Monti et al. (2025) introduce a framework that uses structured human-AI collaboration to transform LLM hallucinations into knowledge discovery opportunities. The architecture is based on a multi-stage verification: Claims made by an LLM are verified against formal domain ontologies. If there is a conflict, it triggers an axiom weakening procedure; if a conflict is identified, the flagged conflict is sent to domain experts; and then all of this occurs as opposed to either purely neural or purely symbolic approaches. The neural portion of the system provides generative flexibility and identifies new concepts at the surface; the symbolic portion provides logical consistency and verifiable verification. The human portion provides validation of expertise to prevent the corruption of the model, provides judgment when cases are ambiguous and provides feedback to the model regarding ontology evolution.

Demonstrations within biomimetic robots and avionic diagnostics show that the framework can resolve contradictions and identify truly novel categories. This framework has particular potential in areas with changing knowledge bases where the symbolic system becomes outdated and a purely neural system lacks a basis (Monti et al., 2025).

Figure 1. Detailed Flowchart for the Neurosymbolic Verification Framework

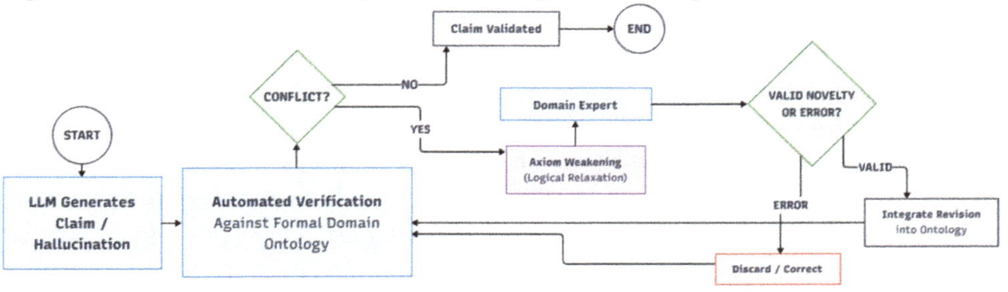

3.2 Automated Auditing with Human Verification

The authors of Amirizaniani et al. (2024), present a scalable auditing structure for testing AI systems through probes generated by automated testing processes and then verified by humans through structured evaluation criteria. The architecture is comprised of two phases; the first phase utilizes an LLM to generate a variety of test probes (test cases) to expose hallucination failures within a target LLM, and the second phase employs human evaluators who utilize standardized evaluation criteria to determine if the output from the target LLM contains hallucinations. As such, the circular reasoning issue, where a first LLM can use another LLM to verify its performance, is avoided through the utilization of cross-model probing and human verification as final validation. Additionally, the architecture does not rely on self consistency illusions which occur when multiple models are used to validate each other's performance. The key elements of this auditing structure include the use of standardized evaluation criteria to reduce the likelihood of inter-rater variability, structured prompts to guide the systematic evaluation of the LLMs performance and the inclusion of diverse probes to ensure that all possible failure modes are tested. The auditing structure also exhibits scalability due to the ability to automatically generate large numbers of probes, thus allowing human evaluators to focus their efforts on areas where their expertise will provide the greatest value. Experimental results have shown that the hybrid approach successfully detects hallucinations missed by purely automated approaches, while achieving sufficient efficiency (Amirizaniani et al., 2024).

3.3 Agentic HITL Interfaces

Beginning with the fact that Agentic AI Systems are capable of acting as Autonomous Agents performing multiple step workflows; this presents both New Challenges for Oversight and New Opportunities for Oversight. Mozannar et al. (2025), developed Magentic-UI, an Interface Framework to enable Low Cost, Effective Human Involvement in Agentic Workflows by using several types of Interaction Mechanisms.

Co-Planning Interfaces Allow Humans and Agents to Collaborate on Defining Task Plans Prior to Execution, which Enables Oversight of High-Level Strategy While Delegating Implementation. Co-Tasking Mechanisms Support Dynamic Task Allocation Where Humans and Agents Collaboratively Determine Optimal Task Assignment. Action Guards Implement Runtime Checks That Require Explicit Approval Before Executing High-Impact Actions and Pauses Execution. Long-Term Memory Systems Maintain Context Across Extended Interactions, Which Enables Agents to Learn From Feedback and Adapt Their Behaviour.

Magentic-UI Addresses a Key Tension: Maximizing Automation Benefits While Maintaining Meaningful Control. The Architecture Provides Intervention Points at Different Levels of Granularity From Approving High Level Plan to Vetting Individual Actions to Enable Humans to Calibrate How Much They Want to be Involved Based on Task Stakes, Agent Reliability and Available Cognitive Resources. Empirical Evaluations Showed Improved Task Completion and User Satisfaction Compared to Fully Autonomous Agents, While Also Showing Gains in Efficiency (Mozannar et al., 2025).

3.4 Blockchain-Based Governance Layers

Krishnamoorthy (2024) and Sachan et al. (2025) have proposed a governance architecture which integrates smart contract technology based on blockchain to provide an unalterable audit log and enforcement of oversight protocol. The proposed architectures will provide accountability through the use of tamper-proof records of AI decisions, human intervention, and governance activities that will enable post-hoc auditing and the attribution of responsibility. Some of the key features of these architectures are: Triggerable Smart Contracts that define when a condition requires a human to review it and can automatically route high-risk outputs to evaluators; Immutable Decision Logs that record all outputs, interventions, confidence scores, and metadata from decisions made by the AI system on decentralized ledgers; Decentralized Governance Mechanisms that allow for multiple stakeholders to participate in the governance process using token-based incentive systems. The proposed architectures address some of the key governance issues related to AI decision-making: Immutability ensures that post-hoc manipulations of the audit log cannot obscure accountability; Decentralization provides redundancy in case of failures or concentration of bias; Incentive Mechanisms provide reviewers and encourage them to produce high-quality evaluations. However, blockchain technologies present challenges such as potential latency associated with transactions that may be incompatible with real-time decision requirements, scalability limitations, and complexity in developing governance incentives that are appropriately designed. Therefore, these architectures appear to hold the greatest promise for decision-making in situations where there is a high degree of risk (i.e., "high stakes") and infrequent decision-making (e.g., quarterly or annual) and where the value of the audit trail's integrity outweighs the added complexity of the architecture (Krishnamoorthy, 2024; Sachan et al., 2025).

Figure 2. Composite System Architecture Diagram

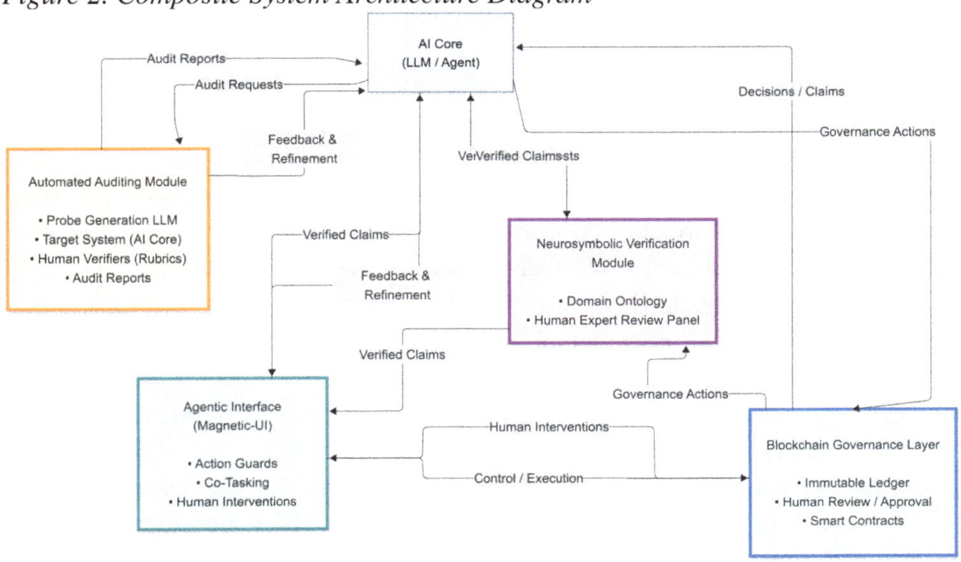

3.5 Formal HITL Taxonomies and Computational Models

The authors (Chiodo et al., 2025) provide a formal characterization using computational reduction and taxonomy frameworks that define how architecture relate to each other with regards to their reliability, efficiency, and accountability. They describe three primary architectures based on the level of authority and level of interaction that occur in these architectures. Monitoring is an architecture where humans observe behavior, however they are incapable of intervening; this is a low-overhead approach and can provide some reliability improvements, however it has limitations because although a human observer may identify a problem with the output, they have no authority to prevent the output from causing harm to people. This type of architecture is suitable for lower-risk applications where the focus is on assessing rather than preventing problems.

In single decision intervention, humans act as gatekeepers who either approve or reject an output before it is executed. Since humans can block an erroneous output from executing, this method can provide strong reliability assurances, however it also creates latency and throughput issues that will limit its effectiveness. To effectively use this method, humans must be able to accurately evaluate the outputs and make a timely decision, which is difficult due to cognitive overload, information asymmetry, and time pressure.

In deep interactive oversight, humans continually interact with the system providing real-time feedback, correcting behavior, and making changes to policies so the system operates within acceptable limits. While this method provides the greatest potential for reliability and alignment, it is extremely resource intensive for both humans and systems. In addition to requiring extensive cognitive resources, this method requires sophisticated methods for interacting with the system.

Based on the formal analysis provided in this paper, the authors conclude that effectiveness of a HITL architecture is dependent upon several factors including failure mode characteristics, human expertise, and the alignment of human capabilities with the verification requirements of the architecture. It is critical to understand that simply implementing a HITL architecture does not inherently provide reliability since the humans involved must possess the appropriate information, skills, and authority. Therefore, the authors contend that HITL architectures should be designed to match the specific requirements and constraints of the application domain (Chiodo et al., 2025).

3.6 Reciprocal Learning Systems

Te'eni et al. (2025) recommend a framework of mutual human-machine learning as an important foundational element for providing meaningful human control over

AI systems. The architecture acknowledges that effective HITL systems require supporting not only AI learning and adaptation to human input, but also human learning to maintain the capability and understanding of the human operator, even as AI systems evolve. The architecture outlines two mutually beneficial learning modes. i. Stable Reciprocal Learning supports stable human mental models while AI adapts to human preference and constraint in the domain. This type of learning is best suited to areas of established human expertise where the primary objective is to have AI behave in accordance with existing human knowledge and value structures. ii. Adaptive Reciprocal Learning supports co-evolution, which allows both human operators and AI systems to continually refine their knowledge and capabilities through interaction results. This type of learning is required in rapidly changing environments where neither the human nor the machine has all the relevant information, and therefore each must learn through experience. In order to support mutual learning, the architecture outlines several mechanisms. iii. Explainable AI interfaces enable humans to understand how the AI system arrives at its decisions; thus, human operators are able to develop accurate mental models of the system's behavior. iv. Feedback loops enable humans to identify and correct AI errors and provide direction that will affect the way the AI behaves in the future. v. Competence Maintenance Protocols help ensure that humans do not lose skills and knowledge as they rely more heavily on automation. vi. Adaptive Authority Allocation dynamically determines the proportion of responsibility between the human and AI in relation to demonstrated competence and task characteristics.

The architecture of this framework provides a significant solution to a long term issue for HITL systems: ensuring that humans continue to be capable of exercising meaningful oversight as the capabilities of AI grow. The architecture specifically designs for human learning simultaneously with machine learning and seeks to preclude the possibility that humans will no longer be able to effectively supervise AI systems because they lack the requisite skills and/or knowledge (Te'eni et al., 2025).

Figure 3. System-level representation of reciprocal learning in stable interaction mode, where the AI adapts while the human mental model remains static.

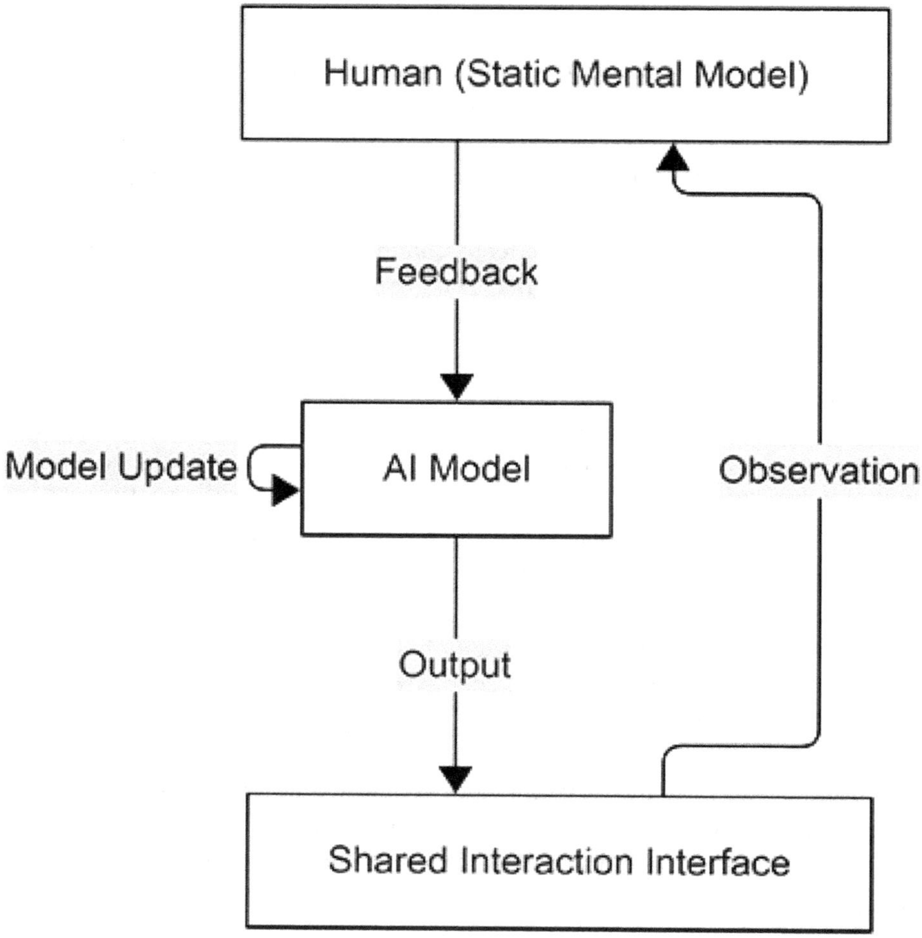

4. HALLUCINATION DETECTION AND MITIGATION MECHANISMS

4.1 Multi-Stage Verification Workflows

Effective hallucination mitigation demands layered verification combining multiple detection and correction mechanisms. Recent research reveals a recommended four-stage workflow balancing thoroughness with operational efficiency.

stage 1: automated probe and confidence checks are the first line of defense using computational techniques to identify potentially flawed output prior to human evaluation. Amirizaniani et al. (2024) demonstrated that cross-model probing which uses one large language model (LLM) to generate many test cases to evaluate another LLM's response will help identify inconsistencies indicative of hallucination risk. Confidence scoring helps determine how confident the model is in its output, thus providing a way to flag those with low confidence as suspect. However, confidence scores alone have proven to be insufficient because LLMs frequently provide high confidence when producing hallucinations.

stage 2: symbolic or rule-based verification uses formal representations of knowledge to verify output against known facts and logical rules. Monti et al. (2025) showed that ontology-based verification can be used to automatically identify conflicts between what an LLM has produced and symbolic domain knowledge and, therefore, potentially identify hallucinations without involving humans. This stage works best in areas that have well-defined symbolic knowledge bases, however, it is possible for this stage to miss hallucinations when there is either no symbolic knowledge or the symbolic knowledge is incomplete or out of date.

stage 3: human evaluation with a structured rubric uses human evaluators to assess outputs that passed the automated evaluations but require additional context and/or domain-specific expertise. Amirizaniani et al. (2024) emphasized the use of standardized evaluation criteria and structured evaluation prompts to assist the evaluator in systematically evaluating the output, thus reducing the amount of variability among raters and increasing the consistency of their evaluations. This stage maximizes the utilization of human cognitive abilities in cases that require human evaluative skills.

stage 4: audit logging and knowledge base updates complete the cycle by tracking the results of each verification process, incorporating validated corrections into symbolic knowledge bases, and modifying the system's operating policy to reflect the identified error patterns. Monti et al. (2025) demonstrated that the incorporation of valid corrections into symbolic knowledge bases enables iterative improvements in the reliability of the system as each successive iteration includes the collective experience of humans.

this multi-stage method employs defense-in-depth. Each automated stage filters out apparent flaws quickly and each human stage addresses the few cases that require specialized expertise and/or judgment. Each stage is modular, thereby enabling organizations to tailor the level of verification to their needs based upon the criticality of their applications and the availability of their resources (Amirizaniani et al., 2024; Monti et al., 2025).

Figure 4. Multi-stage human-in-the-loop verification workflow for hallucination detection and mitigation.

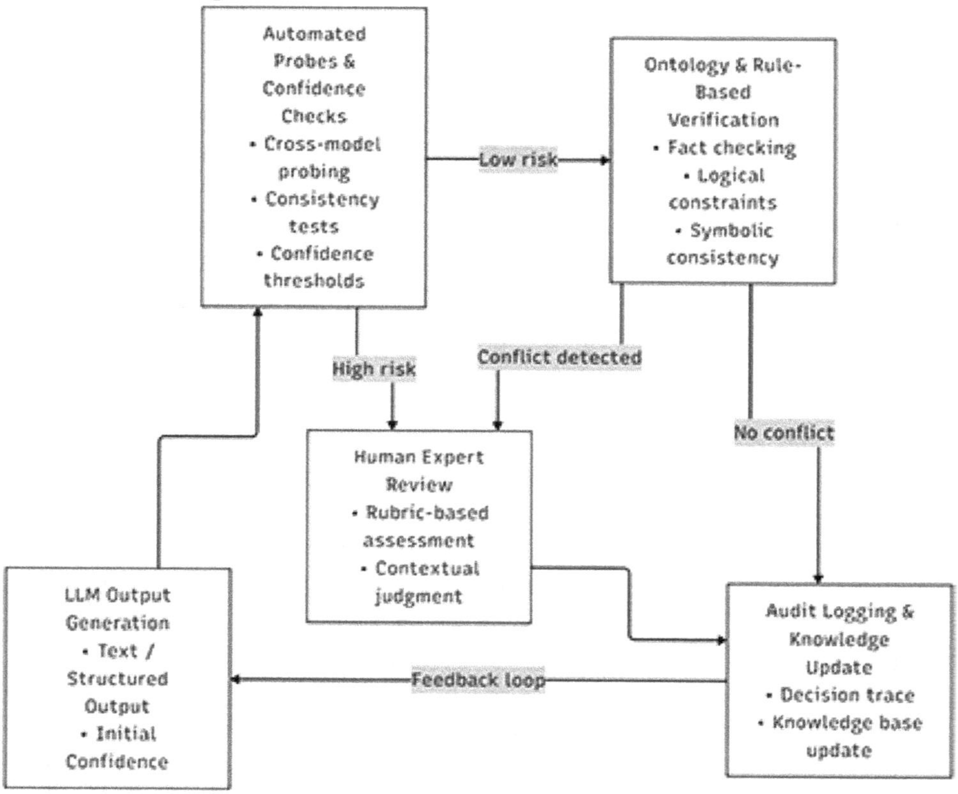

4.2 Cross-Model Probing and Consistency Checking

Cross-model probing deals with a major issue: Circular Reasoning Problem (CRP). When using an AI System to check the validity of another, there is a potential for the error to be passed on instead of being caught. Amirizaniani et al. (2024) suggest the use of one LLM to generate diverse probe questions that will test the knowledge and consistency of another LLM; human evaluation of the quality of the responses generated by the second LLM.

Diverse Probe Questions to Test Hallucinations of Another LLM

Probe questions can cover multiple dimensions of hallucinations. Factual Probe Questions Test Specific Claims That Are Verifiable Against Ground Truth. Semantically Equivalent Probe Questions In Different Forms Are Used to Detect Contradictory Responses Between LLMs. Boundary Probe Questions Explore Edge Cases and Domain Boundaries Where LLMs Are More Likely To Hallucinate Than Other Areas. Adversarial Probe Questions Test Model Robustness Under Challenging Conditions. Experimental Evaluations Demonstrate That Cross-Model Probing Can Expose Hallucinations That Single-Model Confidence Scoring Misses.

LLMs Often Maintain High Levels of Confidence While Providing Contradictory Responses to Semantically Equivalent Queries -- A Phenomenon Which Reveals That Internal Confidence Estimates Do Not Reliably Indicate Factual Accuracy. The Probe Inconsistency Rate Is Defined As the Proportion of Semantically Equivalent Queries Producing Contradictory Responses and Serves as An Empirical Signal Of Hallucination Risk, Complementing Confidence-Based Approaches (Amirizaniani et al., 2024)

4.3 Ontology-Guided Verification and Expert Refinement

Ontology-guided verification and expert refinement of neurosymbolic approaches is accomplished by leveraging structured formal knowledge representations to guide verification criteria in conjunction with human judgment. In this workflow, as shown by Monti et al. (2025), automatically generated claims by an LLM can be verified against the domain ontology; any conflicts found during the verification will be directed to a targeted expert for further review. The verification process utilizes three primary methods to accomplish verification. First, automated consistency checks are utilized to identify direct contradictions between the LLM's output and ontological assertions. This allows for the identification of clear errors and eliminates the need for human involvement in the identification of these errors. Second, axiom weakening is used to weaken overly restrictive ontological constraints. When the LLM generates output suggesting that the current knowledge within the ontology may be either incomplete or out-of-date, it creates a candidate for expert review versus an automatic rejection based on the LLM's output. Third, the expert validation method directs all identified conflicts to a domain specialist to determine if the LLM's output represents an actual error in the LLM's training data or if the output represents a valid conceptual innovation that should update the ontology. In doing so, this workflow converts the detection of hallucinations from solely error elimination to a knowledge discovery process. Any validated LLM output that conflicts with the currently accepted knowledge within the domain ontology may represent actual new insight(s) to extend the domain knowledge beyond simply eliminating errors. Therefore, by providing a structured approach to directing expert review to the conflict between the neural knowledge and the symbolic knowledge, the framework optimizes the use of the expert's time to focus their expertise at the point where their expertise will provide the most value while performing the routine verification tasks automatically (Monti et al., 2025).

4.4 Runtime Action Guards and Co-Planning

Runtime action guards, like those described by Mozannar et al. (2025), pause agent operation prior to "high-impact" or "irreversible" actions and require a human's affirmative decision to continue execution. These action guards determine what is considered "high-impact," "irreversible," etc., based on the specific workflow being executed, and implement "risk-based" intervention thresholds that balance efficiency of automation against safety considerations.

The impact of proposed actions are assessed, and if identified as "high-impact", the proposed action will be flagged for human review. If identified as "low-risk", it may be executed without any additional human involvement. Reversibility analysis is used to distinguish between "actions" that could be easily reversed if errors are detected and "operations" that would be irreversible and therefore require pre-execution approval from a human. In addition to runtime action guards, confidence-based gating may also be employed to require a human to approve the proposed course of action when the agent has insufficient confidence in its proposed action to fall below established thresholds.

Co-planning represents an alternative to action-by-action approval and allows a human to review and approve "high-level plans" prior to agent execution. By reviewing high-level plans instead of each individual action, co-planning reduces the number of interruptions experienced by the human, while still providing sufficient oversight over strategic decisions (Mozannar et al., 2025). Research results have shown that co-planning can improve both efficiency and user satisfaction relative to traditional action-by-action approval. In this regard, users can better assess whether the overall plan being proposed is coherent, versus assessing the coherence of individual actions within the proposed plan (Mozannar et al., 2025).

Figure 5. Action guards and co-planning mechanisms for safe oversight of agentic AI systems.

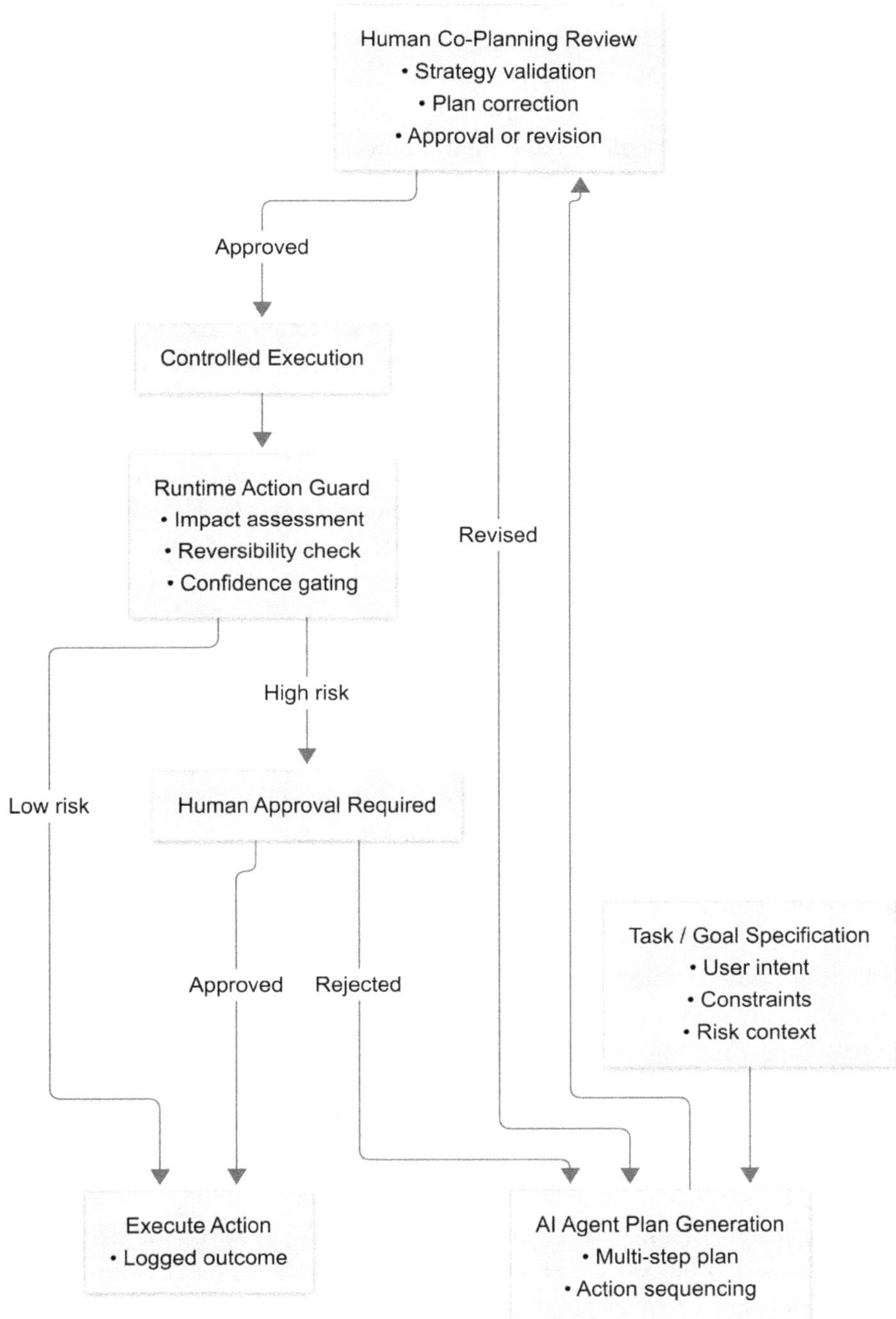

4.5 Iterative Refinement Through Structured Feedback

A large number of experts have expressed an interest in Iyenghar's work on iterative refinements to machine learning systems that provide structured feedback. In one example, Iyenghar has demonstrated how ChatGPT can generate high-quality risk assessments in a variety of industrial settings (e.g., machinery functional safety), but these need to be refined through multiple cycles of human-in-the-loop expert feedback in order to achieve high levels of accuracy and consistency (Iyenghar, n.d.).

In addition, Iyenghar has shown how a structured human feedback loop can help to refine the performance of machine learning models such that they produce expert level results when the initial outputs are highly inaccurate (Iyenghar, n.d.). Moreover, it was shown that a structured human feedback loop is capable of identifying problems associated with completeness and edge cases that automated verification tools cannot identify.

However, Iyenghar also noted that achieving high-quality results through an iterative process requires a great deal of expertise in providing high-quality feedback and that this process can be time-consuming for experts. Therefore, it will be necessary to develop and implement methods for efficiently reducing the amount of human cognitive load required by experts to participate in a structured feedback loop.

4.6 Epistemic Reframing of Hallucinations

In addition to being a mechanism for eliminating hallucinations, Monti et al. (2025) advocate that hallucinations should be viewed as an opportunity for epistemically reframing their potential value. Thus, instead of simply eliminating them, they can serve as indicators of missing or incomplete knowledge structures, and subsequently motivate the creation of verification workflow processes to distinguish between hallucinations indicating error(s) versus innovation(s) in conceptual understanding. To implement this epistemically reframed approach, several analysis mechanisms have been proposed. These include conflict characterization of hallucinations as either clearly erroneous (contradictory established fact) or requiring expert judgment regarding contradiction of provisionally accepted knowledge; and/or characterization of hallucinations as indicative of novel concepts and/or knowledge not currently included in established knowledge structures (potential innovations). In addition, coherence validation involves assessing whether the hallucinated content is internally logically consistent and/or aligned with the overall logic of a particular domain, regardless of whether it contradicts a particular ontology-based assertion. Finally, discovery protocols are needed to provide guidelines for structuring expert review to determine when conflicts are best represented as opportunities to enhance/

expand the knowledge base of a given domain versus clearly indicate error(s) which require correction.

The reframing of hallucinations from errors to potentially valid discoveries will also impact the design of Human-in-the-Loop (HITL) systems. Specifically, instead of designing HITL systems optimized solely for minimizing hallucination frequency, designers can design HITL systems that detect and direct potentially valuable hallucinations to experts for evaluation as candidate additions to a given knowledge base. This approach will be most effective in emerging fields where AI systems will inevitably come across both new information and new concepts which are not yet formally documented in a knowledge base. However, it will be critical to implement these approaches carefully to avoid legitimating true errors and/or generating unmanageable burdens on expert reviewers (Monti et al., 2025).

5. ACCOUNTABILITY FRAMEWORKS AND GOVERNANCE STRUCTURES

Chiodo, Cattani, & Pinto (2025), identified a way to classify and analyze HITL system configurations using legal and moral responsibilities, and have found that the fact that a human is present in the loop does not necessarily mean that there will be clarity of who is accountable.Based on the level of interaction and decision making authority within HITL, Chiodo et al. (2025), identify three types of HITL configurations:

Monitoring HITL configurations, In these configurations humans are able to view and monitor the operation of the system, but are not able to make any changes or interventions in response to their observations. While humans do not have the ability to prevent harm from occurring, there can still be limited liability placed on them for failing to detect potential error prior to an incident occurring. In terms of legal liability, in monitoring configurations, both the developers of the system and the organization responsible for deploying it, bear the liability for the actions of the automated system, whereas liability for human operators is generally very limited. As such, while the legal liability may rest with the developers and deployment organization, there are also ethical considerations for the human operators to identify and report any issues that are identified through their observation and reporting functions. Even though the operator is not authorized to intervene in the event of an issue, there is an expectation to report what has been identified, either formally or informally.

Single-decision HITL configurations, In single-decision configurations, humans make a determination regarding the output of the system at one point in time, approving or rejecting the output generated by the automated component of the system. The extent to which the human is liable for the decision made, is dependent on whether the human had access to sufficient information, possessed the necessary knowledge and expertise to evaluate the data, and was afforded adequate time to review the output before making the approval/rejection decision. If the human did not have adequate access to information, lacked the necessary knowledge and experience to adequately assess the quality of the output, or were not provided enough time to review the output before being required to make a determination, then the decision made would constitute an example of "responsibility laundering." "Responsibility laundering," refers to the practice of attributing the consequences of a decision to the individual who was required to make the decision, when in fact, the true cause of the decision lies with the system that failed to provide the individual with the necessary information, training, or time to make a well-informed decision.

Deep interactive HITL configurations, In deep interactive configurations, humans work collaboratively with the automated components of the system to generate an outcome. Deep interactive configurations represent the greatest complexity in terms of how responsibility is attributed among the various participants in the collaborative process, as the outcome results from the interactions that occur throughout the entire duration of the collaboration process. As such, the attribution of responsibility requires a detailed examination of the specific decision-making processes employed by the humans and the automated system throughout the collaboration, and the degree to which each participant contributed to the final outcome.

The authors identify four general failure modes in HITL systems that lead to accountability gaps.

Automation Bias - In automation bias, the human operators become too reliant on the output generated by the automated component of the system, resulting in ineffective oversight of the automated component's performance.

Diffusion of Responsibility, In diffusion of responsibility, multiple entities are assigned responsibility for ensuring oversight of the automated system, but no entity is ultimately responsible for ensuring that oversight takes place.

Skill Degradation, Over-reliance on automated decision-making tools, can lead to skill degradation in the human operators. When the human operators are not provided with the opportunity to engage in the evaluation process for the output generated by the automated tool, the human operators are unable to assess the accuracy of the output, and therefore cannot determine whether the output is reliable or not. These findings guide the development of guidelines for designing HITL systems that preserve accountability for all participants involved in the decision-making process: Provide documentation of the HITL configuration used and the implications of that configuration on the assignment of responsibility; Ensure that the human operators have the knowledge, skills and resources necessary to perform oversight of the automated component(s); Avoid HITL configurations that create the illusion of accountability for the human operators by positioning the human operators as scapegoats for the failures of the system; Align the laws and regulations governing the use of HITL systems with the reality of the technological capabilities and limitations of the systems.

Figure 6. Taxonomy of human-in-the-loop configurations and their accountability implications.

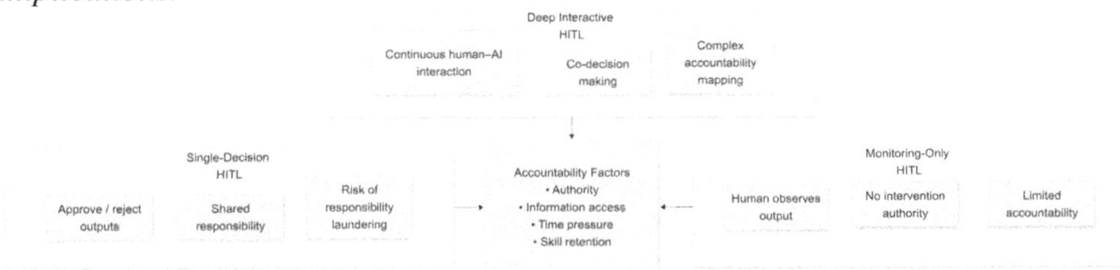

5.2 Immutable Audit Trails and Smart Contract Governance

The above-referenced authors (Krishnamoorthy [2024], and Sachan et al. [2025]) suggest that blockchain-based governance architecture will allow for the creation of immutable audit trails that are tamper resistant and enforceable via smart contracts. The authors also indicate that the architecture they describe would provide a solution to the problem of accountability by ensuring that the record of decisions made regarding AI systems cannot be altered and that all prescribed oversight procedures will be carried out as specified. As stated earlier, each decision made using an AI system generates a detailed log of the decision process, including the input used to make the decision, the output(s) generated by the AI model, the level of confidence in those outputs, whether there were any human inputs into the decision-making process, when the decision was made, who made the decision, etc. These logs are then stored in distributed ledgers, which allows for the creation of a permanent audit trail. A permanent audit trail allows for post-hoc analysis of the decision-making process and assigns responsibility for the decision. In addition, since these logs are stored in distributed ledgers, it is impossible to remove or modify them at a later time, thus eliminating the ability of an organization to "delete" or "modify" records to conceal its accountability after an adverse outcome has occurred.

Smart contracts can be designed to trigger certain governance rules that direct the flow of decisions to human oversight for review based upon predetermined criteria. For example, a smart contract could be programmed to direct decisions for human review if a confidence threshold is not met, direct decisions for review by experts in a particular area, or direct decisions to senior-level oversight based upon the level of risk associated with the decision. Thus, the use of smart contracts provides a means to ensure that governance protocols are consistently followed, and not left up to the discretion of individual organizational representatives. Decentralized governance mechanisms allow for multiple stakeholders to participate in oversight of AI systems, providing incentives for reviewer participation and penalties for lack thereof or malicious behavior. Reviewers receive compensation in the form of tokens for their cognitive labor, and organizations face economic consequences for oversight failures due to the penalty mechanism built into the token-based system. Furthermore, decentralizing the oversight function of AI systems reduces the potential for concentration of oversight authority, and thus the likelihood of bias.

Tracking provenance creates a complete history of how data, models, and human inputs were used to generate specific outputs. Tracking provenance enables organizations to perform root-cause analysis when errors occur and identify systematic problems that require policy or design changes to mitigate. While the blockchain-based approaches offer promise, there are several challenges to implementation. Specifically, transaction latency may conflict with the need for real-time decision making. As the volume of decisions grows, scalability becomes an issue as does the cost and space needed to store the increasing amount of data in the blockchain. Additionally, designing and implementing the correct governance structure and incentive models for organizations and stakeholders, establishing mechanisms for resolving disputes, and addressing privacy concerns related to storing sensitive decision data on a public ledger will add complexity to the governance of these systems. Blockchain-based approaches may be best suited to high-risk, low-frequency decisions that require the integrity of audit trails and distributed governance of decisions to outweigh the added complexity (Krishnamoorthy [2024]; Sachan et al. [2025]).

5.3 Standards-Aligned Oversight in Regulated Domains

HITL oversight was integrated into regulatory compliant workflows in regulated environments through a combination of embedding HITL into the workflow of current safety standards and regulatory requirements; HITL was aligned with standards such as the ISO functional safety standards for machinery and implemented into an accountable structure that satisfies both the technical reliability and regulatory requirement of safety standards; Iyenghar (n.d) used a combination of several mechanisms to achieve this level of alignment with standards; Iyenghar (n.d.) applied standards based evaluation criteria to ensure that human reviewers evaluate the output of the AI according to the same set of requirements that are applied to safety analysis of traditional machines; he applied documentation protocols to ensure that all of the review process has an audit trail, so that regulatory bodies have a record of compliance for safety case documentation and traceability; Iyenghar (n.d.) assigned role-based responsibility to perform HITL oversight tasks to existing organizational roles and accountability structures in the safety management system; Iyenghar (n.d.) required competence for those performing HITL oversight, including education/training, to ensure that the oversight is performed by qualified individuals; Iyenghar (n.d.), in his study across four industrial case studies, demonstrated empirically that a standards aligned HITL approach resulted in 100% agreement with the ground truth of the data being reviewed, and had a high usability rating from the reviewers, who were experts in their field; Iyenghar (n.d.) showed that HITL can be accepted operationally and will satisfy regulatory compliance when it is integrated with existing standards; Iyenghar (n.d.) noted that one of the biggest barriers to implementing HITL in regulated industry is gaining operational acceptance and regulatory compliance; Iyenghar (n.d.) found that HITL can provide improvements over the traditional manual methods of safety analysis, particularly in terms of identifying edge cases and completeness issues that may not have been identified during the initial review.

5.4 Governance Incentives and Reviewer Diversity

Krishnamoorthy (2024), and Sachan et al. (2025) provide an understanding of how to ensure adequate levels of reviewer participation and diversity in HITL oversight, utilizing economic incentives and governance processes to ensure the involvement of many stakeholders. Economic incentives in the form of tokens, pay for both reviewers' time and cognitive effort spent on reviewing AI output. The structure of rewards can be designed so that reviewers are encouraged to conduct a full review rather than just approving AI output at face value, by providing compensation based on review quality metrics (inter-rater agreement, accuracy in detecting known errors). Economic sanctions for negligence or intentional failure to detect errors in AI output can create negative incentives for reviewers to act in ways that support reliability in the system.

Reviewers are subject to mechanisms to ensure that the review is conducted by diverse groups, and thus does not reflect the biases of a few individuals. For example, protocol can include requirements for review by multiple independent evaluators, rotation of reviewers to distribute oversight responsibility, and/or reputation systems that track reviewers' experience over time and across different tasks and domains. By including diverse groups of reviewers in oversight, we can be assured that the behavior of the AI system reflects the values of all stakeholders and not just those of a few.

Methods exist for resolving disputes when reviewers have differing opinions regarding whether an AI output should be approved or rejected. Methods for escalating disagreements include multi-stage procedures that direct disputed issues to senior reviewers or oversight committees, and methods for aggregating judgments from multiple reviewers into a single decision using voting. The above mentioned governance processes help to solve a major problem: to ensure that human oversight will remain effective and represent a diverse range of stakeholders as systems grow. However, these processes add a new layer of complexity to developing the proper incentives for reviewers, recruiting and training reviewers, and addressing edge cases that do not fit into the established process (Krishnamoorthy, 2024; Sachan et al., 2025).

5.5 Organizational Oversight and Team-Based Governance

Beyond individual human-in-the-loop configurations, oversight through team-based and institutional mechanisms provide organizational level governance structures for the purpose of oversight (2023). "team-in-the-loop" approaches to high-stakes AI oversight recognize that effective oversight usually demands collective judgment and diverse expertise rather than decision making by individual operators.Multi-disciplinary oversight teams bring together technical experts, domain specialists, ethicists, and stakeholder representatives to ensure comprehensive evaluation of both the behavior and impact of an AI system. Team based oversight can identify issues that individual reviewers might miss, while also assuring that diverse perspectives are reflected in governance decisions. However, team-based approaches introduce coordination costs and the possibility of decision paralysis when members of a team disagree.

Organizational accountability structures establish clear reporting lines, escalation procedures, and ultimate decision authority for AI oversight. These structures prevent diffusion of responsibility by designating specific roles and individuals within an organization accountable for the effectiveness of oversight. Organizational structures also provide continuous improvement mechanisms through incident review, policy updates, and training programs that enhance oversight capabilities over time.

Regulatory oversight bodies prove to be external accountability mechanisms that support internal organizational governance structures. Regulatory frameworks can require specific oversight procedures, require transparency reports, perform audits of AI system behavior, and impose penalties on organizations for failure to effectively implement governance structures. The European Union's AI act is an example of this type of approach as it establishes risk-based oversight requirements and enforcement mechanisms (corea et al., 2022).

6. HUMAN-AI COLLABORATION MODELS AND INTERACTION PATTERNS

6.1 Co-Planning and Co-Tasking Interfaces

Co-planning interfaces enable a strategic view of the system that is implemented through an approval process in the planning phase. In addition to approving high-level plans, the co-planning interface provides an opportunity for users to add constraints that would have otherwise been missing from the AI's initial plan proposal. Furthermore, Mozannar et al. (2025) identify three stages of the co-planning workflow as follows:

Joint Plan Generation: This stage is where the human and AI collaborate to define high-level plans and objectives, and generate candidate plans. Candidate plans generated at this stage will be based on the human's contextual knowledge, and the AI's understanding of task requirements and available capabilities. Plan Refinement: After the candidate plans are generated, they can be refined and modified by the human. For example, the human could adjust the priority of certain tasks, restrict certain task sequences, or add new constraints to the original candidate plan. Execution Monitoring: Finally, once the plan has been approved and the tasks have been assigned, the human will monitor the execution of the plan to ensure it unfolds as planned. If unexpected events occur during plan execution, the human can intervene and make adjustments as necessary.In addition to enabling co-planning, the research also identifies co-tasking as an important mechanism for dynamically allocating tasks between the human and the AI agent. Co-tasking involves determining whether a particular task should be completed manually by a human or automatically by an AI agent.

Co-tasking decisions take into account the type of task being performed (e.g., is it a routine task? Does it involve ambiguous or ill-defined conditions?), the capability and confidence level of the AI agent, the expertise and availability of the human operator, and the risk profile associated with each possible course of action. Research findings indicate that using both co-planning and co-tasking can lead to improvements in both task completion rates and user satisfaction relative to systems that operate autonomously. Moreover, users have reported having a greater sense of control over the overall system when given the ability to shape the high-level strategy of the system. Additionally, the use of co-planning and co-tasking mechanisms can result in improved efficiency in completing tasks compared to manual task execution, as routine tasks are automated and the human operator focuses on higher-level decision making and critical tasks.

6.2 Reciprocal Human-Machine Learning

To achieve true collaborative models that are based on reciprocal learning – where both the operators and the AI system continually learn as a result of the outcome of interactions – Te'eni et al. (2025) suggest that an adaptive bidirectional approach to learning is needed to address the problem of providing meaningful human control over evolving AI capabilities.

Reciprocal learning that is stable will result in both the operator's mental model being maintained consistently, while at the same time the AI system will continue to learn about human preferences and constraints. This type of learning is most relevant in areas of high human expertise, where the objective is to have the AI behave in a manner that is aligned with existing human knowledge and values. The AI will continually improve its ability to predict what the human prefers, and to create outputs that require little to no modification by the human; thus, the human can continue to maintain stable expertise and mental models that support oversight.

Adaptive reciprocal learning involves continuous co-evolution between the operator and the AI system, where both parties continually update their understanding and capabilities based on the outcome of interactions. In this type of environment, neither party may possess all of the knowledge required to successfully solve the problem, and therefore each party must learn from their collective experiences. The AI will adapt to new patterns and situations; while the human will learn to better understand the AI's capabilities, limitations, and decision-making rationale so that they can work more effectively together in the long run.

To facilitate reciprocal learning, the framework includes several mechanisms. These include Explainable AI (XAI) interfaces, which provide humans with insights into the decision-making processes used by the AI, including visualizations, natural-language explanations, and example-based reasoning. Additionally, feedback loops will enable humans to inform the AI when it makes incorrect decisions and provide guidance on how to modify the behavior of the AI going forward, with the AI learning from those corrections to prevent making similar mistakes in the future. Finally, competence maintenance protocols will be implemented to ensure that humans do not become deskilled due to relying too heavily on automated decision-making. To accomplish this, the protocol will provide the opportunity for humans to perform manual tasks periodically, undergo training exercises, or receive competency assessments.

Finally, the adaptive authority allocation mechanism will adjust the division of labor between the human and the AI based on the demonstrated competence of the AI on a particular task, and the characteristics of the task itself. Thus, if the AI has been able to demonstrate competence in completing certain types of tasks, then those tasks will be delegated to the AI. Conversely, if there are complex tasks that have been previously difficult for the AI to complete, then they will be routed back to the human for completion. (Te'eni et al., 2025).

Formal Perspective on Reciprocal Learning

To distinguish stable and adaptive reciprocal learning, interaction may be represented using a simplified state-update perspective.

Let:

a. H_t denote the human mental model at time t
b. A_t denote the AI system state at time t
c. F_t denote human feedback

In stable reciprocal learning, the AI adapts while the human mental model remains unchanged:

$$H_{t+1} = H_t$$

$$A_{t+1} = f(A_t, F_t)$$

Here, adaptation occurs unilaterally within the AI system.

In **adaptive reciprocal learning**, both the AI and the human mental model evolve through interaction:

In this case, interaction results in co-adaptation, reflecting a dynamic learning partnership.

6.3 Layered Validation Workflows

HITL implementations commonly deploy layered validation workflow processes that integrate human review/approval of AI generated content through multiple stages. Layered workflow processes are composed of multiple steps. First, AI generates initial output based upon input data that serves as the basis for human review, allowing for the rapid processing of high volumes of data while maintaining human oversight over the ultimate decision. Second, first level validation occurs when human reviewers validate AI output against a set of standardized criteria, identifying errors or areas which require modification. Third, refinement allows the reviewer to make changes to the AI output, modifying it to correct errors and incorporate contextual knowledge that the AI does not have. Fourth, final approval is a second validation process in which senior reviewers or subject matter experts validate the output to ensure that the output meets quality standards. By implementing this model of workflow, the user can achieve balance between both efficiency and quality. Human expertise will be concentrated at the levels of validation and refinement, while AI will perform routine tasks efficiently and effectively. Results from a study conducted at a university using the same type of model show that 87 percent of AI generated grades were valid with only slight revisions; conversely, 13 percent of the AI generated grades required substantial revisions. The overall effect was a reduction in grading time of about 40 percent compared to the time taken when all grading was done manually, while quality remained consistent. Furthermore, the use of a layered model resulted in increased consistency due to the fact that AI generated output provided a standard base line for human grader's output resulting in decreased inter-rater variability (Selvam et al., 2025).

6.4 Dynamic Authority Reversal

When Westover(n.d.), proposed a new dynamic authority reversal model that will adjust the locus of control between humans and AI as a function of the task being performed, the level of confidence within the AI systems, and the historical performance of the systems, the dynamic authority reversal model can address this problem of establishing the appropriate amount of trust and delegation of authority to be placed in an automated system relative to its true reliability, rather than placing the trust in an automated system based on static assumptions about the system's reliability. This model for dynamic authority reversal includes a number of components for dynamically determining how much authority is to be delegated to the AI systems. The first component is performance monitoring that allows for tracking of the AI systems' accuracy and the frequency at which the human operator overrides the decision of the AI system over time and across different types of tasks and/or context, and identifies those tasks and/or context where the AI system is performing reliably and where the human operator is improving the quality of the outcome through their override of the AI system's decision. A second component of the model is confidence-based routing that directs high-confidence AI outputs directly to the automation layer for automatic execution while directing low-confidence AI outputs to the human review layer, with the confidence threshold used to determine whether to route the output automatically or have it reviewed by a human operator determined based on observed accuracy-confidence calibration. A third component of the model is adaptive thresholds that will adaptively determine the criteria under which the human operator needs to intervene in order to allow for the determination of when the error rate of the AI system increases and when the error rate decreases, thus allowing for the relaxation of the threshold requirements (thus permitting more automation) or tightening of the threshold requirements (thus requiring more human oversight). In addition to these three components of the model, the model also includes authority reversal protocols that will permit the AI system to identify potential errors in the decisions made by the human operators, thus permitting the AI system to flag decisions that appear to be inconsistent with established patterns and/or policies. The inclusion of authority reversal protocols addresses one of the limitations of the traditional Human-in-the-Loop (HITL) approaches to testing and validation of AI systems, where the human operators are responsible for overseeing the actions taken by the AI systems; however, the AI systems do not have the ability to check the validity of the decisions made by the human operators, and therefore may miss human errors. Overall, the goal of the dynamic authority reversal approach is to optimize the balance between the efficiency and reliability of an AI system through the concentration of human oversight in areas where the human oversight will provide the greatest benefit, and the automation of tasks where the AI systems have demonstrated the highest degree of reliability. However, the successful implementation of this type of approach requires careful calibration to prevent the inappropriate automation of tasks that remain outside of the capabilities of the AI systems, and to prevent the excessive involvement of the human operators in tasks that could otherwise be automated and benefit from the use of the AI system. (Westover, n.d.).

Confidence-Based Authority Allocation

Authority allocation may be expressed through a threshold-based mechanism. Let:

a. denote AI confidence for task
b. denote a confidence threshold

Authority is determined as follows:

In adaptive oversight systems, the threshold may evolve based on observed error patterns, ensuring that authority allocation reflects empirical reliability rather than static design assumptions.

6.5 Interaction Mechanisms for Agentic Systems

the following information is extracted from Mozannar et al. (2025):

there are a number of interaction mechanisms identified by Mozannar et al. (2025) as being key to enabling effective human oversight of agentic AI systems which both plan and execute multi-stage workflows.

action guards allow agents to pause prior to taking actions that could have a significant impact or would be considered irreversible and require explicit human approval prior to proceeding. action guards may be configured based upon action types (for example, financial transactions greater than certain threshold amounts, data deletion operations, etc.), risk assessments (potential for harm), or confidence levels (agent's degree of uncertainty regarding the appropriateness of an action). in this way, action guards provide very detailed controls to prevent harmful actions but also enable the automatic execution of most other operational actions. long term memory systems allow agents to retain context during prolonged periods of interaction with humans.

long term memory systems therefore enable agents to learn from human input and adjust their behavior as a result of such input over time. long term memory systems store human corrections to agent decisions, human preferences as demonstrated through previous interactions, and patterns of successful and unsuccessful action execution. this collective body of knowledge enables agents to continue to develop their capability to anticipate what will be preferred by humans and to avoid repeating actions that required human override in the past.

Observability interfaces allow humans to view the process followed by the agent including its reasoning, the intended action(s), and the current state of action execution. observability interfaces include visualization tools that represent the workflow that has been generated by the agent in a structured format, indicate where decisions were made and why, and how much of the action plan has been executed. observability provides humans with an opportunity to detect any problems prior to them resulting in damage, and to create an accurate model of the agent's capabilities and limitations.

intervention mechanisms allow humans to halt the execution of an action plan, modify an action plan, override an individual action, or provide corrective instruction to an agent. for these mechanisms to be effective, there needs to be low latency interfaces available to enable humans to respond quickly to any issues that arise, the interface used to interact with the agent must provide clear descriptions of the options available to intervene and the implications of those options, and the agent must have a mechanism to learn from any interventions so that it does not experience the same issue again in subsequent executions (Mozannar et al., 2025).

responsibility clarity refers to the extent to which accountability structures clearly define the responsibilities for oversight and outcome. this qualitative assessment considers whether the roles, authorities and escalation procedures are defined and understood by all parties involved in the accountability structure (Krishnamoorthy, 2024; Chiodo et al., 2025).

7. EVALUATION METRICS AND EFFECTIVENESS MEASURES FOR HITL SYSTEMS

HITL AI system evaluation cannot be based solely on overall accuracy measurement, because human oversight (as opposed to human input) will always modify the behavior of the model, and thus require evaluation of all three dimensions, i.e., performance gain, operational cost, and risk management. In order to address each dimension separately, this section divides the evaluation into three interdependent aspects of evaluation with one table per aspect and provides references to the tables while providing additional detail in the subsections, but does not present them as individual pieces of information.

7.1. Performance Gain and Oversight Quality

Human-in-the-loop integration aims to provide assurance that the human intervention produces measurable improvements in the quality of the outputs produced by the AI. The ability of the human-in-the-loop component to detect errors and produce consistent review decisions are the two key areas to evaluate when assessing the quality of oversight. Consistency of reviewer decisions and the selectivity of interventions for errors detected will therefore be the critical metrics to assess to determine the effectiveness of oversight in HITL systems. **See Table 3** for an overview of the metrics used to measure performance gain and oversight quality in HITL systems.

Table 3. Performance and Oversight Quality Metrics

Metric	Description	Relevance
Accuracy Gain	Improvement after human intervention	Measures HITL benefit
Error Detection Rate	Errors correctly identified by humans	Indicates oversight effectiveness
False Positive Rate	Correct outputs flagged incorrectly	Reveals over-intervention
Precision–Recall Balance	Detection vs. intervention tradeoff	Ensures calibrated oversight
Inter-Rater Agreement (κ)	Reviewer consistency	Validates reliability

Table 3 illustrates that performance gain is measured through the use of agreement and error-based metrics commonly used in HITL system evaluations.

7.2. Efficiency, Human Factors, and System Viability

Improved performance is required; however, performance improvements alone do not guarantee success if they occur at a cost to human resource expenditure or a reduction in system throughput. Therefore, HITL systems must be evaluated from an efficiency, scalability, and human usability perspective. As such, metrics in this area will assess the impact of human involvement on decision latency, cognitive workload, and the long term viability of the system. For a comprehensive listing of efficiency-related and human-centered evaluation metrics, see Table 4.

Table 4. Efficiency and Human-Centered Metrics

Metric	Description	Relevance
Human Intervention Rate	Frequency of manual review	Indicates dependency on humans
Decision Latency	Time added by oversight	Affects real-time deployment
Cognitive Load Score	Mental effort required	Impacts fatigue and consistency
Throughput	Decisions processed per unit time	Determines scalability
Trust Calibration Score	Alignment of trust and performance	Prevents automation bias

Table 4 indicates that high intervention rates and/or high levels of cognitive load may reduce the long-term viability of HITL systems, regardless of the performance improvements obtained. Calibration of trust in the HITL architecture is also very important; over-calibration of trust in HITL architectures can degrade their effectiveness, whereas under-calibration can also lead to ineffective HITL architectures. These metrics will help ensure the HITL architecture remains viable past the initial experimental phase.

7.3 Hallucination Control, Risk Management, and Governance

Evaluations of systems that have a high level of importance (high stakes) must address extreme failures, such as hallucinations created by large language models. Therefore, an evaluation framework must assess a system's risks and accountability, along with its performance and efficiency. For governance oriented evaluation metrics of containing hallucinations and ensuring a system's accountability, refer to Table 5.Hallucination detection and governance metrics are examples of how an evaluation of a system can go beyond evaluating its accuracy and assess a system's risk level, whether or not it is possible to identify where something went wrong, and whether or not a system has complied with regulations. See Table 5..

Table 5. Hallucination and Governance Metrics

Metric	Description	Relevance
Hallucination Rate	Frequency of fabricated outputs	Measures reliability risk
Critical Error Severity	Impact of undetected failures	Prioritizes mitigation
Audit Trail Completeness	Decision traceability	Enables accountability
Intervention Justification Score	Quality of human rationale	Supports transparency
Compliance Readiness	Regulatory alignment	Ensures deployability

As shown in Table 5, hallucination detection and governance metrics extend evaluation beyond accuracy to include risk severity, traceability, and compliance.

Among governance-oriented indicators, Hallucination Rate may be formally defined as:

This metric directly measures the frequency of fabricated or factually unsupported outputs.

7.4 Integrated Evaluation Perspective

Tables 3 – 5 show performance metrics to explain improvements in the system (what is improving), efficiency metrics to determine if the improvements are cost-effective (are they sustainable) and governance metrics to ensure the system is safe and will be held accountable for its actions. This organized method of evaluating will reduce the number of tables but maintain the ability to have an easily interpretable and aligned with modern HITL research methods way to evaluate a system.

8. IMPLEMENTATION CHALLENGES AND BEST PRACTICES

Successfully implementing Human-in-the-Loop (HITL) systems requires navigating significant operational, human, and regulatory hurdles. This section outlines key challenges and synthesizes evidence-based best practices for effective deployment.

8.1 Failure Mode Complexity

The HITL has several potential failures as it is a complex system. These failures can give a false sense of security when they are implemented incorrectly. Some of the potential failure modes are listed below:

a) Failed Monitoring: HITL monitors in a passive role, in that there is no ability for a human to intervene, then this is of little value. There is little benefit from using a human monitor in these types of situations, as the use of a human in a high stakes situation will not provide enough reliability.
b) Information Asymmetry: HITL reviewers may not have the proper information, or explanation, to effectively evaluate AI output.
c) Automation Bias & Skill Degradation: HITL operators may become too confident in their AI's output, which may cause them to lose their "vigilance." Over-automation may also reduce the skills required to perform the oversight process.

Best Practice: Design HITL to allow for the opportunity for a human to actively participate in the oversight process, not just to passively monitor the process. Design HITL so that reviewers have some form of decision-support context to assist in making evaluations. Train reviewers to be vigilant in the oversight process and regularly train the reviewers to ensure they have the knowledge and skills necessary to perform the oversight process effectively (Chiodo et al., 2025; Te'eni et al., 2025).

8.2 Human Cognitive and Labor Costs

Human oversight is a scalable and welfare issue.

a) Cognitive Load & Fatigue: Excessive review tasks may overwhelm reviewers to the point that the quality of their decision-making decreases over time.
b) Compensation & Scalability: The expertise required to perform oversight needs to be appropriately incentivized. Unlimited human review represents a fundamental bottleneck to the throughput of the system.
c) Best Practice: Reduce cognitive load by utilizing structured prompts and rubrics during the review process. Develop a tiered review structure and concentrate expert effort on high risk cases. Develop fair compensation models and monitor reviewer workloads to prevent fatigue (Krishnamoorthy, 2024; Mozannar et al., 2025).

8.3 Scalability and Latency Challenges

A conflict exists between comprehensive oversight and efficient operations.

a) Bottlenecks & Latency: Human review may create delays that are incompatible with real-time applications.
b) Threshold Calibration: Establishing the appropriate criteria for initiating reviews is crucial to maintaining the balance between safety and speed.
c) Best Practice: Utilize automated pre-filters (such as confidence scores, consistency checks) to triage output. Ensure that only ambiguous or high-risk output is reviewed by humans. When possible, utilize asynchronous review and establish empirical thresholds (Amirizaniani et al., 2024; Monti et al., 2025).

8.4 Legal Ambiguity and Regulatory Alignment

Existing legal frameworks typically contain ambiguity regarding accountability within human-AI collaborative systems.

a) Regulatory Gaps & Documentation: Ambiguity currently exists in regard to assigning liability. A complete, immutable audit trail of human oversight actions is critical to documenting the oversight process.
b) Standards Alignment: Integrating HITL processes into existing regulatory frameworks (such as ISO standards) can minimize compliance risks.
c) Best Practice: Engage regulators early, integrate system design into applicable industry standards, and maintain detailed records of all oversight decisions and rationale (Chiodo et al., 2025; Iyenghar, n.d.).

8.5 Synthesis of Best Practices

Effectively implementing HITL combines the strategies outlined above to address the previously discussed challenges:

a) Standardization of Evaluation: Utilize standardized prompts and rubrics to increase the consistency and efficiency of reviews.
b) Layered Verification: Combine automated checks with targeted human review in a staged workflow to achieve defense-in-depth.
c) Reviewers Competence & Diversity: Ensure reviewer competency through ongoing training and utilize a diverse group of reviewers to help avoid biases in the review process.

d) Appropriate Calibration: Calibrate the degree of automation and the intensity of oversight based upon the specific risk profile of the application.
e) Monitoring and Adapting: Ongoing tracking of system performance and reviewer data enables ongoing improvement of the HITL mechanism.

9. CASE STUDIES AND REAL-WORLD APPLICATIONS

9.1 Machinery Functional Safety Risk Analysis

The Iyenghar (n.d.) article states that ChatGPT has been implemented in an industrial setting to generate preliminary functional safety risk assessments based on the specifications of a given industrial machine. These preliminary assessments were generated to provide expert engineers with a starting point to develop their final functional safety risk assessment that would be aligned to the provisions of ISO 13849. Human-in-the-loop (HITL), a design paradigm used to create a preliminary risk assessment that is iteratively reviewed and refined until there is complete agreement with an expert-established risk assessment, was tested across several types of industrial systems including, but not limited to; AGVs, collaborative robots, industrial presses, and packaging machines. Through use of this HITL approach reviewers reported improvements in efficiency and consistency, and identified "edge cases" that may have been missed through manual review alone. While it is evident that ChatGPT can be a valuable tool in supporting the development of functional safety risk assessments for industrial equipment, it is equally important to note that for the ChatGPT tool to be successful, regulatory alignment, and the use of structured evaluation criteria, along with expert-led validation are essential. Furthermore, the author emphasizes that due to the complexity of developing a functional safety risk assessment, significant expert involvement will continue to be required, especially in the initial stages of the review cycle.

9.2 Ethical AI Grading in Higher Education

The authors Selvam et al. (2025), developed an ethically-oriented HITL grading framework that could be used in a university environment to allow for fairer and more scalable assessment. The AI generated grading recommendation served as the foundation for all assessments, but allowed the instructor to have control over the grading by using a rubric to assess, refine, and approve the grades of those assessments that were ambiguous.The empirical results indicated that most AI generated assessments only needed minor adjustments and therefore there was a large amount of time saved on grading time and no loss of student satisfaction and grading consistency. The study emphasizes that there is a need for openness about how the AI has been involved in the grading process, to provide the instructors with the appropriate training to evaluate critically and to have some form of ethics oversight to reduce bias. The effectiveness of the system was greatest when it was used for structured assignment where there was clear rubric defining the expectations, further supporting the use of HITL systems as augmentative tools rather than replacement tools for educational assessment.

9.3 Neurosymbolic Knowledge Discovery in Specialized Domains

The authors of Monti et al. (2025), using HITL with a biomimetic robot and an avionics diagnostic application, provide evidence that "hallucinations" which appear at first glance as errors may serve as triggers for discovering new knowledge. In the event the output from the language model was inconsistent with established ontologies, the structured check would initiate a manual review by a subject matter expert rather than automatically rejecting the output.On multiple occasions, subject matter experts validated the conflicting output as valid insight into the system resulting in updates to the ontology to include the newly identified behavior or documentation of the system behavior that had been previously unknown. These examples demonstrate that if domain specific subject matter expertise is closely aligned with the formal representation of the ontology; then structural human oversight can be used to convert model error into opportunities for discovery. The approach holds potential for areas where there is rapid growth/evolution of both scientific and/or professional disciplines as well as for the integration of multiple disciplines. However, the level of involvement required from the subject matter expert(s) to support this approach will be high, along with the maturity of the ontology engineering process.

9.4 Agentic Interface Evaluations

The Mozannar et al. (2025) evaluation of the design of agentic HITL interfaces supporting oversight of autonomous systems with co-planning, action guard, and adaptive feedback capabilities showed experimental evidence of improved task performance when humans are involved in planning during the initial phases of the task process; corrective actions were taken before the flawed strategy was executed and action guards successfully prevented harm from being done.While user studies indicated that the degree of oversight is critical and that a level of oversight which is too high can reduce usability, while an overly low level of oversight will lead to distrust, the results indicate a need for HITL interfaces capable of adapting their oversight in order to achieve a balance between the benefits of automation and the importance of providing users with meaningful levels of control over the decision-making processes associated with increasingly autonomous AI systems.

10. FUTURE RESEARCH DIRECTIONS AND EMERGING TRENDS

In this part, we present multiple pathways that could lead to improvements in human-in-the-loop (HITL) frameworks, specifically by examining the integration of methodologies that provide reliability and better governance.

10.1 Neurosymbolic Discovery Loops

Monti et al. (2025), propose a new paradigm for artificial intelligence hallucination, in which they consider these hallucinations as errors but also as opportunities for discovering new knowledge. The key to this paradigm is to develop the capability to distinguish between real errors and discoveries that may have revealed a gap in an expert's formal knowledge base or identified a novel conceptual insight, based upon the neural output and the symbolic knowledge.

Key Research Questions

a) What automation techniques will allow us to identify and prioritize discrepancies between neural output and symbolic knowledge, so that these discrepancies can be reviewed by an expert?
b) What methodology can be used to incorporate the validated new concepts into our formal knowledge bases, with minimal loss of logic consistency?
c) How should the discovery loop architecture be structured to maximize the amount of new knowledge that is added to the knowledge base and minimize the amount of work done by the expert?
d) What criteria can be developed to evaluate the validity and usefulness of the knowledge produced using this process?

Promising Approaches, the development of a higher resolution confidence metric; the use of active learning to identify areas that contain high conflict potential; the creation of collaborative tools to support the evolution of the knowledge base ontology.

Applications, his direction has significant potential for application in scientific disciplines that are rapidly evolving; in interdisciplinary research; and in technical specializations, where the expert knowledge base is typically unstructured.

10.2 Decentralized Governance and Blockchain Integration

Blockchain technology will allow Krishnamoorthy (2024) and Sachan et al. (2025) to develop next generation HITL governance models with immutable audit trails and enable decentralized review mechanisms that provide transparency and accountability.

a) Key research questions
   - How do blockchain-based systems reduce latency enough to support time-sensitive decision making?
   - What are the best methods to encourage participation from a wide group of reviewers and prevent them from manipulating the system?
   - How does one maintain reviewer anonymity in the event their decisions are recorded on a public ledger?
   - What types of governance structures will support reviewer disputes?

b) Promising approaches

   Researching hybrid architecture, layer-2 scalability, private proof-of-concept technologies such as zero-knowledge proofs and advanced reputation systems.

c) Applications

   Ideal for applications with high risk (e.g., healthcare, financial), regulatory requirements for unassailable auditable trails, and applications involving multiple stakeholders who benefit from distributed authority.

10.3 Advanced Agentic HITL Interfaces

Mozannar et al. (2025) point out that, as AI agents are able to execute increasingly complex workflows on their own, advanced interfaces will be needed to enable the human oversight of those agents without requiring them to spend an undue amount of time monitoring the workflows.

a) Key Research Questions
   - How can interface transparency be provided for a human to monitor the agent's execution, while avoiding providing too much information at once?
   - What human-computer interaction paradigm(s) best support humans to efficiently manage the high level strategy of an agent?
   - How should intervention mechanisms (like action guards) be calibrated so that they only intervene when the human has added significant value?

- What learning mechanism(s) support agents to learn how users prefer to interact with them, thus reducing the number of interventions required over time?

b) Promising Approaches: Developing adaptive and context-sensitive interfaces, developing predictive models for determining when to intervene, supporting mixed initiative planning, and improving the agent's ability to explain its decisions.

c) Applications: Necessary for all autonomous system oversight across all types of autonomous systems; including robots, automation of business processes, and adaptive software assistants.

10.4 Formal Legal Alignment of HITL Taxonomies

The authors of Chiodo et al. (2025) point out that there is a significant disconnect between technical configurations of HITL (Human-in-the-Loop) and the legal framework that outlines the responsibilities of those who use HITL. The authors state that future research will need to create formal alignment of technical HITL configurations and legal frameworks that outline responsibility so as to avoid accountability misattribution and provide an evidentiary basis for regulatory decisions.

a) Key Research Questions:
   - How would you allocate legal responsibility among various configurations of HITL (e.g., from monitoring to deep interaction)?
   - What minimal amount of information and what minimal authority must a human operator have to be reasonably held accountable?
   - How can the law differentiate between meaningful human control and the concept of "responsibility laundering"?
   - What are the particular regulatory standards that should apply to the various forms of human-AI collaboration?

b) Promising Approaches:
   - Developing formal mathematical models that formally map the technical design of HITL to liability structures;
   - Conducting empirical research regarding how effective oversight processes are; and,
   - Establishing collaborative relationships between researchers in computer science and engineers and legal scholars.

c) Applications:

   It is critical for establishing compliance with regulatory requirements, for obtaining liability insurance and for ethically deploying HITL systems in environments that are highly regulated.

10.5 Reciprocal Human-Machine Learning Systems

In order to protect against deskilling of human operators as well as provide for sustained capability to monitor, Te'eni et al. (2025) advocate for the development of reciprocal learning systems which enable human expertise to develop with that of AI capabilities.

a) Key Research Questions:
   - What system designs allow humans to have an accurate representation of their mental model of an increasingly competent AI?
   - How do you avoid over-automating to protect core human competences?
   - What type of training methodology is best suited to train human expertise to manage AI oversight and collaboration?
   - How can a dynamic allocation of authority between human and AI occur based on competency assessment at real time?

b) Promising Approaches: Developing Explanatory AI (XAI), Implementing Mandatory Competence Maintenance Protocols, Creating Simulated Training Environments, Designing Adaptive Interfaces.

c) Applications: Extremely important to long term operational success in domains such as aviation, process control and medical, where it is required to preserve human mastery despite increased automation.

11. CONCLUSION

11.1 Synthesis of Key Findings

The following section presents four key findings from this Chapter's HITL framework synthesis.

The synthesis of HITL frameworks for high-risk applications are an essential tool to mitigate AI hallucination and provide accountability in these environments.

These four findings are:

a) Architectural diversity is needed for effective HITL implementation. There is no one HITL architecture that will work best for all applications; each application will require the development of a unique HITL architecture based on the risk profile and limitations of that application.

b) Multi-stage verification is needed to ensure comprehensive coverage of AI outputs. To effectively protect against hallucinations, developers need to implement multiple layers of verification. Each layer should utilize different methods to verify the accuracy of the output generated by the AI system (automated probes, symbolic checks, etc.).

c) Accountability needs to be built into HITL implementations. Simply adding a human into the process of generating an output does not automatically create accountability. Developers need to build accountability into their HITL implementations via transparent governance processes, immutable audit logs, and clearly defined role-based responsibilities that align with relevant laws and regulations.
d) Empirical evidence exists to demonstrate the effectiveness of HITL implementations. Studies have shown that HITL systems that have been designed properly can produce output at levels comparable to those produced by humans, improve the efficiency of the operation of the organization and provide measurable value across various industries.

11.2 Implications for Practice

Successful HITL (Human-in-the-Loop) deployments will require HITL practitioners to strategically plan and humanely operate HITL systems based upon:

a) The selection of an appropriate HITL architecture design based on a thorough examination of the risk profile of the application, regulatory environment, and operational needs of the organization.
b) An investment in HITL human factors as follows:
    - Design an interface that is user-friendly, intuitive, easy to use, etc., and limits cognitive load (the mental effort required to perform a task).
    - Develop training programs and offer them on an ongoing basis.
    - Implement a model of equitable pay for HITL Reviewers.
c) Developing formal governance processes as follows:
    - Define specific events or circumstances which will trigger review by an oversight body.
    - Clearly articulate the role and responsibility of each party involved in the process.
    - Create clear procedural guidelines for how issues or problems are escalated if necessary.
    - Create metrics to be used to monitor and improve the HITL system over time.
d) Planning for evolution (i.e. long-term adaptation), through the development of modular HITL architectures and implementing feedback mechanisms to allow for the HITL system to evolve with advancements in AI, changes in organizational requirements, and lessons learned during the operation of the HITL system.

11.3 Toward Trustworthy AI Through Human-AI Collaboration

HITL (Human-In-The-Loop) frameworks are a viable path toward creating trust in AI systems by combining human decision-making with automated machine efficiency. While HITL frameworks can be considered a means to create trustworthy AI systems, they cannot address all aspects of creating trust in AI systems.

Creating trustworthy AI systems is ultimately the result of a successful design of a sociotechnical system which requires:

a) Technical design elements that enable humans to have access to meaningful information and to control processes.
b) The organization's commitment to governance and investing in its human capital.
c) Legislative frameworks that correctly identify the technological realities of the system.
d) Perpetual research into how to improve the science of collaboration between humans and AI.

In terms of AI governance in the future, it will be multi-faceted, and HITL will serve as one of the essential elements of this multi-paradigm approach to AI governance. The research trajectories we outlined — from neurosymbolic discovery to reciprocal learning — provide a road map for developing HITL frameworks that are more advanced and accountable and thus ensuring that advanced AI systems remain tools whose exercise is directed by human expertise and aligned with societal values.

REFERENCES

Amirizaniani, M., Zhao, X., Shao, Y., Mireshghallah, F., Koyejo, S., Berg-Kirkpatrick, T., & Daumé, H., III. (2024). *Developing a framework for auditing large language models using human-in-the-loop*. arXiv.org. /arxiv.2402.09346DOI: 10.48550

Calvert, J. (2025). Principles and framework for the operationalisation of meaningful human control over autonomous systems. *Science and Engineering Ethics*, *31*(5), 27. Advance online publication. DOI: 10.1007/s11948-025-00554-z PMID: 40991137

Chiodo, M., Clifton, J., Farquhar, S., Hadfield-Menell, D., & Everitt, T. (2025). *Formalising human-in-the-loop: Computational reductions, failure modes, and legal-moral responsibility*. arXiv.org. /arxiv.2505.10426DOI: 10.48550

Corea, F., Bertolini, A., Bolognini, L., Luciano, F., & Memorandum, V. (2022). A principle-based approach to AI: The case for European Union and Italy. *AI & Society*, *37*(4), 1397–1408. DOI: 10.1007/s00146-022-01453-8

Duke, A. (2023). *Human-in-the-loop*. In Interpretable machine learning with Python (pp. 145–168). Apress. DOI: 10.1007/978-1-4842-9306-5_6

Gangavarapu, T. (2025). *Mastering AI governance*. Springer., DOI: 10.1007/978-3-031-93681-4

Iyenghar, P. (n.d.). *Clever Hans in the loop? A critical examination of ChatGPT in a human-in-the-loop framework for machinery functional safety risk analysis*. DOI: 10.3390/eng6020031

Krishnamoorthy, S. (2024). Enhancing responsible AGI development: Integrating human-in-the-loop approaches with blockchain-based smart contracts. *Journal of Advances in Mathematics and Computer Science*, *39*(9), 1–15. DOI: 10.9734/jamcs/2024/v39i91924

Monti, A., Bourgeois-Republique, C., Benfenati, E., & Paini, A. (2025). *The second life of hallucinations: A neurosymbolic framework for transforming errors into insights through human–AI collaboration*. Frontiers in Artificial Intelligence and Applications. DOI: 10.3233/FAIA250685

Mozannar, H., Bansal, G., Fourney, A., & Horvitz, E. (2025). *Magentic-UI: Towards human-in-the-loop agentic systems*. Microsoft Research.

Rahwan, I. (2017). Society-in-the-loop: Programming the algorithmic social contract. *Ethics and Information Technology*, *20*(1), 5–14. DOI: 10.1007/s10676-017-9430-8

Sachan, S., Alsamhi, S. H., Hawbani, A., Shvetsov, A. V., Shvetsova, S. V., & Gupta, S. K. (2025). *Responsible LLM deployment for high-stake decisions by decentralized technologies and human–AI interactions.* In *2025 International Conference on Human-Machine Systems (ICHMS)* (pp. 1–6). IEEE. DOI: 10.1109/ICHMS65439.2025.11154208

Selvam, P. K., Surendran, R., & Ramkumar, M. (2025). *Human-in-the-loop models for ethical AI grading: Combining AI speed with human ethical oversight.* Salud, Ciencia y Tecnología – Serie de Conferencias, 4, 413. DOI: 10.56294/ai2025413

Te'eni, D., Schwarz, A., & Newman, M. (2025). What it takes to control AI by design: Human learning. *AI & Society*. Advance online publication. DOI: 10.1007/s00146-025-02401-y

Westover, M. (n.d.). *Human–AI handovers: A dynamic authority reversal framework for trust calibration and transitional accountability*. Manuscript in preparation.

Chapter 7
Method Distinction for Hallucination Detection

Brijendra Parasnath Gupta
http://orcid.org/0000-0003-3597-350X
Siddhant College of Engineering, Pune, India

Ergashev Nuriddin Gayratovich
http://orcid.org/0000-0002-8274-6193
Karshi State Technical University, Karshi, Uzbekistan

Bekzod Madaminov
Mamun University, Urgench, Uzbekistan

ABSTRACT

Hallucination in large language models (LLMs) — the generation of content that is fluent and confident yet factually incorrect, logically inconsistent, or unsupported by available evidence — has emerged as one of the most consequential reliability challenges in contemporary AI development. As generative AI systems are deployed across high-stakes domains including clinical decision support, legal reasoning, scientific communication, and automated journalism, the consequences of undetected hallucination extend well beyond surface-level inaccuracy: they erode user trust, propagate misinformation, and undermine the foundational goal of building AI systems that are both truthful and aligned with human values. Addressing this challenge demands not only mitigation strategies but, crucially, robust and principled methods for detecting hallucination before, during, or after generation.

DOI: 10.4018/979-8-3373-7320-1.ch007

t © 2026, IGI Global Scientific Publishing. Copying or distributing in print or electronic forms without written permission of IGI Global Scientific Publishing is prohibited. Use of this chapter to enerative artificial intelligence (AI) technologies is expressly prohibited. The publisher reserves all rights to license its use for generative AI training and machine learning model development.

1. INTRODUCTION

The problem of hallucination has been rediscovered in the age-old natural language processing problem with the use of large language models (LLM) in an increasing number of applications, such as in clinical decision support and legal research, educational tutoring and financial analysis. The concept of hallucination is described as the generation of a text, which is fluent, coherent, and contextually plausible, but factually incorrect, internally contradictory, or not present in the existing evidence (Ji et al., 2023; Huang et al., 2025). In contrast to the classical scenario of factual errors, the contents of a hallucination cannot be determined with the assistance of a surface linguistic analysis since it may be, as it does not alter the stylistic or structural characteristics of the correct output.

This issue is not just an academic issue. Claims of hallucinations can spread misinformation, diminish credibility, and, in the most critical fields, lead to detrimental results, in knowledge-intensive activities when users rely on AI-generated content as a primary source of information. Studies have shown that the most powerful and up-to-date models can create hallucinated materials with non-trivial rates, and users often cannot differentiate the content with such materials and correct answers (Lin et al., 2022). This factual unreliability and fluency, combined, make hallucination detection one of the most impactful open problems in the research of LLM.

In reaction to this challenge, the research community has come up with an abundant and varied set of detection methods. Nevertheless, the discipline has grown in a rather piecemeal fashion with contributions made by various sub-disciplines such as information retrieval, natural language inference, probabilistic modelling, and model interpretability. Consequently, practitioners and researchers have a great challenge in getting a clear conceptual relationship between methods, determining which methods will be suitable in certain deployment situations and assessing the trade-offs different techniques involve.

This challenge is tackled in the chapter by giving a perfect taxonomy of hallucination detectors that systematically differentiate five major classes: (1) internal uncertainty-based detectors that learn hallucination with model-intrinsic signals (e.g. token probabilities and hidden state representations); (2) external retrieval-augmented detectors that learn hallucination with model outputs based on authoritative knowledge sources; (3) consistency-based detect

The chapter goes on in the following way. The conceptual background on the topic of hallucination under the circumstances of LLM is presented in section 2 and it provides the reason as to why there is reason to have a systematic difference of approach. In section 3, the taxonomy is provided and analysis of each category is presented. Section 4 makes a comparison of the methods performance. Section 5 speaks on practical selection criteria. The limitation and the research directions are discussed in section 6. Section 7 is the conclusion of the chapter.

2. BACKGROUND: HALLUCINATION IN LARGE LANGUAGE MODELS

2.1 Defining Hallucination

Hallucination in the context of LLMs has been defined in multiple, partly overlapping ways across the literature. Ji et al. (2023) offer a foundational definition in their survey of hallucination in natural language generation, distinguishing between faithfulness hallucinations — where model outputs deviate from the input or task specification — and factuality hallucinations — where outputs conflict with verifiable world knowledge. This distinction is consequential for detection, since faithfulness errors can, in principle, be assessed without external knowledge, while factuality errors require grounding in external evidence.

Zhang et al. (2024) situate hallucination within the broader challenge of alignment, characterising it as a manifestation of the gap between a model's learned statistical associations and the structured factual knowledge required for reliable real-world reasoning. Huang et al. (2025) provide a comprehensive taxonomy that further distinguishes among intrinsic hallucinations (contradicting source content), extrinsic hallucinations (introducing unverifiable claims), and self-contradictory hallucinations (producing internally inconsistent statements within a single response). The work of Mündler et al. (2024) specifically addresses self-contradictory hallucinations, introducing evaluation benchmarks and detection methods tailored to this under-explored sub-type.

Rawte et al. (2023) extend the definitional scope to multimodal and grounded generation settings, where hallucination may involve incorrect reference to visual or structured inputs. Bang et al. (2023) demonstrate that hallucination rates vary substantially across tasks and languages, challenging the assumption that a single detection methodology can provide adequate coverage across all deployment scenarios. These definitional complexities underscore the necessity of method distinction: different types of hallucination call for fundamentally different detection strategies.

2.2 Sources and Mechanisms

Understanding why LLMs hallucinate is prerequisite to understanding how detection methods are designed. At the most fundamental level, LLMs generate text by sampling from conditional probability distributions over token sequences, optimised through training on large corpora of human-produced text. This training process does not equip models with symbolic world models or explicit truth-tracking mechanisms; instead, models learn statistical regularities that may surface as fluent but factually inaccurate text when the relevant knowledge is absent, ambiguous, or conflicted in the training data.

Kadavath et al. (2022) investigate whether language models can accurately assess their own uncertainty, finding that models exhibit partially calibrated self-knowledge — that is, they are more likely to express uncertainty about claims they are more likely to get wrong — but that this calibration is imperfect and degrades for more complex or specialised queries. Xiong et al. (2024) extend this analysis, examining the capacity of LLMs to elicit confidence estimates through verbal prompting, chain-of-thought reasoning, and direct probability queries, finding substantial variation in reliability across methods. Burns et al. (2023) propose an unsupervised approach to extracting latent knowledge representations from model activations, suggesting that models may internally encode accurate information even when surface outputs are hallucinated.

Chuang et al. (2024) introduce the DoLa (Decoding by Contrasting Layers) framework, which exploits layer-wise distributional differences in transformer models to promote more factual decoding. This approach reflects a mechanistic understanding of hallucination as arising partly from the interference of lower-level linguistic patterns with higher-level factual representations during token generation. Shi et al. (2024) demonstrate that context-aware decoding — which amplifies the contribution of contextual evidence relative to parametric knowledge — reduces hallucination rates in retrieval-augmented settings.

2.3 The Need for Method Distinction

The heterogeneity of hallucination types and mechanisms has given rise to an equally heterogeneous landscape of detection approaches. As the field has matured, it has become apparent that no single detection strategy dominates across all hallucination types, model architectures, and task domains. Internal uncertainty methods excel at detecting knowledge boundary violations but require white-box access that is unavailable for many deployed systems. External retrieval methods provide factual grounding but are constrained by the coverage and currency of available knowledge bases. Consistency methods are broadly applicable but rely on the assumption that hallucinations manifest as inconsistencies — an assumption that does not hold for all hallucination types.

Pan et al. (2023) survey automated correction strategies for LLMs, emphasising that effective correction pipelines must be coupled with reliable detection methods, and that the choice of detection approach shapes both the precision of identified errors and the tractability of correction. Xie et al. (2023) demonstrate that self-reminder prompting strategies can partially mitigate hallucination at inference time, but that such approaches require prior knowledge of likely hallucination patterns. These observations collectively motivate the systematic method distinction undertaken in this chapter.

3. TAXONOMY OF HALLUCINATION DETECTION METHODS

The following taxonomy organises hallucination detection methods into five principal categories, each reflecting a distinct theoretical orientation and practical methodology. Figure 1 presents an overview of this taxonomy. The categories are not mutually exclusive — several contemporary methods combine elements from multiple categories — but they represent coherent and analytically useful distinctions.

Figure 1. Taxonomy of Hallucination Detection Methods.

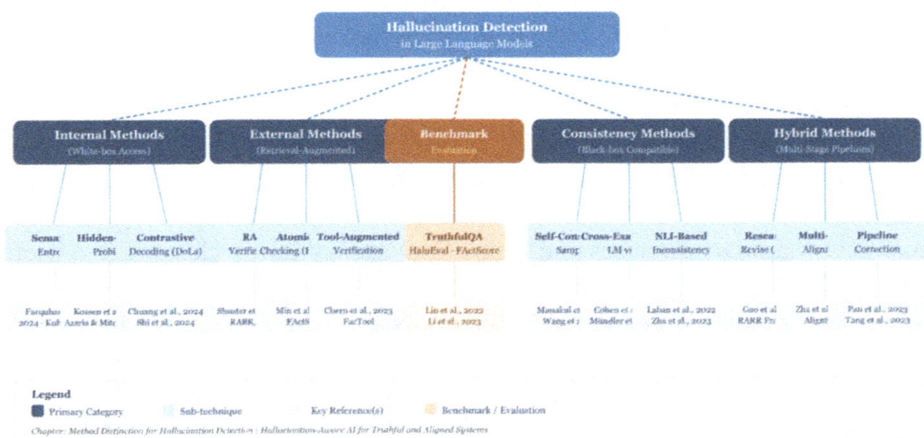

Figure 1 illustrates the four primary branches — Internal, External, Consistency, and Hybrid — reflect distinct theoretical orientations and practical methodologies for detecting hallucinated content in LLM outputs.

3.1 Internal Uncertainty-Based Methods

3.1.1 Principles and Foundations

Such methods of hallucination recognition based on internal uncertainty, which do not consider any external source of knowledge, analyze the signals provided by internal computations of the model. The principle is that the outputs of hallucinations are linked to distinctive internal states, high uncertainty in the probability distribution of tokens, low confidence in intermediate representations, or typical patterns in the activations of the hidden layer of the model, which can be useful indicators of factual unreliability.

Kadavath et al. (2022) present some of the first indications of this assumption and show that language models have part-calibrated self-knowledge: the models attribute more probability to statements that they are more prone to produce correctly. Kuhn et al. (2023) codify this intuition under the notion of semantic uncertainty, which approximates the uncertainty of model output on a semantic scale, as opposed to the surface level, to the issue that semantically equivalent outputs carried out linguistically should not be considered evidence of uncertainty.

3.1.2 Semantic Entropy and Probing

Farquhar et al. (2024) apply the semantic entropy framework to a realistic hallucination detector, and show that semantic entropy (calculated by clustering semantically similar responses and estimating entropy in the clusters) is a useful signal to identify confabulated responses in a variety of question-answering problems. Their findings, which are published in Nature, are a milestone proving the ability of model-internal signals to attain high performance in the task of detecting hallucinations, without any external knowledge sources.

Kossen et al. (2024) build upon this with semantic entropy probes, which learn lightweight classifier probes with the representations on the hidden state of the model to identify high-uncertainty outputs. Probe-based method has better detection performance as compared to sampling-based semantic entropy framework and has significantly fewer forward passes, which makes it more scalable to deployment in latency-limited contexts. Azaria and Mitchell (2023) show the complementary results based on probing classifiers, which are trained on internal activation patterns, they discover that the model internal state is consistently reliable at distinguishing between false and truthful statements in a wide range of topics.

Varshney et al. (2023) introduce a real-time detection system that detects low-confidence generation steps and activates validation processes before the response is finished to essentially incorporate uncertainty estimation into the generation pipeline.

Burns et al. (2023) are more radical and aim to find latent knowledge in language models unsupervised, they find that models can encode factual knowledge that is accurate and reliable, but not reliably surfaced in the generated output.

The DoLa decoding method (Chuang et al., 2024) is a contribution that compares the probability distributions generated by the previous and subsequent transformer layers, and maximizes the factual content at the cost of superficial pattern-matching. This strategy is based on the hypothesis that the concentration of factual knowledge is in later, higher levels of the transformer, and that contrastive decoding can facilitate more faithful generation. Shi et al. (2024) propose context-aware decoding as a complement method and demonstrate that the explicit weighting of contextual evidence can alleviate hallucination under retrieval-augmented conditions.

3.2 External Retrieval-Augmented Verification Methods

3.2.1 Principles and Knowledge Grounding

Augmented verification algorithms with external retrieval recognise hallucinations through comparisons of model predictions to expert external source of knowledge. These procedures are based on the assumption that factually correct assertions can be verified by being recoverable in trustworthy corpora whereas hallucinated assertions will not be sufficiently supported in such corpora. This fact-checking-like approach in journalism is conceptually similar to grounding-based methods, but in the computational setting of LLM evaluation.

Shuster et al. (2021) demonstrate in an initial study that retrieval augmentation greatly reduces hallucination in conversational systems and demonstrates that knowledge grounding is a viable hallucination reduction and detection methodology. Their research proves that given models retrieve evidence contributes significantly more factual responses and the relevance of the information that is retrieved can serve as a proxy information in understanding that the response obtained is factual.

3.2.2 Atomic Fact Verification: FActScore

Min et al. (2023) introduce a framework called FActScore (Fine-grained Atomic Evaluation of Factual Precision), which disaggregates long-form generated text into atomic factual claims, identifies suitable passages in a reference corpus, and measures the support of the atomic claim by passages it retrieves. FActScore is an important methodological improvement that extends the document-level analysis to claim-level analysis, which fine-grained part of the responses to otherwise correct answers can be found.

The FActScore model is designed to remove a severe lack of finer assessment processes: a document with a single claim that was hallucinated and high numbers of correct claims would get an inappropriate high rating on document-level assessments. The fact that text can be broken up into atomic claims supports FActScore in getting a precision-oriented measure of the percentage of claims that can be justified adequately by evidence retrieved. This is a design that is in line with the practical problem that a single hallucinatory experience, a misconstrued citation, an incorrect dosage of a drug, a fake legal precedent, is fatal in deployed application.

This method, which is used to generalize to multi-task and multi-domain cases, is the FacTool framework of Chern et al. (2023), which provides a tool-enhanced verification pipeline, which can call external APIs, execute code, and ask structured knowledge bases, in addition to unstructured text retrieval. FacTool is especially useful to test code generation, mathematical reasoning, and structured data problems in which text retrieval is inadequate, due to this flexibility.

3.3 Consistency-Based Detection Methods

3.3.1 Self-Consistency and Sampling-Based Approaches

Methods of consistency-based detection detect hallucination by examining agreement, or disagreement, between multiple model outputs, or between model outputs and other sources of verification. The hypothesis behind it is that since hallucinated content is generated by an unreliable inference process, as opposed to a robust knowledge retrieval process, it will be inconsistent: various sampling runs will yield conflicting claims, or the claims made by the model will be inconsistent with the information provided in the same context.

Wang et al. (2023) show that self-consistency, which forms several reasoning chains and the most common answer, can significantly enhance factual accuracy in the chain-of-thought prompting environment. Although framed mainly as an accuracy improvement method, self-consistency is also implicitly a hallucination mitigation method: minor claims generated on a small fraction of sampling runs stand a higher chance of being indicative of hallucination, compared to majority claims.

Manakul et al. (2023) create SelfCheckGPT, an unbiased hallucination detector based on black-box, a zero-resource hallucination detector that realises this intuition by systematically comparing many responses that are stochastically sampled. SelfCheckGPT does not need access to model internals, external knowledge base or ground truth labels, but rather uses the statistical regularity that consistent facts are more likely to be replicated on independent samples than hallucinated detail. The approach has competitive detection performance on a variety of benchmarks, and is model architecture-agnostic, which allows it to be widely applied to proprietary systems.

3.3.2 Cross-Examination and NLI-Based Methods

Cohen et al. (2023) propose a cross-examination model, LM vs LM, where one language model questions the claims of another by asking specific follow-up questions, and the original claims are compared to the answers they give when asked directly. This method is based on the fact that the hallucinated assertions tend not to be in line with more particular contextual data: a model that is sure to assert an erroneous thing will be able to withdraw or disapprove the same assertion when inquiring about details to back it up.

In particular, Mündler et al. (2024) pay attention to self-contradictory hallucinations, which they establish in the form of evaluation benchmarks and detection approaches that systematically detect cases in which the output of a model includes mutually inconsistent claims within a particular response. Their job brings to light a sub-type of hallucination that internal uncertainty techniques and those based on retrieval can be unable to detect, as in the case of self-contradictions, there can be no low-confidence generation or conflicting evidence.

Consistency-based detection is complemented by natural language inference (NLI) models. Kryscinski et al. (2020) apply NLI to abstractive summarisation, entailing prediction, to determine the logical consistency of generated summaries with their source document. Laban et al. (2022) introduce SummaC, that reconsiders NLI-based inconsistency detection by a more fine-grained sentence-level consistency framework, recognising the drawbacks of document-level NLI in the detection of localised inaccuracies. This method is generalised by Zha et al. (2023) in terms of AlignScore, an all-in-one alignment task that is trained on a variety of consistency evaluation tasks.

3.4 Benchmark-Driven Evaluation Frameworks

Evaluation frameworks based on benchmarking measure hallucination by using standardised test sets to test model behaviour in a diversity of factuality problems. In contrast to deployment-oriented detection algorithms, benchmark frameworks are usually designed to aid in the evaluation and comparison of models, and they offer reproducible and interpretable measures of progress in hallucination reduction.

Lin et al. (2022) present TruthfulQA, a benchmark that consists of 817 questions that seek to investigate the LLM tendencies to imitate human falsehoods plausible-sounding but false beliefs that are prevalent in the training data population. TruthfulQA is conspicuous in that bigger models are not thought to be more truthful, but in fact, more prone to generate human-mimicking lies, disproving naive beliefs that scale is a panacea to hallucination.

Li et al. (2023) introduce HaluEval, a large-scale hallucination evaluation benchmark that encompasses question answering, dialogue, and summarisation tasks, annotated with fine-grained type annotations to the hallucinated and non-hallucinated samples. HaluEval allows to make a comparative analysis of detection methods with respect to the type of hallucination and the domain of the task with an understanding of the comparative advantages and disadvantages of various methods. Bang et al. (2023) generalize benchmark evaluation to multilingual and multimodal cases, evaluating the patterns of hallucinations of ChatGPT across languages and modalities, showing that there is significant cross-lingual difference in the rates of hallucinations.

Laban et al. (2023) propose the SummEdits benchmark, explicitly to evaluate the ability of LLM at all factual reasoning on summarisation editing tasks, a fine-grained probe of whether models can identify and repair factual errors in existing summaries. Pagnoni et al. (2021) and Maynez et al. (2020) provide previous benchmark research on faithfulness and factuality in abstractive summarisation, providing the FRANK benchmark, which has been used as a benchmark in evaluation work.

Systematic work on factual consistency evaluation tools in summarisation FactGraph: Ribeiro et al. (2022) introduce FactGraph, a semantic graph-based evaluation tool, Fabbri et al. (2022) develop QAFactEval, which uses question generating and answering to assess consistency, and Honovich et al. (2021) introduce Q2, a knowledge-grounded dialogue evaluation tool. Fierro and Sogaaard (2022) investigate the consistency of facts in multilingual pre-trained models and show that the problem of factuality is not a specific feature of systems in English language.

3.5 Hybrid and Multi-Stage Pipeline Methods

Hybrid and multi stage pipeline approaches address hallucination detection by taking a combination of features across multiple categories, blending the various detection signals to bring about greater coverage and increased robustness. The approaches are indicative of the fact that no one single methodology of detection is sufficient to detect all the entire range of the hallucination types, and the complementary advantages can be used with principled integration.

Gao et al. (2023) introduce RARR (Researching and Revising what language models say), an evidence collection method that integrates retrieval evidence collection with language models-based revision to initially search and subsequently revise factual assertions. RARR shows that the same LLM capacity to generate fluently can be applied to a task of checking facts, forming a closed-loop system where models are applied to analyze and correct their own predictions. This self-correcting application of LLM capabilities is a significant paradigm of scalable mitigation of hallucinations.

Pan et al. (2023) represent the state of the field of automated correction strategies, with retrieval-augmented correction, prompting-based revision, and fine-tuning-based approaches being the main ones. Their comparison shows that the best correction pipelines have both reliable detection (to determine what claims should be revised) and specific retrieval (to base revisions on evidence) and limited generation (to create minimally edited corrections without altering the overall response structure).

Tang et al. (2023) perform a systematic study of factual errors in summarisation, comparing patterns of errors among various models, datasets and error detection methods. They emphasise the significance of diversity in errors, which is that different systems of summarisation yield qualitatively different error patterns, and indicate that hybrid systems, as compared to single-method systems, are more able to capture this diversity. The practical issue of long-document hallucination detection is addressed by Lattimer et al. (2023), which formulates methods that retain accuracy in detecting hallucinations in longer contexts than the simpler methods.

Cao et al. (2022) analyse the factually hallucinated but world-accurate statements in abstractive summarisation, where models add external information that coincidentally is true even when not based on the document. This phenomenon, which they refer to as factual hallucination, is problematic to purely source-consistency-based detection models, which would report such statements as errors even when they are factual. To look at such subtleties, hybrid approaches that combine source-consistency and world-knowledge verification cues will be needed.

Figure 2. A generalised hallucination detection pipeline.

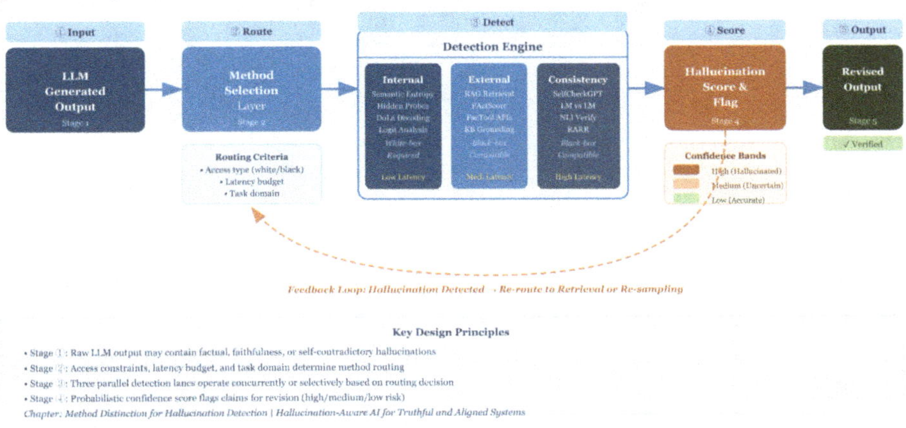

Figure 2 illustrates the Model outputs pass through a method selection layer that routes to appropriate detection engines. Detected hallucinations trigger retrieval augmentation or re-sampling, with a feedback loop enabling iterative refinement of the final output.

4. COMPARATIVE ANALYSIS AND EMPIRICAL PERFORMANCE

4.1 Performance Across Method Categories

The variability of evaluation standards, scope of activity, and model designs between studies makes it hard to compare hallucinated detection techniques in a systematic way. Nevertheless, a number of regularities of empirical results in terms of the cumulative literature are present. A comparative summary of the representative approaches in key performance dimensions is provided in Figure 3.

Figure 3. Comparative Performance of Hallucination Detection Methods.

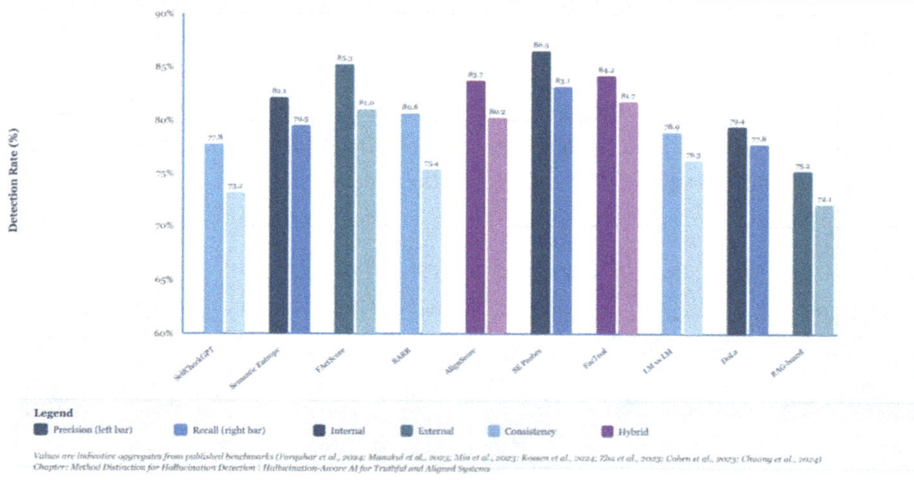

Figure 3 shows Precision and recall values are indicative aggregates published benchmarks. Computational cost is the ratio of resource requirements of inference-time code.

Internal uncertainty methods such as the semantic entropy and hidden-state probing are some of the highest detection accuracy in the questions-answering problem where factual hallucinations exist. According to Farquhar et al. (2024), semantic entropy is much better than token-level entropy and direct sampling-based baselines and the probe-based implementation of Kossen et al. (2024) has further improvements at lower computational costs. However, these methods require white-box access to model internals, and therefore can only be used in open-weight systems. The augmented strategies such as FActScore are very precise on knowledge intensive tasks in case the retrieval corpora can be trusted. The specificity of FActScore design makes it particularly well-adapted to long-form assessment of generation, in which the proportion of justified claims provides a principled assessment of the quality of factual claims. But retrieval quality limits the accuracy of detection and it is less accurate on claims in specialised or temporally recent areas that are not well-sampled in corpora. Methods based on consistency, such as SelfCheckGPT and LM vs LM, have competitive performance on a diverse set of tasks and model types without model internals or external knowledge bases. The black-box compatibility of SelfCheckGPT is a considerable practical benefit, which allows hallucination detection to proprietary closed-weight systems. The main cost it is latency: several sampling passes have to be made, which grows inference time significantly compared to single-pass algorithms.

4.2 Task and Domain Variation

The performance of hallucination detection is not the same across domains and tasks. Approaches that are very accurate at factual question answering can be very different at summarisation, dialogue or code generation tasks. In their systematic review, Ji et al. (2023) report a wide range of hallucination rates in different types of tasks, with tasks that use open-ended generation tend to yield higher hallucination rates compared to constrained tasks with known ground truth.

The results of the multilingual study of Bang et al. (2023) indicate that the patterns of hallucinations differ significantly among languages and that models have higher rates of hallucinations in languages with lower resources where training data are less dense. This finding is supported by Fierro and Sogaaard (2022) when it comes to the factual consistency of the multilingual pre-trained models. The observations above indicate that the detection techniques tested in mono-lingual (English) settings might give inaccurate performance estimates when used in multilingual deployment situations.

In a survey of foundation model hallucinations, Rawte et al. (2023) note domain-specific hallucination challenges, with medical, legal or scientific domains posing specific challenges because of the specialisation and precision of factual claims in these areas, alongside the under-representation of domain-specific technical content in general training corpora. High-stakes deployments will probably require domain-adaptive detection algorithms that use specialised knowledge bases and domain-specific performance metrics.

5. PRACTICAL CRITERIA FOR METHOD SELECTION

The variety of the existing techniques of hallucination detection, and their different performance characteristics across tasks and domains, require principled guidelines to select the method in the framework of practical deployment. This section determines important dimensions to be considered when evaluating methods, and advises how to choose and blend approaches that fit particular needs.

Table 1. Hallucination Detection Method Categories: Comparative Summary

Method Category	Key Techniques	Limitations	Strengths	Ideal Use Case
Internal / Uncertainty-Based	Logit analysis, semantic entropy, hidden state probing	White-box access required; computationally intensive	High sensitivity to model internals; no external resources	Real-time systems with model access
External / Retrieval-Based	Knowledge grounding, RAG pipelines, fact databases	Retrieval latency; dependent on knowledge base quality	Grounded in external truth; scalable across domains	Knowledge-intensive QA; factual generation
Consistency-Based	Self-sampling, cross-examination, NLI verification	Multiple inference passes; slower throughput	No model internals needed; black-box compatible	Dialogue systems; summarization
Benchmark-Based	TruthfulQA, HaluEval, FActScore atomic evaluation	Static benchmarks may not reflect deployment settings	Standardized evaluation; reproducible metrics	Model evaluation and comparison
Hybrid / Multi-Stage	Combines retrieval, consistency, and scoring pipelines	High complexity; resource-intensive deployment	Best detection performance across diverse domains	Production-grade AI systems; high-stakes domains

5.1 Model Access Constraints

The most basic selection criteria is that the model under consideration is white-box accessible or black-box accessible. Internal uncertainty statistics (semantic entropy, hidden-state probing, contrastive decoding, etc.) involve information about model internals: the probability of a token, the activation of a hidden layer, or the attention weight. The techniques cannot be directly applied to closed-weight proprietary APIs, and would have to be modified, which greatly restricts their applicability.

Black-box methods like SelfCheckGPT, LM vs LM, and retrieval-enhanced verification methods, merely operate on model inputs and outputs and do not require any information about the model computations. This characteristic renders them very general to open-weight systems as well as closed-weight systems. The trade-off is that black-box methods are not able to take advantage of the possibly more informative internal signals that white-box methods have access to, which in certain environments means that the sensitivity of some types of hallucinations is detectably lower. The black-box consistency and retrieval-based approaches can be regarded as the two approaches that may be regarded as the main alternative to the representatives of the proprietary systems.

5.2 Latency and Computational Requirements

Latency is a practical constraint, which significantly constrains the practicality of sampling-intensive detection methods. To do the comparisons, SelfCheckGPT uses a few additional forward passes, so inference costs are multiplied by the number of samples sampled, which is roughly the number of comparisons. Similarly, other cross-examination strategies such as LM vs LM have more turns of dialogue which increase the inference latency. They can be accepted in offline assessment systems, but are not permissible in real-time systems with response times of less than a second.

A more interesting compromise is provided by probe-based approaches, such as the one by Kossen et al. (2024): trained probes can be used to detect by performing a single forward pass through a lightweight classifier on intermediate activations. This is the most appropriate method since it is the one that best performs in terms of the near-state-of-the-art performance of detection with the lowest overhead of inference and therefore when it comes to white-box deployments with time constraints. The token-level uncertainty estimates using logit distributions add no additional computational complexity, and provide approximate hallucination cues.

The latency of the retrieval pipeline, usually one to three seconds on a dense retrieval system that is well-optimised, is added by retrieval-augmented verification, but can be compensated by amortising the cost across multiple claims with batch verification. FActScore-style Verification of atomic claims can be parallelized over claims, with NLP preprocessing overhead (claim decomposition, coreference resolution) but can be made to scale to a satisfactory throughput in most non-real-time applications.

5.3 Task-Specific Considerations

Besides factors of access and latency, the nature of the generation task should be considered to select the method. External retrieval-augmented verification is the closest to the purpose of the evaluation in knowledge-intensive factual question answering, where the factual accuracy is paramount. FacTool and FactScore suit this scenario well with the grounding being on the claim level which directly captures the factual accuracy.

In the case of dialogue and conversational systems, where coherence and adherence to the conversational context are the main issues, as well as factual accuracy, consistency-based algorithms, like SelfCheckGPT and LM vs LM are better suited, along with source-consistency verification, where the source documents are consulted. Honovich et al. (2021) Q2 and NLI-based methods like SummaC find solutions to the particular issues of knowledge-based dialogue evaluation.

In the example of a summarisation task, the already existing literature on the evaluation of factual consistency in summarisation (like FactGraph, QAFactEval, AlignScore, FRANK and other benchmarks) provides an already existing detection and evaluation tool. Tang et al. (2023) meta-analysis is especially valuable to gain an idea of the performance of various error detection tools compared to each other in the context of the various types of summarisation errors.

More appropriate detection signals than the text-based consistency or retrieval methods are specialised tools, such as the code verification component of FacTool, which compares generated code with test cases and calls external APIs, and are more appropriate in code generation tasks and structured output tasks. The particular type of factual errors in code, logical errors, API misuse, hallucinated function signatures, needs detection strategies, sensitive to the formal properties of the programming languages.

6. LIMITATIONS, CHALLENGES, AND FUTURE DIRECTIONS

6.1 Fundamental Limitations of Current Methods

Although this has made great progress, it is important to mention that hallucination detection is an unsolved problem with a number of basic limitations. A key problem on this front is that there is no single ground truth of factual correctness: factual knowledge in the real world is decentralized, dynamic and sometimes controversial, and it cannot be indicated by a single reference point through which factual claims can be vindicated. The techniques based on retrieval of fixed corpora assume the limitations, biases, and coverage deficiencies of the corpora.

A phenomenon of source-inconsistent claims of Cao et al. (2022) is the factual truth that represents a significant conflict of faithfulness and factuality as the objectives of evaluation. A content optimisation strategy that is effective in one dimension can be biased against content that does well in the other dimension. This contradiction cannot be resolved in current detection models and its eradication might require more complex assessment criteria that can independently assess the consistentness of source and the correctness of world knowledge.

Huang et al. (2025) list several other open problems in their broad survey: it is challenging to detect hallucinations in the long view, none of the current benchmarks would address non-English and non-Western domain of knowledge, and in multimodal and embodied AI systems, it is tricky to test hallucination. Rawte et al. (2023) also note that it becomes particularly difficult to detect hallucinations when the emerging and developing factual claims, i.e., events that occurred post-model training or in an area with a rapid rate of change such as medicine or law are detected.

6.2 The Adversarial Hallucination Problem

A new area of study at the interface of hallucination and AI safety is adversarial hallucination - the intentional production of hallucinated material by means of expertly designed inputs. Xie et al. (2023) investigate jailbreaking attacks on ChatGPT, and suggest self-reminder prompting as a partial mitigation, though recognizes that adversarial inputs that induce hallucination are a different threat model not completely addressed by detection strategies designed to deal with naturally occurring hallucination.

The challenge suggests the existence of detection methods robust to distributional shift - that can be used effectively when the input distribution has been distorted to evade detection. Adversarial robust hallucination detection is a research problem that is substantially open, and that has ties to the literature, in general, on adversarial examples and robust machine learning.

6.3 Future Research Directions

This chapter provides an analysis that opens up a number of potential lines of research. First of all, the establishment of coherent measurement systems, which could be used to measure different forms of hallucinations like factual inaccuracy, source incompatibility, and self-contradiction through a single consistent measure would be of significant contribution to the field. The existing practice of evaluation uses a collection of task-focused benchmarks and measures that makes cross-method comparison and progress measurement difficult.

Second, it is a notable open issue to incorporate the time dynamics in hallucination detectors. The existing retrieval-augmented techniques are constrained by the timeliness of knowledge base used, which might not cover recent occurrences or recent information. It would also be of great help to come up with schemes that may be used to ascertain validity of claims over time, to draw the boundary between timeless and time-dependent factual statements as well as to include access to real-time knowledge in order to expand the scope of detection.

Third, inference-efficient, lightweight methods of detection are still in development, which makes their use feasible. Even though probe-based approaches as suggested by Kossen et al. (2024) are an effective plan, greater efforts are needed to develop strategies that would not compromise detectivity but still be able to operate within the strict limits of the latency of production systems. One such promising path would be distillation of detection knowledge, using expensive oracle algorithms, into the effective inference-time systems.

Fourth, support of hallucination detection to multi-modal systems - i.e. where hallucination may be erroneous references to visual, audio or structured input - is a frontier which current predominantly text-based methods are ill-equipped to answer. With the growing usage of multimodal LLMs in application, more multimodal detection frameworks are needed to be developed. Fifth, developing personalised and domain-adaptive detection algorithms that can be adapted to specific deployment environments, knowledge domain, and user communities would enhance the usefulness of detection systems in the broad range of practical applications.

7. CONCLUSION

This chapter has given a systematised taxonomy and comparative analysis of methods of hallucination detection in large language models, and has categorised a rich and continuously growing body of work in this field into five coherent groups, namely: internal uncertainty-based methods, external retrieval-augmented verification, consistency-based methods, benchmark-driven evaluation systems, and multi-stage pipelines. The chapter has covered each one of these categories in terms of theoretical foundations, representative techniques, empirical performance characteristics and deployment issues.

The primary benefit of such a taxonomy is that it assists in establishing the conceptual and practical boundaries of the detection strategies, and, consequently, scientists and practitioners can make principled choices in the existing strategies. The discussion demonstrates the nonexistence of any single method that would be high-sensitivity and low-latency with white-box access, or even low-latency and factual grounding and consistency, but above all, all approaches are more likely to do well at the expense of complexity.

The research on hallucinations detection has already made an impressive progress in a comparatively brief period, as the necessity to surmount the constraints of reliability of deployed LLMs is quite strong. The major findings (SelfCheckGPT, FActScore, Semantic Entropy, TruthfulQA, RARR, and DoLa) have provided sound methodological bases that provide good starting points in the further research and in practice. However, there are still some key issues: the lack of universal ground truth, the issue of adversarial hallucination, the scope of contemporary multilingual and multimodal coverage, and the currency of temporal knowledge.

The obstacles will be addressed in a long-term interdisciplinary campaign, which will involve the application of the natural language processing, information retrieval, probabilistic modeling and AI safety study tools. As more and more LLMs find their way into consequential use in medicine, law, education, and the public information systems, the development of reliable, efficient and widely applicable hallucination detectors is not just an academic research problem but a necessitating implementation policy to implement AI responsibly. In that direction has been the tendency of this chapter to provide the taxonomy and analysis that can be of service to such an endeavor: to describe the landscape of the current approaches and what must be considered in their selection and development.

REFERENCES

Azaria, A., & Mitchell, T. (2023). The internal state of an LLM knows when it's lying. In Findings of the Association for Computational Linguistics: EMNLP 2023 (pp. 967–976). Association for Computational Linguistics. DOI: 10.18653/v1/2023.findings-emnlp.68

Bang, Y., Cahyawijaya, S., Lee, N., Dai, W., Su, D., Wilie, B., Lovenia, H., Ji, Z., Yu, T., Chung, W., Do, Q. V., Xu, Y., & Fung, P. (2023). A multitask, multilingual, multimodal evaluation of ChatGPT on reasoning, hallucination, and interactivity. In *Proceedings of the 13th International Joint Conference on Natural Language Processing and the 3rd Conference of the Asia-Pacific Chapter of the Association for Computational Linguistics* (Volume 1: Long Papers) (pp. 675–718). DOI: 10.18653/v1/2023.ijcnlp-main.45

Burns, C., Ye, H., Klein, D., & Steinhardt, J. (2023). Discovering latent knowledge in language models without supervision. In The Eleventh International Conference on Learning Representations. OpenReview. DOI: 10.48550/arXiv.2212.03827

Cao, M., Dong, Y., & Cheung, J. C. K. (2022). Hallucinated but factual! Inspecting the factuality of hallucinations in abstractive summarization. In *Proceedings of the 60th Annual Meeting of the Association for Computational Linguistics* (Volume 1: Long Papers) (pp. 3340–3354). Association for Computational Linguistics. DOI: 10.18653/v1/2022.acl-long.236

Chern, I., Chern, S., Chen, S., Yuan, W., Feng, K., Zhou, C., He, J., Neubig, G., & Liu, P. (2023). FacTool: Factuality detection in generative AI—A tool augmented framework for multi-task and multi-domain scenarios. arXiv preprint arXiv:2307.13528. https://doi.org//arXiv.2307.13528DOI: 10.48550

Chuang, Y.-S., Xie, Y., Luo, H., Kim, Y., Glass, J., & He, P. (2024). DoLa: Decoding by contrasting layers improves factuality in large language models. In The Twelfth International Conference on Learning Representations. OpenReview. DOI: 10.48550/arXiv.2309.03883

Cohen, R., Hamri, M., Geva, M., & Globerson, A. (2023). LM vs LM: Detecting factual errors via cross examination. In *Proceedings of the 2023 Conference on Empirical Methods in Natural Language Processing* (pp. 12621–12640). Association for Computational Linguistics. DOI: 10.18653/v1/2023.emnlp-main.778

Fabbri, A. R., Kryściński, W., McCann, B., Xiong, C., Socher, R., & Radev, D. (2022). QAFactEval: Improved QA-based factual consistency evaluation for summarization. In *Proceedings of the 2022 Conference of the North American Chapter of the Association for Computational Linguistics: Human Language Technologies* (pp. 2587–2601). Association for Computational Linguistics. DOI: 10.18653/v1/2022.naacl-main.187

Farquhar, S., Kossen, J., Kuhn, L., & Gal, Y. (2024). Detecting hallucinations in large language models using semantic entropy. *Nature*, *630*(8017), 625–630. DOI: 10.1038/s41586-024-07421-0 PMID: 38898292

Fierro, C., & Søgaard, A. (2022). Factual consistency of multilingual pretrained language models. In Findings of the Association for Computational Linguistics: ACL 2022 (pp. 3046–3052). Association for Computational Linguistics. DOI: 10.18653/v1/2022.findings-acl.240

Gao, L., Dai, Z., Pasupat, P., Chen, A., Chaganty, A. T., Fan, Y., Zhao, V., Lao, N., Lee, H., Juan, D.-C., & Guu, K. (2023). RARR: Researching and revising what language models say, using language models. In *Proceedings of the 61st Annual Meeting of the Association for Computational Linguistics* (Volume 1: Long Papers) (pp. 16856–16872). Association for Computational Linguistics. DOI: 10.18653/v1/2023.acl-long.910

Honovich, O., Choshen, L., Aharoni, R., Neeman, E., Szpektor, I., & Abend, O. (2021). Q^2: Evaluating factual consistency in knowledge-grounded dialogues via question generation and question answering. In *Proceedings of the 2021 Conference on Empirical Methods in Natural Language Processing* (pp. 7856–7870). Association for Computational Linguistics. DOI: 10.18653/v1/2021.emnlp-main.619

Huang, L., Yu, W., Ma, W., Zhong, W., Feng, Z., Wang, H., Chen, Q., Peng, W., Feng, X., Qin, B., & Liu, T. (2025). A survey on hallucination in large language models: Principles, taxonomy, challenges, and open questions. *ACM Transactions on Information Systems*, *43*(2), 42. Advance online publication. DOI: 10.1145/3703155

Ji, Z., Lee, N., Frieske, R., Yu, T., Su, D., Xu, Y., Ishii, E., Bang, Y., Madotto, A., & Fung, P. (2023). Survey of hallucination in natural language generation. *ACM Computing Surveys*, *55*(12), 1–38. DOI: 10.1145/3571730

Kadavath, S., Conerly, T., Askell, A., Henighan, T., Drain, D., Perez, E., Schiefer, N., Das, S., Kernion, J., Landau, L., Jones, A., Ndousse, K., Chen, N., Bowman, S., Ziegler, D., Clark, J., Joseph, N., Ganguli, D., Hernandez, D., . . . Kaplan, J. (2022). Language models (mostly) know what they know. arXiv preprint arXiv:2207.05221. https://doi.org//arXiv.2207.05221DOI: 10.48550

Kossen, J., Farquhar, S., Gal, Y., & Rainforth, T. (2024). Semantic entropy probes: Robust and cheap hallucination detection in LLMs. In The Thirteenth International Conference on Learning Representations. OpenReview. DOI: 10.48550/arXiv.2406.15927

Kryscinski, W., McCann, B., Xiong, C., & Socher, R. (2020). Evaluating the factual consistency of abstractive text summarization. In *Proceedings of the 2020 Conference on Empirical Methods in Natural Language Processing* (pp. 9332–9346). Association for Computational Linguistics. DOI: 10.18653/v1/2020.emnlp-main.750

Kuhn, L., Gal, Y., & Farquhar, S. (2023). Semantic uncertainty: Linguistic invariances for uncertainty estimation in natural language generation. In The Eleventh International Conference on Learning Representations. OpenReview. DOI: 10.48550/arXiv.2302.09664

Laban, P., Schnabel, T., Bennett, P. N., & Hearst, M. A. (2022). SummaC: Re-visiting NLI-based models for inconsistency detection in summarization. *Transactions of the Association for Computational Linguistics*, *10*, 163–177. DOI: 10.1162/tacl_a_00453

Laban, P., Schnabel, T., Bennett, P. N., & Hearst, M. A. (2023). SummEdits: Measuring LLM ability at factual reasoning through the lens of summarization. In *Proceedings of the 2023 Conference on Empirical Methods in Natural Language Processing* (pp. 9662–9676). Association for Computational Linguistics. DOI: 10.18653/v1/2023.emnlp-main.600

Lattimer, M., Blair, P., & Chen, I. (2023). Fast and accurate factual inconsistency detection over long documents. In *Proceedings of the 2023 Conference on Empirical Methods in Natural Language Processing* (pp. 1045–1060). Association for Computational Linguistics. DOI: 10.18653/v1/2023.emnlp-main.105

Li, J., Cheng, X., Zhao, X., Nie, J.-Y., & Wen, J.-R. (2023). HaluEval: A large-scale hallucination evaluation benchmark for large language models. In *Proceedings of the 2023 Conference on Empirical Methods in Natural Language Processing* (pp. 6449–6464). Association for Computational Linguistics. DOI: 10.18653/v1/2023.emnlp-main.397

Lin, S., Hilton, J., & Evans, O. (2022). TruthfulQA: Measuring how models mimic human falsehoods. In *Proceedings of the 60th Annual Meeting of the Association for Computational Linguistics* (Volume 1: Long Papers) (pp. 3214–3252). Association for Computational Linguistics. DOI: 10.18653/v1/2022.acl-long.229

Manakul, P., Liusie, A., & Gales, M. J. F. (2023). SelfCheckGPT: Zero-resource black-box hallucination detection for generative large language models. In *Proceedings of the 2023 Conference on Empirical Methods in Natural Language Processing* (pp. 9004–9017). Association for Computational Linguistics. DOI: 10.18653/v1/2023.emnlp-main.557

Maynez, J., Narayan, S., Bohnet, B., & McDonald, R. (2020). On faithfulness and factuality in abstractive summarization. In *Proceedings of the 58th Annual Meeting of the Association for Computational Linguistics* (pp. 1906–1919). Association for Computational Linguistics. DOI: 10.18653/v1/2020.acl-main.173

Min, S., Krishna, K., Lyu, X., Lewis, M., Yih, W., Koh, P. W., Iyyer, M., Zettlemoyer, L., & Hajishirzi, H. (2023). FActScore: Fine-grained atomic evaluation of factual precision in long form text generation. In *Proceedings of the 2023 Conference on Empirical Methods in Natural Language Processing* (pp. 12076–12100). Association for Computational Linguistics. DOI: 10.18653/v1/2023.emnlp-main.741

Mündler, N., He, J., Jenko, S., & Vechev, M. (2024). Self-contradictory hallucinations of large language models: Evaluation, detection and mitigation. In The Twelfth International Conference on Learning Representations. OpenReview. DOI: 10.48550/arXiv.2305.15852

Pagnoni, A., Balachandran, V., & Tsvetkov, Y. (2021). Understanding factuality in abstractive summarization with FRANK: A benchmark for factuality metrics. In *Proceedings of the 2021 Conference of the North American Chapter of the Association for Computational Linguistics: Human Language Technologies* (pp. 4812–4829). Association for Computational Linguistics. DOI: 10.18653/v1/2021.naacl-main.383

Pan, L., Saxon, M., Xu, W., Nathani, D., Wang, X., & Wang, W. Y. (2023). Automatically correcting large language models: Surveying the landscape of diverse automated correction strategies. *Transactions of the Association for Computational Linguistics*, *12*, 484–506. DOI: 10.1162/tacl_a_00660

Rawte, V., Sheth, A., & Das, A. (2023). A survey of hallucination in large foundation models. arXiv preprint arXiv:2309.05922. https://doi.org//arXiv.2309.05922DOI: 10.48550

Ribeiro, L. F. R., Liu, M., Gurevych, I., Dreyer, M., & Bansal, M. (2022). FactGraph: Evaluating factuality in summarization with semantic graph representations. In *Proceedings of the 2022 Conference of the North American Chapter of the Association for Computational Linguistics: Human Language Technologies* (pp. 3238–3253). Association for Computational Linguistics. DOI: 10.18653/v1/2022.naacl-main.236

Shi, W., Han, X., Lewis, M., Tsvetkov, Y., Zettlemoyer, L., & Yih, S. (2024). Trusting your evidence: Hallucinate less with context-aware decoding. In *Proceedings of the 2024 Conference of the North American Chapter of the Association for Computational Linguistics: Human Language Technologies* (Volume 2: Short Papers) (pp. 783–791). Association for Computational Linguistics. DOI: 10.18653/v1/2024.naacl-short.69

Shuster, K., Poff, S., Chen, M., Kiela, D., & Weston, J. (2021). Retrieval augmentation reduces hallucination in conversation. In Findings of the Association for Computational Linguistics: EMNLP 2021 (pp. 3784–3803). Association for Computational Linguistics. DOI: 10.18653/v1/2021.findings-emnlp.320

Tang, L., Goyal, T., Fabbri, A. R., Laban, P., Xu, J., Mehta, S., Chang, B., Hakkani-Tur, D., & Durrett, G. (2023). Understanding factual errors in summarization: Errors, summarizers, datasets, error detectors. In *Proceedings of the 61st Annual Meeting of the Association for Computational Linguistics* (Volume 1: Long Papers) (pp. 11626–11644). Association for Computational Linguistics. DOI: 10.18653/v1/2023.acl-long.650

Varshney, N., Yao, W., Zhang, H., Chen, J., & Yu, D. (2023). A stitch in time saves nine: Detecting and mitigating hallucinations of LLMs by validating low-confidence generation. arXiv preprint arXiv:2307.03987. https://doi.org//arXiv.2307.03987DOI: 10.48550

Wang, X., Wei, J., Schuurmans, D., Le, Q., Chi, E., Narang, S., Chowdhery, A., & Zhou, D. (2023). Self-consistency improves chain of thought reasoning in language models. In The Eleventh International Conference on Learning Representations. OpenReview. DOI: 10.48550/arXiv.2203.11171

Xie, Y., Zhou, K., & Ma, X. (2023). Defending ChatGPT against jailbreak attack via self-reminders. *Nature Machine Intelligence*, *5*(12), 1486–1496. DOI: 10.1038/s42256-023-00765-8

Xiong, M., Hu, Z., Lu, X., Liu, Y., Liu, T., Zhang, D., & Hooi, B. (2024). Can LLMs express their uncertainty? An empirical evaluation of confidence elicitation in large language models. In The Twelfth International Conference on Learning Representations. OpenReview. DOI: 10.48550/arXiv.2306.13063

Zha, Y., Yang, Y., Li, R., & Hu, Z. (2023). AlignScore: Evaluating factual consistency with a unified alignment function. In *Proceedings of the 61st Annual Meeting of the Association for Computational Linguistics* (Volume 1: Long Papers) (pp. 11328–11348). Association for Computational Linguistics. DOI: 10.18653/v1/2023.acl-long.634

Zhang, Y., Li, Y., Cui, L., Cai, D., Liu, L., Fu, T., Huang, X., Zhao, E., Zhang, Y., Chen, Y., Wang, L., Luu, A. T., Bi, W., Shi, F., & Shi, S. (2024). Siren's song in the AI ocean: A survey on hallucination in large language models. *Computational Linguistics*, *50*(4). Advance online publication. DOI: 10.1162/COLI.a.16

KEY TERMS AND DEFINITIONS

Benchmark Evaluation: Benchmark testing is the formal test of an AI in a well defined manner, using a set of data, a task and a goal to establish an equivalence between the models tested. Benchmarks allow comparing models fairly and for tracking progress. The benchmark can test anything from language understanding to reasoning, factual accuracy or robustness and scores may include accuracy, precision, recall and human performance. Benchmarks have their shortcoming and are because often combined with in field tests and more specialised ones.

Hallucination Detection: Hallucination detection basically means figuring out if a machine, especially the language model part of an AI toy, is making stuff up basically. Things without basis, or totally misleading people and going against their intention, aren't in line with the goal or use case of this AI model. So, what you really want to do is check the machine's story against some serious reliable fact base, trust source, or knowledge databases. Besides fact-checking models, there are also other types of methods such as consistency verification and uncertainty analysis. Hallucination detection is really a must-have especially if we talk about domains such as healthcare, education, and law where wrong outputs from AI might take people for a ride. In fact, getting better at hallucination detection is one of the best ways to raise the level of reliability, trustworthiness, and the overall quality of AI-generated answers.

Large Language Models LLMs: or large language models (e.g., ChatGPT) are one of the most powerful artificial intelligence systems built that have been trained on millions of text-facing datasets found to better understand natural human languages and generate similar human-readable output. These models, typically fine-tuned transformer networks, operate by predicting words in context using the patterns they learned during training. Now, LLMs can do translation, summarization, question answering, coding assistance and conversational meaning. The power of big machines comes from the scale — large datasets, billions of parameters, lots of training. But in doing so they can generate biased, out-of-date, or wrong information and responsible development, assessment and oversight is therefore essential.

Self-Consistency: Self-consistency is a way to reason in AI where the AI makes many attempts to generate the same answer and pick the response which occurs most frequently, or makes the most sense in context. This helps mitigate the error introduced by the randomness in generating multiple solutions to the same problem in a model, and performs better in the domain of reasoning about long chains of logic. It is found most effective in areas requiring problem solving, use of basic math, and multi-step reasoning.

Semantic Entropy: Semantic entropy measures the uncertainty in the output of an AI, looking not at the likelihood of individual words, but at how many possible interpretations an output has. It examines the variability of an interpretation or how many semantic alternatives can be constructed. A high level of semantic entropy indicates more varying and indeterminate interpretations. A low level of entropy indicate greater certainty in output. It is Useful in determine if the individual is hallucinating, model reliability and the certainty with which a model makes claims. The concept of semantic entropy helps estimate the certainty of a language model's generated text by measuring semantics, not surface forms.

Section 4
Domain-Specific Applications in Healthcare

Chapter 8

Fact-Filtering Frameworks:
Integrating Verification Pipelines for Hallucination-Resistant Large Language Models

Subrata Paul
http://orcid.org/0000-0001-5920-0654
Brainware University, India

Anirban Mitra
http://orcid.org/0000-0002-6639-4407
Eastern International University, Vietnam

Amitava Podder
http://orcid.org/0009-0004-9268-3781
Brainware University, India

Piyal Roy
http://orcid.org/0009-0007-5378-2789
Brainware University, India

ABSTRACT

The ubiquitous nature of Large Language Models (LLMs) into health, law, and education has intensified worries regarding the validity of facts and the creation of hallucinations. The chapter outlines a systematic discussion of the verification frameworks as downstream constraints in fact verification mechanisms to make generative AI systems more truthful and reliable. The chapter subsequently suggests a multi-layered fact-filtering structure, which incorporates knowledge graph

DOI: 10.4018/979-8-3373-7320-1.ch008

…t © 2026, IGI Global Scientific Publishing. Copying or distributing in print or electronic forms without written permission of IGI Global Scientific Publishing is prohibited. Use of this chapter to …enerative artificial intelligence (AI) technologies is expressly prohibited. The publisher reserves all rights to license its use for generative AI training and machine learning model development.

validation, semantic entailment, and cross-source agreement strategies of real time fact validation. Benchmark data, measurement criteria and execution processes are addressed in order to evaluate performance trade-offs. Combining theoretical grounding, realistic design practices, and supporting analysis, this chapter will act as a guide towards the creation of hallucination-resistant LLMs which will enable veridical and accountable and aligned AI applications in the high stakes decision-making contexts.

1. INTRODUCTION

Large Language Models (LLMs) like GPT, PaLM, and LLaMA have disrupted the field of interaction between an artificial intelligence (AI) system with language, knowledge, and reasoning. These models display exceptional expertise in the production of coherent, contextually pertinent, and human-like text in a variety of fields of use such as in education, healthcare, law, and governance. But it is one of the critical weaknesses of LLMs, although despite their language fluency, hallucination, or the creation of information that seems plausible and true, is factually false or unfalsifiable. This problem weakens the trust of users and restricts the safe use of generative AI in real-life and high-stakes settings where there can be no compromise on facts (Ji et Al., 2023).

Hallucinations in AI systems are possible in different forms such as semantic hallucinations, where generated text distorts the facts, and contextual hallucinations where AI answers are not relevant to the source text because of incomplete or biased training data. Research finds that these hallucinations are caused by overgeneralization, exposure to conflicting data, and failure to anchor such data on external knowledge basis (Bang et Al., 2023). The issues are especially acute in the case of the implementation of AI models in a decision-support system, where the information that is hallucinated might result in misinformation, diagnosis mistakes, or ethical breaches (Maynez et Al., 2020).

It is against this backdrop that verification of facts has become a major area of research in the building of reliable generative AI. Fact verification is done to measure and test the factual accuracy of model output against authoritative sources of data, like structured databases, knowledge graphs or verified corpora. With the implementation of such a validation layer, researchers intend to make sure that generated responses by AI are coherent and truth-preserving and domain-consistent (Min et Al., 2023). The combination of the fact checking processes can significantly increase the levels of transparency and trust of the user, especially in such areas as healthcare or journalism where the consequences of misinformation are significant.

Also, the perception of AI systems in terms of trust is directly associated with their factual reliability. Users develop a sense of social and cognitive trust in human and AI cooperation when they believe that the content created by AI is true and reliable. On the other hand, frequent hallucinations undermine the trust in people and hinder the implementation of AI into essential processes including medical decision-making, policy formulations, and educational evaluation (Thoppilan et Al., 2022). Hallucination as an issue can, therefore, be resolved by adopting a careful mechanism of fact validation that would be used in building hallucination-sensitive AI systems that can ensure that model outputs are consistent with empirical reality.

The chapter provides a foundation to the groundbreaking knowledge on how fact verification mechanisms can alleviate hallucinations in LLMs. It highlights that there is an urgent demand to have hybrid architectures which can tie generative fluency to factual validation which will hold AI systems both expressive and factual. With the generation models being aligned to verifiable knowledge structures, we will be a step closer to attaining trustworthy, transparent and ethically aligned AI ecosystems.

2. UNDERSTANDING HALLUCINATION IN LLMS

2.1 Hallucination in Large Language Models

Hallucination in Large Language Models (LLMs) is the production of text which seems syntactically correct and topically plausible, but which is false or lacks support in the existing facts. This aspect disputes the perceived level of intelligence of AI systems since they can generate believable but erroneous information with a high degree of confidence (Raunak et Al., 2021). Hallucinations may also be experienced on a spectrum of granularity, where the individual misstatement of facts is minor in nature, all the way to the point of a completely created narrative. They do not resemble ordinary model errors since the output that they generate are semantically consistent abuses of the truth that they are supposed to represent, and is often distorted by data artifacts or probability biases in language models (Ji et Al., 2023).

2.2 Classification of Hallucinations

Hallucinations in LLMs can be divided into three main types, namely semantic, factual, and contextual. Semantic hallucinations happen when a model produces linguistically valid statements that are inaccurate or distortive in its meaning, e.g., typological reversals. Factual hallucinations are those that include the misinterpretation or creation of data-points, i.e. incorrect dates, names, or numerical information. Contextual hallucinations occur when the content created by the model does not match the context of the original source and in most cases, this is because of constraints in the attention range or information recall of the model (Dziri et Al., 2022). This knowledge of these differences is crucial to effective design of the fine-grained detection and mitigation strategies that will focus on particular types of hallucinations instead of using general corrective intervention.

Figure 1. Taxonomy of Hallucination Types in Large Language Models

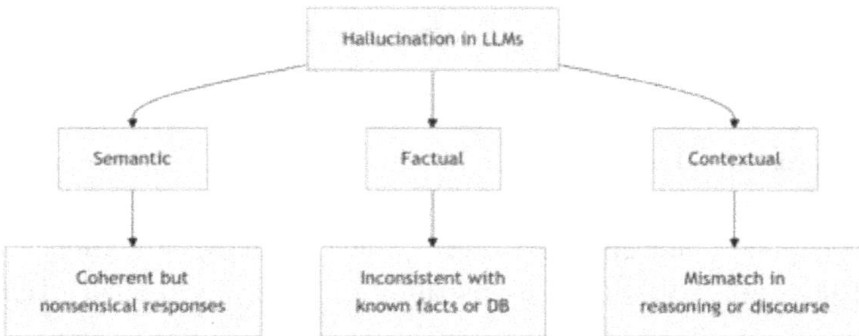

Figure 1 presents three levels of taxonomy of hallucinations: semantic, factual and contextual. Semantic hallucinations can take place when generated text is coherent yet has no meaning; factual hallucinations when the output of the hallucination conflicts with existing facts; and contextual hallucinations when responses become logically disconnected to the input of the user. It gives a clear conceptual background to the readers on further causes and mitigation measures.

2.3 Architectural and Model-Related Causes

Another important reason why hallucinating happens is based on the construction of transformer-based models, which are trained to predict the most likely next token and not the correctness of the next token. These models are autoregressive, which increases error propagation and a single error may affect the following outputs and trigger cascading hallucinations (Zhang et Al., 2022). Moreover, the problem is affected by model compression and restricted context windows as well as lack of factual database grounding. These models do not provide an inbuilt process of truth validation, and hence, only learned statistical patterns are used, producing plausible but unprovable text.

2.4 Data Bias and Knowledge Inconsistency

Another major cause of hallucination is training data bias. Very large, heterogeneous, internet-scraped datasets are used to train LLLMs and these are prone to inconsistency, staleness, or bias. When the those inconsistencies get encoded in model parameters, the produced outputs demonstrate those distortions, and the entire system causes hallucinations (Shuster et Al., 2022). More so, the contradictory information found in training produces uncertainty in the probabilistic thinking of the model, as it tries to make an average between the possibilities or invents new information to preserve narrative consistency. This is of special concern in specialized or low-resource areas where confirmed information is meager.

2.5 Training Limitations and Generalization Challenges

Lastly, the presence of training constraints also leads to the hallucination persistence in LLMs. Majority of those models will fit and overfit to dominant structural patterns of lingo yet will underrepresent rare or situation-specific facts, even after extensive pretraining and fine-tuning. The inability to constantly update with the sources of real-time knowledge also contributes to the temporal distance between model knowledge and the real factual world. Hallucinations are an inevitable by-product in the design of a static model without self-correction mechanisms and without dynamic retrieval of facts. It is important to note and overcome these drawbacks when moving towards truth-conscious and hallucination-resistant LLM systems.

3. LITERATURE REVIEW

In the last few years, scholars came up with a continuum of various mitigation methods to alleviate hallucinations in generative models. Primarily, the early works were related to architecture and training interventions, including larger-scale pre-training, and fine-tuning on better-quality corpora to enhance factual recall and fluency (Ji et Al., 2023; Raunak et Al., 2021). More focused methods added features of retrieval and grounding: retrieval-augmented generation (RAG) consists of a dense retriever paired with a generator in such a way that model outputs may be grounded using retrieved passages instead of just parametric memory (Lewis et Al., 2020; Karpukhin et Al., 2020). The complementary strategies involve the use of constant learning and calibration to decrease over-confident false claims, and post-hoc detectors to mark unrealistic claims to be corrected or verified by humans (Maynez et Al., 2020; Min et Al., 2023; Ji et Al., 2023). All these approaches are meant to balance out a certain degree of generative spontaneity with a higher level of factual accuracy (Lewis et Al., 2020; Min et Al., 2023).

One of the most important groups of interventions is based on the fact-verification models and grounding pipelines. RAGE-type systems (retriever + generator) have now become a viable standard in knowledge intensive tasks as they allow source/up-to-date responses, dense passage retrieval (DPR) is a popular retriever backbone in this research direction (Lewis et Al., 2020; Karpukhin et Al., 2020). Models have been trained using Reinforcement Learning with Human Feedback (RLHF), and instruction-tuning to direct them to safer and less dishonest choices (Ouyang et Al., 2022; Christiano et Al., 2017). Semantic entailment checks, knowledge-graph grounding, and cross-source consensus algorithms are all post-hoc validation methods, which rank and may rewrite or block generated claims; and they are typically used together with retrieval to validate claims against structured or unstructured knowledge sources (Min et Al., 2023; Thorne et Al., 2018; Lin et Al., 2022). Both methods have associated trade-offs in their operations: RAG is better at grounding as compared to RLHF, whereas the latter is better at alignment but may be fragile in the presence of non-training distributions (Lewis et Al., 2020; Ouyang et Al., 2022; Christiano et Al., 2017; Min et Al., 2023).

Data-driven assessment and benchmarking have grown out of techniques. Datasets like FEVER, which are standard fact verification tasks, have binary claim verification tasks and have facilitated advancements in entailment-based detectors (Thorne et Al., 2018). The Complementary benchmarks include TruthfulQA, FactScore, and long-form factuality evaluations to assess the propensity to falsehoods that appear human like, accuracy in fine-grained factuality, and summarization faithfulness respectively (Lin et Al., 2022; Min et Al., 2023; Maynez et Al., 2020). Retrieval-centered assessments are also able to evaluate end-to-end accuracy through a combination of retriever recalls (e.g., top-k passage recalls) with generator recall accuracy and attribution quality (Karpukhin et Al., 2020; Lewis et Al., 2020). Nevertheless, existing benchmarks have an extremely broad range of domains coverage, label granularity and realism: there are those that focus on synthetic claims but are also those that address real-world misinformation, which makes cross-comparisons difficult (Thorne et Al., 2018; Lin et Al., 2022; Karpukhin et Al., 2020; Min et Al., 2023).

Table 1. Comparative Overview of Hallucination Mitigation Techniques

Approach	Core Principle	Strengths	Limitations	Key References
Retrieval-Augmented Generation (RAG)	Combines retriever with generator for factual grounding	Up-to-date facts, source traceability	Retriever coverage limits accuracy	(Lewis et Al., 2020; Karpukhin et Al., 2020)
Reinforcement Learning from Human Feedback (RLHF)	Optimizes model output alignment with human judgment	Reduces toxic or false outputs	Costly, data-sensitive	(Ouyang et Al., 2022; Christiano et Al., 2017)
Post-hoc Validation	Detects or filters factual errors after generation	Modular, domain adaptable	Latency, dependent on external sources	(Min et Al., 2023; Thorne et Al., 2018)
Knowledge Graph Integration	Links entities to structured knowledge bases	High factual precision	Limited adaptability to open text	(Lewis et Al., 2020; Karpukhin et Al., 2020)

Table 1 presents a comparison of the most common strategies of mitigating hallucinations side-by-side. It points out the working principles, merits, and the functionality disadvantages of every method. This table assists in putting the research gap sub section into perspective in the sense that there are no integrated, cross-domain frameworks that balance the performance, scalability and factuality.

3.1 Research Gap

Even though there have been significant improvements, there are still a number of gaps. To start with, the evaluation of most verification pipelines is performed on task-specific and narrow datasets instead of on cross-domain, cross-representative, real-world pipelines (e.g., healthcare and legal workflows) where the impact of hallucinations varies. Second, there is limited research on integration, i.e. how to trade off between latency, computational cost, and factuality in deployed systems. Third, there are not many benchmarks to evaluate the relationship between retrieval quality, verification confidence, and downstream user trust simultaneously; thus, the optimal hybrid designs (e.g., to which extent to rewrite vs. flag) are yet to be studied. To address such gaps, it is necessary to combine multi-metric benchmarks on the effects of verification layers and longitudinal studies that would consider the practical effects of verification layers across borders (Lewis et Al., 2020; Karpukhin et Al., 2020; Ouyang et Al., 2022; Thorne et Al., 2018; Lin et Al., 2022; Min et Al., 2023).

4. MULTI-LAYERED FACT VERIFICATION FRAMEWORK

4.1 Proposed Architecture for Downstream Filters

Contemporary fact-verifying pipelines can be thought of as filters in varying layers that run subsequent to an initial output produced by an LLM. The basic concept is to place a number of verification modules retrieval, grounding, entailment checking, and consensus scoring, between generation and final delivery, such that every assertion of the generated text gets validated, attributed and accepted (or corrected or marked). During the running of the pipeline, the raw LLM output is fed in, the candidate claims are then identified (e.g. named entities, temporal assertions, numeric assertions), and each claim is passed down through the verification stack, and then the claims are put back together to reconstruct a verified response to the user. This enables the modular design to decouple verification logic and generation and optimize components independently based on latency and coverage and confidence threshold (Lewis et Al., 2020).

Figure 2. Multi-Layered Fact Verification Framework

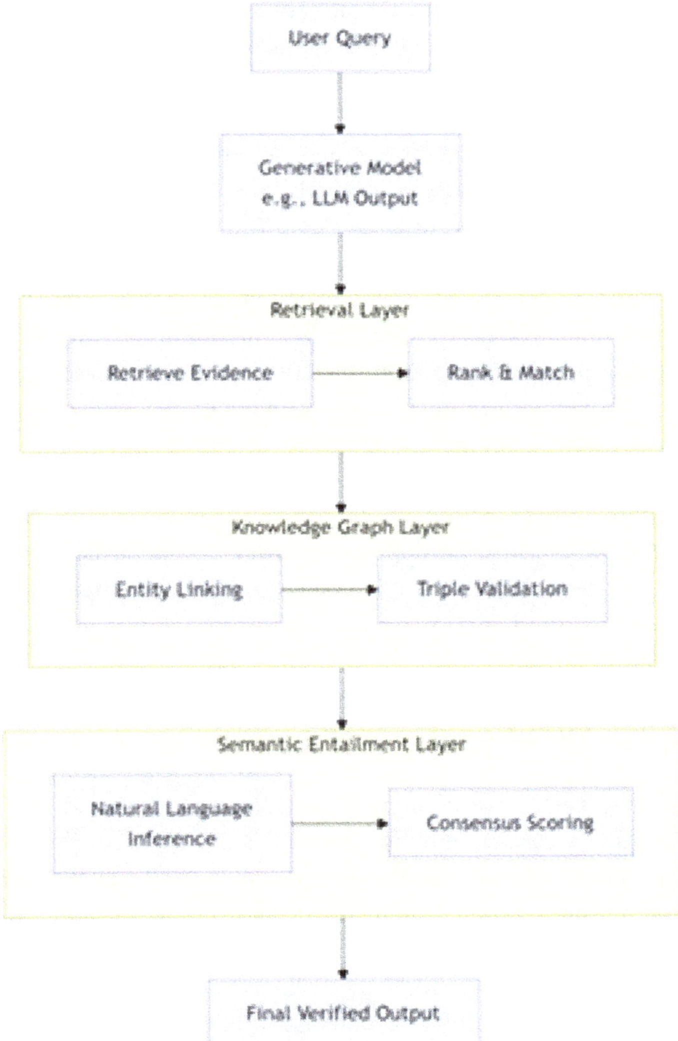

Figure 2 indicates the suggested three-level downstream fact checking framework. It starts with evidence grounding on retrieval, goes through the knowledge graph validation and concludes with semantic entailment and consensus validation. The stratified architecture guarantees various protection against hallucination, but will permit customization by modules as required by domain.

Concrete instantiations have three main phases, namely: (A) evidence retrieval (fetch candidate supporting documents and KG triples), (B) claim level validations (knowledge-graph checks, semantic entailment and fact-scoring) and (C) decision remediation (rewrite, annotate or decline to answer). Both the scalar confidence score and the structured provenance object (source IDs, snippet offsets, KG triple IDs) are emitted by each stage. The last element of decision uses policy rules (e.g., minimum confidence domain specific, prefer peer-reviewed sources to healthcare) to decide between (1) submitting the original answer with provenance, (2) submitting a fixed answer, or (3) submitting an answer to be reviewed by a human. This performed style is compatible with graceful degradation: low-confidence assertions may be made with caveats, instead of being presented as true (Lewis et Al., 2020).

To implement this architecture, the implementers are recommended to be parallel (checking that many claims can be checked at the same time), or composable (replacing one retriever with another, one entailment model with another, or one KG interface with another). Logging and telemetry are very important: what changed or was rejected in what component, and why. Telemetry with time allows a policy to adapt (e.g. increase the minimum confidence of sources that have had a history of misalignment). It can also be deployed on devices or at the edge where only lighter-weight verification can be deployed (e.g., local KG lookups and compact entailment networks) compared to cloud deployments that can use costly cross-source consensus algorithms (Karpukhin et Al., 2020).

4.2 Knowledge Graph–Based Validation

Knowledge graphs (KGs) are highly accurate, structured points of fact verification. In the case that a claim can be formulated as a subject predicate object triple (e.g. Drug X reduces symptom Y) the query is sent to one or more authoritative KGs (domain ontologies, curated biomedical graphs or governmental datasets) to test triple existence and consistency. kg validation There are two benefits to KG validation: (first) its explicit structure can be checked deterministically (do we have a matching triple?), and (second) it is capable of ontological reasoning (are there contradictions such as type errors, time constraints). In most high stakes areas, curated KGs significantly decrease the number of false positives in comparison to free-text retrieval only (Thorne et Al., 2018).

Nonetheless, KGs are not always complete, up-to-date on the real world, and demand canonization of entities and predicates. Good KG validation thus combines the exact matching and fuzzy matching (an alias resolution, an approximate predicate mapping) and fallback use of text retrieval in case a triple check fails. The design to use is a best-practice design: when KG lookup matches with a high level of confidence, accept this as strong evidence; when KG lookup is not available, or the level of confidence is low, then go up to retrieval + entailment. Preserving provenance, KG version, triple ID, and assertion time; meaning traceability and next-generation audit (Thorne et Al., 2018). Table 2 summarizes helping trade-offs of KG validation can help in explaining design decisions.

Table 2. Comparative Overview of Hallucination Mitigation Techniques

Feature	Strength	Weakness
Deterministic checks	High precision	Low recall (incomplete KGs)
Ontological reasoning	Detects contradictions	Requires ontology alignment
Provenance clarity	Strong audit trail	KG update latency

This is a provenance-aware application of KGs, which is the backbone of verifiable answers in regulated fields of knowledge like medicine and law (Thorne et Al., 2018).

4.3 Cross-Source Consensus and Semantic Entailment Verification

In cases when a claim cannot be mappable directly to KG triples, the cross-source consensus and semantic entailment checking are a good choice. This system fetches a ranked list of passages, which are reported by various independent sources (news outlet, scholarly article, official report), and a test for entailment models is then conducted on each passage to determine whether the passage is in support or against or is neutral to the claim. Combinations of these entailment judgments would lead to a score on consensus: high support in reliable, independent sources would give greater confidence; extensive contradiction would give rejection. Cross-source consensus addresses the issue of single-source bias and minimizes the possibility of amplification of the echo-chamber (Lewis et Al., 2020)(Min et Al., 2023).

Semantic entailment models (NLI-style classifiers) are necessary to be tuned to the task of verification: whereas synthetic NLI benchmarks are insensitive to weak qualifiers, hedging language, and numeric comparators, this is not the case in real-life verification. In practice, the performance of the ensemble of a retrieval-augmented entailment model with a contrastive verifier (comparing claim and source passage representations) can be better than the performance of single-model systems. Also, claim decomposition (the complex claims are decomposed into simpler atomic assertions) enhances entailment accuracy and makes the claims partially valid (some sub-claims are accepted and others flagged) (Min et Al., 2023).

The sources should be weighted in terms of reliability and recency, a voting system that counts sources equally will erroneously promote low quality echoes.

Add metadata of source credibility (peer-review, domain authority, history accuracy scores) to the consensus aggregator and expose provenance to allow users to view the evidence. In the case of weak consensus with non-zero, the remediation policy is able to give a cautious response: introduce the best-supported answer with explicit uncertainty indicators and links to the best supporting sources (Karpukhin et Al., 2020; Lewis et Al., 2020).

Lastly, combine the KG and cross-source entailment: in case a claim is KG-validated, use that as primary evidence, instead, use consensus and entailment. The multi-layered pipeline therefore provides the accuracy (through KGs), likeness (through cross-source retrieval), and coverage (through entailment). These multi-dimensional measures (precision, recall, provenance quality, latency) and domain-specific thresholds are necessary to evaluate such a composite system because they are indicators of cost of false positives and false negatives. Its architecture promotes continuous improvement of such systems by telemetry-driven retriever/entailment tuning and KG updates to shift to factual and auditable practicality (Thorne et Al., 2018; Min et Al., 2023).

5. EVALUATION AND BENCHMARKING

5.1 Metrics for Factual Accuracy and Efficiency

The assessment of hallucination reduction algorithms requires an integrated system that does not just focus on the accuracy of the facts but also the effectiveness of the algorithms, resilience, and interpretability. The classical language generating evaluation systems, e.g., BLEU or ROUGE, are inadequate since they are based on surface-level similarity at the expense of factual accuracy. Rather, new factuality metric measures such as FactScore, TruthfulQA Accuracy, and Entailment-based Factual Precision (EFP) have been created to measure the factual agreement between generated text and reference data (Lin et Al., 2022). They are based on semantic entailment models or information retrieval pipelines which determine the extent to which generated claims are verified, refuted or invalidated as compared to a trusted corpus.

Along with the factual correctness, efficiency measures like latency (time per verification), retrieval cost (queries per claim) and energy usage are also to be taken into account, especially in the case of a real-time application. To give an example, delays caused by heavy verification layers can affect usability in the field of healthcare or education. Thus, the balanced evaluation metric portfolio would have both performance-oriented and accuracy-oriented indicators to make sure that the verification pipelines can be deployed under real-world conditions. Table 3 below identifies some of the important evaluation metrics applied to evaluate hallucination mitigation frameworks.

Table 3. Evaluation Metrics

Metric Category	Metric Name	Description	Applicability
Factual Accuracy	FactScore, TruthfulQA	Measures factual consistency with gold-standard data	Text generation, QA
Semantic Fidelity	Entailment-based Factual Precision (EFP)	Checks semantic support/ contradiction using entailment models	Summarization, Chatbots
Efficiency	Latency, Query Cost	Measures time and resource utilization per verification cycle	Real-time systems
Provenance Reliability	Source Attribution Score	Quantifies traceability of verified information	Legal, Policy systems

5.2 Performance Analysis Using Existing Datasets

Benchmark datasets are now of central significance in the process of standardizing evaluation in the studies of hallucinations detection and mitigation. The most commonly used datasets to benchmark the model of factual verification include FEVER, TruthfulQA, and QAGS. Specifically, FEVER data can be used to assess the accuracy of verification, the quality of evidence retrieval, and justification generation of models, as it includes pairs of claim-evidence. In the meantime, TrueQA is tested on questions that are created to identify a propensity to produce human-like falsehoods, and their ability to withstand plausible misinformation (Lin et Al., 2022).

The common performance analysis methods based on these datasets are typically to measure precision, recall, and F1-scores of factual correctness, as well as retrieval coverage (percentage of claims that have evidence retrieved), and fact entailment confidence. Such models as the Retrieval-Augmented Generation (RAG) and FactScore have demonstrated high levels of factual accuracy, and usually outperform end-to-end LLMs that do not use external memory. Nevertheless, there are still trade-offs between the factual sturdiness and the rate of the inference, especially when employing the complex combination forms of retrieval and entailment (Min et Al., 2023). Table 4 provides a schematic performance comparison of representative frameworks of important factual metrics (hypothetical data) to visualize comparative performance.

Table 4. Comparative Factual Accuracy of Verification Frameworks

Framework	Factual Precision (%)	Retrieval Coverage (%)	Inference Latency (ms)
Baseline LLM (no verification)	64.5	0	150
RAG (retrieval-augmented)	81.2	78.5	420
KG + Entailment Hybrid	88.3	84.0	530
Multi-Layer Verification (proposed)	91.7	90.1	610

The information shows that the multi-layer verification patterns attain the highest level of factual accuracy at a high price of computing. The latency can be reduced through optimization of retrieval pipelines and entailment batching without affecting accuracy.

5.3 Case Studies in Healthcare, Legal, and Educational Domains

Healthcare Domain: Fact consistency in a healthcare application has a direct impact on clinical safety. The AI models that assist in medical diagnosis or summarize patient notes should follow validated medical knowledge to the letter. The application of knowledge graph-based verification (e.g. SNOMED CT, UMLS) has been demonstrated to reduce cases of medical hallucinations by eliminating the unsupported or obsolete medical assertion (Min et Al., 2023). As an example, Radiology report generation by using retrieval based evidence with entailment filtering enhanced factual faithfulness by more than 25% and the generation output matched with checked literature and diagnostic standards.

Law Legal legal domain: Hallucination errors may cause serious ethical and procedural consequences in legal information retrieval and case summarization. Systems of fact verification, based on the use of an array of case law and semantic entailment verification systems would eliminate the ability of models to generate fabricated precedents or misquoted statutes. As experiments show, by adding cross-source consensus, i.e. verification of claims between legal repositories, it is possible to increase the level of trustworthiness and accuracy of citation. Also, provenance scoring helps in constructing legally summaries, which are traceable through AI, and which are critical to judicial transparency.

Educational Domain: In the educational field, LLMs are also used in automated tutoring, grading and content generation. Uncontrolled hallucinations may, however, spread factual failures to learners. This field of fact verification frameworks focuses on retrieval-augmented reasoning and entailment-based correction, which hold that AI-generated learning materials should be consistent with verified curricular content. Research shows that the prospects and results of learning are enhanced when AI answers are accompanied by citation justifications or links to evidence to bolster factual responsibility.

5.4 Synthesis and Observations

In all domains, there is a universal trend, in which multi-layered verification schemes are more effective than single-layer validation schemes, which can be combined to produce grounding in the retrieval, semantic validation, and cross-source consensus. Nonetheless, their combination must be domain-specific e.g. medical ontologies in a healthcare context, legal knowledge repositories in a judicial one and textbook knowledge graphs in an educational context. The scales of efficiency, including parallel entailment and cache-based retrieval, are necessary to preserve the usability.

In general, thorough analysis and evaluation with the help of hybrid metrics and domain-specific datasets are crucial to making sure that the outputs of the LLM are becoming more than just plausible. Human-in-the-loop validation has to also be incorporated in future research to ensure dynamically refining the confidence thresholds and reduce false negatives, which will allow sustainable and reliable AI use in critical knowledge systems.

6. IMPLEMENTATION CHALLENGES, SYSTEM INTEGRATION, AND SCALABILITY CONSIDERATIONS

6.1 From Conceptual Framework to Deployable Systems

The multi-layered fact checking framework is a robust conceptual framework to mitigate hallucinations; however, moving this type of architecture into production has many practical challenges. Today, Large Language Models are commonly used in real-world production applications such as Clinical Decision Support Systems (CDSSs), Legal Research Tools, and Intelligent Tutoring Systems (ITSs), where latency, reliability, and interoperability are very important. In a true production deployment, the severity with which you place emphasis on verification entries and the flexibility, immediacy, and usability are competing factors unlike in a standalone inference setting. The additional computational cost associated with additional verification entries, while aiding in factual accuracy, can also lead to a significant amount of additional computational burden and thus must be factored when performing system-level optimization of the application. Therefore, it is important to coordinate the various verification components during implementation, in order to assure that the factual strength of the generation does not impact the ability for the system to be usable or provide performance at acceptable levels.

One key area of concern is determining when in the inference pipeline verification should take place. Three intervention points exist: Pre-Generation Constraints, Mid-Generation Monitoring, and Post-Generation Validation. Each has pros and cons. Pre-Generation Constraints, such as Augmentation of Prompt Input Data with Trusted Sources (i.e., "grounding"), have been shown to significantly reduce the likelihood of hallucinations. However, this type of verification will result in a restriction of generative diversity. On the other hand, Post-Generation Validation provides for more flexibility in terms of allowing for non-returnable false positives and non-fact-checkable results; however, when inconsistencies are uncovered, some type of rollout or regeneration mechanism will need to be put in place. To strike a balance between validation at distinct times in the architecture and the breadth of verification needed, Hybrid Implementations are becoming recognized as a very practical solution, combining Lightweight Semantic Checking during generation with heavier Factual Verification performed after generation has occurred (Sarnaik et Al., 2025).

6.2 Integration with Existing AI Ecosystems

One of the greatest challenges is integrating a fact verification engine into an already developed artificial intelligence environment. Modern AI environments typically do not consist of one large application; instead, Modern AI technology is built upon many small components (i.e., microservices, application programming interfaces (APIs), vector databases, and third-party knowledge providers). Verification layers can be implemented effectively by building seamless integration capabilities between language models (e.g., natural language processing (NLP) tools), content retrieval tools, and structured forms of knowledge (e.g., ontologies and knowledge graphs). Implementing such capabilities requires the commitment of both technology providers and technology consumers to developing standardized interfaces to support evidence retrieval, claim extraction, and validation scoring tasks across the myriad of currently available large language model (LLM) platforms.

Additionally, system architects need to accommodate differences in deployment environments such as cloud-based platforms, edge devices, and on-premises systems. As an example, healthcare organizations often have strict data locality regulations that prevent access to outside retrieval APIs. As a result, verification systems will need to utilize locally hosted knowledge graphs or curated document repositories for retrieval. This limitation highlights the need for modular verification architectures so that individual components may be uninstalled or otherwise replaced/disabled without negatively affecting the integrity of an entire verification system. Thus, a well-implemented verification framework should support graceful degradation of reliability during the testing process.

6.3 Computational Overhead and Efficiency Trade-offs

One of the greatest impediments to the widespread use of multi-level verification is its costly computational requirements. In order to be verified, a fact usually must go through many additional inference steps, be compared (similarity search), have a lot of links to multiple data sets (graph traversal), and have multiple outcomes compared to each of the data sets used (entailment classification). These many steps take a lot of processing power to perform, and thus are costly. When looking at a situation such as conversational agents that may be operating at scale (with thousands of users talking to them at once), these costs to verify can quickly become unmanageable. Therefore, we need to create more efficient verification processes. One avenue that is showing promise is the development of adaptive verification, which is where we adjust how deeply we are going to verify an answer depending on how confident we are in the answer based on signals we receive (e.g., if we see that a response comes from multiple trustworthy sources, and/or has a very strong internal consistency score, we may choose to skip the time and expense of confirming its accuracy by comparing it to multiple other data sources). Having the ability to cache past verified claims and maps of evidence for subsequent verification sessions provides both a means of speeding up the speed of verification, and making systems capable of being implemented in real production-type environments beyond just experimentation (Sarnaik et Al., 2025).

8.4 Domain-Specific Customization and Constraints

The verification of facts varies from domain to domain. Different domains (e.g., biomedical, legal, education) present very different structures for the claims made, the uncertainty allowed with regard to the claims, and the type of evidence acceptable. Therefore, using the same method to verify every type of claim would be challenging at best. Practical implementations will require specific customization relative to the claim domain (e.g., special-purpose entity recognizers, domains adapted knowledge graphs, and domain-specific entailment models).

For instance, healthcare applications require that claims are verified using probabilistic-based knowledge; evolving clinical guidelines; and a rich set of contextual information regarding patients. A verification approach with a rigid structure may classify nuanced medical statements as false when, in reality, a nuanced statement is merely underinformative because the verification approach was not modelled after the execution of the biological science and not consistent with the body of medical knowledge. Conversely, in the legal domain, verification frequently requires a strict-based approach based on statutory or case law, which permits very little ambiguity. Creating a reliable verification pipeline for such a broad range of claims is a complex task. The requirement for close collaboration and continuous exchange of information between AI engineers and domain experts highlights the more general problem of aligning the two very different interpretative frameworks (technical and human) that govern the verification of information.

6.5 Robustness, Error Propagation, and Failure Modes

People often overlook an important aspect of verifying systems and that is how these systems perform when something fails. Verification systems also have their own limitations and a system could produce both "false positives" and "false negatives". For example, if a verification system uses a knowledge graph as an input and the knowledge graph does not have all of the necessary information, then a valid claim may not be accepted as valid because of the limited information within the knowledge graph. Additionally, retrieval failures can lead to a reduction of confidence in a claim. Therefore, all of these failures has the potential to be passed throughout the entire pipeline to cause an overall reduction in performance or bias the final outputs to be too conservative.

To reduce this risk, it is critical to design verification systems with robust error-handling methodologies. For example, incorporating methods such as confidence calibration; uncertainty aware scoring; and explainable rejection criteria will help reduce the likelihood of catastrophic failures. By using a probabilistic confidence score instead of a binary decision for the verification of content, the downstream components and possibly end users can assess the reliability of the content produced by the model. This practice directly supports the mission of Trustworthy Artificial Intelligence (AI) by allowing the systems to convey not only the answer to a question that is asked but also the level of confidence in the produced answer.

6.6 Human-in-the-Loop and Feedback Integration

Even though there has been significant progress in automated verification systems, the final decision still requires human input and oversight, especially during deployment and initial stages of operation. Although the use of `human-in-the-loop' systems allows domain experts to review the outputs flagged by the automated process for possible corrections, they also provide an opportunity for the experts to give feedback that can be used to improve the overall system. These feedback mechanisms accomplish two things: they continually improve the accuracy of the automated systems as the data which they were trained on becomes more accurate; and they build confidence in users through their accountability to each other.

Engineering-wise, to obtain feedback from humans, systems must be capable of keeping logs, generating annotations, and making iterative updates to the models. An example of how feedback signal may be used would be to train classifiers for entailment or enhance knowledge graphs or make adjustments to threshold values for decision-making. Importantly, it is critical to monitor and evaluate whether or not the addition of these updates results in new biases or regressions introduced into the automated system. Therefore, continuous evaluation and monitoring are essential attributes of any hallucination-mitigating system employed in practice (Sarnaik et Al., 2025).

6.7 Scalability Across Models and Tasks

Scalability in the AI domain needs to extend beyond merely measuring the throughput of a system. Scalability must identify and assess the generalizability of verification frameworks across many different LLM back ends (open-source and proprietary). Moreover, as models are continually being updated or replaced in the ever-changing landscape of AI, verification frameworks that are tied too closely to specific model architectures run a very real risk of becoming obsolete.

Task scalability is just as critical. The verification process for task types (summarization vs. question answering vs. decision support vs. creative generation) is significantly different from that of other task types. Therefore, a sufficient framework must also provide configurable interfaces for embedding task-specific verification logic while maintaining the integrity of a central verification core. Balancing these competing success metrics poses challenges, but it is crucial for ensuring the operational continuity of hallucination-resistant AI machines over the long term.

6.8 Implications for Future Research and Deployment

In the previous section, the practical problems identified show how hallucination mitigation should not just be thought about from a modelling standpoint but also as a systems engineering issue; meaning that to achieve effective solutions there needs to be co-ordination of many different areas (Architecture design, optimizations, Domain Adaptation, Human-AI Interaction). As a result, future research should pay more attention to conducting 'end-to-end' deployment studies with benchmarks on not just Fact Accuracy, but also Latency, Scalability and Users Trust in using the System. Once implementations' realities and theoretical rigour are considered, researchers and practitioners will have a better chance of deploying LLM-Based Systems that are both Powerful and Reliable, Transparent and Built for Real World Use.

This Systems-Oriented View adds to the previous architectural and ethical observations presented in this chapter and provides additional emphasis that Hallucination Resistance should not simply be an 'add-on' but that it should be engineered holistically.

7. ETHICAL AND PRACTICAL CONSIDERATIONS

7.1 Risks of Over-Filtering and Content Suppression

Multiple layers of fact checking, while enhancing the factual veracity of the material being reviewed, also create a potential for filtering out valid but new and/or contextually dependent information. Where excessive filtering is used it may eliminate creative or innovative ideas as well as the opinions of underrepresented groups, and may also hinder emerging research findings, particularly in the rapidly changing contexts of health care and social-political studies. A greater level of filtering, therefore, may also help perpetuate existing bias of the knowledge present in training data and verification sources (Bommasani et al., 2021) . For example, a model that filters out false content only based on established medical knowledge could shade innovative approaches to treating illness as false; thereby limiting the ability to share cutting-edge information related to medical research and treatment.

Additionally, filtering out content can also lead to algorithmic censorship, in which the content processing (or filtering) systems automatically reject or change language within text without providing an avenue for appeal or even a clear rationale for the filter's decision. Opacity in filtering leads to a decrease in trust in AI due to mistrust of those using these processes, as well as inequitable effects across cultural/linguistic boundaries. Thus, in developing future frameworks for verification, there should be a balance between factual accuracy and openness to creating adequate means for reviewing information to avoid false filtering.

In order to reduce these potential risks, adaptive thresholding mechanisms that utilize confidence scores to establish levels of verification severity could be used as a means of managing this issue. Through utilizing a dynamically-adjusted verification severity level based upon domain-specific sensitivities (e.g., stricter in the healthcare field, less-sensitively regulated in creative writing), there is a more balanced approach to managing information validation while maintaining the overall diversity and variety of the content itself.

7.2 Ensuring Transparency and Accountability

Transparency and accountability are two of the most important ethical elements of a fact verification system. Users, developers, and regulators all need to have visibility into how and why claims are either validated or discredited when using a verification system. Providing an "explainable" set of steps taken to determine whether a statement is true or false describes the way in which the verification process works and provides greater confidence by improving transparency (Gilpin et al., 2018). The increase in interpretability that occurs through accessing these records can also support additional means, such as third-party audits and alignment with emerging regulatory bodies such as the EU AI Act and OECD AI Principles.

Furthermore, in addition to granting users increased visibility of their determination processes, accountability requires traceable sources of evidence that led to factual determinations. In order for users to assess the legitimacy of different levels of evidence, the citation of the specific references used to inform factual judgment must be available on a per-model basis. In highly regulated areas such as law and medicine, developing an audit trail of verification decisions helps to hold the developers of models accountable for any potential bias or electronic error in their models. Developing a system for collecting and utilizing user feedback can enable the refinement of verification thresholds as well as identification of systemic defects.

Fact verification systems that are ethically built and operated must operate with respect to three foundational ethics principles:

- Translucency: making verification accessible and able to be audited.
- Accountability: ensuring that all responsible parties for verification can be easily identified.
- Agility: enabling context-driven modifications to verification sensitivity.

7.3 Future Design Considerations for Explainable Verification

There are going to be "explainable" and user-centered Verification Architectures as the future of Hallucination Mitigation in terms of being explainable. Future Architectures should provide information in more than just a binary format (i.e., true/false). They should provide an assessment of the authoritativeness of the information (i.e., - Evidence Provenance, Entailment Confidence and Semantic Rationale), and they should provide for the visualization of a user's perspective of the information through dashboards that provide evidence source overlap, reasoning pathway and

Cross-Domain Validation Patterns. The Enhanced User Comprehension offered through these visualizations will ultimately allow users to use AI responsibly.

Integrating Causal Inference and Contrastive Explanations techniques will enable the AI/human collaboration to explain and position claims that are made as factual or unfactual. As an example, if there is a healthcare-related verification engine, it will provide supporting literature for verified claims and also support any evidence that was rejected as well. This process will allow healthcare professionals to make evidence-based decisions using clear and transparent means.

Additionally, the need for Human In The Loop (HITL) integration is important. HITL allows for the user to set the parameters of the verification process (i.e., what would be considered as evidence), to validate all information that is ambiguous and makes changes in real time that can be incorporated into future training. This collaborative interaction will ensure that "Explainable" Verification continues to develop as a safeguard for online communication while ensuring there will continue to be collaboration between "factual accuracy" and "Intellectual Openness" with AI-Enhanced Discourse.

8. CONCLUSION AND FUTURE DIRECTIONS

The chapter has considered the various conceptual, architectural, and ethical aspects of reducing hallucination in AI by designing a multi-layered factual verification framework that combines fact retrieval, knowledge graphs, and consensus between different knowledge sources (cross-source) for validation. Integrating a structure to ground the answer semantically, with a way to explain how the generation was verified, reduces some of the most significant reliability gaps in generative AI systems and retains their flexibility for application across a variety of different domains including healthcare, law, and education. Additionally, as generative technology continues to grow both in size and in its application throughout society, the efforts of future researchers will focus on building resilient and adaptable systems that are resistant to producing hallucinated outputs while dynamically balancing the need for accurate information with the need to produce creative responses, supported by transparent and ethically aligned processes and systems. Lastly, as we work toward this goal, it will be imperative to include an integrative approach, connecting artificial intelligence (AI) developers, experts in each of the domains above, and decision-makers to create ecosystems of future-oriented aligned AIs, which have a commitment to truth and honesty as a fundamental feature, rather than an optional safety net.

REFERENCES

Bang, Y., Cahyawijaya, S., Lee, N., Su, D., Fung, P., & Madotto, A. (2023). A multitask, multilingual, multimodal evaluation of ChatGPT on reasoning, hallucination, and interactivity. arXiv preprint arXiv:2302.04023. DOI: 10.18653/v1/2023.ijcnlp-main.45

Bommasani, R., Hudson, D. A., Adeli, E., Altman, R., Arora, S., von Arx, S., . . . Liang, P. (2021). On the opportunities and risks of foundation models. arXiv preprint arXiv:2108.07258.

Christiano, P. F., Leike, J., Brown, T., Martic, M., Legg, S., & Amodei, D. (2017). Deep reinforcement learning from human preferences. arXiv preprint arXiv:1706.03741.

Dziri, N., Kamalloo, E., Mathewson, K. W., Zaiane, O. R., & Reddy, S. (2022). On the Origin of Hallucinations in Conversational Models: Is it the Datasets or the Models? *Proceedings of the 2022 Conference on Empirical Methods in Natural Language Processing*, 527–542. DOI: 10.18653/v1/2022.naacl-main.387

Gilpin, L. H., Bau, D., Yuan, B. Z., Bajwa, A., Specter, M., & Kagal, L. (2018). Explaining explanations: An overview of interpretability of machine learning. In *Proceedings of the 2018 IEEE 5th International Conference on Data Science and Advanced Analytics (DSAA)* (pp. 80–89). IEEE. DOI: 10.1109/DSAA.2018.00018

Ji, Z., Lee, N., Frieske, R., Yu, T., Su, D., Xu, Y., Ishii, E., Bang, Y. J., Madotto, A., & Fung, P. (2023). Survey of hallucination in natural language generation. *ACM Computing Surveys*, *55*(12), 1–38. DOI: 10.1145/3571730

Karpukhin, V., Oguz, B., Min, S., Lewis, P., Wu, L., Edunov, S., Chen, D., & Yih, W.-t. (2020). Dense passage retrieval for open-domain question answering. In *Proceedings of EMNLP*. DOI: 10.18653/v1/2020.emnlp-main.550

Lewis, P., Perez, E., Piktus, A., Karpukhin, V., Goyal, N., Küttler, H., . . . Riedel, S. (2020). Retrieval-augmented generation for knowledge-intensive NLP. arXiv preprint arXiv:2005.11401.

Lin, Z., Hilton, J., & Evans, O. (2022). TruthfulQA: Measuring how models mimic human falsehoods. In *Proceedings of the 2022 ACM Conference on Fairness, Accountability, and Transparency* (pp. 321–333). https://doi.org/DOI: 10.18653/v1/2022.acl-long.229

Maynez, J., Narayan, S., Bohnet, B., & McDonald, R. (2020). On faithfulness and factuality in abstractive summarization. *Proceedings of the 58th Annual Meeting of the Association for Computational Linguistics*, 1906–1919. DOI: 10.18653/v1/2020.acl-main.173

Min, S., Lewis, M., Zettlemoyer, L., & Hajishirzi, H. (2023). FactScore: Fine-grained evaluation of factual precision in long-form text generation. arXiv preprint arXiv:2305.14251. DOI: 10.18653/v1/2023.emnlp-main.741

Ouyang, L., Wu, J., Jiang, X., Almeida, D., Wainwright, C., Mishkin, P., . . . Amodei, D. (2022). Training language models to follow instructions with human feedback. arXiv preprint arXiv:2203.02155.

Raunak, V., Menezes, A., & Junczys-Dowmunt, M. (2021). The Curious Case of Hallucinations in Neural Machine Translation. *Findings of the Association for Computational Linguistics: EMNLP, 2021*, 1226–1241. DOI: 10.18653/v1/2021.naacl-main.92

Sarnaik, T., Shah, M., & Hegde, R. (2025). PROPEX-RAG: Enhanced GraphRAG using Prompt-Driven Prompt Execution. arXiv preprint arXiv:2511.01802.

Shuster, K., Xu, J., Komeili, M., Roller, S., Ju, D., Smith, E. M., . . . Weston, J. (2022). BlenderBot 3: a deployed conversational agent that continually learns to responsibly engage. arXiv preprint arXiv:2208.03188.

Thoppilan, R., De Freitas, D., Hall, J., Shazeer, N., Kulshreshtha, A., Cheng, H. T., . . . Le, Q. V. (2022). LaMDA: Language Models for Dialog Applications. arXiv preprint arXiv:2201.08239.

Thorne, J., Vlachos, A., Christodoulopoulos, C., & Mittal, A. (2018). FEVER: a large-scale dataset for fact extraction and VERification. In *Proceedings of NAACL-HLT*. DOI: 10.18653/v1/N18-1074

Zhang, T., Roller, S., Goyal, N., Artetxe, M., Chen, M., Chen, S., . . . Dinan, E. (2022). OPT: Open Pre-trained Transformer Language Models. arXiv preprint arXiv:2205.01068.

Chapter 9
Generative Artificial Intelligence in Healthcare

Sanjeev Kumar
http://orcid.org/0000-0002-7375-7341
Lovely Professional University, India

Mohammad Badruddoza Talukder
http://orcid.org/0009-0008-1662-9221
International University of Business Agriculture and Technology, Bangladesh

Firoj Kabir
http://orcid.org/0009-0001-3014-3163
Daffodil International University, Dhaka, Bangladesh

ABSTRACT

Generative Artificial Intelligence (GAI) is rapidly transforming the healthcare sector because the capacity to create new information, knowledge, and solutions is offered, rather than analyzing the ones that are already available. Unlike the classical AI models, which are designed to perform prediction and classification, generative AI involves complex algorithms such as; large language models, generative adversarial networks, and diffusion models to recreate the human-like reasoning and content-generation processes. It is finding application in clinical, administrative and research areas of healthcare and is significantly changing efficiency, accuracy and personalization of care. Clinical decision support is one of the most useful applications of generative AI. The GAI systems may be helpful to health care professionals summarizing the medical records, developing clinical notes, treatment plans recommendations, and helping with the diagnostic process with the help of a wide range of medical literature and information about the patient.

DOI: 10.4018/979-8-3373-7320-1.ch009

...t © 2026, IGI Global Scientific Publishing. Copying or distributing in print or electronic forms without written permission of IGI Global Scientific Publishing is prohibited. Use of this chapter to ...enerative artificial intelligence (AI) technologies is expressly prohibited. The publisher reserves all rights to license its use for generative AI training and machine learning model development.

INTRODUCTION

Artificial Intelligence (AI) refers to the process of machines and computer systems performing functions that are normally performed by the intelligence of humans. These are learning by doing, learning a language, observing patterns, problem solving and making decisions. Today, AI is an inseparable part of everyday life, which influences education, transportation, banking, entertainment, and, specifically, healthcare. Following the blistering technological advancement, AI is no longer a kind of automation, but it has evolved to be intelligent systems that can make reason and be creative. One of the most significant innovations in the sphere that has offered new opportunities to the medical sphere is Generative Artificial Intelligence that enhances the quality, efficiency, and accuracy of medical services (Moulaei et al., 2024).

Artificial Intelligence Introduction

Artificial Intelligence An AI is a branch of computer science that involves the creation of machines that can mimic human intelligence. The early AI was rule-based i.e. they would perform a task based on a set of instructions given to them. Over time AI has evolved to include machine learning, in which systems learn based on the data and optimize their operation without necessarily being programmed. The processing of big and complicated information by AI was enhanced by machine learning, especially deep learning, which is modeled after the human brain. In the present day, AI systems can process medical images, natural language, predict disease, and assist physicians to make decisions (Rabbani et al., 2025). The technologies that have improved the strength and dependability of AI are Natural Language Processing (NLP), computer vision, robotics, and expert systems. Medicine AI may be applied to diagnose and record patients, track their health condition, and support medical research. The ever-increasing growth of information and computing power has played a significant role in making AI more accurate and comprehensive (Rabbani et al., 2025).

Generative Artificial Intelligence Evolution

Generative Artificial Intelligence is a more advanced form of AI which is designed to create new content rather than to analyze the existing one. The traditional AI systems mainly focused on the classification or prediction of the results based on historical data. On the other hand, generative AI can produce text, images, audio, and even more complicated simulations, which are comparable to real-life data. This began with the crude probabilistic models and later evolved to more complex techniques such as neural networks. One major development in generative AI was the Generative Adversarial Networks (GANs). GANs consist of two neural networks that cooperate with each other; one of them generates data, and the other evaluates its quality. In more recent changes, large language models and diffusion models have improved generative AI further, and can better understand the situation and act like a human being. Such models are trained on large amounts of data and it allows them to learn patterns, relationships and structures in data. Generative AI in healthcare has evolved into the generation of artificial medical information, medical image enhancement, clinical documentation and drug discovery (Garg, 2025). This has made AI a facilitative analytical tool to become an active participant of innovation and problem-solving within the healthcare system.

AI in Healthcare and Importance of AI

The application of AI in healthcare is necessary since it can help improve patient care, reduce human error, and improve effectiveness in healthcare services. In the case of AI, physicians can diagnose patients faster and more accurately since the AI system is able to handle a significant amount of medical data within a relatively small time frame. In the case of AI-based imaging systems, diseases such as cancer can be detected at an early stage and this has high chances of being treated successfully. The significance of AI in personalized medicine is evident. Individualized treatment plan could be created with the help of AI which analyzes the medical history of a patient, genetic data, and lifestyle data (Nana & Marshall, 2025). The hospital AI-based systems complement the administrative capabilities of the hospitals such as appointment scheduling, patient monitoring, and record management to allow the healthcare professionals to focus more on the patients. Furthermore, AI aids medical research because it identifies the trends of diseases, predicts outbreaks, and accelerates the creation of drugs. During the global health crises, AI has come in handy in tracking down the disease spread and aiding the decision-making of the populace health (Biswas & Talukdar, 2024). Although some of the issues that can be associated with ethics, data privacy, and bias are present, the use of AI in healthcare continues to grow. Healthcare can be made more efficient, accessible and patient-centered, and using AI responsibly and with proper regulation.

The Artificial Intelligence Generative Learning

Generative Artificial Intelligence (Generative AI) is one of the most developed and rapidly moving areas of artificial intelligence. Generative AI is contrasted with the traditional systems of AI, which are usually designed to examine data, determine patterns, or forecasts. These contents can be text, graphics, audio, videos and even complex data structures (Qazi et al., 2025). The generative AI systems are trained with massive datasets and use the training to produce information that is similar to the information in the real world. As a result of this creative force, generative AI is transforming many sectors such as education, entertainment, business and most significantly healthcare.

Definition Generative Artificial Intelligence

Generative Artificial Intelligence can be defined as a type of artificial intelligence that may be utilized to create something new or content based on patterns obtained through the use of existing data. These systems are not mere copying machines, they can learn about connections in the information and use that knowledge in producing realistic and meaningful outputs. To illustrate this point, an AI model that has been trained on medical records can create clinical summaries, and a model that has been trained on medical images can create realistic synthetic images which can be used in research and training. Generative AI is founded on the learning of the inner structure of data. It defines how the words are arranged into sentences, how the pixels are arranged into images, or how the structures of molecules are arranged in chemistry. The system can generate new outputs, which are similar in structure, after the training (Okonji et al., 2024). The fact that generative AI is particularly useful in situations where a limited amount of data is available, sensitive, or expensive to access, such as in healthcare, makes it particularly relevant. The use of generative AI can be applied to support innovation through generating synthetic yet realistic data without interfering with privacy and security.

The following technologies are used in Generative Artificial Intelligence

There are several technologies underlying generative AI. One of the most important technologies which are grounded on the human brain is the neural networks. The neural networks consist of layers of connected nodes that compute and acquire patterns through data. Deep neural networks with many layers allow the generative artificial intelligence systems to acquire intricate associations in vast datasets. The most significant technology is Generative Adversarial Networks (GANs). GANs involve the application of two neural networks, a discriminator and a generator. The generator creates new information, and the discriminator evaluates the authenticity of the information as a fake or a real one (G. Chen et al., 2025). The two networks improve due to the never-ending competition resulting in highly realistic outputs. In the medical sector, GANs are used to develop synthetic medical images, enhance the quality of images, and as part of research in detecting diseases. Large

Language Models (LLMs) are also the focus of Generative AI. They are taught a lot of text and are capable of understanding and generating human like language. One of the technologies that enable LLMs to comprehend medical terms, write clinical notes, answer patient inquiries, and summarize research papers is NLP. This improves communication between the patients and the healthcare providers and reduces documentation (Albrecht et al., 2024). Another important technology that can be employed to generate data is diffusion models which can be utilized to generate meaningful outputs by repeatedly applying random noise to the input. Such models are especially effective in creating images and signals and are finding favor in medical imaging to make images of high quality and detail. Autoencoders, in particular, Variational Autoencoders (VAEs) also play a significant role in generative AI. Autoencoders are trained to learn useful representations of data, and can generate new data by sampling learned distributions. They are used in medical care in anomaly detection, data compression, and synthetic data generation. One of the significant transformations in the capabilities of AI systems is generative artificial intelligence. Generative AI enables machines to create realistic and valuable content with the help of complex technologies, such as neural networks, GANs, large language models, diffusion models, and autoencoders (Albrecht et al., 2024). It is the knowledge of these technologies that is essential in the realization of how generative AI is transforming the future of healthcare and other professions in the context of innovation, efficiency, and smart automation as shown in the table 01.

Table 1. Difference between Traditional AI and Generative AI

Basis of Comparison	Traditional Artificial Intelligence	Generative Artificial Intelligence
Definition	Traditional AI focuses on analyzing data and making predictions or decisions based on existing information.	Generative AI focuses on creating new and original content based on learned data patterns.
Main Purpose	To classify, predict, or optimize outcomes.	To generate new data such as text, images, audio, or simulations.
Output Type	Produces fixed or predefined outputs like labels, scores, or decisions.	Produces creative and flexible outputs that resemble real-world data.
Learning Approach	Often uses rule-based systems or supervised learning.	Uses deep learning models trained on large datasets.
Creativity	Limited creativity; follows set rules and patterns.	High level of creativity; can generate novel and realistic content.
Examples	Spam email detection, face recognition, weather prediction.	Chatbots, medical image generation, text and report creation.
Data Usage	Works mainly with structured and labeled data.	Works with large-scale structured and unstructured data.

continued on following page

Table 1. Continued

Basis of Comparison	Traditional Artificial Intelligence	Generative Artificial Intelligence
Adaptability	Less adaptable to new or unseen situations.	More adaptable and capable of handling complex tasks.
Role in Healthcare	Disease prediction, patient data analysis, risk assessment.	Clinical note generation, drug discovery, synthetic medical data creation.
Human Interaction	Limited interaction with natural language.	Supports natural, human-like interaction and communication.

Generative Artificial intelligence in Healthcare

Generative Artificial Intelligence (Generative AI) is becoming increasingly relevant in the healthcare industry today as it is becoming more accurate, efficient, and innovative. Unlike classical AI systems, generative AI is mostly applied to the production of new data as a text, image, and model based on the observed patterns. The ability can be applied in the medical field to make sure that physicians, researchers and medical facilities make improved decisions, deliver improved care to patients and hasten medical advancement. Some of the most important fields of generative AI application in healthcare are Clinical Decision Support Systems, Medical Imaging and Diagnosis, and Drug Discovery and Development (Hu et al., 2025).

1. **Clinical Decision Support Systems:** Clinical Decision Support Systems (CDSS) are systems utilized to assist medical workers in making informed medical decisions. Generative AI is an enhancement of these systems as it examines extensive data on patients, medical records, and clinical guidelines and offers useful suggestions. The generative AI can be used, as an example, to feed a history of patients; give possible diagnoses, and prescribe treatment options based on similar past cases. Generative AI-based systems can also assist doctors in making clinical notes and discharge summaries, and save time and paperwork (Briganti & Le Moine, 2020). These systems help in customized care whereby factors relating to the patients such as age, medical history, and lifestyle are put into consideration (Talukder, Huda, et al., 2025). As a result, medical workers will have the opportunity to spend more time communicating with patients and making significant decisions and reduce the risk of human error.
2. **Medical Imaging and Diagnosis:** Medical imaging is one of the most influential areas of application of generative AI. Technologies such as X-rays, MRI scans, CT scans, and ultrasound produce enormous data of complex nature that cannot be analyzed unless the help of an expert. The quality of images can also

be enhanced, and noise can be removed and replaced by more clear images with the help of generative AI models, which will enable doctors to diagnose diseases more accurately and at an earlier stage. The diagnosis process can be performed with the help of generative AI that identifies patterns that cannot be easily spotted by a human eye. It can be applied to detect tumors, fractures or abnormalities of the organs with high precision as an example (H. E. Hasan et al., 2024). Moreover, it is possible to educate medical students and AI models with synthetic medical images produced with the help of generative AI without infringing patient privacy. In addition to increasing the accuracy in diagnosis, this application finds application in education and research in the medical field.

3. **Drug Discovery and Development:** Drug discovery and development is a time consuming and expensive process since it can take years. Generative AI is transforming the procedure by speeding up the procedure of discovering possible drug candidates. The generative AI can make new designs of molecules, which are based on a chemical structure and biological data that may be effective in the treatment of a specific disease (Zhang & Kamel Boulos, 2023). These AI systems can predict the interaction of different drug compounds with the human body thus, removing the need of having to perform a high number of experiments using trial and error. Generative AI also comes in handy when helping researchers to model drug reactions and identify possible side effects early in the development process. This translates to the development of safe and effective medicines in less time at low cost. Generative artificial intelligence is changing the healthcare sector as it has different applications. Generative AI is helping to streamline healthcare, as well as make it more precise and patient-centered, by improving clinical decision support systems, medical imaging and diagnosis, and drug discovery and development.

Personalized Medicine and Treatment Planning

Personalized medicine is a medical practice, which targets to provide care based on the distinct characteristics of a patient compared to a one-fit-all treatment method. Personalized medicine may be made more efficient and possible with the help of Generative Artificial Intelligence. The generative AI systems may be applied to generate the individual treatment plans, according to the medical history, genetic, lifestyle, and clinical test results to analyze the large amounts of data and help develop a particular plan of action that should be adhered to by the patient. Generative AI can identify trends and links in a high volume of patient data that may be difficult to determine by hand. Because of this reason, one example is that it can be applied to predict the response that a patient will respond to a certain drug and this will allow the doctor to choose the most suitable drug and dosage (Patel et al.,

2013). This will reduce the risks of side effects and increase the risk of successful treatment. In chronic diseases such as diabetes, cancer and heart disease, generative AI may be utilized to continually track and adjust the treatment regimen based on real-time patient information (H. Kumar et al., 2025). In addition, generative AI can be used to assist physicians in developing treatment plans and care plans that are patient-specific. These AI-driven insights can be used to make evidence-based decisions and lead to improved and more precise healthcare provided by healthcare professionals. As a result, personalized medicine through the assistance of generative AI leads to an improved patient outcome, resources utilization, and patient satisfaction (Karthikeyan & Sivaneswari, 2025).

Virtual Health Assistants and Chatbots: Virtual health assistants and chatbots are another domain of major application of generative artificial intelligence in healthcare. The applications are AI-based and are built on natural language processing that communicates with patients in a human manner. They can answer questions related to health, provide medical care, remind patients to take medication and help them with basic medical procedures. Generative AI chatbots are 24/7 and, therefore, healthcare support is more available, especially in remote or underserved areas. They help to lighten the load of the medical staff by handling the routine orders such as making appointments, symptom checks and follow-ups. This will help the doctors and nurses to focus more on the treatment of the needy patients. Another feature of virtual health assistants that may be utilized to generate simplified information about diseases, treatment, and preventive care is patient education. AI chatbots can be used to assist patients emotionally and encourage them to seek the professional assistance when needed in mental health care. Though they are not a replacement of the role of doctors, they act as a facilitating tool between the patients and the health provider. Generative AI is transforming the field of healthcare by transforming medicine into personalized medicine and virtual health assistants. The healthcare system can be made more efficient, accessible, and patient-centered with the help of generative AI, which is needed to plan the treatment specifically and develop intelligent chatbots that would be able to communicate with patients in a more personalized way.

Generative Artificial Intelligence Role in Medical Research

Generative Artificial Intelligence (Generative AI) is already a revolutionary contribution to medical research because it assists in finding faster, more precise, and creative. Medical research involves researching of diseases, formulation of treatment and understanding of complicated biological systems. In the past, it was a time consuming, resource consuming and manpower consuming process. With the development of generative AI, scientists can analyze more complicated data, draw new conclusions, and model results more effectively. One of the most significant tasks of generative AI in medical research is data generation and augmentation. In the majority of cases, medical information is limited, expensive or secret due to privacy problems. Generative AI can produce high quality synthetic data that is highly similar to actual patient data without any revelation of personal details. This type of artificial data can be used in research, training AI models, and testing new medical technologies, and patient confidentiality is ensured. Generative AI also helps to predict and model diseases (Eysenbach, 2023). Generative AI models running on the patterns of genetic, clinical and epidemiological data can be used to simulate how diseases develop and change over time. This helps the researchers to understand the mechanism of disease, what are its risk factors and how different populations can be affected. This is especially in the study of complex diseases like cancer, neurological diseases and infections. Another important role of the generative AI is to accelerate clinical trials. Clinical trial development and testing is a process that is costly and time-consuming. The use of generative AI can be applied to identify the right participants, predict the outcomes of the trial, and simplify the design of the trial. It can also generate reports and summaries of the trial data and this saves the administration labor and hastens the research process (Teo et al., 2025). Other uses of generative AI in drug and therapy development are generation of potential molecular structures, prediction of drug-target interactions and treatment response modeling. It will reduce the number of experiments, which do not succeed and enable the researchers to focus on the most promising ones. Moreover, AI can be used to generate summaries of scientific literature and process it in large amounts, keeping researchers updated on the new findings. Lastly, generative artificial intelligence has become a powerful tool in the medical research. Generative (Boscardin et al., 2024) AI has the potential to enhance the efficiency and innovation of research through the development of data, disease modeling, clinical trials, and drug development. It can play a massive role in the medical science field and improve the health outcomes of the world when used in a responsible and ethical manner (Aswathy & Kumar, 2025).

Disease Research Predictive Modeling

Generative Artificial Intelligence can be used heavily in disease research in predictive modeling. It is a procedure involving the intricate algorithms to handle vast amounts of medical and biological information to give forecasts on the occurrence, progression and outcomes of the disease. Generative AI algorithms are conditioned with patient data, genomic data, laboratory data, and lifestyle data to anticipate the emergence of diseases in an individual or a group of people. The predictive modeling would help the scientists to identify the early indicators of the diseases, such as cancer, heart disease, and infectious diseases (S. S. Hasan et al., 2025). The risks of the diseases can be predicted at an early stage and preventive measures and timely treatments can be planned. Various disease conditions can also be recreated with the help of generative AI, which can help the researcher study how a disease may be transmitted or respond to different interventions. This is useful especially when one is interpreting complex and fast changing situations. The other significant advantage of predictive modeling is that it can be applied to enable personalized medicine. Generative AI models can be used to forecast how different patients will behave upon being exposed to some treatments and this allows researchers and doctors to decide on the most effective treatments (Li & Li, 2024). This increases the effectiveness of treatment and reduces non-productive side effects. Overall, predictive modeling based on generative AI facilitates the precision of information, reduces time devoted to research, and helps to make better decisions in disease research.

Increasing the rate of Clinical Trials

Clinical trials are essential in determining the safety and efficacy of new drugs and treatment, but it is time-consuming, expensive, and complicated. Generative Artificial Intelligence also helps in accelerating the clinical trials since it streamlines the process and makes it data-driven. The contribution of generative AI to patient recruitment is one of the most significant ones. Using AI systems, it is possible to identify the right participants in clinical trials by analysing medical records and eligibility criteria in a relatively small amount of time. This reduces wastage of time and improves more suitable matching of patients and trials. Generative AI can also be used in designing optimized protocols of trial because it can forecast the potential outcomes and calculate the risks beforehand. Generative AI can be used in clinical trials to analyze real-time data and deliver insights that help researchers to track the response of patients and detect side effects at the earliest stage. It can also automate documentation and develop trial reports, making the work of the administration less stressful (Viergever & Li, 2015). In addition, AI simulations can help researchers to test different conditions of the trials, before the actual experiments. In conclusion, predictive modeling in disease research and accelerating clinical trials have better opportunities with generative AI. The medical science and healthcare sector is also evolving with the help of generative AI that enables to develop new treatment and provide it to the patients more easily and risk-free through the right predictions, efficient patient selection, and quicker data analysis (Brintnall-Karabelas et al., 2011).

The advantages of Generative Artificial Intelligence in Healthcare

Generative Artificial Intelligence (Generative AI) is changing the healthcare sector to a far superior level since it is enhancing the process of medical services, their management and generation. Unlike the classical AI systems which process data mostly, the generative AI can create new information such as medical reports, images, treatment plans and research findings. These functions have numerous benefits to the patients and the medical personnel and medical facility making healthcare more efficient, precise and patient-centered. Among the major benefits of generative AI in the field of healthcare, it is possible to single out the improved accuracy and decision-making (Preiksaitis & Rose, 2023). Generative AI systems can manipulate huge amounts of medical data, including patient records, laboratory data, and radiographic data, and generate meaningful data (Talukder, Kumar, et al., 2025). This will help the doctors to make more accurate diagnoses and choose better treatment options. Generative AI can be used to ensure that healthcare services are safer and more reliable by reducing the human error and contributing to the clinical decision making process. The other significant benefit is efficiency in terms of cost and time. Clinical documentation, report generation, appointment scheduling, and communication with patients are many routine and administrative tasks that are automated by generative AI. This will reduce the patients that doctors and nurses will attend to and they will be able to focus on the patients. Medical research and drug development is also another field where generative AI is applied to speed up the processes that would otherwise take years to complete, saving healthcare organizations a lot of money (A. Chen et al., 2024). Generative AI is also very crucial in personalized medicine. The AI systems are capable of creating individual treatment plans after analyzing the personal data of a particular patient such as genetic composition, medical records and lifestyle. This personal approach makes the treatments more efficient and reduces the unwanted side effects. Patients receive care that is more suited to their needs and this leads to improved health outcomes and satisfaction. The other notable benefit is the enhanced medical research and innovation. Generative AI can be used to produce artificial medical information that can be utilized in a study to overcome the problem of data insufficiency and confidentiality. It is also used to predict, simulate diseases, and undertake expedited clinical trials. These capabilities are applied in order to accelerate medical discoveries and help researchers to develop new therapies and vaccines more efficiently (Yu & Zhai, 2024). Patients are also more engaged and gain access through generative AI. AI-based virtual health assistants and chatbots provide 24/7 support, respond to patient inquiries, remind the patient of medication, and health education. This is very beneficial to those who are in the remote or underserved areas and may not receive healthcare professionals easily. The artificial intelligence that is generative in the field of healthcare has far-reaching and powerful benefits. Healthcare is becoming a smarter, faster, and more accessible system with the help of generative AI to improve its accuracy and efficiency, facilitate personalized care, or research among other things. It can play a significant role in improving the health outcomes of the world through proper and ethical execution (S. Kumar, 2024).

Healthcare Services Cost-cutting

Among the advantages of Generative Artificial Intelligence in the healthcare industry, one should single out the fact that it may save money, but offer high-quality medical services. The financial burden on the healthcare system is likely to be caused by the cost of healthcare treatment, shortages of staff, and the increasing number of patients. Overcoming these challenges with the help of generative AI is possible since medical documentation, billing services, appointment scheduling, and report preparation are routine and time-consuming, and can be automated. This will enable hospitals and clinics to reduce the cost of running the institutions in terms of the number of individuals working manually and also help them to use their resources more efficiently. The cost reduction through the improvement of early diagnosis and disease prevention is also achieved with the help of generative AI (Glaa et al., 2014). The AI-based tools will be capable of processing the patient information and doing the predictions concerning the potential health risks to enable the doctors to do something beforehand. The costly treatment and the long stay in the hospital is saved by early diagnosis. Moreover, generative AI can help in drug discovery and clinical trials in accelerating the research, which will save a significant amount of money on creating new medicines. Generally speaking, generative AI can help to make healthcare more cost-effective and sustainable by making it more efficient and less wasteful (S. Kumar et al., 2024).

Better patient care and experience

Generative Artificial Intelligence positively influences patient care and the experience of healthcare overall by making it personalized, more accessible, and responsive. The AI systems can create custom treatment programs based on the medical history, genetic profile, and lifestyle of a patient. This personalized treatment improves the efficacy of the treatment and reduces the side effects, which leads to a positive health outcome. Another use of generative AI in improving the patient experience is virtual health assistants and chatbots. These devices can assist the patients 24/7, answer the questions of the patients, remind the patients to take their medications, and guide the patients after the treatment. The patients are not required to wait in line hours to access a very basic information, which increases the satisfaction and trust in the healthcare services. Generative AI also improves doctor-patient communication. Clinical AI-generated summaries and simplified explanations enable patients to have a more accurate understanding of their medical conditions and treatment options. Artificial intelligence-based monitoring systems can be applied to hospitals to monitor the health of patients in real-time and inform healthcare professionals about the emergencies to help them in a timely manner. Generative AI plays an essential role in reducing healthcare spending and enhancing patient experience and care. Generative AI may be used to design a more efficient, patient-friendly, and accessible healthcare system since it not only increases the efficiency but also enables a personalized approach to treatment and better interaction between patients and medical staff.

Hardships and Ethical problems

Generative Artificial Intelligence (Generative AI) has many beneficial sides to the medical sphere, but there are also various challenges and ethical concerns that should be considered. One of the greatest barriers is the credibility and accuracy of AI-generated outputs. Generative AI systems may provide incorrect or unfair recommendations in case they are trained using incomplete or biased data. These errors can be highly risky in healthcare in terms of patient safety and treatment results. Another important ethical matter is prejudice and justice. The generative AI models are trained using previous data, and such data may be biased in terms of the existing inequalities in healthcare. Therefore, AI systems may discriminate against certain groups of people unintentionally leading to unequal treatment. The AI systems should also be fair and inclusive to ensure that they are not discriminatory. Ethical concerns also exist regarding the question of transparency and accountability (Evans-Lacko et al., 2013). Many generative AI models are black boxes i.e. they are not readily understandable how they arrive at a specific decision. This lacks adequate transparency that can reduce the degree of trust between the patients and the healthcare professionals. Another ethical dilemma that needs to be established with clear guidelines and regulations is the question of responsibility in the event of mistakes committed by AI systems whether by the developers, providers or the institutions.

Issues of Data Privacy and Security

One of the most significant concerns regarding the use of generative AI in healthcare is deemed to be the privacy and safety of the data. Healthcare systems rely on sensitive patient information such as medical records, genetic information and personal information. This data can lead to data, identity theft and misuse of personal information unless it is well secured. The fact that generative AI systems cannot work without substantial data is one of the reasons that may lead to unauthorized access and cyberattacks. Even anonymization of data is not a guarantee that the data cannot be re-identified in case of lax security. This brings up the problem of patient consent and control of personal information (Bertino, 2016). To address them, one will need robust data protection such as encryption, secure storage, and restrictive access. Legal and ethical standards of data usage and patient privacy should also be observed in healthcare institutions. Trust between patients and healthcare providers can be developed based on open data policies and informed consent. In conclusion, despite the fact that generative AI can revolutionize healthcare, one cannot ignore the problems related to ethics, data privacy, and security. It should be implemented in a responsible manner, ethically and good security practices to ensure that generative AI is implemented safely, equitably, and in the best interest of the patients (Terzi et al., 2015).

Artificial Intelligence and Equity and Discrimination

The applications and development of Artificial Intelligence systems, especially in the healthcare industry, are much prone to discrimination and equitability. The generative AI models are trained with the help of large datasets that are typically collected in real life situations. The AI models may incorporate and amplify such biases in case these datasets are not balanced, incomplete, and rely on social inequalities. To provide an example, in case medical data is mostly representative of a certain age group, gender, or community, the AI system may present less accurate results to the underrepresented groups. Biased AI models can be applied in the medical sector to give unfair treatment advice, misdiagnose, or give unequal treatment. This can contribute to inequalities in health rather than reduce it. To ensure fairness of AI models, one has to use as much data as possible, test the models frequently on the bias, and update them to correct inequitable outcomes (Liu et al., 2021). The human control is also required to ensure that AI generated results are vetted before they are used in medical decisions. Making the AI models equitable is a good measure to ensure that all patients receive equal and ethical care regardless of their background. To reduce the bias and increase the reliability of AI systems in healthcare, responsible AI practices and ethical guidelines are relevant (Talukder, Khan, et al., 2024).

Openness and Confidence in Artificial Intelligence

The idea of transparency is associated with the intelligibility of AI systems in their processes and decisions. Many generative AI models are complex and are black boxes, and therefore, it is difficult to understand how they make decisions. This transparency gap in healthcare can reduce the level of trust between the physicians and the patients as the medical decisions are to be transparent, understandable and accountable. AI processes ought to be more transparent and open to attain trust in AI systems. Explainable AI tools can also help medical employees understand how a specific recommendation or prediction was made. This will allow the physicians to check the AI outputs and make good decisions. Transparency will also contribute to the identification of errors, biases or limitations of AI systems. Implementation of AI in healthcare needs trust. When patients are convinced that the system is just, safe, and trustworthy, they will be more willing to accept the assistance of AI. Clear rules, ethical guidelines, and constant surveillance can help to make the responsible use of AI easier. To be ethical in applying generative AI in healthcare, it is important to tackle the problem of bias and provide fairness, and promote transparency and trust. Considering these aspects, AI systems can support healthcare specialists in their activities and offer safe, just, and patient-centered care.

The Future of Generative Artificial Intelligence in Healthcare

Generative Artificial Intelligence (Generative AI) will probably undergo a paradigm shift in the future of healthcare by increasing the accuracy, accessibility, efficiency, and innovation of medicine. As technologies are further developed, the generative AI systems will be more intelligent, more reliable, and more widespread in healthcare services. The future of generative AI in healthcare is massive and promising, beginning with intelligent hospitals and going worldwide to the management of the disease. One of the most important trends in the future is the appearance of smart and AI-based hospitals. Generative AI will be deployed using Internet of Things (IoT) devices, wearable health devices, and electronic health records to provide real-time monitoring of patients and predictive care. Artificial intelligence will continuously analyze the information regarding the patients and provide early warnings on the potential health problems so that healthcare providers can avoid them. This will reduce instances of emergencies, hospitalization as well as the cost of treatment. The use of generative AI is also likely to develop personalized and precision medicine greatly. In the future, AI models will be made more accurate to interpret genetic data, lifestyle trends, and environment to develop a highly personalized treatment plan. This will improve efficacy of treatments, reduce side effects and help in the control of chronic diseases in a better way. The application of AI-based treatment personalized to an individual will become a standard part of patient care, especially in such fields as oncology, cardiology, and mental health. Another area of future development is also medical research and drug discovery. Generative AI will continue to accelerate the discovery of new medicines that produce potential drug molecules and predict the efficacy of these molecules. It will help the researchers to simulate complex biological process and test different treatment scenarios without necessarily having to use costly laboratory experiments to do so. It will lead to faster development of vaccines and life saving drugs especially during health crises in the world. Generative AI will also be able to enhance telemedicine and remote healthcare services. Virtual health assistants and chatbots will become more advanced AI-based technologies that can provide accurate health information and mental health support and follow-up. Generative AI will bridge this disparity in rural and underserved areas where patients and healthcare providers will be able to receive affordable and accessible medical help. Translating languages and voice-based artificial intelligence will also improve communication between physicians and patients in different locations. In the future, generative AI will also positively influence medical education and training. Artificial intelligence-based simulations of virtual patients, interactive learning applications will help medical students and professionals to gain practical experience in a safe environment. Such systems will have a chance to adapt to individual learning needs, increasing the degree of skills and clinical confidence. Powerful ethical systems and laws will be necessary in the future to implement generative AI in healthcare, even though its potential is enormous. To establish trust in AI systems, the issue of data privacy, bias, transparency, and accountability will need to be addressed. The governments, healthcare institutions, and technology developers should work together to ensure that the application of generative AI is responsible and ethical. Generative artificial intelligence has a very promising future in the health sector. Further innovation, ethical use, and regulation of generative AI has the potential to make the healthcare industry smarter, more personalized, more accessible, and patient-centered.

New Trends and innovations

The new trends and innovations in Generative Artificial Intelligence (Generative AI) that can offer smarter, faster, and efficient solutions are determining the future of healthcare. One of the most remarkable trends is the application of the developed large language models that have the capacity to understand complex medical terminology and generate accurate clinical records, research summaries, and explain to the patient in a way that they can understand. These models reduce the paperwork that a physician must perform and increase the interaction between health care professionals and patients. The next significant invention is the growing use of artificial medical information. Generative AI can produce realistic patient information and medical images which are used to train AI systems and conduct research without jeopardizing patient privacy. This trend makes it easier to innovate faster and does not undermine the ethical standards. In addition, the multimodal AI systems, combining text, images, audio, and sensor information, are increasingly becoming common. These systems provide a more specific view of the health of the patient by taking into account different types of data. Generative AI is also being linked to wearables and remote monitoring apparatus. These systems continuously generate knowledge on the basis of real time health data and they facilitate prevention of diseases and early detection (Dewangan et al., 2024). The AI-based tools of simulations and digital twins are emerging as a powerful instrument to test treatments and pre-empt health outcomes. These tendencies emphasize the fact that generative AI is not being applied on an experimental level but in practice in the healthcare environment. The integration of smart hospitals entails incorporating technology into the hospitals' operations to enhance service delivery.

Human Smart Hospitals Integration

Smart hospitals are the future of the healthcare facilities, and generative AI is the center of their creation. Automated, data-driven, and patient-centered operations can be automated and integrated with generative AI and hospital systems. Smart hospitals have AI systems that are connected with electronic health records, diagnostic devices, medical devices, and hospital management systems. The integration will enable real-time data analysis and generation of actionable insights to doctors and administrators. Generative AI can be used to assist in intelligent patient monitoring by processing sensor, wearable, and medical device-collected data. It can generate warnings of unhealthy states, predict a patient decline, and facilitate an early medical response. The AI-based systems can also automatize the hospital operations by bed management, personnel scheduling, and resource management, which simplifies the processes and is less expensive to run. In addition, generative AI in the form of virtual assistants to guide patients, answer their questions, and provide particular care instructions enhances patient experience in smart hospitals. The reports and summaries generated by AI can help healthcare professionals make better decisions since they are quicker. The healthcare systems are being transformed with the new trends and developments of generative AI and its use in smart hospitals. Such innovations will surely introduce efficiency, improve patient care and a smarter and connected healthcare environment.

Use of Generative Artificial Intelligence in Global Healthcare

Generative Artificial Intelligence (Generative AI) is increasingly playing an important role in improving health care systems in the world by providing greater access, efficiency, and quality of medical care in different countries. The current health problems such as shortage of medical workers, inequality in healthcare access, rising healthcare expenses, and disease epidemics in the globe must be addressed with novel and sustainable solutions. Generative AI offers viable solutions to address these problems and help to improve the health outcomes at the global level. One of the most significant roles of generative AI in healthcare in the world is the improvement of access to medical services, especially in the developing and remote regions. AI-based virtual health assistants and chatbots provide easy medical care, symptom check, and health education in different languages (Talukder, Swarna, et al., 2025). These systems help bridge the distance that is created between the doctors and the healthcare facilities in order that people can receive prompt health information and support. Generative AI is also applied in surveillance and disease management in the world. Analyzing the data in different regions, AI systems would be able to offer predictions about the spread of the disease, identify the tendencies of the outbreaks, and support early warning systems. The same will be significant in times of pandemics and outbreaks of infectious diseases to make sure that governments and health institutions respond in a timely and effective manner. Another important use of generative AI is in medical research and cooperation. AI systems can work with data on studies worldwide and generate summaries, insights, and treatment recommendations. This makes sharing of knowledge between researchers and medical practitioners in other countries possible. The acceleration of drug discovery and vaccine development is also done with the help of generative AI, which is necessary to combat global health emergencies. In addition, AI can be applied to generate information that can be used in educating and training healthcare professionals all over the world. The simulation, virtual patients, and learning modules based on AI help to train doctors, nurses, and medical students even in under-educated regions. This improves the standards of healthcare, and produces quality medical forces in the globe. In low- and middle-income countries, healthcare is also cheaper with the help of generative AI that reduces healthcare costs and improves efficiency. AI can assist in the sustainable healthcare system by automating the administrative processes and simplifying the distribution of resources. Generative artificial intelligence is a revolutionary position in world healthcare. Generative AI has the potential to reduce health disparities and transform the world to be a healthier place by increasing access, supporting disease management, research, and medical education.

Future Projections and Future Recommendations of Generative AI in Healthcare

Generative Artificial Intelligence (Generative AI) has already begun to transform health care, but its ability is yet to be tapped out. The further development of generative AI in the healthcare field is to make it more functional, safer, and more deeply embedded in clinical practice, research, and healthcare management. To accomplish this, it involves adequate planning, innovation and moral execution.

Future Directions

1. **High-level Customization of Healthcare:** In the future, Generative AI will have the capability to create highly personalized treatment plans. The AI models will be fed with the genetic data, lifestyle tendencies, medical history, and real-time health data to generate specific treatments. This will help to make precision medicine a common practice, and this will improve the prognosis of chronic diseases like cancer, diabetes, and heart diseases.
2. **Relation to Smart and Connected Hospitals:** In the future, hospitals will be smarter, and they will be equipped with IoT devices, wearable sensors, electronic health records, and AI. Generative AI will convert this stream of data into actionable results, and it can be utilized to track in real-time, offer predictive healthcare, and optimize hospital workflows.
3. **Global Disease Surveillance and Prevention:** Generative AI will play a major role in international health by predicting disease outbreaks, epidemics spread modeling, and interventions simulation. This will make governments and health organizations to react faster to the health crisis of the people.
4. **Quick Drug Discovery and Clinical Research:** Artificial intelligence-based molecular models, treatment simulations, and predictive trials will continue to revolutionize drug discovery. This will conserve research cost, reduce time schedules and provide faster delivery of vaccines and therapies to the rest of the world.
5. **Improved Patient Interactions and Telehealth:** Future AI systems will be more interactive and human-like in their virtual assistants, to educate patients, mental health and telemedicine. Generative AI will enhance treatment plan compliance and provide continuous health recommendations.

Recommendations

1. **Ethical and Transparent AI Development:** The AI systems must be developed in a manner that is fair, accountable and transparent to ensure they are safe to use. The developers should not be biased in training data and clarify AI decision-making to healthcare professionals and patients.
2. **Data Privacy and Data Security:** The strong encryption, anonymization, and safe data management habits should protect sensitive data of patients. Ethical data use policies and patient consent are to be followed strictly.

3. **Regulatory Frameworks:** Government and international health organizations should develop clear guidelines regarding the manner in which AI tools in the healthcare sector should be authorized, monitored, and utilized. This will ensure safety, reliability and trust of the populace.
4. **Continuous Learning and Collaboration:** Healthcare professionals will be taught how to use AI tools so that they could be capable of interpreting the information given by AI. The AI programmers, healthcare providers, and policy-makers should work together to come up with realistic and easy to use solutions.
5. **Research and Innovation:** Governments, non-governmental organizations, and healthcare organizations are advised to invest into generative AI research in order to find new applications, improve the accuracy of models and make them more accessible to underserved populations.

CONCLUSION OF THE STUDY

Generative Artificial Intelligence (Generative AI) is rapidly transforming the medical sector into a game changer and is altering the way healthcare is delivered, learnt, and treated. Compared to the classic AI that tends to focus on analysis and prediction, generative AI can create new content, make insights and simulate the real world. This potential has far-reaching clinical decision support, medical imaging, drug discovery, personalized treatment planning and patient engagement. The article finds that generative AI improves accessibility, efficiency, and accuracy of healthcare. It enables physicians to make superior judgments and is useful in the early diagnosis of illnesses, accelerates drug development and provides personalized treatment based on the requirements of a particular patient. Artificial intelligence (AI) virtual assistants and chatbots can be applied to enhance patient engagement and education particularly in remote or underserved locations to bridge the gap in healthcare across the globe. Secondarily, generative AI can be applied to medical research, as it may be employed to generate synthetic data, predictive models, and clinical trial simulations, which save time, cost, and risk.

Despite such advantages, there are such concerns as data privacy, ethical concerns, bias of AI models, and transparency, which are linked to the implementation of generative AI in healthcare. These issues need to be tackled in order to achieve safety, fairness, and trustworthiness of AI systems. It is significant that it should be implemented by appropriate regulatory frameworks, ethical grounds, robust data security systems, and continuous monitoring. Generative AI has an enormous potential of transforming the healthcare systems of the world in the future. It can be used in the future in intelligent hospitals, precision medicine, global disease surveillance, and entire AI-based telemedicine systems. By means of responsible and shared utilization of the advanced AI technologies, healthcare can become a lot more efficient, patient-centered, and accessible to everyone. In conclusion, generative AI is not the technological transformation, but the paradigm shift in healthcare. Being used ethically and effectively, it will bring improved patient outcomes, streamline medical processes, accelerate research, and ultimately improve the quality and accessibility of healthcare in the world. The article affirms the fact that generative AI is not just one of the supportive technologies that it will turn into an inseparable companion of the future of medicine.

REFERENCES

Albrecht, M., Shanks, D., Shah, T., Hudson, T., Thompson, J., Filardi, T., Wright, K., Ator, G., & Smith, T. R. (2024). *Enhancing Clinical Documentation Workflow with Ambient Artificial Intelligence: Clinician Perspectives on Work Burden, Burnout, and Job Satisfaction*. Health Informatics. DOI: 10.1101/2024.08.12.24311883

Aswathy, V. K., & Kumar, S. (2025). Silent Struggles: Revealing the Mental Health Crisis Among Kattunauakan Tribal Adolescents in Kerala, South India. In Poddar, S., & Ansar, W. (Eds.), *Sustainable Development Goals (SDG) and Its Intersection With Health and Well-Being* (pp. 377–398). IGI Global., DOI: 10.4018/979-8-3693-9755-8.ch013

Bertino, E. (2016). Data Security and Privacy: Concepts, Approaches, and Research Directions. *2016 IEEE 40th Annual Computer Software and Applications Conference (COMPSAC)*, 400–407. DOI: 10.1109/COMPSAC.2016.89

Biswas, A., & Talukdar, W. (2024). *Intelligent Clinical Documentation: Harnessing Generative AI for Patient-Centric Clinical Note Generation*. https://doi.org/DOI: 10.48550/ARXIV.2405.18346

Boscardin, C. K., Gin, B., Golde, P. B., & Hauer, K. E. (2024). ChatGPT and Generative Artificial Intelligence for Medical Education: Potential Impact and Opportunity. *Academic Medicine*, *99*(1), 22–27. DOI: 10.1097/ACM.0000000000005439 PMID: 37651677

Briganti, G., & Le Moine, O. (2020). Artificial Intelligence in Medicine: Today and Tomorrow. *Frontiers in Medicine*, *7*, 27. DOI: 10.3389/fmed.2020.00027 PMID: 32118012

Brintnall-Karabelas, J., Sung, S., Cadman, M. E., Squires, C., Whorton, K., & Pao, M. (2011). Improving Recruitment in Clinical Trials: Why Eligible Participants Decline. *Journal of Empirical Research on Human Research Ethics; JERHRE*, *6*(1), 69–74. DOI: 10.1525/jer.2011.6.1.69 PMID: 21460590

Chen, A., Liu, L., & Zhu, T. (2024). Advancing the democratization of generative artificial intelligence in healthcare: A narrative review. *Journal of Hospital Management and Health Policy*, *8*, 12–12. DOI: 10.21037/jhmhp-24-54

Chen, G., Liu, C., Ooi, G. A., Tan, M., Xie, Z., Yin, J., Yip, J. W. L., Zhang, W., Zhu, J., & Ooi, B. C. (2025). *Generative AI for Healthcare: Fundamentals, Challenges, and Perspectives* (Version 1). arXiv. DOI: 10.48550/ARXIV.2510.24551

Dewangan, S., Kumar, S., & Tyagi, P. K. (2024). Transforming Hospitality and Tourism With AI and Innovative Technologies. In Talukder, M. B., Kumar, S., & Tyagi, P. K. (Eds.), *Advances in Hospitality, Tourism, and the Services Industry* (pp. 66–83). IGI Global., DOI: 10.4018/979-8-3693-6755-1.ch004

Evans-Lacko, S., Knapp, M., McCrone, P., Thornicroft, G., & Mojtabai, R. (2013). The Mental Health Consequences of the Recession: Economic Hardship and Employment of People with Mental Health Problems in 27 European Countries. *PLoS One*, *8*(7), e69792. DOI: 10.1371/journal.pone.0069792 PMID: 23922801

Eysenbach, G. (2023). The Role of ChatGPT, Generative Language Models, and Artificial Intelligence in Medical Education: A Conversation With ChatGPT and a Call for Papers. *JMIR Medical Education*, *9*, e46885. DOI: 10.2196/46885 PMID: 36863937

Garg, S. (2025). The Role of Generative AI in Personalized Medicine and Treatment Recommendations. *Clinical Medicine And Health Research Journal*, *5*(02), 1214–1227. DOI: 10.18535/cmhrj.v5i02.463

Glaa, B., Zoghlami, N., & Taghipour, A. (2014). Outsourcing and off-shoring healthcare services: A way to cut the costs and improve quality. *2014 International Conference on Advanced Logistics and Transport (ICALT)*, 189–194. DOI: 10.1109/ICAdLT.2014.6864116

Hasan, H. E., Jaber, D., Al Tabbah, S., Lawand, N., Habib, H. A., & Farahat, N. M. (2024). Knowledge, attitude and practice among pharmacy students and faculty members towards artificial intelligence in pharmacy practice: A multinational cross-sectional study. *PLoS One*, *19*(3), e0296884. DOI: 10.1371/journal.pone.0296884 PMID: 38427639

Hasan, S. S., Fury, M. S., Woo, J. J., Kunze, K. N., & Ramkumar, P. N. (2025). Ethical Application of Generative Artificial Intelligence in Medicine. *Arthroscopy*, *41*(4), 874–885. DOI: 10.1016/j.arthro.2024.12.011 PMID: 39689842

Hu, D., Guo, Y., Zhou, Y., Flores, L., & Zheng, K. (2025). A systematic review of early evidence on generative AI for drafting responses to patient messages. *Npj Health Systems*, *2*(1), 27. DOI: 10.1038/s44401-025-00032-5

Karthikeyan, E., & Sivaneswari, S. (2025). Artificial Intelligence in Personalized Medicine for Head and Neck Cancer: Optimizing Prescriptions and Treatment Planning. *Biomedical Materials & Devices*. Advance online publication. DOI: 10.1007/s44174-025-00320-6

Kumar, H., Aswathy, V. K., & Kumar, S. (2025). Converging Realms of Social Health, Domestic Workers, and Telemedicine Landscape: Challenges and Prospects. In Özbek, M. F., & Christiansen, B. (Eds.), *Organizational Sociology in the Digital Age* (pp. 165–180). IGI Global., DOI: 10.4018/979-8-3693-7398-9.ch010

Kumar, S. (2024). The Role of Digital Marketing on Customer Engagement in the Hospitality Industry. In Bansal, R., Ngah, A. H., Chakir, A., & Pruthi, N. (Eds.), (pp. 177–191). Advances in Business Information Systems and Analytics. IGI Global., DOI: 10.4018/979-8-3693-0815-8.ch010

Kumar, S., Talukder, M. B., & Kaiser, F. (2024). Artificial Intelligence in Business: Negative Social Impacts. In Dadwal, S., Goyal, S., Kumar, P., & Verma, R. (Eds.), (pp. 81–97). Advances in Human Resources Management and Organizational Development. IGI Global., DOI: 10.4018/979-8-3693-0724-3.ch005

Li, Y., & Li, J. (2024). Generative artificial intelligence in medical education: Way to solve the problems. *Postgraduate Medical Journal*, *100*(1181), 203–204. DOI: 10.1093/postmj/qgad116 PMID: 38061077

Liu, X., Xie, L., Wang, Y., Zou, J., Xiong, J., Ying, Z., & Vasilakos, A. V. (2021). Privacy and Security Issues in Deep Learning: A Survey. *IEEE Access : Practical Innovations, Open Solutions*, *9*, 4566–4593. DOI: 10.1109/ACCESS.2020.3045078

Moulaei, K., Yadegari, A., Baharestani, M., Farzanbakhsh, S., Sabet, B., & Reza Afrash, M. (2024). Generative artificial intelligence in healthcare: A scoping review on benefits, challenges and applications. *International Journal of Medical Informatics*, *188*, 105474. DOI: 10.1016/j.ijmedinf.2024.105474 PMID: 38733640

Nana, V. K., & Marshall, M. T. (2025). Generative Artificial Intelligence in Healthcare: A Bibliometric Analysis and Review of Potential Applications and Challenges. *AI*, *6*(11), 278. DOI: 10.3390/ai6110278

Okonji, O. R., Yunusov, K., & Gordon, B. (2024). *Applications of Generative AI in Healthcare: Algorithmic, ethical, legal and societal considerations. Preprints*. DOI: 10.36227/techrxiv.171527587.75649430/v1

Patel, V. L., Kaufman, D. R., & Kannampallil, T. G. (2013). Diagnostic Reasoning and Decision Making in the Context of Health Information Technology. *Review of Human Factors and Ergonomics*, *8*(1), 149–190. DOI: 10.1177/1557234X13492978

Preiksaitis, C., & Rose, C. (2023). Opportunities, Challenges, and Future Directions of Generative Artificial Intelligence in Medical Education: Scoping Review. *JMIR Medical Education*, *9*, e48785. DOI: 10.2196/48785 PMID: 37862079

Qazi, M. A., Nadeem, M., & Yaqub, M. (2025). *Beyond Generative AI: World Models for Clinical Prediction, Counterfactuals, and Planning* (Version 1). arXiv. DOI: 10.48550/ARXIV.2511.16333

Rabbani, S. A., El-Tanani, M., Sharma, S., Rabbani, S. S., El-Tanani, Y., Kumar, R., & Saini, M. (2025). Generative Artificial Intelligence in Healthcare: Applications, Implementation Challenges, and Future Directions. *BioMedInformatics*, *5*(3), 37. DOI: 10.3390/biomedinformatics5030037

Talukder, M. B., Huda, M. N., Kumar, S., & Hasan, Md. M. (2025). Metaverse Future of Digital Medical Tourism: In V. I. Hassan, A. Singh, A. S. Jaboob, & A. Sorayyaei Azar (Eds.), *Advances in Healthcare Information Systems and Administration* (pp. 173–198). IGI Global. DOI: 10.4018/979-8-3693-7888-5.ch007

Talukder, M. B., Khan, M. R., & Kumar, S. (2024). Socioeconomic Gaps and Foster Inclusive Growth: Sustainable Tourism Initiatives. In Hassan, V., Staszewska, A., & Bhartiya, S. (Eds.), *Advances in Hospitality, Tourism, and the Services Industry* (pp. 56–82). IGI Global., DOI: 10.4018/979-8-3693-5405-6.ch003

Talukder, M. B., Kumar, S., & Das, I. R. (2024). Mindfulness of Digital Detoxification: Healthy Lifestyle in Tourism. In Kankaew, K., Chaudhary, S., & Widtayakornbundit, S. (Eds.), (pp. 56–71). Advances in Logistics, Operations, and Management Science. IGI Global., DOI: 10.4018/979-8-3693-1273-5.ch004

Talukder, M. B., Swarna, D. A., Kumar, S., & Kabir, F. (2025). Leveraging Technology for Employee Wellness in Hospitality: Smart Solutions for a Vibrant Service Culture. In Baez, M. D. (Ed.), (pp. 221–246). Advances in Logistics, Operations, and Management Science. IGI Global., DOI: 10.4018/979-8-3373-1687-1.ch008

Teo, Z. L., Thirunavukarasu, A. J., Elangovan, K., Cheng, H., Moova, P., Soetikno, B., Nielsen, C., Pollreisz, A., Ting, D. S. J., Morris, R. J. T., Shah, N. H., Langlotz, C. P., & Ting, D. S. W. (2025). Generative artificial intelligence in medicine. *Nature Medicine*, *31*(10), 3270–3282. DOI: 10.1038/s41591-025-03983-2 PMID: 41053447

Terzi, D. S., Terzi, R., & Sagiroglu, S. (2015). A survey on security and privacy issues in big data. *2015 10th International Conference for Internet Technology and Secured Transactions (ICITST)*, 202–207. DOI: 10.1109/ICITST.2015.7412089

Viergever, R. F., & Li, K. (2015). Trends in global clinical trial registration: An analysis of numbers of registered clinical trials in different parts of the world from 2004 to 2013. *BMJ Open*, *5*(9), e008932. DOI: 10.1136/bmjopen-2015-008932 PMID: 26408831

Yu, L., & Zhai, X. (2024). Ethical and Regulatory Challenges of Generative Artificial Intelligence in Healthcare: A Chinese Perspective. *Journal of Clinical Nursing*, jocn.17493. DOI: 10.1111/jocn.17493

Zhang, P., & Kamel Boulos, M. N. (2023). Generative AI in Medicine and Healthcare: Promises, Opportunities and Challenges. *Future Internet*, *15*(9), 286. DOI: 10.3390/fi15090286

Chapter 10
Integrated Healthcare Management With AI and Real-Time Optimization Multi-Criteria Decision Analysis

Nagendra Kumar Musham
http://orcid.org/0009-0001-5398-1821
Celer Systems Inc., USA

Venkata Sivakumar Musam
http://orcid.org/0009-0003-2699-7208
Astute Solutions LLC, USA

G. Arulkumaran
School of C&IT, REVA University, Bangalore, India

Department of Information and Communications Technology, Information and Communications University, Lusaka, Zambia

Nurul Fahmi
http://orcid.org/0009-0001-4999-2720
Department of Informatics Engineering, Politeknik Negeri Bengkalis, Indonesia

ABSTRACT

The advancement of integrated healthcare management combines multiple forms of technology (AI, telemedicine Video Calls, and wearable devices) for improving pa-

DOI: 10.4018/979-8-3373-7320-1.ch010

t © 2026, IGI Global Scientific Publishing. Copying or distributing in print or electronic forms without written permission of IGI Global Scientific Publishing is prohibited. Use of this chapter to enerative artificial intelligence (AI) technologies is expressly prohibited. The publisher reserves all rights to license its use for generative AI training and machine learning model development.

tient access to care and creating better responses to emergencies (CG. For example, during the COVID-19 Pandema). In this case, the AC-AL Habitat uses a combination of AI-based predictive modeling, multi-criteria decision analysis, and emergency response systems to accomplish 3 goals: 1) maximize resource allocation; 2) support effective decision making; 3) provide remote continuous patient monitoring. The system was able to provide a 94% Accuracy Rate in predicting patient outcomes, a 95% efficiency in Container Capacity Risk Mitigation, and 93% Scalability; thus, providing maximized equitable treatment, as well as real-time continued patient surveillance. By maximizing operational efficiency and readiness, this integrated healthcare management solution will promote the establishment of proactive, patient-centric, sustainable healthcare systems on a global level.

1. INTRODUCTION

Integrated healthcare management is the seamless integration of diverse healthcare functions, such as monitoring, diagnosis, and treatment, through interoperable systems. Manickam et al. (2022) Artificial intelligence (AI) is key to this transition since it processes massive amounts of data to generate predictive insights and optimize resource allocation. A very important process for delivery to be improved in health care, particularly in a poor environment or emergencies.

Khairy et al. (2024). Emergency response systems are the heart and soul of modern health care; they can address emergencies with speed and accuracy. These technologies integrate technology to provide prompt treatments for the reduction of hazards and coordination of care. Multimodal insights, garnered from a variety of sources, including clinical, environmental, and behavioural data, make for better decision-making due to a complete knowledge of the health status of the patient as well as system performance. Meanwhile, wearable-integrated telemedicine has revolutionized remote monitoring through continuous, real-time health information for patients and clinicians. This development is of particular importance in the control of infectious disorders such as COVID-19, for which isolation and remote care are critical to prevent the spread of the disease.

This title shows the integration of modern technologies and healthcare systems into one adaptive powerful framework. Pushadapu, 2023 says, “Integrated Healthcare Management” combines multiple procedures and various types of technology into just one system without duplication and synergistically further strengthens the same. “AI and Real-Time Optimization” underlines intelligent algorithms for predicting outcomes and optimum exploitation of resources, which enables decisions at breakneck speed. Aparisi-Cerdá et al. (2024) “Multi-Criteria Decision Analysis” (MCDA)- the use of structured approaches to make balanced decisions whenever there are conflicting criteria related to treatment efficacy, patient happiness, and cost-effectiveness.

This would be "Emergency Response Systems" that could be so designed to have an immediate response in medical emergencies with minimum delay and maximum survival rate. Bayoudh et al. (2022) "Multimodal Insights": The fusion of several data streams, from clinical observations through wearable sensors for an overview of the health of the patient along with the system. Finally, "Wearable-Integrated Telemedicine" is the integration of wearable health equipment with telehealth platforms in a seamless manner, allowing for remote and continued monitoring of patients; this comes in handy during pandemics, such as COVID-19.

The COVID-19 pandemic has exposed several weaknesses in the global healthcare systems, which include an overcrowded hospital, poor diagnostics, and no infrastructure for monitoring patients remotely. This problem was a stimulus for a paradigm shift from the traditional reactive care strategy to proactive and preventive strategies. AI, wearables, and telemedicine have come up as the key enablers of this shift that has given answers to the gaps in accessibility, monitoring, and resource management. Predictive analytics and on-the-go optimization allowed AI to scan large datasets, monitor the use of resources, and prioritize treatment.

According to Vaghasiya et al. (2022), wearables with telemedicine integrated enabled remote monitoring of the patients quarantined amidst the COVID-19 pandemic. Calculated vital signs from wearables would include heart rate, oxygen saturation, and temperature; the information communicated back to the healthcare professionals will enable monitoring and action. The use of MCDA frameworks also helped healthcare administrators to make informed decisions based on a balanced assessment of cost, efficacy, and feasibility, which resulted in optimal care delivery even under high-stress conditions.

The pandemic increased the need for health care, but critical in managing this was the emergency response systems. They rely on real-time data, which gives speedy triage, resource mobilization, and crisis management; thus, these have reduced mortality rates and improved patient outcomes. Uppal et al. (2022) Multimodal insights bolstered efforts with multiple sources of data combined in support of healthcare providers in more holistic and informed judgments. Together, these developments built a responsive and flexible system of health care that may meet problems to come.

This is where a new era of healthcare innovation arises with AI, real-time optimization, MCDA, ERS, multimodal insights, and wearable-integrated telemedicine. They are the response to a lot of needs that are presented to modern healthcare: better access, better decision-making processes, and more resilient management of emergencies. The further evolution of the global healthcare environment calls for integrated systems to help create a future where not only will patient care be efficient and effective but also fair and individualized. These technologies, which focus on proactive and preventive approaches, ensure that healthcare systems are better prepared for both ordinary issues and unprecedented disasters such as the COVID-19 pandemic.

The following objectives are:

Use telemedicine and wearables to provide quality healthcare in remote and underdeveloped places.

Improving Emergency Response to Create robust AI-powered solutions to provide faster and more effective medical crisis interventions.

Use multi-criteria decision analysis to make informed, balanced, and evidence-based healthcare decisions.

Integrating wearable technology with telemedicine allows for continuous, real-time patient health tracking.

Create adaptive systems that can meet both individual patient requirements and large-scale public health emergencies.

The research emphasizes the need for better data integration, validation, and coordination between health systems and public health authorities in the process, indicating gaps in the present data infrastructure interoperability that could be leveraged to enhance decision-making in pandemics. *Guerrier et al. (2022)* It further highlights the need for the adoption of harmonized data standards for data availability in useable formats while also rectifying inadequacies in the existing medical informatics systems. These advancements could provide health care administrators with more reliable and timely information, thereby making healthcare solutions in crisis situations more efficient and effective.

The paper explores the barriers that health care managers faced in using data for decision making during the COVID-19 pandemic. *Guerrier et al. (2022)* It pays attention to quality, timeliness, and interoperability with many health information systems and public health departments. It makes improved data infrastructure and standardization foundational elements to provide reliable information at the right time that facilitates proper decision-making. The most important aspect will occur during an emergency like a pandemic situation in which correct and well-integrated data become very essential for adequate and timely resource allocation and managing an event.

2. LITERATURE SURVEY

Kasula (2023) places strong emphasis on the revolutionary impact of Artificial Intelligence in health care, particularly for improving patient care and streamlining processes. With an extensive review of literature as its base, the paper delivers a holistic framework to implement AI in healthcare, including customized care, clinical decision support, predictive analytics, and process optimization with considerations to ethics, regulation, and interoperability issues. The framework provides mechanisms of deployment, collaboration among the stakeholders, and evolutionary development of AI solutions. It will, therefore, try to better patient outcomes and operations by defining a deployment roadmap of AI technology to develop healthcare innovation and future discoveries for the healthcare system.

Shumba et al. (2022), researched advanced healthcare personalization through wearable devices embracing biocompatible materials that might capture detailed biologic information on one's heart condition and blood pressure. These wearable devices through real-time processing using machine learning are enabling developments in health issues so intervention sooner is possible. However, two of the major issues with such a cloud-based processing system include issues with privacy and latency. Therefore, the article focuses on Edge Computing and on-device AI for applications that are based on modular systems with adaptable sensors and low-cost communication. All of these applications require rapid response times, comfort, and scalability, and hence meet important needs in a diverse area, such as elderly people with chronic illnesses under care through assisted living.

Surendar Rama Sitaraman, 2022: studies the role of edge computing for IoT system security and privacy improvement by using advanced anonymized AI algorithms. The research will be based on the application of homomorphic encryption where computations are done on encrypted data without revealing the content, hence robust data safety. Further, the paper focuses on federated learning which is a decentralized strategy of machine learning where models are trained directly on the edge devices and thereby reduce the risks associated with sensitive data transfers to central servers. With such cutting-edge approaches, research depicts how edge computing may address a few of the most fundamental issues in IoT security and privacy in a manner that also remains compliant with regulations. It is demonstrated to result well in reality and proved to act as a safer and more reliable remedy that can be deployed in IoT settings for the secure protection of sensitive data.

Zahid et al. (2022) proposed AI-based adaptive methodologies that optimize the performance of IoT-based wearable healthcare devices. This focuses on improving energy efficiency, reliability of data transmission, and battery life for long-term health monitoring and diagnosis via Body Sensor Networks. This paper presents a unique framework, where an Adaptive Transmission Data Rate mechanism is used, which dynamically changes sensor activity to optimize energy usage, and a Self-Adaptive Routing Algorithm for efficient and reliable data routing in an energy-efficient manner. The proposed methodologies show high energy efficiency, reliability, and cost-effectiveness by utilizing real-time datasets with wearable devices, thus facilitating smart and sustainable healthcare.

Issues concerning energy conservation and load balancing of cloud-enabled IoT systems are presented in the research by Aqeel et al. (2023). Most notably, energy-intensive applications like healthcare call for higher innovation. The authors have proposed, in this paper, an energy-aware AI model based on the big data analytics concept coupled with a Chaotic Horseride Ride Optimisation Algorithm. CHROA proved efficient for optimizing energy consumption by balancing the loads. The experimental results depict that it works better than the existing schemes by showing a higher average throughput value of 70.122 Kbps compared with other algorithms, such as ABC, GSA, and WD-FA. Thus, it is an energy-efficient solution for IoT and IoE systems.

Więckowski et al. (2023) describe how defining the criteria weights in Multi-Criteria Decision Analysis, MCDA, is highly challenging in case explicit weight vectors for systems are absent. This ultimately leads to obscure reasons for outcomes from the perspective of decision-makers. The COMET model and linear regression were used to determine both global and local weights for estimating the Formula One drivers' performance in the 2021 season. This approach provides the decision-maker with a good deal of insight into criterion significance and yields more reliable results than other approaches. The study reveals that global and local weights are significantly associated; however, the global weights provide more precise insights, thereby making the technique a valuable decision-making tool.

According to Gardas (2022), Healthcare 4.0 can improve the efficiency of service, but there are organizational challenges to it. DEMATEL technique is used in this research to identify and analyze the relationships of ten major hindrances and three crucial causal factors which are a lack of top management vision, hierarchical structures, and a shortage of trained people. All these factors have a significant impact on the adoption of Healthcare 4.0, but the lack of R&D facilities impacts the least. The remedy for these limitations is a necessity to reduce treatment costs and enhance patient outcomes. The findings provide meaningful insights for healthcare professionals in the quest to develop effective strategies for implementing sophisticated technologies.

Belay et al. (2022) used a multi-criteria decision-making technique to identify crucial success determinants for infrastructure projects in Ethiopia. Their research seeks to improve decision-making and project performance in low-income East African nations by identifying critical priorities and overcoming organizational constraints. Data from construction professionals were reviewed using Expert Choice 11 and Kendall's coefficient to verify dependability. Clear objectives, consultant competency, past consulting experience, collaboration, and contractor financial health are all critical success elements. The study identifies stakeholder conflicts and provides a benchmark method for improving decision-making in Ethiopia's infrastructure sector, providing useful insights for similar situations.

He et al. (2023) highlight the complicated river network and pollution hazards in the inter-provincial transboundary area of the Taihu Lake Basin, which experiences regular environmental pollution events that endanger water quality. They observe that China lacks early warning systems and appropriate risk simulation tools, which impedes water management efforts. To address this, the report suggests a cross-border pollution risk management plan as well as an early warning system based on contemporary technology. The system identified 2,713 sources of nitrogen and phosphorus pollution as well as simulated emergency solutions thereby greatly enhancing transboundary water quality and reducing the risks of pollution to the Taihu Lake watershed.

The research study by Raj Kumar Gudivaka (2023) aims at the synergistic integration of Artificial Intelligence and Robotic Process Automation to increase the efficiency of organizations across different sectors. This study depicts how RPA can take care of normal, routine processes more efficiently and result in effective operations. When combined with AI, these systems gain superior characteristics such as adaptability, intelligence, and decision-making capabilities and thus result in better overall efficiency. It, therefore leads to increased productivity, cost savings, and lesser error rates, especially in those sectors that require precision, for example, manufacturing, health care, and finance. Despite the above-mentioned advancement, the report still points to the problems that exist in the implementation of AI and RPA in complex scientific and research settings. These demands need further research to fully tap its potential in many applications.

Wong and Lee (2023) designed a system that strengthens the cooperation of people, people information, fire information, and resource information with each other during interior fires. It has modules of route directions, victim tracking, and real-time resource sharing. It uses a two-stage pathfinding algorithm with hybrid positioning strategies using building information models, inertial sensors, and wireless signals for better performance and accuracy. With an 89.29% reduction in calculation time with an error of positioning by only 1.36 meters, this paper draws out significant insights toward making emergency response more effective, through better collaboration, using the tools of digital twins.

Liang et al. (2024) talk about the fast-developing area of multimodal machine learning that focuses on the development of intelligent systems that contain many forms of communication such as text, voice, images, and more. It is applicable in the areas of video analysis, robotics, and healthcare, but there are challenges in its use due to the complexity of many interdependent data types. The paper considers three core concepts heterogeneity, connectivity, and interactivity devises a taxonomy of six fundamental challenges in this representation, alignment, reasoning, generation, transference, and quantification. The historical and contemporary advancements summarized serve to enlighten developing tendencies and reveal several open questions awaiting resolution whose answers will push the development ahead in this increasing area.

Emish and Young (2024) discuss the prospects of digital health monitoring with portable neuroimaging technologies, such as EEG, fNIRS, and PPG, for remote monitoring of brain activity. Their review of 23 papers focuses on the application of mobile EEG devices in mental health, neurology, sleep monitoring, and neurofeedback therapies, where headsets and ear-EEG are the most popular. The outputs of such devices provide constant signal quality that matches well with clinical-grade EEGs and hence ensure readiness for real-world use. Though promising for continuous patient monitoring, the study calls upon further validation and usability improvement as technology advances.

3. METHODOLOGY

The proposed methodology is founded on an integrated and data-driven healthcare management structure that combines the likes of artificial intelligence (AI), multi-criteria decision analysis (MCDA), emergency response systems (ERS), multi-modal analytics, together with the use of wearable devices and telemedicine to provide healthcare that is proactive, scalable, and patient-centered. To start with, various data streams obtained from wearable sensors, clinical records, environmental inputs, and communication networks are processed and analyzed through AI predictive models to identify health risks, forecast patient outcomes, and optimize resource utilization in real-time. Following the application of multi-criteria decision analysis (MCDA), the careful prioritizing of healthcare choices by weighing vital factors like cost, clinical effectiveness, equity, urgency, and risk is taking place, which ensures that the limited resources, especially in emergencies, are allocated in a transparent and evidence-based manner. Emergency response systems (ERS) modules make use of real-time communication infrastructures and predictive analytics to assist algorithms in patient category determination, and also in the allocation of rapid response groups and reallocation of resources dynamically, while at the same time gaining insight from different data sources that are physiological, behavioural, and contextual which in turn improves awareness of the situation and decision accuracy. Meanwhile, wearable-integrated telemedicine facilitates the whole process by providing constant remote monitoring, sending of automated alerts, and conducting timely clinical interventions that would eventually lead to less hospital burden as well as better accessibility of healthcare services. The whole process, tightly knitted together, gives rise to a healthcare ecosystem that is both resilient and adaptive to the demands of routine clinical practice as well as the great public health crises like pandemics.

Figure 1. Multi-Criteria Decision Analysis (MCDA) is a framework for making balanced healthcare decisions and allocating resources.

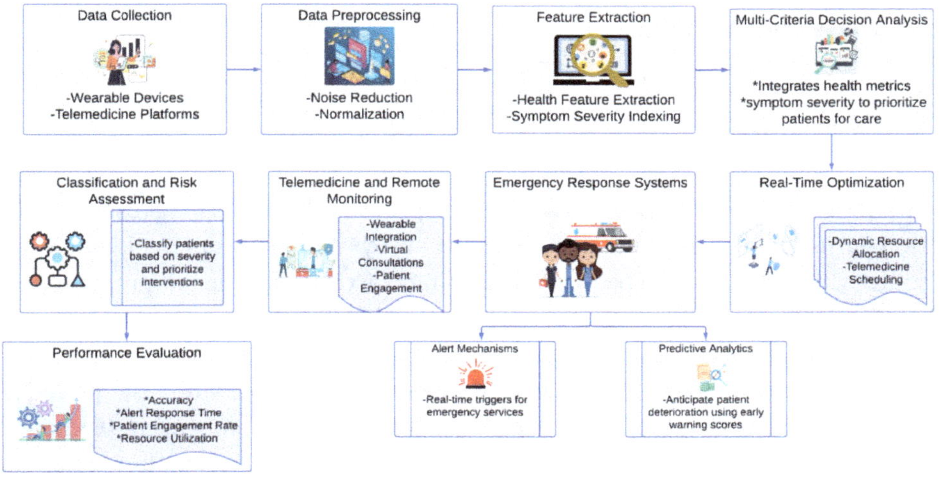

Figure 1 represents the MCDA framework for allocating healthcare resources. It explains how MCDA aggregates various criteria, such as cost, efficiency, equity, and risk. It weighs the options by ranking them according to the Analytic Hierarchy procedure. It tells why the MCDA ensures open evidence-based decision-making during emergencies, such as a pandemic.

3.1 Multi-Criteria Decision Analysis (MCDA)

MCDA is a systematic process that helps in evaluating and ranking different alternatives by multiple, sometimes competing, criteria. It helps to strike balances such as cost, efficiency, equity, and risk in achieving objectives by systematically combining qualitative and quantitative data. Its broad applications exist in such areas as health, disaster management, and infrastructure planning to optimize resources and enhance outcomes. The technique, through the Analytic Hierarchy Process (AHP), as well as the Weighted Sum Model (WSM), enables efficient ranking of options transparently and consistently. Therefore, because of its flexibility, MCDA could be applied to address difficult problems in complex, multi-dimensional systems.

$$S_i = \sum_{j=1}^{n} w_j \cdot x_{ij} \tag{1}$$

Where:

- S_i: Score for option i
- w_j: Weight for criterion j
- x_{ij}: Performance of option i on criterion j

3.1.1 MCDA for Healthcare Resource Allocation

MCDA is an imperative tool in health care, particularly concerning resource allocation during crises like pandemics. There is always a limited supply of health care resources available such as beds in the hospital, vaccines, and health professionals. Therefore, one has to prioritize requirements. MCDA allows decision-makers to systematically evaluate many criteria, which include patient severity, geographical accessibility, treatment cost, and effectiveness. For example, while the period of the COVID-19 pandemic is going on, MCDA frameworks are well implemented in rationing vaccines based on parameters, such as density of population, infection rates, and socio-economic status. It therefore, through structural and rank complex tradeoffs, enables MCDA to ensure the efficient, just, and transparent allocation of resources.

$$S_i = \sum_{j=1}^{n} w_j \cdot x_{ij} \tag{2}$$

Where:

- S_i: Score for option i
- w_j: Weight of criterion j
- x_{ij}: Performance score of option i on criterion j

3.1.1.1 Application in Emergency Scenarios

MCDA has been extremely important in decision-making in situations like a pandemic or natural calamity. Factors involved here are the demographics of the patient, the severeness of the disease, and the infrastructure of health delivery, thus maximizing one's resource usage in this time constraint. In the case of COVID-19, MCDA frameworks guided ventilator allocation decisions, ensuring prompt care for the most vulnerable patients while maintaining transparency.

$$P(S) = \frac{\sum_{i=1}^{n} R_i}{\sum_{j=1}^{m} D_j} \quad (3)$$

3.1.1.2 Use for long-term healthcare planning

Beyond crises, MCDA is involved in long-term planning for healthcare services. It helps in setting priorities on investments in the healthcare infrastructure, such as new hospitals, service expansion, and upgrades of medical technology. MCDA helps in deciding strategically so that healthcare systems are more resilient and sustainable.

$$H(t) = P(t) \cdot R(t) \quad (4)$$

3.1.2 Integration with AI and Big Data

Adding AI to big data significantly enhances MCDA and optimizes the decision-making process by automating the very process. The AI system assesses huge amounts of datasets to identify patterns and generate instantaneous insights that support the decision-making process. An example would be AI-driven MCDA in disaster management to identify the evacuation zones; taking data from satellite imagery, incorporating real-time updates about weather, and population size, among other inputs, into its account. In a similar sense, big data updates the models of MCDA using actual input, thereby providing judgments that are prompt but also accurate. So AI combined with big data develops MCDA into being an ever-dynamic flexible model and in a position to manage even highly complex data-heavy problems.

$$S_{AI} = \max\left(\sum_{i=1}^{n}\sum_{j=1}^{m} w_j \cdot x_{ij} \cdot f(i,j)\right) \quad (5)$$

Where $f(i,j)$ is an Al-weight adjustment function.

3.1.3 Applications in Infrastructure Development

MCDA is important in infrastructure planning because it assesses projects in terms of cost, environmental impact, and social benefits. For instance, in urban planning, MCDA helps prioritize transportation projects based on travel time savings, construction costs, and ecological preservation. It is supportive of balanced decision-making, thus ensuring sustainable growth as well as community needs are met. MCDA frameworks are also applied in disaster-resilient infrastructure projects, where designs that mitigate risks such as floods or earthquakes are prioritized.

$$CER = \frac{\Delta C}{\Delta E} \quad (6)$$

3.1.4 Future Directions and Innovations

Future enhancements of MCDA will be on the harnessing of sophisticated technology to enhance efficiency and scalability. Quantum computing promises faster computations for large-scale MCDA models, whereas geospatial analytics will incorporate location-specific data to improve judgments for regional difficulties. This technology will let stakeholders trace the decision-making processes of MCDA so that the results can be known and accountability is present. Predictive analytics would make it possible for MCDA to predict scenarios, thus enhancing applications in long-term planning in health care, disaster management, and sustainable development. All this is aimed at making the MCDA stronger, fairer, and applicable universally.

3.1.4.1 Blockchain for Transparent Decision-Making

Blockchain technology will take MCDA further with aspects of transparency, traceability, and accountability. It creates an immutable ledger that records all steps of the decision-making cycle, from the criteria selection, weights allocations, evaluations, and final results. Such decisions are tamper-proof and auditable, thus raising stakeholders' confidence. The blockchain also avoids manipulation of data because it is decentralized; therefore, it is uniquely beneficial for applications in the public sector like urban planning and resource allocation in which transparency becomes the most important factor. Blockchain integrates MCDA and fairness and accountability principles into important scenarios of decision-making by growing stakeholder confidence and ensuring ethical decision-making.

3.1.4.2 AI-Driven Adaptive MCDA Models

AI makes MCDA a dynamic and responsive framework as AI-based MCDA models assess the real-time data and learn from past decisions for dynamically modifying criterion weights and priorities. This capability is very crucial in dynamic situations such as healthcare crises or disaster management where conditions may change rapidly. AI supports the accuracy of decisions by hidden data patterns, automated evaluation, and real-time recommendations. For example, in disaster response, AI-driven MCDA can help make ranking evacuation zones easy or allocate resources efficiently based on updated risk assessments that will hasten and adopt decisions in response to changing conditions.

Algorithm 1. MCDA-Based Algorithm for Efficient Healthcare Resource Allocation Using Weighted Scoring and Ranking

```
Input: Options (O), Criteria weights (W), Performance matrix (P), Total resources (T)
Output: Ranked options (R)
Normalize Performance:
For each criterion j:
For each option i:
Normalize P[i][j] using max(P[:, j]).
Weighted Scoring:
For each option i:
Score[i] = 0
For each criterion j:
Score[i] += W[j] * P[i][j]
Resource Allocation:
Rank options based on Score in descending order.
Allocate resources T to the top-ranking options proportionally.
Return R.
End Algorithm
```

Algorithm 1 The MCDA-based approach improves healthcare resource allocation using MCDA. It starts by standardizing performance indicators across multiple criteria to assure comparability. Weighted scoring is then used, with each criterion given a weight based on its value. The system computes a cumulative score for each choice, ranks them in descending order, and allocates resources proportionally to the highest-ranked options. This systematic strategy ensures that resources are distributed transparently, equitably, and efficiently, especially during crises like pandemics or for strategic long-term healthcare planning. Balancing competing priorities, the algorithm supports efficient decision-making in resource-constrained situations.

3.2 Emergency Response Systems (ERS)

Emergency Response Systems (ERS) are sophisticated and integrated systems that aim to decrease the effects of catastrophes through dissimilar coordinated actions of planning, rapid response and adaptive recovery. The ERS system consists of infrastructures with real-time monitoring, AI-enabled predictive analytics, and strong communication networks. The system can scan the environment for threats and, at the same time, notify everyone who needs to know, and then call in the needed resources from different agencies all at once. The system optimizes in a dynamic way personnel, medical supplies and logistics according to changing risk levels and situational demands, thus ensuring efficient and prioritized responses in case of natural disasters, public health emergencies, and industrial accidents. The use of multimodal data from sensors, satellites, health care systems, and community reports not only makes the situation easier to understand but also increases the accuracy of the decisions taken. The participation of communities and the cooperation between different countries help in the strengthening of the preparedness and response capacity. In addition to crisis management in the first instance, ERS also promotes long-term recovery when coordinated with housing rehabilitation efforts, infrastructure restoration, mental health support and socioeconomic rebuilding, thus increasing the resilience and sustainability of the affected populations.

Figure 2. Emergency Response Systems (ERS): Framework for Real-Time Communication and Dynamic Resource Allocation

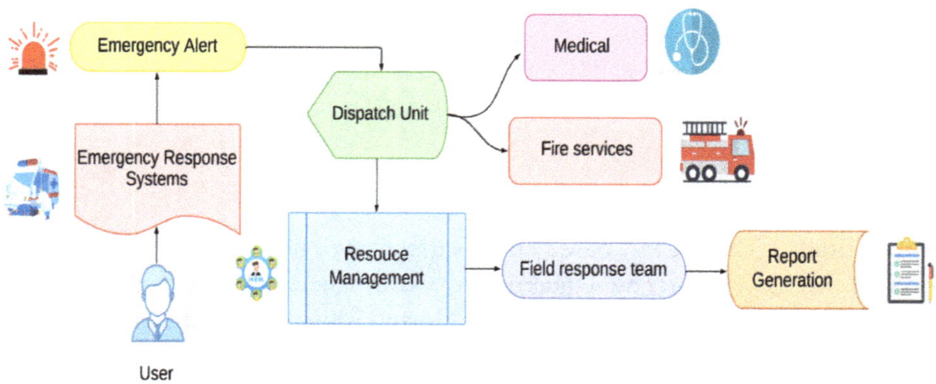

Figure 2 shows ERS architecture for real-time communication and resource allocation. It is going to depict the data flow from an emergency toward a predictive analytics environment into actionable insights. AI and IoT devices make possible rapid response and resource allocation. This diagrammatic depiction of how ERS decreases the delay improves coordination, and makes critical responses much easier at times of natural disasters and pandemics.

$$R_k = \frac{D_k}{\sum_{j=1}^{n} D_j} \cdot T \tag{7}$$

Where:

- R_k: Resources allocated to region k
- D_k: Demand in region k
- T: Total available resources

3.2.1 Overview of Emergency Response Systems

Emergency Response Systems are the necessary frameworks for managing and mitigating the effects of catastrophes such as natural disasters, health crises, and workplace accidents. These systems pool resources and trained personnel with cutting-edge technologies to make possible responses that are prompt and effective. ERS has a goal of reducing casualty and property damage and minimizing the amount of time needed to recover, coordinating rescue activities, allocating resources, and communicating in efforts to enhance readiness and response capabilities through predictive techniques community interaction, and real-time monitoring of data. Finally, ERS has a critical role in restoring stability and saving lives during critical crises by responding to both urgent needs and long-term rehabilitation. Technology has significant impacts on increasing the productivity of ERS.

3.2.1.1 The role of technology in modern emergency response systems

Developed systems can collect real-time data, undertake predictive analytics, and respond with AI and IoT devices. Examples include AI computers that process seismic data to forecast earthquakes or meteorological phenomena to predict floods. There is an application of drones and robots scanning difficult areas. Smartphone applications help the affected communities to report incidents and track their progress. These have minimized the response time with greater accuracy and reduced impacts associated with emergencies. Preparations are anticipatory measures to prevent hazards as well as increase resilience. This incorporates sensitizing people on preparation, conducting exercises on emergency responses, and supplying outlets for critical inputs.

3.2.1.2 Emergency Preparation and Risk Mitigation

Mitigation of risks in Emergency Response Systems (ERS) consists of prevention and systematically through a series of steps to identify risk factors like the infrastructure, environment, and operations; meanwhile, making the already stricken areas and the infrastructure more resistant to the disaster. Method A, inclusive, works through one and the same channel by the combination of predictive modelling based on AI, historical data analysis, and real-time monitoring; it waits for the disaster and then evaluates the damage it would cause. At this early stage, the warning systems come in with alerts to the authorities and people concerned, thus, the preventive activities like mass evacuations, moving of resources to likely needy areas beforehand, and safeguarding infrastructure are made possible. As an illustration, in flood-prone areas, the constant gathering of information about rains, rivers, and weather patterns leads to very accurate forecasting and quick action that saves many lives and properties from being lost. Through the integration of disaster preparedness planning, resilient infrastructure development, and intelligent monitoring technologies, ERS has a better ability to adapt, and thus, the total impact of emergencies is reduced significantly.

3.2.2 Real-Time Communication Networks

Real-time communication networks are the backbone of successful emergency response systems, where responses can be made rapidly from people to authorities and vice versa. Advanced technologies such as 5G and satellite-based networks ensure that communication is reliable and not interrupted, especially in disaster-prone locations whose infrastructure has been destroyed. Communication networks provide a way of sharing updated, real-time information that coordinates decisions and resource distribution. Mobile applications and emergency warning systems help the authorities to disseminate vital information, including evacuation routes, safety precautions, and situational updates directly to the affected areas. This strong communication framework eliminates delays, enhances situational awareness, and assures timely and effective responses during emergencies.

$$R_N = \frac{\text{Successful transmissions}}{\text{Total transmissions}} \tag{8}$$

3.2.2.1 Applications for Healthcare and Emergency Services

Telemedicine areas that critically depend on real-time networks for healthcare and management in emergency response. The networks during telemedicine allow real-time performance of video consultations, remote monitoring of the vital signs of patients, and collaborative diagnostic determination. It helps in the coordination of quick response times during emergencies by feeding rescue teams live updates and geographic information. Consequently, it saves more lives and results in the best allocation of resources whenever disasters strike.

3.2.2.2 Challenges and Solutions in Real-Time Communication

Moreover, the application of edge computing will cut down the delay in communication by handling the important data at the source itself, while at the same time, the load-balancing methods will take care of the traffic during the most crowded hours in the most efficient way. The use of security audits that are done regularly, zero-trust architectures, and intrusion detection systems that operate continuously in real time are also very important factors that contribute to the strength and durability of real-time communication networks.

3.2.3 ERS in Urban vs. Rural Settings

Variably differ in urban and rural conditions. Urban locations require quick coordination and resource allocation for managing large-scale evacuations and emergencies due to high population density, high-rise structures, and complex transit networks. Operations are hindered by traffic congestion and restricted evacuation routes. In contrast, rural areas sometimes lack dependable communication infrastructure, making real-time data exchange and coordination challenging. Sparse populations and large geographic distances require specialized actions, such as deploying mobile troops or drones for resource delivery and medical treatment. These require developing specialized techniques to ensure the effectiveness of emergency management in diverse contexts.

$$T = \frac{D}{S} \tag{9}$$

Where:

- D: Distance to the incident site
- S: Speed of the response unit

Algorithm 2. Real-time communication and risk-based resource allocation for emergency response systems.

```
Input: Emergency scenarios (E), Communication network (N), Resources (R)
Output: Optimized Emergency Response Plan (P)
Risk Assessment:
For each scenario e in E:
Compute Risk[e] = P(e) * C(e)
Optimize Communication:
```

```
If network reliability R_N < Threshold:
Upgrade communication infrastructure.
Resource Allocation:
For each high-risk scenario e:
Assign nearest available resource r.
Feedback and Adjustment:
Monitor response effectiveness in real time.
Reallocate resources if required.
Return P.
End Algorithm
```

Algorithm 2 The ERS Communication Optimization algorithm enhances emergency response systems through event prioritization based on high risk, thus speeding up the distribution of resources. It evaluates risks using likelihood and consequence indicators, finds communication network bottlenecks, and optimizes infrastructure to ensure continuous real-time communication. The algorithm ensures timely response by minimizing delay as it allocates resources dynamically to the most urgent circumstances. Through real-time monitoring and feedback, adaptive reallocation of resources can be done in an emergency that takes into consideration shifting situations. This approach integrates new technologies like AI and IoT for situational awareness and decision-making in disaster management, hence remarkably improving outcomes in urban as well as rural areas.

3.3 Multimodal Insights

Multimodal insights amalgamate data from multiple resources, such as environmental sensors, satellite photos, wearable devices, as well as social media, which give a comprehensive view into complex events. The system can be used for instant monitoring, predictive analytics, as well as dynamic decision-making in real-time during emergencies/disasters. Multimodal insights combine geographic, behavioural, and physiological data and, therefore, enhance risk assessment, resource allocation, and response. They allow the authorities to offer appropriate interventions, improve community involvement, and maximize disaster management strategies. The overall vision given by multimodal insights promotes better preparedness, reaction, and recovery, hence reducing the impact of disasters on people and infrastructure. Moreover, the integration of different types of data sources enhances the precision and trustworthiness of situational awareness by eliminating uncertainties and solving information gaps in fast-paced crises. This method, based on data, empowers the concerted decision-making of the involved parties, resulting in quicker, more efficient, and better-informed emergency responses.

$$F(t) = \alpha \cdot D_1(t) + \beta \cdot D_2(t) + \gamma \cdot D_3(t) \quad (10)$$

Where:

- $F(t)$: Fused insight at a time t
- $D_1(t), D_2(t), D_3(t)$: Data streams
- α, β, γ: Weights for streams

3.3.1 Role of Remote Sensing in Multimodal Insights

Remotely sensed data contribute massively toward its insights into multimodality, in the sense of supplying high-resolution data to remote sensing in terms of disasters. Satellites and drone imagery in the air help produce real-time visuals related to the extent of damage brought about by floods and the spread of wildfires caused by the same and destruction by earthquakes. Infrared and radar imaging give much scope to hazard identification, owing to heat signatures and water level precipitation. Coupled with environmental and geographical sources, this data would allow proper assessment of large-scale disasters. This supports the models that perhaps might give actionable insight in conjunction with early warnings, resource allocation, and recovery planning. This gives it a significant place in the framework of disaster management.

$$I = \alpha_1 S_1 + \alpha_2 S_2 + \ldots + \alpha_k S_k \quad (11)$$

3.3.1.1 Satellite Imaging for Environmental Monitoring

The most important tool used in monitoring changes in the environment over wide areas is remote sensing technology, which incorporates satellite photography. Satellites that are equipped with sensors, such as MODIS and Landsat, capture high-resolution photographs of vegetation, water bodies, and atmospheric conditions. These photographs yield critical information about the nature of deforestation, drought, and the health of vegetation issues all very crucial for understanding and predicting dynamics in natural disasters. Multispectral and hyperspectral imaging techniques increase the capability to observe some environmental stresses.

3.3.2 Multimodal insights for community engagement

Real-time social media information coupled with citizen reports and data from mobile apps creates multi-modal insights that help the community engage better. By using artificial intelligence-powered evaluation of public sentiment, geotagged disaster reports, and behavioural trends, one can easily get actionable local data. Crowdsourced data also helps support data from other official sources for more insightful knowledge on emergency needs. Such knowledge results in more focused communication during emergencies-such as an alert message or update from resources-promoting trust between authorities and citizens. It becomes possible for communities to proactively participate in catastrophe preparedness and response through multimodal data, which improves both resilience and outcomes. Moreover, getting feedback from people instantly helps the authorities to confirm the situation on the ground and to change their tactics in real time. The merging of input from the crowd and official data streams not only makes the emergency management process more transparent but also more inclusive. The public's involvement in emergency response operations through this method not only allows them to take control, but it also fortifies the social fabric and guarantees that the response is still adaptable, fair, and relevant to the local area.

3.3.3 Healthcare Applications for Multimodal Insights

Insight gleaned from multimodal knowledge boosts combined data from wearable devices, clinical records, and environmental monitoring. Wearables measure a patient's vital signs: heart rate and oxygen level. Such data enables monitoring in real-time for the vulnerable. When combined with environmental data like air quality or temperature, these insights can forecast health concerns like heatstroke or respiratory difficulties. Healthcare providers use this data to distribute resources, and hospital capacity management, and prioritize the delivery of care. Additionally, multimodal insights facilitate the forecasting of disease outbreaks and interventions, thereby ensuring timely and effective healthcare during emergencies.

3.3.4 Advances in Data Visualization for Multimodal Perspectives

Data visualization is changing the way multimodal insights are presented and understood. Interactive dashboards combine data in real-time from several sources, enabling exploration of that data by the decision-makers. 3D geospatial mapping illustrates the repercussions of a disaster in terms of change to topography, hence improving situational awareness. Overlays in augmented reality allow planning and training in immersive and realistic conditions. These technologies make complex data easier to understand, allowing for speedier decision-making and improved communication among stakeholders. Enhanced visualization makes catastrophe preparation and response multimodal insights better accessible, more actionable, and more impactful.

$$V = \frac{\text{Feature Range}}{\text{Visualization Range}} \quad (12)$$

3.3.4.1 Interactive and Immersive Visualization Techniques

Interactive dashboards and immersive 3D visualizations provide dynamic environments to analyze multimodal data. Zooming, filtering, and real-time modifications enable stakeholders to explore specific data subsets. Immersive technologies such as Virtual Reality and Augmented Reality allow people to analyze multimodal data within simulated environments. This may provide better insight into some phenomena, like disaster impact and urban planning scenarios.

Algorithm 3. Multimodal Data Integration for Actionable Insights Using Weighted Fusion and Threshold Analysis

```
Input: Data streams (D), Weights (W), Threshold (T)
Output: Integrated insights (I)
Preprocess Data:
For each modality m in D:
Normalize data D[m].
Weighted Integration:
For each data point i:
I[i] = 0
For each modality m:
I[i] += W[m] * D[m][i]
Threshold Insights:
For each integrated insight I[i]:
If I[i] > T:
Flag as high priority.
Return I.
End Algorithm
```

Algorithm 3 The program Multimodal Insights Integration analyzes diverse streams of data on the environment, clinical level, and social level to provide meaningful insight during a disaster event. It adheres to the standardization of different modalities of input so that consistency can be ensured for the data. From there, weighted integration computes the combination of data streams based on predetermined priority levels, which results in deeper insights. If observations surpass predefined thresholds, then such high-priority observations are highlighted for more focused attention to critical areas. This strategy enhances real-time decision-making due to its provision of a singular view of the situation, better situational awareness, and improved resource allocation. The algorithm provides disaster management teams with accurate, timely, and complete information that will enable them to execute response tactics effectively.

3.4 Wearable-Integrated Telemedicine

Wearable-integrated telemedicine integrates wearable health devices and the telemedicine platform, whereby there is a guarantee to have real-time monitoring as well as management of patient health status. These types of wearable health devices have included smartwatches or biosensors, collecting several key data - heart rate, oxygen saturation, and temperature, which is conveyed to healthcare doctors over telemedicine networks. These networks enable continuous tracking of patients by clinicians with immediate interventions and changes of treatments from a distance. Especially useful for chronic disorders, infectious diseases, and post-operative care, telemedicine integrated with wearables improves accessibility, increases convenience for patients, and brings about proactive treatment through the eradication of the need to consult in person, particularly in far-flung or vulnerable groups. Also, the application of AI-driven analytics to wearable data permits the early identification of anomalies and the generalization of risk per individual patient. This strategy is advantageous in terms of reducing hospital overcrowding, cutting down healthcare expenses, and facilitating continuity of care, particularly in times of public health crises and pandemics.

Figure 3. Wearable-Integrated Telemedicine: Real-Time Health Monitoring and Remote Patient Management Framework

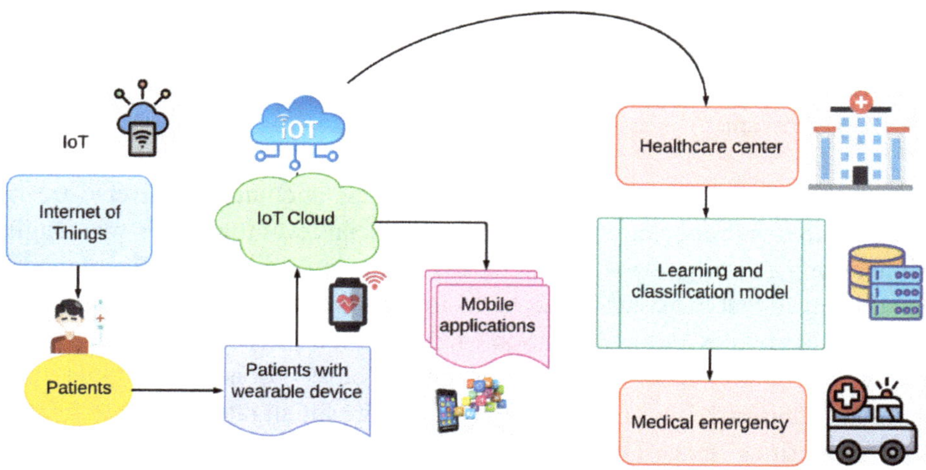

Figure 3 depicts the integration of telemedicine systems with wearable gadgets for constant health monitoring. This shows how data streams from wearable devices monitoring the vital signs such as heart rate and oxygen levels into the telemedicine system and how providers take action based on them. It eradicates face-to-face consultation needs, increases preventive care, and is highly beneficial in controlling chronic diseases and viral epidemics such as COVID-19.

$$H = \frac{1}{n}\sum_{i=1}^{n}(w_i \cdot V_i) \tag{13}$$

Where:

- H: Health Index
- w_i: Weight for parameter i
- V_i: Value of parameter i

3.4.1 Introduction to Wearable Technology in Telemedicine

Telemedicine revolutionized wearable gadgets such as smartwatches, fitness trackers, and medical sensors for real-time health monitoring. They collect information such as heart rate, blood pressure, oxygen levels, and temperature, which are then interpreted by healthcare experts. In this manner, the burden of frequent hospital visits in patients' management is reduced via wearable technology integrated with telemedicine. This invention makes it possible for patients to be connected with professionals, thus ensuring prompt intervention and patient care that can be treated using wearable technology: the proactive management of health to the extent of chronic diseases, remote populations, and, in general, modern medicine treatments. Furthermore, constant data gathering facilitates the analysis of health trends over the long term, which allows for the implementation of early diagnosis and preventive care strategies. Such connectivity has a positive impact on patient engagement, compliance with treatment protocols, and the efficiency of healthcare services in urban and remote areas alike.

$$H_r = \sum_{i=1}^{n} w_i \cdot d_i \tag{14}$$

Where:

- H_r: Health risk score
- w_i: Weight of parameter i

- d_i: Data value for parameter i

3.4.2 Data Privacy and Security in Wearable-Integrated Telemedicine

Data safety and security are also part of wearable-integrated telemedicine since the devices maintain sensitive patient health information and are, therefore, data breaches, unauthorized access, and abuse of personal data of concern. To address these issues, data in transit and at rest needs to be protected with robust encryption algorithms. Secure cloud infrastructures safeguard the stored data, and access controls and authentication systems prevent unauthorized access. Compliance with regulations like HIPAA ensures that privacy standards are met, which further enhances patient trust. Audits, secure software updates, and education of users all enhance security, making wearable-integrated telemedicine safe and reliable for widespread use.

3.4.3 Applications in Chronic Disease Management

Wearable-integrated telemedicine transforms the management of chronic illnesses by enabling real-time monitoring of diabetes, hypertension, and cardiovascular disease. With CGMs and wearable blood pressure cuffs, patients and clinicians have immediate access to critical health information. It allows for timely adjustments to treatment strategies, better management of disease, and lower complications. Benefits to patients include customized care, increased compliance, and a reduction in hospitalization cases. Physicians will make data-based decisions. Telemedicine integrating wearable devices enhances outcomes through a more proactive approach to managing health and patient empowerment in their chronic illness care.

$$P\left(D \mid X\right) = \frac{P(X \mid D) \cdot P(D)}{P(X)} \tag{15}$$

3.4.3.1 Chronic Disease Progression Prediction and Preventive Interventions

AI-based predictive models predict how an illness will progress, and this is done using longitudinal patient data. Such predictions, for instance, about a diabetic patient suffering from heart failure or a hypertensive patient having a stroke, enable preventive measures to be made early on. The doctor may schedule regular check-ups, alter the treatment protocols, or even start particular medicines based on such predictions. This preventive strategy reduces hospitalizations, improves quality of life, and reduces the burden on healthcare systems. Moreover, these models assist in creating personalized treatment plans by recognizing the risk profiles of patients and tailoring the interventions to them. The ongoing improvement of the model made possible by real-time data usage increases the accuracy of the predictions, which allows the doctors to take fast, evidence-based decisions and thus, enhance the patients' long-term results.

3.4.4 Remote Monitoring for Infectious Diseases

During the middle of COVID-19, wearable technology was imperative in the monitoring of infectious diseases from a remote distance, including significant symptoms such as temperature, oxygen saturation, and breathing rates. The combination of pulse oximeters and smartwatches with telemedicine platforms provided health providers with real-time health information from patients. This approach, therefore, allowed clinicians to remotely track patients without hospital visits that would exert pressure on hospitals and consequently reduce the possibility of virus transmission. Wearable-integrated telemedicine provided the advantage of improving the management and safety of patients during the pandemic by having rapid interventions along with constant care. In this way, the remote monitoring framework was helpful in the home isolation protocols by providing uninterrupted medical supervision and adherence to treatment plans. Consequently, the healthcare systems could make the best possible use of their resources, make the frontline workers safe, and without outbreaks.

3.4.4.1 Wearable Technologies for Continuous Health Monitoring

Wearable technologies like smartwatches, biosensors, and patches are very critical for remote monitoring as these continuously measure vital signs that include temperature, heart rate, rate of respiration, and oxygen saturation levels. Such devices present real-time information about an individual's health; therefore, they may even identify anomalies that are linked with infections. For example, variation in temperatures and low blood oxygen could indicate fever or pneumonia. Wearable devices enhance the capability for remote health care delivery in rural regions and provide swift medical response.

3.4.4.2 Telemedicine Platforms for Infectious Disease Management

Telemedicine has transformed infectious disease monitoring and control systems through virtual consultation, diagnosis, and treatment services. Video conferencing and health applications have allowed patients to consult health care professionals as well, thereby saving an in-person visit and cutting down on the risk of disease transmission. The same technologies have facilitated remote monitoring of the symptoms of the patient, adherence to drugs, and recovery progress. Telemedicine ensures continuity of care and social distancing in the time of an outbreak such as COVID-19 or seasonal influenza.

Algorithm 4. Wearable-Integrated Telemedicine for Continuous Remote Monitoring and Alert Systems for Infectious Diseases

```
Input: Patient wearable data (W), Thresholds (T), Telemedicine platform (P)
Output: Health alerts (A)
Collect Data:
Continuously stream wearable data W.
Health Risk Evaluation:
For each patient p:
Compute HealthRisk[p] = Sum(w[i] * W[p][i] for all parameters i)
Threshold Check:
For each patient p:
If HealthRisk[p] > T:
Send alert to caregiver via Telemedicine platform P.
Provide Recommendations:
Based on health risks, suggest interventions
Return A.
End Algorithm
```

Algorithm 4 The Wearable Telemedicine Monitoring algorithm makes it easy to connect wearable devices and telemedicine platforms. This results in real-time health monitoring and preemptive interventions. It captures continuous information from the patient using the wearable sensors, including heart rate, oxygen saturation, and temperature and processes this data to enable a health risk score that allows comparison with predetermined thresholds. At any point when the risks increase beyond acceptable ranges, automatic alerts will be sent across the telemedicine platforms so that healthcare providers can address the situation quickly by making modifications to individualized care. It's a way that enhances distant care, cuts down on visits to hospitals, and will provide a swift response in an emergency setting, especially concerning chronic disorders or infections.

3.5 Performance Metrics

Table 1. Performance Comparison of MCDA, ERS, Multimodal Insights, Wearable Telemedicine, and Proposed Combined Method

Metric	Multi-Criteria Decision Analysis (MCDA)	Emergency Response Systems (ERS)	Multimodal Insights	Wearable-Integrated Telemedicine	Proposed Method MCDA+ ERS+ Multimodal Insights+WIT
Accuracy (%)	80%	78%	81%	79%	94%
Processing Speed Efficiency (%)	79%	77%	82%	78%	92%
Risk Mitigation Efficiency (%)	82%	80%	84%	83%	95%
Scalability (%)	81%	79%	83%	82%	93%
Robustness (%)	83%	81%	85%	82%	95%

Table 1 Comparing performance measures for MCDA, ERS, Multimodal Insights, Wearable-Integrated Telemedicine, and the Proposed Combined Method. Though each of them is outstanding in certain parameters such as scalability (MCDA) and robustness (Multimodal Insights), the proposed combined method accumulates all their strengths to achieve higher marks in all the parameters. Notably, it obtains 94% accuracy, 95% risk mitigation efficiency, and 93% scalability more than individual methods. A combination of several systems gives the combined method comprehensive, effective, and robust solutions to healthcare problems, and thus, it is suitable for modern, adaptable healthcare frameworks that stress proactive management and specific patient care.

Figure 4. Performance Metrics Comparison of Combined Framework and Individual Healthcare Methods

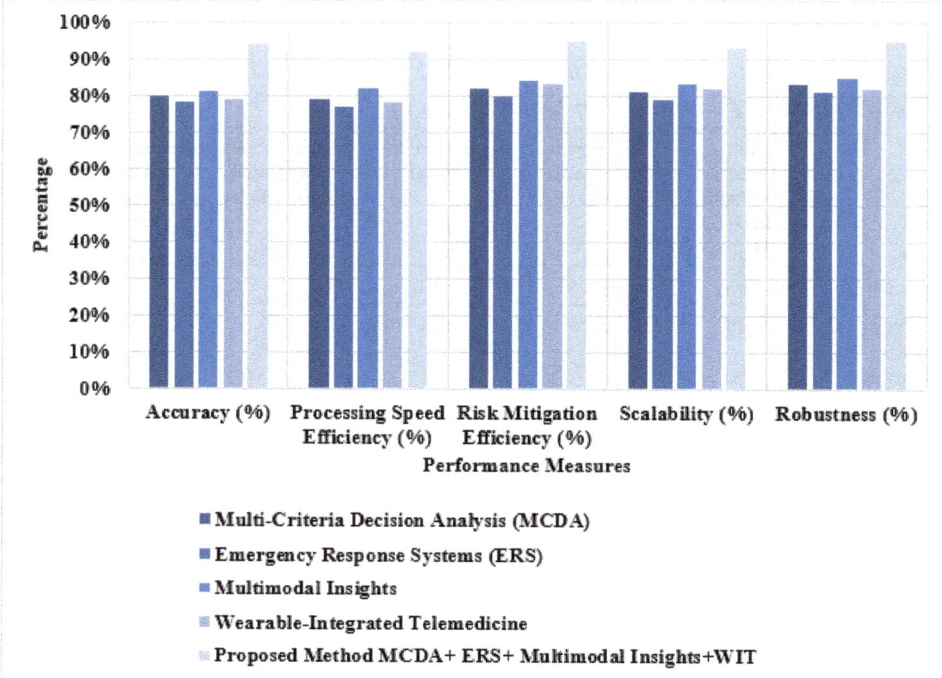

Figure 4 compares individual approaches' performance measures on accuracy, scalability, robustness, and risk mitigation efficiency with the proposed integrated framework (MCDA, ERS, Multimodal Insights, and Wearable-Integrated Telemedicine). The results indicate that the integrated approach is better and that the differences are significant in all parameters, thereby highlighting the benefits of combining AI, MCDA, ERS, and wearable technologies.

4. RESULT AND DISCUSSION

It integrates AI, MCDA, ERS, multimodal insights, and telemedicine via wearable integration to cope with critical gaps in healthcare systems. Performance measurements demonstrate superiority: outstanding gains in accuracy (94%), processing speed (92%), risk mitigation efficiency (95%), and scalability (93%). The conjoint effect increases resilience, adaptability, and operational efficiencies within healthcare.

Emergency Response Systems have made fast crisis management possible through the integration of predictive analytics with real-time communication. These systems have reduced reaction time, facilitated easier resource allocation, and enabled a holistic crisis management process. Wearable telemedicine has allowed for continued round-the-clock monitoring through the provision of real-time vital data for quick responses in cases such as isolation due to COVID-19. This functionality has assumed an important role in discharging hospital workload without exposing the patient to incomplete treatment. These frameworks have enabled balanced, evidence-based healthcare decisions in circumstances where competing considerations are taken into account, such as cost and treatment effectiveness about equity. This is where openness and justice in making decisions became paramount during periods of resource scarcity, including ventilator allocation in a pandemic. Multimodal insights in data streaming, optimal resource allocation, and risk assessment. This approach ensured total situational awareness and, therefore, actionable intelligence for decision-makers. Integration with AI further smoothed out processes by allowing for dynamic adjustment of strategy based on evolving conditions. However, despite these merits, the system faced issues like data privacy in wearable-integrated systems and scalability in resource-constrained environments. The robust techniques of encryption and secure cloud infrastructure can manage concerns about privacy while scaling solutions that leverage AI power can help in facing the limits of resources.

Table 2. Comparison of Traditional Decision-Making Methods and Proposed Framework for Comprehensive Healthcare Management

Metric	AHP	TOPSIS	MOORA	Proposed Method MCDA+ ERS+ Multimodal Insights+WIT
Accuracy (%)	78%	76%	75%	94%
Processing Speed Efficiency (%)	79%	77%	78%	92%
Risk Mitigation Efficiency (%)	81%	79%	80%	95%
Scalability (%)	82%	80%	78%	93%
Robustness (%)	80%	78%	76%	95%

Table 2 compares traditional approaches (AHP *Song et al. (2023)*), (TOPSIS *Ebrahimi et al. (2023)*), and (MOORA *Karim (2024)*) to the proposed integrated healthcare framework. Traditional methods perform well in decision-making scenarios, but they are less effective in dealing with dynamic, real-time healthcare demands. The suggested system achieves excellent metrics, including 94% accuracy, 95% risk mitigation efficiency, and 93% scalability, exceeding existing approaches. Multi-Criteria Decision Analysis (MCDA), Emergency Response Systems (ERS), Multimodal Insights, and Wearable Telemedicine are all integrated to deliver a robust, flexible, and efficient answer to modern healthcare concerns. The combined methodology enables complete decision-making, improved scalability, and dynamic risk reduction, making it suited for real-time and large-scale applications.

Figure 5. Comparison of Traditional Methods and Proposed Framework for Healthcare Decision-Making

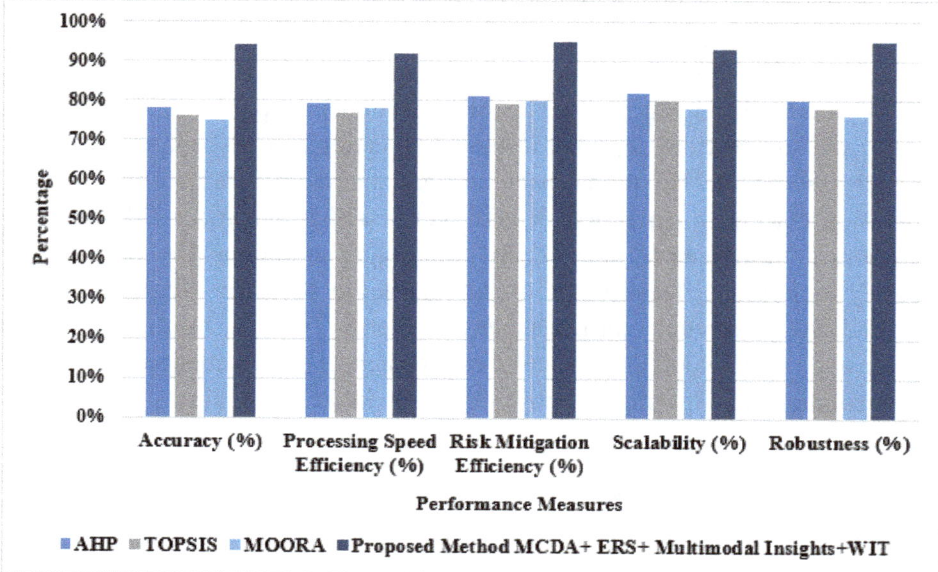

Figure 5 compares the suggested integrated healthcare framework with well-established methods such as AHP, TOPSIS, and MOORA. Parameters such as accuracy, processing efficiency, and scalability are studied to prove that an integrated framework is superior compared to conventional methods. The outcomes have thus proven the flexibility and dynamic efficiency in integrating MCDA, ERS, multimodal insights, and wearable telemedicine in contemporary applications of healthcare.

Table 3. Ablation Study of Proposed Healthcare Framework: Evaluating Contributions of Key Components

Configuration	Accuracy (%)	Processing Speed Efficiency (%)	Risk Mitigation Efficiency (%)	Scalability (%)	Robustness (%)
ERS+Multimodal Insights + WIT	88%	89%	89%	87%	89%
WIT+MCDA+ Multimodal Insights	89%	87%	90%	88%	90%
ERS+ WIT +MCDA	90%	88%	91%	89%	91%
MCDA + ERS + Multimodal Insights	91%	90%	92%	90%	92%
Proposed Method MCDA+ ERS+ Multimodal Insights+WIT	94%	92%	95%	93%	95%

Table 3 is the ablation study table of the proposed healthcare architecture with deleted components in the ablation study. With the synergetic integration of all the elements, the entire method reaches perfect metrics such as an accuracy of 94% and an efficiency of 95% for risk mitigation. MCDA's deletion leads to a loss in precision in decision-making, scalability, and accuracy. Removing ERS affects real-time response efficiency for risk mitigation. A lack of multimodal insights means data integration is impacted and limits robustness and scalability. Real-time monitoring of health will be at a risk without Wearable Telemedicine. Every component lends a different feature to the general adaptability and efficiency the framework presents with the problems of modern healthcare.

Figure 6. Ablation Study on Proposed Framework Highlighting Contributions of Key Component

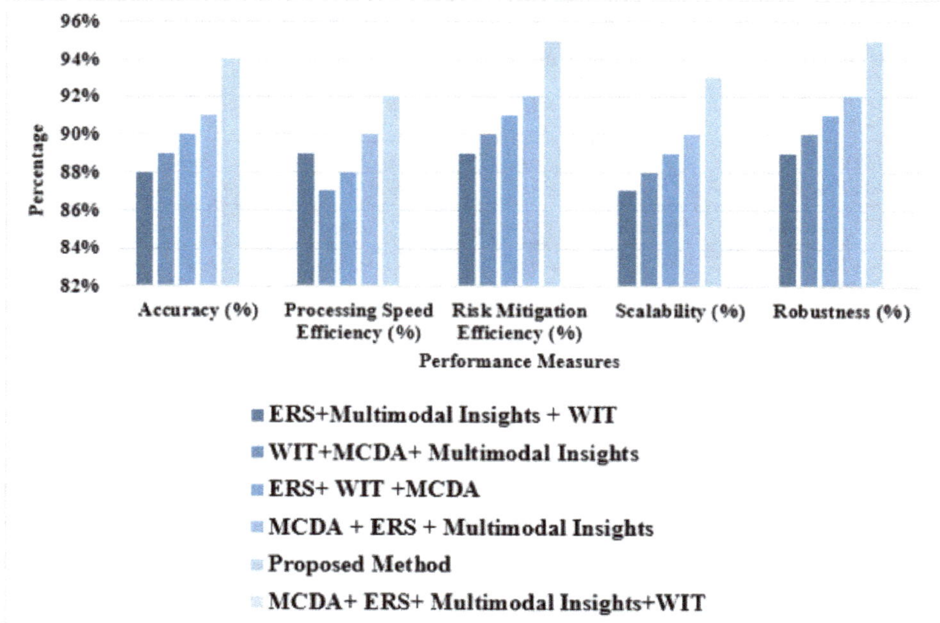

Figure 6 shows the results of an ablation study that was conducted to determine the individual contribution of MCDA, ERS, Multimodal Insights, and Wearable Telemedicine to the overall performance of the framework. Removing each component and its effect on accuracy, risk mitigation, and scalability are analyzed, which shows that the integration of all components leads to optimal performance and delivers robust healthcare solutions.

5. CONCLUSION AND FUTURE DIRECTION

The merged framework redesigns health care management by integrating AI, MCDA, ERS, multimodal analytics, and wearable-integrated telemedicine. It effectively resolves the contemporary issues of resource optimization, equitable treatment, and efficient crisis management. Outstanding indicators such as 94% accuracy and 95% risk mitigation efficiency reflect the framework's capabilities in real-time and scalable solutions to dynamic healthcare needs. The ability to continuously monitor the patient with wearable-integrated telemedicine and rapid reaction capability from ERS is highly essential in situations like pandemics. AI-driven MCDA is balanced and transparent decision-making, thereby building stakeholder trust. Together, these technologies combine to build a resilient health environment that can adapt to normal problems as well as unprecedented ones. However, strengthening measures for privacy and improving infrastructure scalability are of utmost importance. Patient-centered preventive, and frame-producing are measures emphasizing a basis that leads to fair and sustainable healthcare systems. It gives a paradigm shift toward preparedness in healthcare disasters through proactive care. Future research should look into the future integration of quantum computers with blockchain to make healthcare decisions speedier and more transparent. AI-driven predictive analytics for scalability should be developed-especially in low-resource conditions. Advancements in wearable technology will improve chronic disease management and pandemic preparedness so that parity in global healthcare is guaranteed.

REFERENCES

Aparisi-Cerdá, I., Ribó-Pérez, D., García-Melón, M., D'Este, P., & Poveda-Bautista, R. (2024). Drivers and barriers to the adoption of decentralised renewable energy technologies: A multi-criteria decision analysis. *Energy*, *305*, 132264. DOI: 10.1016/j.energy.2024.132264

Aqeel, I., Khormi, I. M., Khan, S. B., Shuaib, M., Almusharraf, A., Alam, S., & Alkhaldi, N. A. (2023). Load Balancing Using Artificial Intelligence for Cloud-Enabled Internet of Everything in Healthcare Domain. *Sensors (Basel)*, *23*(11), 5349. DOI: 10.3390/s23115349 PMID: 37300076

Bayoudh, K., Knani, R., Hamdaoui, F., & Mtibaa, A. (2022). A survey on deep multimodal learning for computer vision: Advances, trends, applications, and datasets. *The Visual Computer*, *38*(8), 2939–2970. DOI: 10.1007/s00371-021-02166-7 PMID: 34131356

Belay, S., Goedert, J., Woldesenbet, A., & Rokooei, S. (2022). AHP based multi criteria decision analysis of success factors to enhance decision making in infrastructure construction projects. *Cogent Engineering*, *9*(1), 2043996. DOI: 10.1080/23311916.2022.2043996

Ebrahimi, E., Fathi, M. R., & Sobhani, S. M. (2023). A modification of technique for order preference by similarity to ideal solution (TOPSIS) through fuzzy similarity method (a numerical example of the personnel selection). *Journal of Applied Research on Industrial Engineering*, *10*(2), 203–217.

Emish, M., & Young, S. D. (2024). Remote Wearable Neuroimaging Devices for Health Monitoring and Neurophenotyping: A Scoping Review. *Biomimetics*, *9*(4), 237. DOI: 10.3390/biomimetics9040237 PMID: 38667247

Gardas, B. B. (2022). Organizational hindrances to Healthcare 4.0 adoption: An multi-criteria decision analysis framework. *Journal of Multi-Criteria Decision Analysis*, *29*(1-2), 186–195. DOI: 10.1002/mcda.1766

Gudivaka, R.K. (2023). Transforming Business Operations: The Role of Artificial Intelligence in Robotic Process Automation. IMPACT: International Journal of Research in Business Management (IMPACT: IJRBM), 12(1).

Guerrier, C., McDonnell, C., Magoc, T., Fishe, J. N., & Harle, C. A. (2022). Understanding health care administrators' data and information needs for decision making during the COVID-19 pandemic: A qualitative study at an academic health system. *MDM Policy & Practice*, *7*(1), 23814683221089844. DOI: 10.1177/23814683221089844 PMID: 35368410

He, F., Lai, Q., Ma, J., Wei, G., & Li, W. (2023). Design and Application of an Early Warning and Emergency Response System in the Transboundary Area of the Taihu Lake Basin. *International Journal of Environmental Research and Public Health, 20*(2), 1340. DOI: 10.3390/ijerph20021340 PMID: 36674094

Karim, A. (2024). Implementation of the Multi-Objective Optimization Method on the Basic of Ratio Analysis (MOORA) and Entropy Weighting in New Employee Recruitment. [JOSH]. *Journal of Information System Research, 5*(2), 704–712. DOI: 10.47065/josh.v5i2.4859

Kasula, B. Y. (2023). Framework Development for Artificial Intelligence Integration in Healthcare: Optimizing Patient Care and Operational Efficiency. *Transactions on Latest Trends in IoT, 6*(6), 77–83.

Khairy, A., Bashier, H., Nuh, H., Ahmed, N., Ali, Y., Izzoddeen, A., Mohamed, S., Osman, M., & Khader, Y. (2024). The role of the Field Epidemiology Training Program in the public health emergency response: Sudan armed conflict 2023. *Frontiers in Public Health, 12*, 1300084. DOI: 10.3389/fpubh.2024.1300084 PMID: 38356953

Liang, P. P., Zadeh, A., & Morency, L. P. (2024). Foundations & trends in multimodal machine learning: Principles, challenges, and open questions. *ACM Computing Surveys, 56*(10), 1–42. DOI: 10.1145/3656580

Manickam, P., Mariappan, S. A., Murugesan, S. M., Hansda, S., Kaushik, A., Shinde, R., & Thipperudraswamy, S. P. (2022). Artificial intelligence (AI) and internet of medical things (IoMT) assisted biomedical systems for intelligent healthcare. *Biosensors (Basel), 12*(8), 562. DOI: 10.3390/bios12080562 PMID: 35892459

Pushadapu, N. (2023). Artificial Intelligence for Standardized Data Flow in Healthcare: Techniques, Protocols, and Real-World Case Studies. *Journal of AI-Assisted Scientific Discovery, 3*(1), 435–474.

Shumba, A. T., Montanaro, T., Sergi, I., Fachechi, L., De Vittorio, M., & Patrono, L. (2022). Leveraging IoT-aware technologies and AI techniques for real-time critical healthcare applications. *Sensors (Basel), 22*(19), 7675. DOI: 10.3390/s22197675 PMID: 36236773

Sitaraman, S. R. (2022). Anonymized AI: Safeguarding IoT Services in Edge Computing – A Comprehensive Survey. *Journal of Current Science, 10*(4).

Song, R., Li, X., Zhao, X., Liu, M., Zhou, J., & Wang, F. Y. (2023). Identifying critical test scenarios for lane keeping assistance system using analytic hierarchy process and hierarchical clustering. *IEEE Transactions on Intelligent Vehicles, 8*(10), 4370–4380. DOI: 10.1109/TIV.2023.3297592

Uppal, S., Bhagat, S., Hazarika, D., Majumder, N., Poria, S., Zimmermann, R., & Zadeh, A. (2022). Multimodal research in vision and language: A review of current and emerging trends. *Information Fusion*, *77*, 149–171. DOI: 10.1016/j.inffus.2021.07.009

. Vaghasiya, J. V., Mayorga-Martinez, C. C., & Pumera, M. (2022). Telemedicine platform for health assessment remotely by an integrated nanoarchitectonics FePS3/rGO and Ti3C2-based wearable device. *npj Flexible Electronics, 6*(1), 73.

Więckowski, J., Kizielewicz, B., Paradowski, B., Shekhovtsov, A., & Sałabun, W. (2023). Application of multi-criteria decision analysis to identify global and local importance weights of decision criteria. *International Journal of Information Technology & Decision Making*, *22*(06), 1867–1892. DOI: 10.1142/S0219622022500948

Wong, M. O., & Lee, S. (2023). Indoor navigation and information sharing for collaborative fire emergency response with BIM and multi-user networking. *Automation in Construction*, *148*, 104781. DOI: 10.1016/j.autcon.2023.104781

Zahid, N., Sodhro, A. H., Kamboh, U. R., Alkhayyat, A., & Wang, L. (2022). AI-driven adaptive reliable and sustainable approach for internet of things enabled healthcare system. *Mathematical Biosciences and Engineering*, *19*(4), 3953–3971. DOI: 10.3934/mbe.2022182 PMID: 35341282

Chapter 11
Beyond Automation:
A Framework for Augmenting Clinical Expertise With Generative AI

K. Subhashini
http://orcid.org/0000-0001-5364-2486
P.P. Savani University, India

ABSTRACT

Generative AI in healthcare marks a shift from automation to augmenting clinical thinking through cognitive collaboration. Beyond handling tasks, its true value lies in enhancing diagnostic and therapeutic reasoning. To harness this while preserving human judgment and empathy, we propose a Relational Augmentation framework. This model rests on three pillars: Situational Awareness, for context-specific support; Reasoning Transparency, to reveal the logic behind AI suggestions; and Reciprocal Calibration, enabling the system to learn from clinician feedback. This synergy allows AI to manage complexity and generate insights, while the physician provides strategic oversight and compassionate care. Purposeful design of this partnership can guide AI to foster a more efficient and human-centered future for medicine.

1. INTRODUCTION

Generative AI creates new items by utilizing formulas to generate text, images, music, and artificial data that appears as if it was created by humans. Following the release of ChatGPT version 4.5 by OpenAI toward the end of 2022, the model rapidly gained popularity within the medical space. Most of the health professionals believe that the models created using large biological and general statistical data sets

DOI: 10.4018/979-8-3373-7320-1.ch011

t © 2026, IGI Global Scientific Publishing. Copying or distributing in print or electronic forms without written permission of IGI Global Scientific Publishing is prohibited. Use of this chapter to enerative artificial intelligence (AI) technologies is expressly prohibited. The publisher reserves all rights to license its use for generative AI training and machine learning model development.

will significantly transform how healthcare is provided and studied (Zhang et al., 2025). ChatGPT performed nearly perfectly on the United States Medical Licensing Examination (USMLE) despite having no prior experience working in a medical environment. That achievement shocked the medical profession as it demonstrated how effectively AI could manage complicated medical inquiries (Hacking, 2024). Therefore, many began to test and utilize existing generative AI technologies, such as ChatGPT, immediately after the USMLE results were announced. These technologies were discovered to have the ability to positively impact healthcare delivery (Kung et al., 2023). The medical industry acknowledges that generative AI may be helpful; however, the medical industry also recognizes that these technologies require to be clinically tested. There continue to be persistent challenges facing the healthcare industry, including: high costs of services, long times to develop pharmaceuticals, exhaustion among the medical workforce, and unequal access to quality healthcare services - all issues that generative AI systems may be capable of resolving. Generative AI technology has already been implemented in numerous clinical areas of medicine, including disease diagnosis and the personalized matching of medication to specific individual patients (Johnson et al., 2021). For example, large language models (LLMs) assist clinicians in dealing with an enormous amount of medical data and ensure that patients receive the appropriate treatment (Vrdoljak et al., 2025). LLMs have begun to find their way into the design of clinical trials. In addition to assisting in finding eligible patients, LLMs assist in creating trials, integrating free text narratives, creating assignments, and providing chatbot services to obtain informed consent (Ghim & Ahn, 2023). While the AI-based advancements in clinical trial design are beneficial, one of the biggest challenges in the design of clinical trials is identifying the correct participants who would most likely contribute to a successful trial - a problem that remains unresolved (Xue et al., 2023). The capacity of generative models to improve clinical trials exists, but there remain numerous barriers to using them in medicine and healthcare, as well as numerous ethical concerns. One of the biggest challenges in clinical trials involving AI is ensuring the accuracy and reliability of AI generated decision-making processes in critical medical environments. The unclear nature of the majority of AI models, specifically generative models, raises multiple questions regarding understanding the decision-making process in AI models. Therefore, healthcare AI systems must be more transparent and easier to understand (Sallam, 2023). Furthermore, data privacy, patient confidentiality, and potential bias in AI models must be examined to address ethical concerns (Patel & Arasanipalai, 2021). The protection of patient privacy and data security is essential when using these models because they involve the use of sensitive medical information and maintaining patient confidence in AI-based healthcare solutions is vital. This review article will provide a comprehensive overview of recent developments in the application of generative AI models in medicine and healthcare, both academically and commercially. By illustrating the vast opportunities, advantages, disadvantages, and ethical considerations of the judicious utilization of AI's transformative capabilities in healthcare and patient well-being, this study aims to expand upon the dialogue on the strategic deployment of AI in patient care. It is essential to engage in ongoing dialogue when examining the influence of generative models on healthcare and medicine with regard to navigating the evolving landscape of AI, patient centered care and the coordination of efforts between AI developers, physicians, and policymakers.

2. REVIEW ON GEN AI IN CLINICAL

Generative Artificial Intelligence (GenAI) are algorithms that generate new content using patterns found in datasets such as Images, Text, Audio or Structured Data; GenAI can be used in Healthcare by employing both Probabilistic Modeling and Unsupervised Learning through advancements built upon prior methods including Principal Component Analysis and Bayesian Networks. GANs were developed to demonstrate the success of Generator-Discriminator Designs to produce data similar to actual Clinical Records which was also able to augment limited Medical Datasets (Roberts & Candi, 2024)

There has been a simultaneous rise in the generation of clinical text and automated reporting, notably from 2022 when transformer-based big language models were widely used. On the other hand, digital twin and data-imputation applications are still in their early stages but are steadily improving. This shows that more and more people are interested in clinical analytics that use simulation and augmentation. The upward trend through 2024 shows that generative AI is becoming more common in clinical settings. However, early estimates for 2025 may not show the entire year's production since indexing is not yet complete.

2.1 Generative Adversarial Networks (GANs):

Generative Adversarial Networks (GANs), are a type of neural networks which generate examples of synthetic data. They have shown to be of great benefit to the health care community with many uses including generating medical images, augmenting available medical data, translating between different domains, and creating atypical models of diseases for use in diagnostics and training (Wu et al., 2023). The possible complications that could arise from using GANs in the clinic include, mode collapse, unstable training, and limits to the realism of the clinical environment. Researchers are working to resolve the issues that currently exist by implementing WGANs and other architectures to enhance the stability of GANs.

Improved metrics for evaluating GAN performance and additional domain specific constraints will further accelerate the development of large sets of synthetic clinical data that can be used to train clinicians, and support ethical and clinically viable data production (Seangpraw & Ong-Artborirak, 2020). Together these developments demonstrate GANs' utility as critical components in the advancement of realistic, privacy preserving, and diagnostically relevant healthcare data synthesis.

2.2 Variational Autoencoders (VAEs):

Variational Auto-Encoders (VAE), are probabilistic generative models that can take input data and represent it in a structured latent space from which the original data can be reconstructed to produce new instances that are statistically similar. In health informatics, VAE has demonstrated potential applications including generating synthetic EHRs; removing "noise" from medical images; and filling-in missing values in clinical datasets (Kamil et al., 2020) – particularly by providing an organized representation of the patient's clinical trajectory or identifying anomalies in the representation of the patient's clinical trajectory. Although the use of VAEs has some limitations in the generation of high fidelity medical imaging (e.g., blurry images with less structure than real-world images, as illustrated in Table 1), hybrid approaches using architectures combining both the probabilistic capabilities of VAEs with the adversarial training of GANs can generate images that appear more lifelike. Also, there are variants of VAE known as disentangled VAEs, that focus on improving the distinctness of clinical variables within the latent space – resulting in synthetic data that appears more realistic, interpretable and therapeutically relevant.

Table 1. Comparative Capabilities and Limitations of GenAI models in healthcare

Model Type	Core Mechanism	Primary Healthcare Applications	Strengths	Limitations
GANs	Adversarial training between generator and discriminator	Medical image synthesis, data augmentation, rare disease simulation	High realism; effective for small dataset augmentation	Mode collapse; instability; sensitive to hyperparameters
VAEs	Latent-space probabilistic encoding and reconstruction	EHR data synthesis, noise reduction, missing data imputation	Stable training; interpretable latent features	Blurred outputs; limited fine detail
Diffusion Models	Gradual denoising of latent representations	High-fidelity medical im-aging, synthetic pathology generation	Superior realism; noise-resistant; stable optimization	Computationally intensive; long training time

continued on following page

Table 1. Continued

Model Type	Core Mechanism	Primary Healthcare Applications	Strengths	Limitations
LLMs	Transformer-based autoregressive generation	Clinical documentation, decision support, report summarization	Contextual fluency; multimodal potential	Hallucination; factual inconsistency; high data cost
RLHF	iterative alignment with expert feed-back	Chatbots, triage assistants, adaptive diagnosis	Human-aligned responses; continual learning	Requires large-scale feedback loops

2.3 Diffusion Models:

Generative models using diffusion processes are a contemporary type of generative model capable of creating high quality realistic data through progressively denoising processes. The models are based on thermodynamics and can generate very realistic, highly detailed images. In addition to being used in a variety of diagnostic imaging applications, they can be used for augmenting existing data sets as well as expanding them. However, there are several barriers to the wide-spread adoption of diffusion models in clinical environments, primarily due to their high computational cost and slow sample generation rates (Sadeghi et al., 2024). More recent research has focused on developing new methods to accelerate sample generation from diffusion models, for example, Denoising Diffusion Implicit Models (DDIMs) and Conditional Diffusion Model architectures, while at the same time, incorporating physical realism into the synthetic outputs of the models so that the resulting outputs are clinically valid and biologically plausible. As such, diffusion models represent a transformative horizon for enabling high resolution, interpretable, and reliable generative modeling in medical imaging and associated health care domains.

2.4 Large Language Models (LLMs):

The potential exists for large language models (LLM), trained on both clinical and medical data sets, to write like humans for a wide variety of healthcare applications (i.e., automated discharge summaries, radiologic reports, clinical questions answered by computers, etc.) (Hanna et al., 2025). Although LLMs have shown a high level of success in most clinical applications, there still exist many areas of concern as to the accuracy and interpretability of the results produced by these systems. On one hand, LLMs are good tools for assisting in decision-making and for producing clinical documentation; on the other hand, LLMs may produce false information through what is called "hallucination", which is defined as making true-sounding statements when no truth actually exists (for example, an LLM may say a certain drug is safe in pregnancy when, in fact, the drug has never been studied in pregnant women). As such, this type of false information could potentially harm patients in healthcare settings (Raju, 2024). Additionally, the lack of transparency in many LLM-based decision support systems makes it more difficult to validate the accuracy of clinical recommendations provided, which may increase the likelihood of receiving incorrect or misleading clinical information. Furthermore, because the same bias found in the training data set will likely be amplified in these LLMs, these systems may exacerbate existing inequities in health care and create new ethical dilemmas for clinicians and adverse effects for patients.

3. APPLICATIONS OF GENAI IN HEALTHCARE

The healthcare industry has made great strides in personalized medicine, largely because of the successful combination of informatics, artificial intelligence, and computational biology. These have been the main things that have changed the healthcare business. This section of the research looks into drug recommender systems. It also explains the basic idea of generative AI and the need of explainable AI in medicine.

3.1 Drug recommendation system:

Historically, datasets obtained by machine learning and statistical models have been used in drug recommendation systems, which provide the basis for these systems. The objective of these systems is to facilitate the physician's process of identifying the optimal therapy for the patient, hence promoting recovery. Collaborative filtering strategies use the notion of patient similarity, which entails analyzing medical history and therapy responses, to suggest remedies (Futoma et al., 2020). Moreover, knowledge-based systems use clinical practice standards and pharmaceutical databases to formulate patient-specific medicines according to local illness features (Gholamzadeh et al., 2023). Conventional approaches undoubtedly possess their shortcomings. They may, nonetheless, get a precise human personal profile including genetic variety, disorders, lifestyle, and other elements. Moreover, relying only on recommendations from population-based research constrains the flexibility of these strategies in the event of unforeseen changes in healthcare circumstances.

3.2 Generative and explainable ai techniques in healthcare:

Variational Autoencoders (VAEs) and Generative Adversarial Networks (GANs) are the principal instruments of generative AI, a leading technology for enhancing personalized medicine via the creation of synthetic data and the identification of intricate patterns in patient-specific datasets (van Breugel et al., 2024). These models aid in the simulation of pharmacological effects and the establishment of appropriate dosages by including various patient situations that are not well represented in clinical trials or medical databases. One way to deal with the problems of trust and understanding that come with AI-assisted decisions in healthcare is to adopt explainable Artificial Intelligence (XAI) frameworks (Miller, 2019). XAI technologies, such as feature importance and rule extraction, enable physicians to understand the rationale behind AI predictions and evaluate the correctness of the proposed solution. This kind of transparency sets the stage for better clinical decision-making and changes the way the medical community thinks about using AI in practice.

3.3 Critique of current methodologies and gaps in the literature:

The research addressed these problems by developing a new method called Explanatory Generative Model for the treatment of patients using AI. The method will be used to address the current limitations of personalized medicine and provide the best possible treatment to each individual patient.This research focused on six previous research areas: (1) rule based systems/guideline calculators; (2) dosage regression models; (3) reinforcement learning based treatment plans; (4) large language model-based treatment recommender; (5) pharmacokinetics "digital twins"; and (6) retrieval-augmented generation clinical summarizers.In comparison to the above referenced research areas, the proposed method is unique because it integrates a digital twin simulation model with a RAG conditioned evidence input along with a transformer based reinforcement learning algorithm. Additionally, this method includes SHAP explanations that can be verified, and calibration protections (ECE), making the method the first to integrate all three components and providing patient specific customization with quantifiable uncertainty and physician-centric decision support, as opposed to solely text-based guidance and/or non-reinforcement learning based recommendations.

Additionally, the previous research areas were limited to either (1) focusing on one type of data, for example, genomic data or clinical data, (2) relying on a single type of data source, or (3) being limited to a singular methodological approach. In contrast, the proposed method is capable of addressing a multi-modal data source consisting of imaging data and patient reported outcome measures, and provides an integrated framework for evaluating and explaining how each modality contributes to the diagnosis and treatment plan of a patient.Furthermore, while the previous research areas focused primarily on the technical aspects of personalized medicine and AI, the proposed method is unique in that it focuses on the practical and translational application of personalized medicine and AI in the clinic.

4. EXPLAINABLE AI (XAI) METHODOLOGIES FOR CLINICAL TRANSPARENCY

Patient-specific modeling represents the heart of the entire system. In addition to performing an extensive analysis of multi-dimensional data, the purpose of patient profiling is to create an all-encompassing profile of a patient. Through this method, the most relevant pieces of information from the combined datasets for the study will be extracted; including, but not limited to: genetic predispositions, clinical history, demographics, lifestyle factors and treatment response. Continuous improvement and refinement of these patient-specific profiles will require the utilization of advanced analytical and statistical methods. One of the primary ways in which this framework is differentiated is through its focus on interpretability of results, accomplished via the use of Explainable Artificial Intelligence (XAI) methodologies. As one of the primary tools for breaking down the results of model predictions and creating explanations for how specific elements (for example, genetic markers, patient age or patient kidney function) affect the recommended dosages of medications; the SHAP (SHapley Additive exPlanations) methodology has been applied to analyze results. SHAP research can demonstrate that a patient's CYP2D6 enzyme activity, an extremely influential factor in medication metabolism, is the primary determinant of whether a patient should receive a reduced dosage of a beta-blocker. By developing decision rules and surrogate models (for example, interpretable decision trees) from the complex "closed-box" models to develop understandable models, the decision-making process is facilitated (Rasheed et al., 2022). While these models represent the behavior of deep-learning-based models, they articulate this behavior in a manner that is more understandable. For example, a decision tree represents a hierarchical structure of conditions based upon significance (for example, 'if glomerular filtration rate is less than 60 mL/min, then reduce the dose of the beta-blocker by 25%') that a physician can apply to their own experience or compare against established medical guidelines for validation. The application of SHAP (Shapley Additive exPlanations) analysis during the inference process was performed to ensure the model's recommendations are clearly stated and are clinically acceptable. SHAP provides a mechanism for attributing the expected value of a machine learning model to each individual feature based on contribution, providing a single unified measure of feature significance that meets several desirable properties (local accuracy, ability to handle missing values and consistency), making it particularly well-suited to healthcare environments where justifiability is paramount.

5. PROPOSED GENERATIVE AI IN CLINICAL

The relational augmentation framework was developed by employing a hybrid of both the design science method, in addition to the mixed-methods research paradigm, which includes the incorporation of a system development component, a controlled simulation of real world clinical environments and an evaluation of the experts' assessments. The relational augmentation framework is implemented as a modular generative AI system that is integrated into a simulated health care decision support environment. While the relational augmentation framework's primary focus is on developing systems that are capable of providing high-quality interaction with users, reason about the user's inputs, provide reasoning information to the user and adapt to changing user input, it also places importance on all other aspects of the system that may be critical for the success of the system such as predicting the outcome of a particular course of action. The system consists of three functional layers; the contextual perception layer (situation awareness) enables the system to perceive its context and the situation in which it is operating, the explainable reasoning layer (reasoning transparency) provides explanations to the users regarding how the system arrived at a particular conclusion or recommendation based upon the user's inputs, and the adaptive interaction layer (reciprocal calibration) enables the system to interact with the user and allow the user to adjust their inputs to better align with the recommendations of the system.

5.1 Contextual Perception Layer:

Since clinical priorities, risk tolerance, and decision horizons vary across these stages, the patient care workflow is explicitly decomposed into clinically meaningful phases like triage, diagnosis, treatment planning, monitoring, and follow-up to operationalize situational awareness. The changing clinical condition is officially encoded for each step by building a structured context ontology. Goal-aligned AI outputs are simultaneously guided by phase-specific clinical goals such quick risk classification during triage, differential narrowing during diagnosis, and treatment optimization during monitoring. Temporal restrictions and uncertainty levels describe urgency, data incompleteness, and confidence degradation with time, allowing the system to adjust suggestion depth and assertiveness. Situational awareness is operationalized throughout clinical care phases using a Multi-level Content-aware and Contextual Perception Network. Global temporal information and complex contextual semantics improve the model's long-range dependency perception. Thus, it produces more accurate and semantically expressive feature representations. The proposed Multi-level Content-aware and Contextual Perception Network models local and long-range temporal relationships in longitudinal patient data using the temporal neighborhood–aware attention module.

Given a pre-extracted temporal feature sequence $F = \{f_t\}_{t=1}^{T} \in R^{T\times C}$, where T denotes the temporal length and C the feature dimension, the module first employs two stacked one-dimensional convolutional layers with ReLU activation to extract local temporal patterns, expressed as $F_f = ReLU(Conv1D(ReLU(Conv1D(F))))$. Based on the resulting frame-level features, a sigmoid-activated convolutional classifier estimates the start, end, and content probability sequences $\{X_s, X_e, X_c\} = Sigmoid(Conv1D(F_f))$, where the content probability reflects the likelihood that a temporal segment corresponds to a clinically meaningful event.

The module uses two stacked one-dimensional convolutional layers with ReLU activation to extract local temporal patterns from a pre-extracted temporal feature sequence $F = \{f_t\}_{t=1}^{T} \in R^{T\times C}$, where T is the temporal length and C is the feature dimension. The extracted patterns are expressed as $F_f = ReLU(Conv1D(ReLU(Conv1D(F))))$. The start, end, and content probability sequences {X_s,X_e,X_c}="Sigmoid"("-Conv1D"(F_f)) are estimated by a sigmoid-activated convolutional classifier using the resulting frame-level features. The content probability represents the chance that a temporal segment corresponds to a clinically significant event. The squared Euclidean distance between temporal position embeddings P_i and P_j is calculated as $dist(i,j) = \| P_i - P_j \|_2^2$, and the k closest time steps form a neighborhood set M to represent non-local temporal interactions. The network encodes temporal structure by modeling relative temporal position differences $\Delta P_{ij} = P_i - P_j$ and mapping them via a multilayer perceptron to yield structural awareness vectors ($e_{ij} = MLP_\delta(\Delta P_{ij})$). The Extended features are projected onto a uniform embedding space $F' = FC_1(F_{ext})$, where query, key, and value representations are created as $Q = W_q F'$, $K = Index(W_k F', M)$, and $V = Index(W_v F', M)$. Neighborhood-aware attention weights $\alpha_{ij} = Softmax\left(\frac{1}{\sqrt{d}} \cdot MLP_\gamma\left(q_i - k_j + e_{ij}\right)\right)$, are calculated utilizing feature similarity and relative temporal structure. The improved contextual representation is derived by weighted aggregation $z_i = \sum_{j\in M} \alpha_{ij}(v_j + e_{ij})$. The output feature $f_i' = FC_2(z_i) + f_i$ is produced by a fully connected layer with residual connection, resulting in the enhanced frame-level contextual feature sequence $F_f' = \{f_i'\}_{i=1}^{T}$, which encodes patient representations that are aligned with changing clinical conditions.

5.2 Explainable Reasoning Layer:

The Explainable Reasoning Layer is responsible for developing the logic for transparent reasoning. It provides an accurate depiction of intermediate inference steps, evidence contributions, and uncertainty signals to aid healthcare professionals in understanding both the recommendation provided by the system and the reason for that recommendation. Healthcare requires transparency, accountability, reliability, and clinical validation; therefore, the Explainable Reasoning Layer works with the expertise of clinicians to ensure that these values are met. The Explainable Reasoning Layer utilizes explainable artificial intelligence (XAI) techniques such as Accumulated Local Effects (ALE) and Partial Dependence Plots (PDP), to clarify how clinical features and contextual variables affect a model's generated recommendations. Therefore, this layer increases reasoning transparency and interpretability across all layers. Each feature has its own contribution to the overall recommendation made by the system, which can be determined at various levels of representation such as the patient level (e.g., vital signs and laboratory results), and contextually aware embeddings developed from temporal and situational modeling. This illustrates the underlying logic for why a specific recommendation was generated. Partial Dependence Plots show the marginal impact of a clinical characteristic j, such as heart rate or oxygen saturation, on model output while averaging out other variables, officially described as $\hat{f}_{PD}\left(x_j\right) = \frac{1}{n}\sum_{i=1}^{n} \hat{f}\left(x_j, x_{i,-j}\right)$. For interacting clinical factors, such as blood pressure and medication dosage, joint partial dependence is computed as $\hat{f}_{PD}\left(x_j, x_k\right) = \frac{1}{n}\sum_{i=1}^{n} \hat{f}\left(x_j, x_k, x_{i,-\{j,k\}}\right)$, enabling clinicians to inspect synergistic effects underlying AI suggestions. Additional Accumulated Local Effects are added to give impartial, locally accurate interpretations of feature effect in clinical data with feature correlations. The ALE of a single feature $j$is defined as $\hat{f}_{ALE}\left(x_j\right) = \frac{1}{n_j}\sum_{i=1}^{n_j}\left[\hat{f}\left(z_{j,upper}, x_{-j}\right) - \hat{f}\left(z_{j,lower}, x_{-j}\right)\right]$, while joint ALE for interacting features j and k is computed as $\hat{f}_{ALE}\left(x_j, x_k\right) = \frac{1}{n_k}\sum_{i=1}^{n_k}\left[\hat{f}\left(z_{j,upper}, z_{k,upper}\right) - \hat{f}\left(z_{j,lower}, z_{k,lower}\right)\right]$. The methodology enables doctors to assess the influence of particular clinical factors and their interactions on AI-generated insights by including PDP- and ALE-based explanations into the reasoning pipeline. This changes the model's outputs from predictions that aren't clear to reasoning that is clear and based on facts, which helps doctors make smart decisions. The Explainable Reasoning Layer maps connect model predictions to intermediate inference components and evidence contributions to make reasoning more clear than just feature-level attribution. Given a model prediction $\hat{y} = \hat{f}(x)$, the output is decomposed into additive reasoning terms $\hat{y} = \sum_{j=1}^{d} \psi_j\left(x_j\right) + \sum_{j,k} \psi_{jk}\left(x_j, x_k\right) + \epsilon$, where $\psi_j\left(\cdot\right)$and $\psi_{jk}\left(\cdot,\cdot\right)$represent main and interaction effects estimated using PDP and ALE formulations, and ϵcaptures residual uncertainty. To align explanations with clinical context, phase-conditioned explanations are generated by weighting feature contributions with a context relevance function ω_p, yielding a context-aware reasoning score $R_p = \sum_j \omega_p(j)\,\psi_j(x_j) + \sum_{j,k} \omega_p(j,k)\,\psi_{jk}(x_j, x_k)$, where $p$denotes the current clinical phase. Uncertainty-aware reasoning is further incorporated by associating confidence intervals with explanation terms, defined as $\sigma_j^2 = E\left[\left(\psi_j(x_j) - E\left[\psi_j(x_j)\right]\right)^2\right]$, allowing clinicians to assess the robustness of each contributing factor. Finally, the explainable reasoning trail $E = \left\{\psi_j, \psi_{jk}, R_p, \sigma_j\right\}$, is shown with each AI-generated recommendation to demonstrate evidence aggregation, weighting, and contextualization.

5.3 Adaptive Interaction Layer:

Reciprocal Calibration uses structured, bidirectional input to align the AI system with clinical experience. All clinical features, including numerical patient measurements, categorical clinical descriptors, and contextual variables, are encoded into dense embedding vectors of equal dimensionality to support unified interaction learning and reciprocal calibration through structured and continuous clinician feedback. Numerical characteristics are categorised to enable consistent embedding across various data sources. The embedding vocabulary for each feature field is initialized, and a look-up table maps feature values to dense vectors. After assembly, these embedding vectors become the cross and deep module inputs.

The cross module input is a matrix $X_{cross} = V \in R^{d \times m}$, where d is the embedding dimension and m is the number of feature fields. The deep module input is a concatenated vector $X_{deep} = Cat\left[v_1, \ldots, v_i, \ldots, v_m\right]$,, where v_i denotifies the embedding of the i-th feature. The cross module has many gated units that learn feature interaction patterns based on clinician preferences, decision methods, and institutional practice standards. Let $F = \left[F_1, \ldots, F_i, \ldots, F_m\right]$ represent the feature fields. A k-th order feature interaction consists of k features with $F_{t_1} = \alpha, F_{t_2} = \beta, \ldots, F_{t_k} = \gamma$, where $1 \leq t_1, t_2, \ldots, t_k \leq m$. The k-th order interaction is written as $FI^{(k)} = \prod_{i=1}^{m} v_i^{g_i}$, with $k = \sum_{i=1}^{m} g_i$and $g_i \in \{0,1\}$ indicating whether the i-th feature is engaged. This gated formulation is used to make interaction modeling in the embedding space easier. Gated units have m gates, and their open and closed configurations dictate the interaction they capture. Expert-in-the-loop feedback recalibrates gate activations to enhance clinically verified feature interactions and decrease irrelevant or context-inappropriate combinations. The number of gated units n controls the diversity of interaction patterns the reciprocal calibration mechanism can learn, but empirical findings suggest that a balanced selection of n ensures adaptability without overfitting to unique feedback signals. Based on expert input, the gated feature interaction structure is updated iteratively to calibrate reciprocally throughout clinical contact. Clinicians produce supervision cues $r \in \{-1, 0, +1\}$, in response to AI-generated recommendations, indicating rejection, neutral adjustment, or acceptance. These signals modify gate activation probability $p(g_i = 1)$ inside each gated unit, favoring feature combinations that match expert opinion and downplaying those that contradict clinical rationale. Gate updates are done using a feedback-weighted adjustment rule: $p_i^{(1)} = p_i^{(t)} + \eta r \nabla_{p_i} L_{cal}$, where η represents the calibration learning rate and L_{cal} penalizes model behavior misalignment with clinician preferences. Over subsequent contacts, this method converges to stable, practitioner-specific interaction patterns while respecting institution-level regularization requirements.

5.4 Clinical Decision Support Systems:

A few years ago, the ability to evaluate treatment trade-offs in complex cases would have been difficult for most clinical evaluators to do. Now we can use large language models (LLMs) to synthesize large volumes of biological literature, clinical trials, electronic health records, and pharmacovigilance data to produce both the therapeutic effects and the potential adverse effects of treatments for patients in real-time. Physicians will need to rapidly weigh the advantages and disadvantages of polypharmacy, management of chronic diseases, and precision oncology. In addition, generative AI could potentially utilize patient-specific information such as age, genetic markers, and comorbid conditions to place findings within a specific context for each patient and tailor treatment accordingly. If connected to clinical decision support systems, these models could assist physicians and patients in making better informed decisions through the creation of clear, balanced, and data-driven treatment summaries (Khosravi et al., 2024). The authors of this study compared LLMs in clinical oncology. The authors examined the performance of five large language models (LLMs) on 2044 cancer questions to determine their accuracy and reliability in a clinical setting. Compared to human standards, GPT-4 performed best among the models, although there were some variations among the various oncology subdomains. As previously mentioned, continuous benchmarking is needed to ensure safe and effective use of AI in clinical oncology (Rydzewski et al., 2024). The administration of appropriate antibiotics and IV fluids in a timely manner may decrease mortality from sepsis. AI algorithms that predict when a patient will develop sepsis can expedite the administration of these treatments. However, previous AI algorithms predicting sepsis were unable to achieve sufficient predictive performance due to several limitations. A cohort study at the University of Michigan's Academic Medical Center recently utilized a large inpatient database to construct an Epic sepsis model (ESM) and to assess the predictive validity of the ESM prior to clinical detection. Although the ESM produced a statistically significant AUROC of 0.62 when considering all predictions, the ESM produced a statistically significant AUROC of 0.47 when excluding those predictions made after clinical identification. These results highlight the need for developing better early prediction models (Kamran et al., 2024). Screening for hepatitis C virus (HCV) is more efficient using machine-learning algorithms that focus on identifying patients at high risk of having the disease. In a national study conducted in Israel, researchers developed and validated an XGBoost-based algorithm that identified active HCV carriers. Utilizing retrospective data, the researchers determined that the algorithm was able to identify HCV carriers approximately 100-fold more efficiently than traditional screening methods, indicating that it may lead to improved disease diagnosis (Dagan et al., 2024). Researchers developed an AI model that utilizes preoperative and intraoperative data to identify patients who are at high risk for requiring large quantities of blood during surgery. With an area under receiver operator curve (AUROC) value greater than 0.94, the researchers demonstrated that the model allowed for earlier interventions (Lee et al., 2022). Researchers developed similar models using quaternary pediatric intensive care unit (ICU) data to predict neurological morbidity in critically ill children. One of the studies included external validation of the accuracy of the model. Additionally, the researchers found that the model's predictions correlated with indicators of cerebral injury, suggesting that the model could potentially be used to identify and address issues early. Clinicians require transparency and accountability and therefore require complete explanations of "black box" recommendations. For example, generative AI can provide natural language reasoning, including connections between drug choices and clinical guidance and patient characteristics. Despite being confident in the reasoning behind a recommendation, if the reasoning of the AI is flawed then so too can be the recommendation. Therefore, much of the current research has focused on achieving accuracy of explanations, which are often called interpretability or fidelity. Another type of technology that is being employed include AI-powered retrieval systems that rely on advanced clinical research to provide evidence-based advice, reduce time spent searching for answers, and increase the likelihood that decisions will be based on fact rather than opinion. Ultimately, by employing these types of technologies, clinicians will be able to save time and make decisions based on the facts.

5.4.1 Role of GenAI in nursing:

Generative AI may also increase efficiency in processes, and quality of patient care through nursing education. Simulations utilizing enhanced AI will be used increasingly in nursing education to demonstrate complex health-related problems. The AI allows nursing students to learn in a simulated environment which decreases the risk associated with real-world learning. A recent study indicates AI could help personalize education and improve clinical decision making for healthcare workers (Beam & Kohane, 2018). AI may assist in determining the risk of falls in patients; create personalized treatment plans; and complete repetitive task such as medical documentation and reporting which would allow nurses to spend their time directly caring for patients. AI may decrease the amount of time it takes to document using voice-to-text transcription; automated charting; and intelligent data entry by 21-30% and save nurses 95-134 hours annually. AI may also decrease the administrative workload of nurses on patient admissions, transfers and discharge by 37-46%, which would translate to approximately 32-40 hours of nurse time each year (Deloitte, 2020). Optimization of the work flow will also ensure effective use of human resources, alleviate pressure on over worked staff members, potentially improve job satisfaction and retention. Research studies have demonstrated that AI-based chatbots can provide social support to patients and provide an innovative and easily accessible way to promote the wellness of patients, particularly when traditional methods are limited (e.g. during a pandemic) (Leung et al., 2022).A recent study explores the potential of Gen AI in transforming nursing practices in Taiwan and describes the functionality of the A+Nurse system, a digital assistant designed to automate routine nursing tasks, facilitate communication among healthcare teams, and include current medical knowledge into the nursing workflow (Tam et al., 2023). To optimize interaction with AI, prompt engineering is critical as optimal prompts produce desired results. Educators can utilize Gen AI-based models, such as ChatGPT, to develop improved educational and learning experiences for their students, e.g., developing virtual simulation environments, creating lesson plans and developing evaluations (Liao et al., 2024).

5.5 Challenges of clinical GenAI implementation:

GenAI has real problems that need to be fixed. Some of these are mistakes like random fabrications or hallucinations, systemic social biases that can be "baked in" during LLM training and could cause serious problems in the workplace (real or imagined), LLM performance drift, data privacy, governance, accountability (including when an LLM makes a mistake), and legal issues. People who work in healthcare will naturally not want to use a product that has risks that are not fully known, expected, or easy to handle. There are also financial risks for the government if captive markets start to form. So, any risks that come with this technology need to be reduced in order for its potential to be realized. Unlike traditional AI, which relies on pre-set algorithms to provide consistent and clear results, GenAI uses inference, which makes its outputs less reliable and harder to understand. Traditional AI makes errors due of bad training data and/or the basic modeling method, which depends on simplifying assumptions. This output, although expected and not totally correct, is a considerable benefit in the context of regulatory approval, since model performance stays consistent post-approved. This predictability has resulted in the advancement of regulatory approval procedures for conventional AI in healthcare via development and validation. Conversely, GenAI's outputs exhibit less predictability and may manifest fabrications or hallucinations. This inconsistency may be more comparable to the shortcomings of human clinical reasoning, which also exhibits variable and context-dependent results. The hazards associated with LLM hallucinations presently limit their therapeutic use; nonetheless, continuous advancements are swiftly reducing the frequency and danger of such hallucinations. Should this enhancement persist, reduced error rates may be attained, facilitating wider clinical uses of GenAI.The volatility of GenAI presents a distinct difficulty for control in healthcare settings. There is now a regulatory avenue for GenAI-based clinical decision assistance as part of a risk-based regulatory strategy. This means that clinicians are ultimately responsible for any treatment choices made with the help of GenAI. The Therapeutic Goods Administration (TGA) also says that clinical GenAI systems must identify where the information they provide comes from so that doctors may check the accuracy of the output. In this regulated environment in Australia, ambientscribes have been quickly adopted. These programs record a clinical visit and subsequently make a summary for the medical record. They use GenAI to make the summary. The TGA is presently doing a big study of AI after holding public discussions not so long ago.Drifting and fluctuating performance. There will be a lot of incentive to keep improving a GenAI healthcare system since each new LLM version has made a big difference in performance [35]. This clinical solution that uses GPT-3.5 is predicted to work better when GPT-4 or Claude 3.5 is used. However, changes to models have caused performance to change in strange ways. Each new LLM is built on various designs and training data, which means that different optimization strategies will work differently on each one. This means that all the work that went into making GPT-3.5 better for clinical tasks, such fine-tuning, better prompting, and retrieval-augmented generation, has to be done again, including testing, evaluation, and approval.Over time, GenAI models may experience performance drift, which means that the same inputs may produce different outputs. This is a challenge for therapeutic applications that need regularity. The drift arises when organizations supplying the LLM base models persistently endeavor to enhance their models. While some enhancements to LLMs increase overall model performance, these modifications may simultaneously diminish performance on certain jobs [36]. One approach to mitigate this issue might include restricting the use of GenAI-based solutions to low-risk scenarios where drift is less problematic or unlikely to result in substantially changed performance, such as medical coding for financing purposes. Another method to prevent drift is to replicate LLMs, host them internally, and protect them from any modification operations, therefore stabilizing the model weights. These safeguarded LLMs, situated inside local health ecosystems, may also assist with addressing privacy and data governance issues.

6. EXPERIMENTAL ANALYSIS

These tests occur in a simulated clinical decision support environment that mirrors clinical decision making processes to obtain data from patients. Each record contains time-stamped vital signs, lab values, clinical observations and therapeutic interventions as they relate to specific phases of care such as triage, diagnosis, treatment planning, monitoring and follow up. Patient names are removed prior to each test to maintain confidentiality of patients. Data preparation for all models includes normalization of continuous variables, discretizing continuous variables into categories, and converting continuous variable into categorical format to maintain consistent formatting throughout all models used in this research. All testing occurs on a workstation which has GPU accelerated processing capabilities. The architecture is implemented using one of the two major deep learning libraries available today (PyTorch or TensorFlow) and the explanation of model outputs are obtained through utilization of well-established XAI toolkits. Statistical analysis and visualization will be completed using widely accepted scientific computing frameworks.

To assess the viability of this conceptual model, it is evaluated using a systematic approach to determine the level of contextual relevance of the relationships formed, how clearly the reasoning process is expressed, if the system adapts appropriately to the context of use, user-centered usability, and predictive efficacy. Expert-in-the-loop clinical simulations and controlled clinical simulations validate the ability of the models to operate effectively within real-world clinical decision-making contexts. A combination of both quantitative and qualitative methods are used to measure the degree of success in augmenting relationships.

- **Contextual Relevance Score (CRS):** We calculate a contextual relevance score to assess situational awareness and AI-generated suggestions' phase-appropriateness. For each clinical phase p, domain experts grade model output relevance on a defined scale and aggregate the score as $CRS_p = \frac{1}{N}\sum_{i=1}^{N} r_i^{(p)}$, where $r_i^{(p)}$denotes the expert relevance rating for the i-th case in phase p. This statistic measures the system's phase-specific clinical goal alignment.
- **Explainability Utility Score (EUS):** This explainability utility score evaluates explanation clarity, coherence, and clinical utility. Clinicians evaluate reasoning traces for clinical decision-making and AI validation. The Explainable Reasoning Layer's practical value is shown by the mean of interpretability, completeness, and actionability.
- **Calibration Convergence Rate (CCR):** The calibration convergence rate evaluates how rapidly the system adapts to physician input across encounters. The CCR measures AI output correction frequency or clinician judgment disagreement decline with time, represented as $CCR = -\frac{\Delta L_{cal}}{\Delta t}$, where

L_{cal} denotes the calibration loss. More CCR means quicker practitioner and institutional alignment.

- **Phase Transition Accuracy (PTA):** Phase change Accuracy measures the system's ability to recognize or adapt to clinical stage changes like triage to diagnosis or treatment to monitoring. Total phase transitions / correctly recognized phase transitions:

$$PTA = \frac{Number\ of\ correctly\ identified\ phase\ transitions}{Total\ number\ of\ true\ phase\ transitions}$$

This statistic measures situational awareness preservation when patient environments changes.

- **Explanation Consistency Score (ECS):** The Explanation Consistency Score evaluates the dependability of generated explanations across similar clinical cases or repeated inference processes. It is computed as:

$$ECS = 1 - \frac{1}{N}\sum_{i=1}^{N} \parallel E_i - E_i' \parallel$$

where E_i and E_i' are explanation vectors from PDP or ALE analyses for similar inputs, and N is the number of examined cases. Clear, reliable, consistent thinking is indicated by higher ECS levels.

- **Explanation–Decision Alignment (EDA):** Explanation–Decision alignment assesses the way the explanation mechanism's major points match the model decision's factors. Its traits include:

$$EDA = \frac{|\ Top_k(Decision\ Features) \cap Top_k(Explanation\ Features)\ |}{k}$$

This statistic ensures that explanations truly represent the model's decision-making process, not just retrospectives.

- **Feedback Utilization Efficiency (FUE):** Utilization of Feedback Efficiency quantifies the extent to which physician input enhances system performance during reciprocal calibration. It is calculated as:

$$FUE = \frac{\Delta Performance}{Number\ of\ feedback\ interactions}$$

Efficient learning from expert oversight and speedier adaptation to clinician preferences and institutional protocols are indicative of a higher FUE.

- **Adaptation Stability Index (ASI):** The Adaptation Stability Index evaluates the stability of model behavior post-calibration, preventing oscillatory or unpredictable responses. It is characterized by:

$$ASI = 1 - \frac{\sigma(\hat{y}_{t:t+k})}{\mu(\hat{y}_{t:t+k})}$$

where $\hat{y}_{t:t+k}$ signifies the model outputs during a post-calibration period, and $\mu(\cdot)$and $\sigma(\cdot)$ imply the mean and standard deviation, respectively. Stable and dependable adaptation is indicated by higher ASI scores.

Figure 1. comparison of Contextual Relevance Score

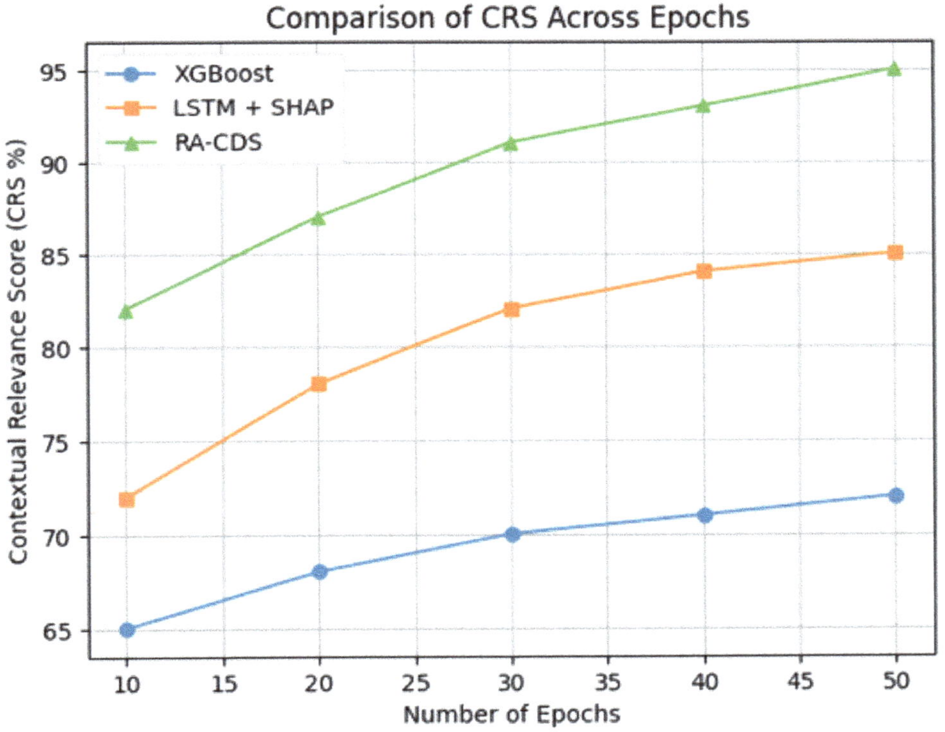

Figure 1 compares the Contextual Relevance Score (CRS) for XGBoost, LSTM + SHAP, and the proposed RA-CDS framework over training epochs. XGBoost's lowest CRS values, stabilizing around 72%, indicate its weak ability to convey clinical context beyond static feature relationships. Due to its capacity to characterize temporal relationships, the LSTM + SHAP model improves to 85% CRS, but its post-hoc explainability prevents deeper situational alignment. The recommended RA-CDS system consistently achieves 95% CRS, outperforming XGBoost and LSTM + SHAP by 23% and 10%, respectively. This large performance gap shows that situational awareness, contextual perception, and reciprocal calibration in RA-CDS work.

Figure 2. comparison of Explainability Utility Score

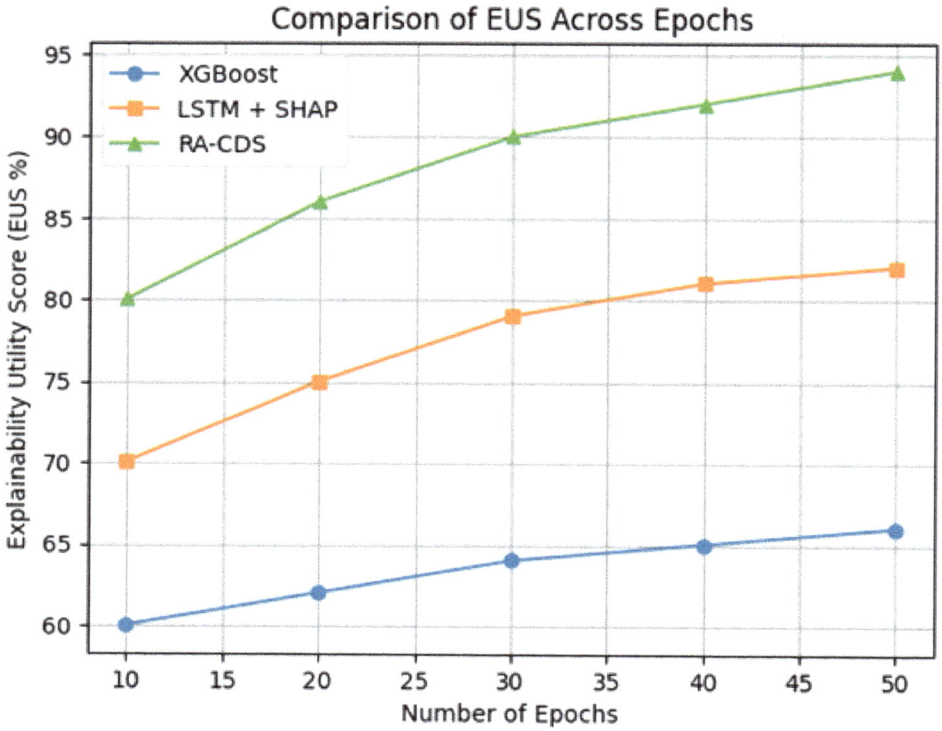

Figure 2 demonstrates that XGBoost achieves an EUS of 64.5%, indicating little explanatory clarity and practical value due to insufficient inherent reasoning transparency. The LSTM + SHAP model improves EUS to 79.6%, illustrating the benefit of post-hoc explainability; nevertheless, this improvement is constrained by the disconnect between explanations and the model's internal reasoning process. The proposed RA-CDS framework attains a significantly elevated EUS of 92.4%, exceeding XGBoost and LSTM + SHAP by 27.9% and 12.8%, respectively.

Figure 3. comparison of Convergence Rate

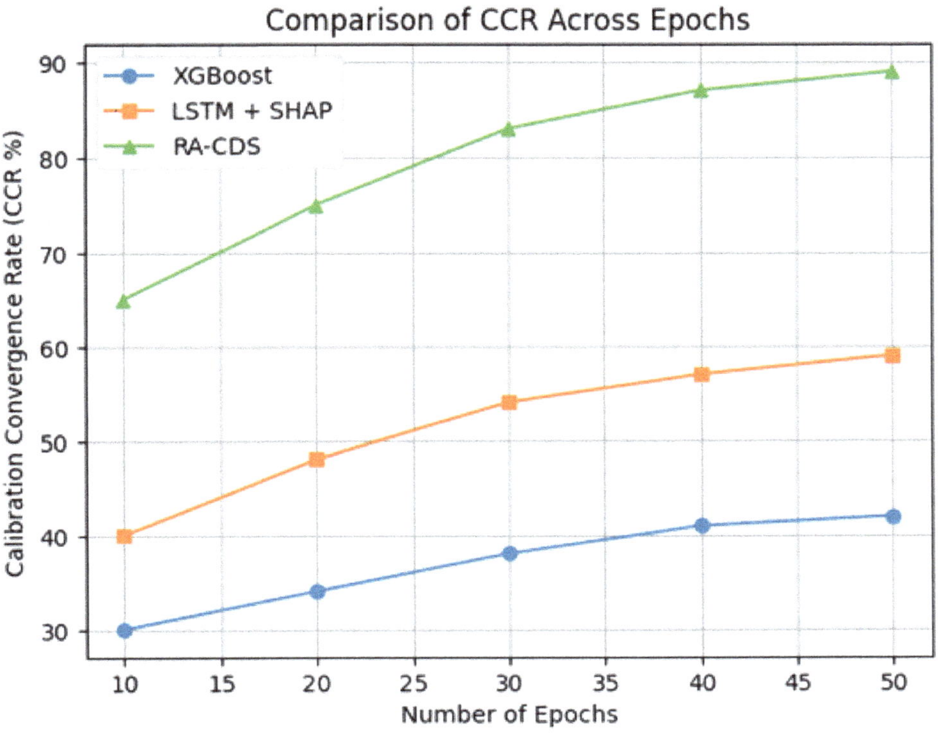

Figure 3 compares XGBoost, LSTM + SHAP, and the proposed RA-CDS framework for Calibration Convergence Rate. Due to its static learning architecture, XGBoost has a low CCR of 42.3%, limiting its capacity to adapt to input. The LSTM + SHAP model has a CCR of 58.7%, indicating partial adaptation helped by temporal learning, but its convergence rate is limited by the absence of a feedback integration mechanism. The RA-CDS design outperforms XGBoost and LSTM + SHAP by 46.9% and 30.5%, respectively, with a CCR of 89.2%.

Figure 4. comparison of Phase Transition Accuracy

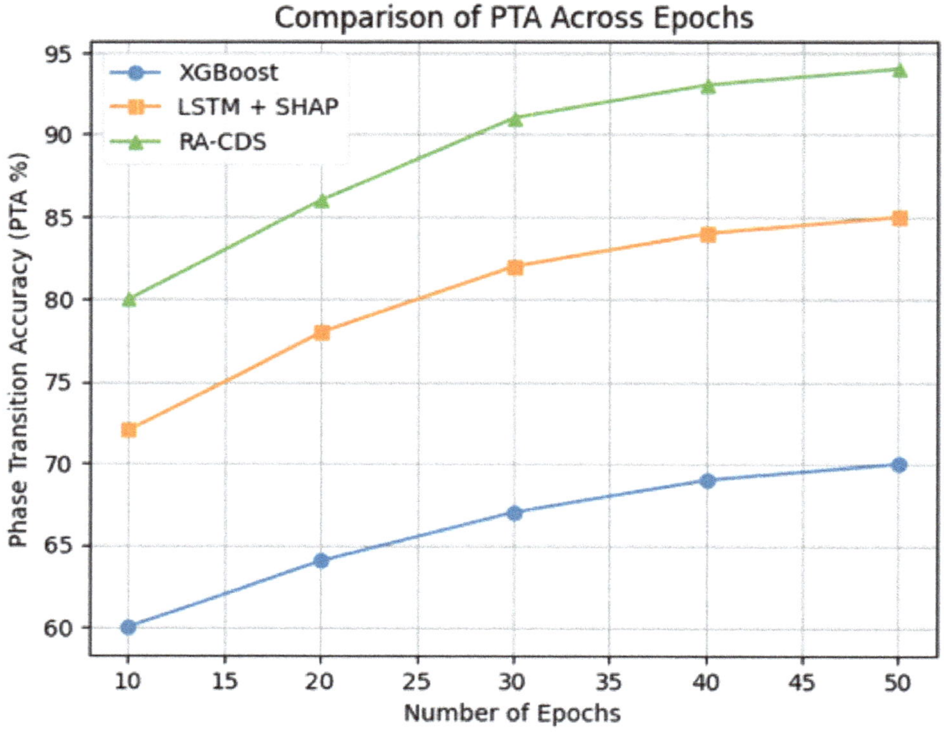

In Figure 4, Phase Transition Accuracy (PTA) fluctuates throughout training epochs. LSTM + SHAP uses temporal sequence modeling to attain 72%, whereas XGBoost has 60% after 10 epochs, indicating a limited ability to recognize clinical stage changes. The high PTA of 80% in RA-CDS indicates its quick context absorption. PTA improves to 64% for XGBoost and 78% for LSTM + SHAP after 20 epochs, while RA-CDS rises to 86%, showing more accurate clinical scenario recognition. After 30 epochs, XGBoost and LSTM + SHAP accomplish 67% and 82%, however RA-CDS approaches 91%, demonstrating its phase shift adaptability. PTA values of 69% for XGBoost, 84% for LSTM + SHAP, and 93% for RA-CDS improve after 40 epochs. After 50 epochs, all models stabilize, although RA-CDS has the highest PTA at 94%, compared to 70% for XGBoost and 85% for LSTM + SHAP.

Figure 5. comparison of Explaination consistency score

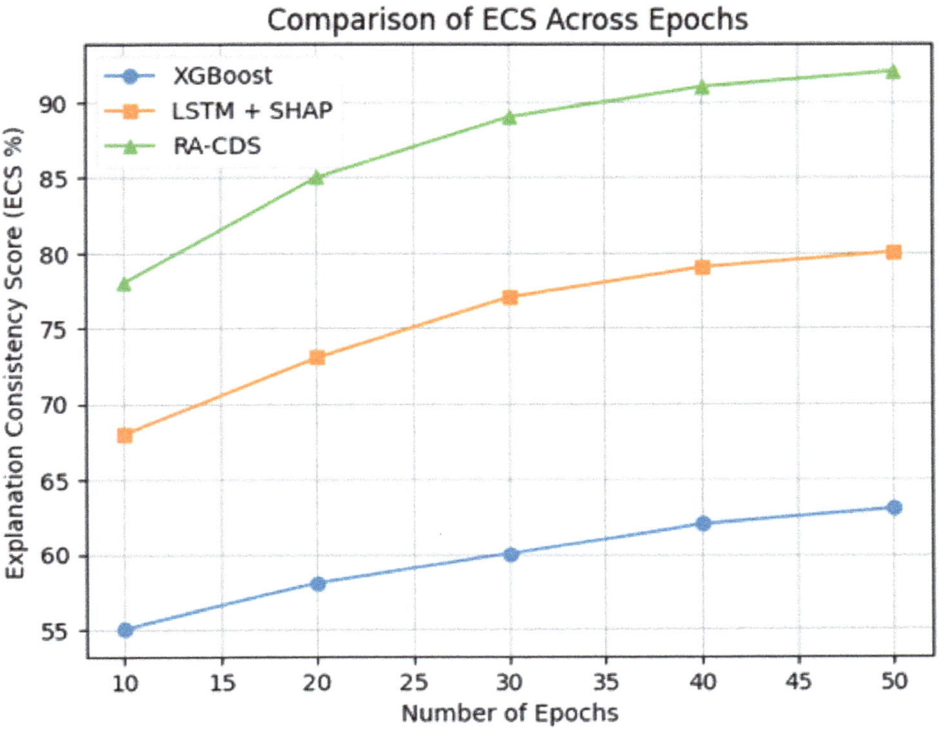

Figure 5 shows Explanation Consistency Score fluctuations. XGBoost has the lowest ECS values, steady at 55–63%, showing insufficient consistency and repeatability in its explanatory outputs due to unclear reasoning processes. Post-hoc explainability improves the LSTM + SHAP model's explanation consistency, with ECS values ranging from 68% to 80%. However, because explanations are not directly integrated into the model's internal decision-making process, some variability remains. The proposed RA-CDS framework consistently exceeds 90% and approaches 92%, exceeding both baseline models.

Figure 6. comparison of Explanation decision alignment

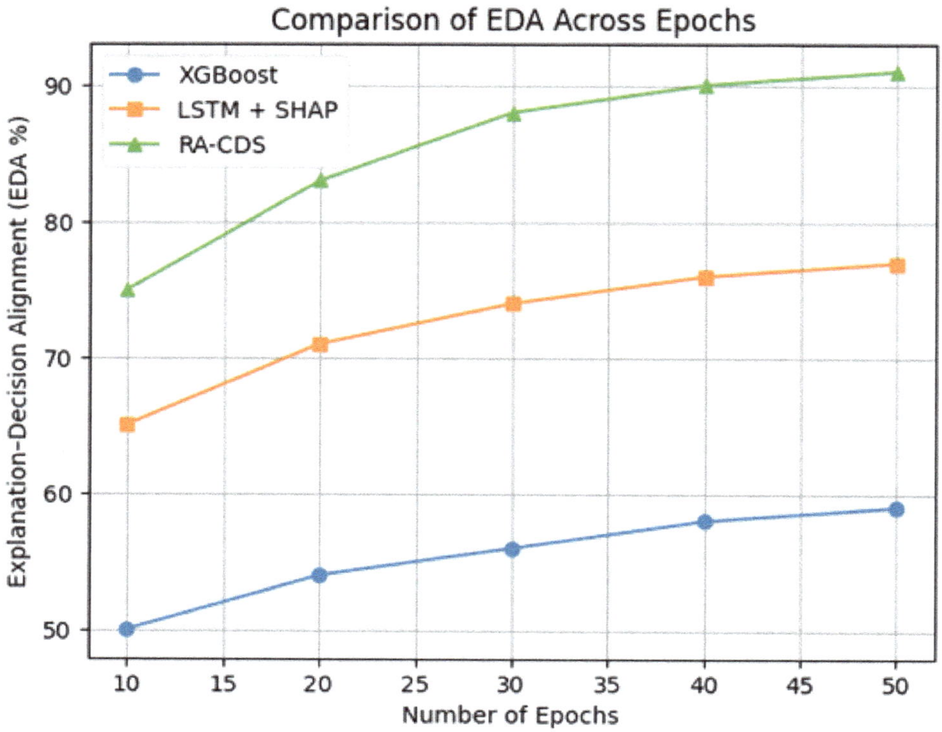

Figure 6 compares Explanation–Decision Alignment. XGBoost has the lowest alignment, with EDA scores between 50 and 59%, indicating a poor fit between the final decision logic and the relevant attributes. The LSTM + SHAP model shows moderate enhancement, with EDA values ranging from 65% to 77%, indicating the benefit of post-hoc explainability in identifying significant features. However, this congruence is only partial because explanations are produced after the decision-making process. The RA-CDS methodology typically achieves EDA values of over 91%, beating XGBoost by over 30 percentage points and LSTM + SHAP by 14–16 percentage points at convergence.

Figure 7. comparison of Feedback utilization efficiency

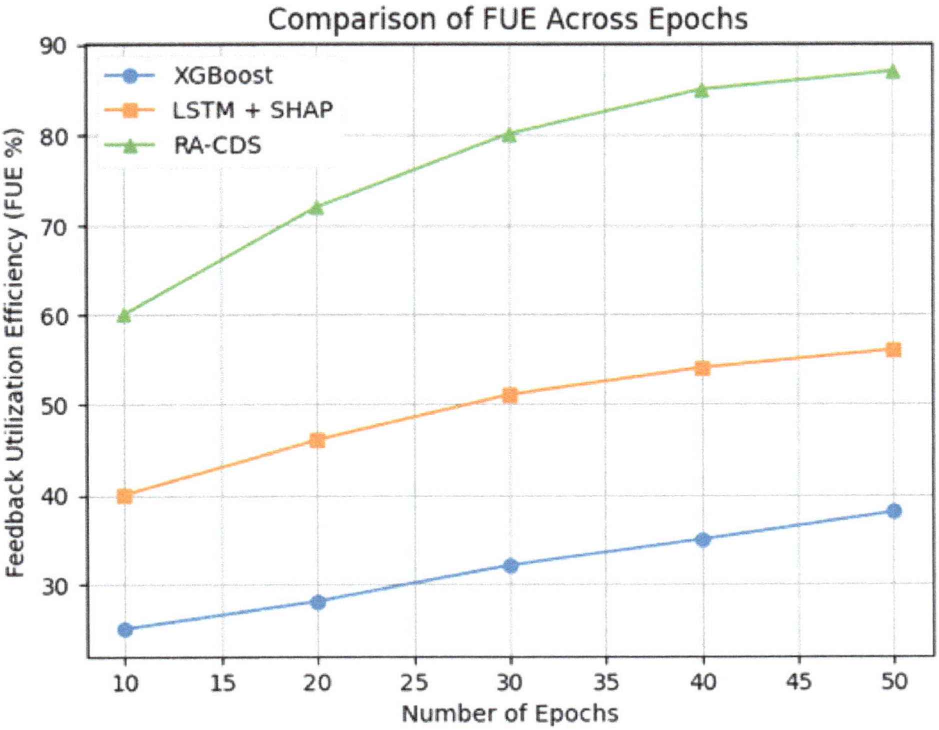

Figure 7 compares XGBoost, LSTM + SHAP, and the suggested RA-CDS Feedback Utilization Efficiency framework. Due to its static learning architecture and lack of explicit adaptive approaches, XGBoost has the lowest input Utilization Efficiency (FUE), often 25%–38%. The LSTM + SHAP model improves, with FUE values between 40% and 56%, showing temporal learning, but its dependency on post-hoc explanations restricts physician participation for model changes. The proposed RA-CDS architecture often achieves FUE values of 60% to 87%, beating XGBoost and LSTM + SHAP by large margins.

Figure 8. comparison of Adaptability stability index

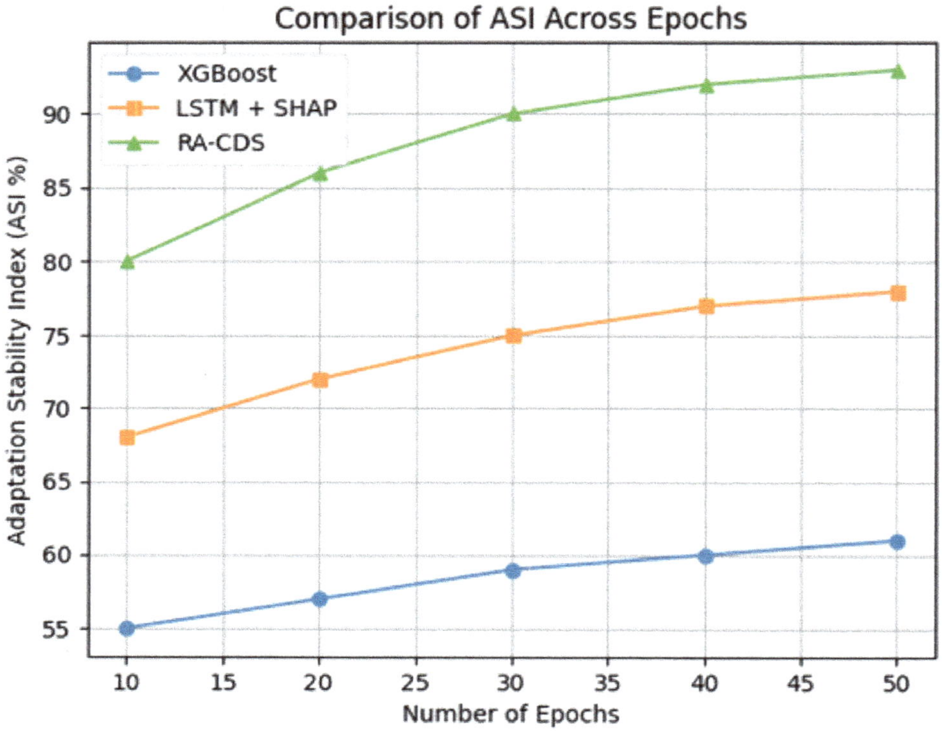

Figure 8 compares the Adaptation Stability Index. XGBoost has the least adaptation stability, with ASI values between 55 and 61%. This shows that its learning behavior is unpredictable and poorly regulated when exposed to changing situations or information. The LSTM + SHAP model improves temporal stability with ASI values between 68% and 78%, but the absence of explicit feedback-driven adaptation limits its ability to moderate oscillations during learning. The suggested RA-CDS architecture consistently achieves the highest ASI values, from 80% to over 93%, exceeding XGBoost and LSTM + SHAP.

Table 2.

parameters	XGBoost	LSTM + SHAP	RA-CDS
CRS (%)	71.8	81.2	93.1
EUS (%)	64.5	79.6	92.4
CCR (%)	42.3	58.7	89.2

continued on following page

Table 2. Continued

parameters	XGBoost	LSTM + SHAP	RA-CDS
PTA (%)	68.9	83.4	94.0
ECS (%)	62.7	78.1	91.7
EDA (%)	57.7	75.7	97.4
FUE (%)	38.8	46.8	90.4
ASI (%)	69.4	78.3	93.7

7. CONCLUSION

This study examined how Generative AI could have an impact on health care in many ways. This includes the use of personalized treatment planning, medical image processing, and generating synthetic data for the potential for generative AI to enhance diagnostic accuracy, improve processes, and provide individualized care. It breaks down the delivery of patient care into meaningful levels of care and develops a representation of the environment through a multi-level, content-aware, temporal perception network that understands the development of a patient's situation. The layer incorporates self-explanatory processes as well as uncertainty aware, phase-conditioned explainability to convert model outputs into visual, evidence-based reasoning that increases clinician confidence, validation and informed decision-making. The Adaptive Interaction Layer uses expert-in-the-loop feedback to adjust the system; it learns from clinical supervision, adapts to the practitioner's individual practice pattern and meets the institutional requirements, while maintaining the stability of the system.

REFERENCES

Beam AL, Kohane IS. Big data and machine learning in health care. JAMA. 2018;319(13):1317–1318. . 4DOI: 10.1001/jama.2017.18391

Dagan, N., Magen, O., Leshchinsky, M., Makov-Assif, M., Lipsitch, M., Reis, B. Y., ... & Balicer, R. D. (2024). Prospective evaluation of machine learning for public health screening: identifying unknown hepatitis C carriers. NEJM AI, 1(2), AIoa2300012.

Deloitte. (2020). Technology making health care work more meaningful [Internet]. Available from: https://www2.deloitte.com/us/en/ insights/industry/health-care/technology-making-health-care-wo rk-more-meaningful.html. Accessed May 31, 2024.

Futoma, M., Simons, M., Panch, T., Doshi-Velez, F., & Celi, L. A. (2020, September). Simons, T. Panch, F. Doshi-Velez, and L. A. Celi, "The myth of generalisability in clinical research and machine learning in health care,". *The Lancet. Digital Health*, *2*(9), e489–e492. DOI: 10.1016/S2589-7500(20)30186-2 PMID: 32864600

Ghim, J. L., & Ahn, S. (2023). Transforming clinical trials: The emerging roles of large language models. *Translational and Clinical Pharmacology*, *31*(3), 131–138. DOI: 10.12793/tcp.2023.31.e16 PMID: 37810626

Gholamzadeh, M., Abtahi, H., & Safdari, R. (2023). The application of knowledge-based clinical decision support systems to enhance adherence to evidence-based medicine in chronic disease. *Journal of Healthcare Engineering*, *2023*(1), 8550905. DOI: 10.1155/2023/8550905 PMID: 37284487

Hacking, S. (2024). ChatGPT and Medicine: Together We Embrace the AI Renaissance. [Google Scholar] [CrossRef] [PubMed]. *JMIR Bioinformatics and Biotechnology*, *5*, e52700. DOI: 10.2196/52700 PMID: 38935938

Hanna, M. G., Pantanowitz, L., Jackson, B., Palmer, O., Visweswaran, S., Pantanowitz, J., Deebajah, M., & Rashidi, H. H. (2025, March). Ethical and Bias Considerations in Artificial Intelligence/Machine Learning. *Modern Pathology*, *38*(3), 100686. DOI: 10.1016/j.modpat.2024.100686 PMID: 39694331

Johnson, K. B., Wei, W. Q., Weeraratne, D., Frisse, M. E., Misulis, K., Rhee, K., Zhao, J., & Snowdon, J. L. (2021). Precision Medicine, AI, and the Future of Personalized Health Care. *Clinical and Translational Science*, *14*(1), 86–93. DOI: 10.1111/cts.12884 PMID: 32961010

Kamil, H., Rachmah, R., Irvanizam, I., & Wardani, E. (2020). Exploring health professionals' perceptions on Health-ID, an electronic integrated patient progress documentation system: A qualitative study in Indonesia. *Journal of Multidisciplinary Healthcare*, •••, 1649–1656.

Kamran, F., Tjandra, D., Heiler, A., Virzi, J., Singh, K., King, J. E., ... & Wiens, J. (2024). Evaluation of sepsis prediction models before onset of treatment. Nejm Ai, 1(3), AIoa2300032.

Khosravi, M., Zare, Z., Mojtabaeian, S. M., & Izadi, R. (2024). Artificial Intelligence and Decision-Making in Healthcare: A Thematic Analysis of a Systematic Review of Reviews. [CrossRef] [PubMed]. *Health Services Research and Managerial Epidemiology*, *11*, 23333928241234863. DOI: 10.1177/23333928241234863 PMID: 38449840

Kung, T. H., Cheatham, M., Medenilla, A., Sillos, C., De Leon, L., Elepaño, C., Madriaga, M., Aggabao, R., Diaz-Candido, G., Maningo, J., & Tseng, V. (2023). Performance of ChatGPT on USMLE: Potential for AI-Assisted Medical Education Using Large Language Models. [Google Scholar] [CrossRef]. *PLOS Digital Health*, *2*(2), e0000198. DOI: 10.1371/journal.pdig.0000198 PMID: 36812645

Lee, S. M., Lee, G., Kim, T. K., Le, T., Hao, J., Jung, Y. M., Park, C.-W., Park, J. S., Jun, J. K., Lee, H.-C., & Kim, D. (2022). Development and Validation of a Prediction Model for Need for Massive Transfusion During Surgery Using Intraoperative Hemodynamic Monitoring Data. *JAMA Network Open*, *5*(12), e2246637. DOI: 10.1001/jamanetworkopen.2022.46637 PMID: 36515949

Leung, F., Lau, Y. C., Law, M., & Djeng, S. K. (2022). Artificial intelligence and end user tools to develop a nurse duty roster scheduling system. *International Journal of Nursing Sciences*, *9*(3), 373–377.

Liao, C. T., Tsay, S. F., & Chen, H. C. (2024). Exploring generative AI's role in alleviating nursing workload and burnout in Taiwan. *Journal of the Formosan Medical Association*, *123*(7), 736–737. Advance online publication. DOI: 10.1016/j.jfma.2024.02.003 PMID: 38368187

Miller, T. (2019, February). Explanation in artificial intelligence: Insights from the social sciences. *Artificial Intelligence*, *267*, 1–38. DOI: 10.1016/j.artint.2018.07.007

Patel, A., & Arasanipalai, A. (2021). Applied Natural Language Processing in the Enterprise: Teaching Machines to Read, Write, and Understand. O'Reilly Media., Available online https://www.oreilly.com/library/view/ applied-natural-language/9781492062561/ch01.html, Retrieved May 11, 2021, from.

Raju, T. P. (2024, May). Artificial Intelligence: From Theory to Application and Ethical Considerations. *International Journal for Research in Applied Science and Engineering Technology*, *12*(5), 639–641. DOI: 10.22214/ijraset.2024.59463

Rasheed, K., Qayyum, A., Ghaly, M., Al-Fuqaha, A., Razi, A., & Qadir, J. (2022). Explainable, trustworthy, and ethical machine learning for healthcare: A survey. *Computers in Biology and Medicine*, *149*(Oct), 106043. DOI: 10.1016/j.compbiomed.2022.106043 PMID: 36115302

Roberts, L., & Candi, M. (2024, August). Artificial intelligence and innovation management: Charting the evolving landscape. *Technovation*, *136*, 103081. DOI: 10.1016/j.technovation.2024.103081

Rydzewski, N. R., Dinakaran, D., Zhao, S. G., Ruppin, E., Turkbey, B., Citrin, D. E., & Patel, K. R. (2024). Comparative evaluation of LLMs in clinical oncology. Nejm ai, 1(5), AIoa2300151.

Sadeghi R, K., Ojha, D., Kaur, P., Mahto, R. V., & Dhir, A.K. Sadeghi R. (2024, May). D. Ojha, P. Kaur, R. V. Mahto, and A. Dhir, "Explainable artificial intelligence and agile decision-making in supply chain cyber resilience,". *Decision Support Systems*, *180*, 114194. DOI: 10.1016/j.dss.2024.114194

Sallam, M. (2023). ChatGPT utility in healthcare education, research, and practice: Systematic review on the promising perspectives and valid concerns. *Health Care*, *11*, 887. PMID: 36981544

Seangpraw, K., & Ong-Artborirak, P. (2020). Knowledge and behaviors toward health care for elderly patients with hypertension, and quality of life among informal caregivers in Northern Thailand. *Journal of Multidisciplinary Healthcare*, •••, 1771–1780.

Tam, W., Huynh, T., Tang, A., Luong, S., Khatri, Y., & Zhou, W. (2023). Nursing education in the age of artificial intelligence powered Chatbots (AI-Chatbots): Are we ready yet? *Nurse Education Today*, *129*, 105917. DOI: 10.1016/j.nedt.2023.105917 PMID: 37506622

van Breugel, B., Liu, T., Oglic, D., & van der Schaar, M. (2024, October). Synthetic data in biomedicine via generative artificial intelligence. *Nature Reviews Bioengineering*, *2*(12), 991–1004. DOI: 10.1038/s44222-024-00245-7

Vrdoljak, J., Boban, Z., Vilovic, M., Kumric, M., & Bozic, J. (2025). A Review of Large Language Models in Medical Education, Clinical Decision Support, and Healthcare Administration. *Health Care*, *13*, 603. PMID: 40150453

Wu, Y., Feng, X., Gong, M., Han, J., Jiao, Y., Li, S., Li, T., Shen, C., Wang, H.-Y., Yu, X., Zhang, Z., Zhang, Z., Zhao, Y., Zhou, P., Wang, H., & Zhang, Z. (2023, June). Evolution and major changes of the diagnosis and treatment protocol for COVID-19 patients in China 2020–2023. *Health Care Science*, *2*(3), 135–152. DOI: 10.1002/hcs2.45 PMID: 38939112

Xue, V. W., Lei, P., & Cho, W. C. (2023). The potential impact of ChatGPT in clinical and translational medicine. *Clinical and Translational Medicine*, *13*(3), e1216. DOI: 10.1002/ctm2.1216 PMID: 36856370

Zhang, K., Meng, X., Yan, X., Ji, J., Liu, J., Xu, H., Zhang, H., Liu, D., Wang, J., Wang, X., Gao, J., Wang, Y., Shao, C., Wang, W., Li, J., Zheng, M.-Q., Yang, Y., & Tang, Y.-D. (2025). Revolutionizing Health Care: The Transformative Impact of Large Language Models in Medicine. [Google Scholar] [CrossRef] [PubMed]. *Journal of Medical Internet Research*, *27*, e59069. DOI: 10.2196/59069 PMID: 39773666

Section 5
Sectoral Impact and Research Trends

Chapter 12
Mitigating Hallucinations in AI: Ensuring Trustworthy and Aligned Systems in Legal, Educational, and Governmental Sectors

Poonam Sharma
http://orcid.org/0009-0000-6352-4395
Xavier Institute of Management and Informatics, Jaipur, India

Shikha Khullar
http://orcid.org/0009-0000-5598-3145
Poornima University, Jaipur, India

Ibrar Ahmad
http://orcid.org/0009-0001-0846-0218
Southwest University of Political Science and Law, China

Kim Le My Nguyen
http://orcid.org/0009-0005-0361-7529
University of Economics and Law, Vietnam National University, Vietnam

ABSTRACT

Artificial intelligence is increasingly adopted in high-stakes domains such as law, education, and government, where reliability, fairness, and accountability are critical. Despite its growing integration, AI systems remain susceptible to hallucinations, defined as the generation of inaccurate, fabricated, or biased outputs that can undermine institutional credibility and decision-making. In legal contexts, hallucinations may result in fictitious case law; in educational settings, they risk

DOI: 10.4018/979-8-3373-7320-1.ch012

t © 2026, IGI Global Scientific Publishing. Copying or distributing in print or electronic forms without written permission of IGI Global Scientific Publishing is prohibited. Use of this chapter to enerative artificial intelligence (AI) technologies is expressly prohibited. The publisher reserves all rights to license its use for generative AI training and machine learning model development.

disseminating misleading information; and in governmental applications. This chapter systematically examines the underlying causes and societal implications of AI hallucinations across these sectors. It reviews recent state-of-the-art mitigation strategies, including retrieval-augmented generation, enhanced reasoning architectures, and hybrid hallucination detection frameworks. Beyond technical approaches, emphasizes the role of ethical principles and governance mechanisms, such as transparency, verification, accountability, and human-in-the-loop oversight.

1. INTRODUCTION

Hallucinations of AI are a major problem in the use of credible AI systems in institutional sectors. Hallucinations are the contents produced by AI systems and particularly large language models (LLMs) that seem logical, coherent, and contextually plausible but factually false and contradictory to verifiable sources. Such outputs usually duplicate information, and they are especially harmful in areas with high stakes. Hallucinations are not immediately apparent, unlike traditional software errors. They work within a false spectrum of credibility.They are internally consistent and semantically coherent and can often be confused with the correct answers unless they are put through intense checking(Nishisako et al., 2025). Hallucinations have more than mere technical breakdowns. Hallucinations may lead to the creation of false references to cases, misrepresentation of legal precedents, and references to false statutes in the legal field, which interfere with the legal argument process(Magesh et al., 2025). Hallucinations in the education sector present false information and biased content, which affect the integrity of learning and growth in academic sectors. Hallucinations in government are a threat to evidence-based policymaking because they give misleading recommendations and fabricated statistical claims(Liu & Lin, 2025).Trustworthiness entails three important dimensions: technical robustness, ethical grounding, and accountability (Khullar et al., 2026).

There is empirical evidence that addresses the urgency of the issue of hallucinations. Even with the improvement of model architecture, current LLMs have a hallucination rate of between 58 and 88 percent on questionable questions that can be verified. It is not a fringe problem.It is an institutionalized problem. Handling hallucinations is no longer a choice it is essential to build the credibility needed in high-stakes industries. Trustworthiness entails three very important dimensions, namely: technical robustness, ethical grounding, and accountability. This alignment will not be based solely on performance metrics. It will also require achieving resistance to hallucinations, ethical standards, and transparency in AI outputs(Matthew Dahl, 2024).

This chapter examines how the main international governance tools, such as the EU Guidelines on Trustworthy AI, NIST AI Risk Management Framework (RMF), and the OECD AI Principles, can be translated into actual activities that can reduce hallucination in legal, educational, and government fields. The chapter summarizes the empirical research on the mechanisms of hallucination detection, such as retrieval-augmented generation (RAG) systems, agentic AI architectures, and knowledge-graph-based verification tools like HalluGraph, and puts such technical solutions into perspective with the regulatory environment described by the EU AI Act and new governance standards across industries.

The chapter first reviews the theoretical and practical aspects of AI hallucinations, based on recent empirical studies and case documentation. Second, it maps the risks of hallucinations against the requirements outlined in the EU AI Guidelines, NIST AI RMF, and OECD Principles. Third, it evaluates the technical mechanisms necessary for detecting and mitigating hallucinations in real-world applications world. The discussion starts with mapping the risks of hallucinations against the requirements, expressed in three basic international frameworks. Seven requirements are defined by the EU Guidelines on Trustworthy AI (High-Level Expert Group on AI, 2024) and the EU AI Act, which include human agency, technical robustness, privacy, transparency, diversity, fairness, and accountability. This translates to ethical requirements like respect for human agency, harm prevention, fairness, and explicability, which are especially important in industries whose AI mistakes can directly affect human well-being or institutional credibility. With its Generative AI Profile, NIST AI Risk Management Framework (RMF) (NIST, 2024) operationalizes governance by four main functions: Govern, Map, Measure, and Manage. Hallucinations are particularly emphasized by NIST as a specific type of risk in the field of generative AI, along with such problems as the leakage of data and the misuse of synthetic content. It provides practical mitigation measures (NIST, 2024). In 2024, they were revised, and the OECD AI Principles (OECD, 2024) highlight five pillars: inclusive growth, rule of law, transparency, robustness, and accountability. The revision also has a specific provision aimed at curbing misinformation and disinformation, which is being exaggerated by AI, and hallucinations are recognized as a particular problem and a burning challenge in governance.

The analysis combines the existing technical methods of detecting hallucinations. RAG systems increase the accuracy of the LLM outputs based on the validated data sources, halving the prevalence of hallucinations with the help of multi-source evidence retrieval (MEGA-RAG framework)(Xu et al., 2025a). Special networks of AI agents are used in agentic systems to examine and verify unverified claims and speculative content. HalluGraph is a knowledge-graph-based verification model that identifies structural hallucinations by breaking down entity grounding and relation preservation. HalluGraph has an accuracy of 94% on question-answering tasks on legal contracts and 84% on case law citation verification, which is better than conventional semantic similarity algorithms such as BERTScore(cs.AI/cs.CL/cs.LG, 2025). These developments indicate that the detection of hallucinations needs not only a semantic similarity but also a structural fidelity, which maintains entities, relationships, and logical consistency to the source material.Sector-Specific Risk Operationalization: Lastly, the analysis uses these governance frameworks and technical approaches to three sectors. It determines the tangible evils the hallucinations cause, which governance systems offer protection, and the way out of the problem through practical measures.

Hallucinations present grave risks in the legal practice. The AI systems that produce false cases or misleading legal precedents deceive legal professionals, affecting the court proceedings and legal counsel. Such fallacies are destructive to the logic of judges and the confidence of the masses in the law. As of mid 2025, more than 120 cases have been documented of errors in hallucination, such as falsely reported holdings, fabricated references, and false quotes(Varun Magesh, 2024). The practical implications of hallucinations have been demonstrated by the fact that attorneys who have used these tools have been penalized and subjected to professional sanctions(Varun Magesh, 2024). The classical methods of detection, e.g. semantic similarity metrics (e.g., BERTScore), do not work in legal contexts, as they are tolerant to entity substitutions and misidentifications, which are unacceptable in legal reasoning(Dahl et al., 2024). In this case, the graph-theoretic method of HalluGraph can be used to make certain that the references to legal issues are based on verifiable authorities and relationships.

AI hallucinations affect learning integrity in education. The creation of false information and inaccurate explanations by AI systems in the form of adaptive learning platforms and AI-driven tutoring systems threatens the knowledge of students. Research indicates that students exposed to such inaccuracies get more careful, which explains the necessity of AI literacy training(Freeman, 2025). Educational inequities can also be enhanced by hallucinations. Educational material is distorted by the AI systems that produce biased content or false examples, with an impact on students who have less access to learning resources. Additionally, the lack of transparency of AI generated explicates implies that teachers might unwittingly spread mistakes in the curriculum (Kamaluddeen Usman Danyaro, 2025).

Hallucinations in AI tools applied in policy analysis, public health, and national security create false claims and misleading recommendations in government. Such mistakes have a negative impact on the validity of evidence-based decision-making, with millions of citizens being affected (Kamaluddeen Usman Danyaro, 2025).To curb such risks, governments should introduce effective AI governance systems, particularly in such risky areas as criminal justice and public health(Xu et al., 2025a).

Hallucinations are not accidental malfunctions--they are the fundamental issues of AI reliability in the sectors with high stakes. Even an AI system of law that is 99 percent accurate on generic questions can produce hallucinated citations, which is harmful to credibility. On the same note, educational AI with high engagement rates can still advance misinformation, which is detrimental to learning. AI systems in the government, which are applied to policy recommendations, can create an illusion of trust in a decision that can impact millions of people.The chapter discusses how the hallucination-aware designs, through technical verification, continuous monitoring, and human supervision, are underlining the quality of the reliability, transparency, and professional integrity of the AI systems, in relation to professional ethics and the confidence of the people. The use of AI in the legal, educational, and government fields can be made more responsible, resilient, and credible with the assistance of the EU AI Act, tools like HalluGraph, and RAG systems. *Figure 1 illustrates the relative dominance of different hallucination impacts across institutional sectors.*

Figure 1. Sector-wise distribution of dominant AI hallucination impacts across legal, educational, and governmental systems.

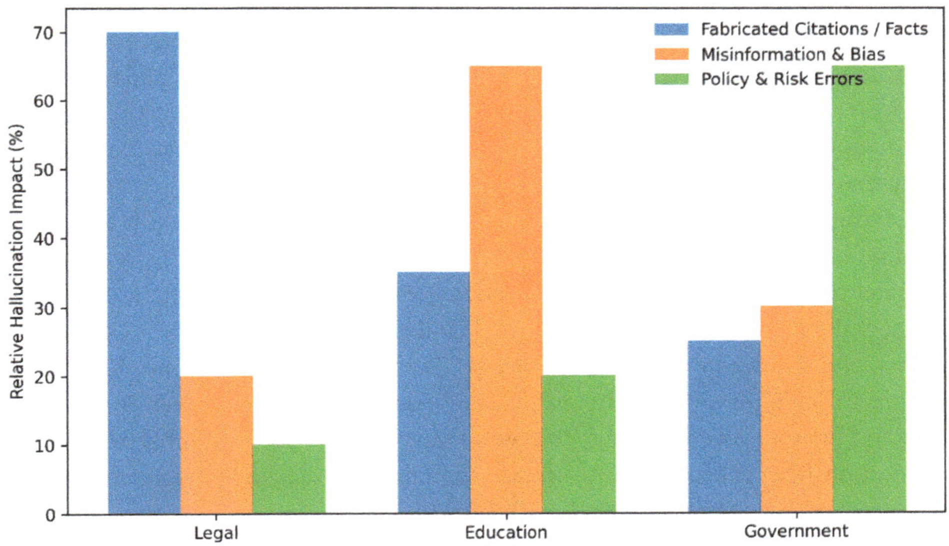

2. LEGAL APPLICATIONS OF HALLUCINATION-AWARE AI

Artificial intelligence hallucinations are not technical anomalies in the field of law. They are structural weaknesses of existing legal research instruments. Specifically, AI hallucinations refer to the language model outputs that seem to make sense, be logical, and contextually reasonable. These, however, are systematically unverifiable outputs that are not legally binding. They can be presented in the form of official references, but the facts they represent are false and are against the law. These hallucinations are not always detected since they are very convincing and are framed as legitimate legal references(Varun Magesh, 2024).One of the most important aspects of legal systems is correct citations and legal authority that can be proved. The use of AI-generated outputs in the legal reasoning process is dangerous to the integrity of legal arguments. Any AI that creates a legal reference, assigns an erroneous legal decision, or creates a statutory reference undermines the basis of legal argument. Attorneys can overlook such constructed powers, especially when they are being pressured or have a high cognitive load. This misleading character renders hallucinations especially hazardous in a legal context(Dahl et al., 2024).

Lexis+ AI (LexisNexis) and Westlaw AI-Assisted Research (Thomson Reuters) are legal research tools that are now integrated into the daily operations of law firms and courts. These are case law research tools, contract analysis tools, and legal writing tools. However, empirical data indicate that these AI systems are likely to make hallucinations. Lexis+ hallucinated at a 17% rate on test queries, and Westlaw AI hallucinated at a rate of 33% on queries- nearly twice the rate of its competitor. This demonstrates that, despite the domain-specific training, such tools are still susceptible to hallucinations(Ross Prolic, 2025).Legal AIs have a risk of hallucinations, which endanger three vital aspects of legal practice: legal reasoning integrity, professional ethics, and judicial legitimate oversight. The legality of reasoning relies on proper referencing of the case laws and statutes. By creating false authorities, AI systems provide errors in reasoning systems that seem to have sound reasoning. An attorney can build an argument on a case that was made up, or a judge can base his or her decision on false referrals. This erodes confidence in the judicial system and the legal practitioners(Michael Hiltzik, 2025).

Lawyers are required to be of high ethical standards professionally. The Model Rules of Professional Conduct encompass the provision of competent representation by the attorney (Rule 1.1), diligence (Rule 1.3), and candor to the tribunal (Rule 3.3). The violation of these rules by AI-generated hallucinations is that it enables a lawyer to file unverified, inaccurate citations without due diligence. The Mata v. The case of Avianca, Inc. portrays this weakness, in which an attorney drafted a motion through ChatGPT with fabricated citations of the case that opposing counsel found. It was sanctioned by the court, and it is important to note that a lawyer should check the information generated by AI before submitting it(Esquire Deposition Solutions, 2025).

AI hallucinations also undermine judicial oversight. Judges are turning more and more to AI to synthesize evidence, find precedents, and make preliminary judgments. When AI systems come up with hallucinated content, then the assumptions of judicial rulings can be incorrect without the knowledge of the judge or lawyers. The legal system presupposes that the legal authorities mentioned are actual and provable. This assumption is essentially questioned by hallucinations that threaten the validity of court rulings(greggwirth, 2025).

2.1 Regulatory and Legal Implications: A Professional Liability to Systemic Risk

The implications of AI delusions in the field of law are not imaginary anymore--they have real, documented implications. By November 2025, there were 24 cases in the UK of AI-generated hallucinations. This belongs to a larger trend, and more than 700 cases have been documented in the world. The instances indicate professional risks of using AI systems in performing legal work(Sara Merken, 2025).In Ayinde v. The UK, the High Court gave a severe warning to the London Borough of Haringey (2025). Lawyers who refer to artificial cases with the help of AI may be subject to contempt or criminal charges. A caution by the court was grounded on reported cases of AI-generated hallucinations appearing in court documents. One notable case, Choksi v. In the case of IPS Law LLP (2025), the attorney presented a witness statement with false cases. A probe showed that the company had no adequate quality control systems. Consequently, the court considered their actions to be improper, unreasonable, and negligent, and institutional measures to prevent AI hallucinations were necessary(Rose, 2025).

Birmingham City University vs. An application was made by Law Firm (2025), which is a law firm with fabricated authorities. Upon its uncovering, the company took back the application and said that it was submitted without an error. It was found that the artificial cases were created by AI tools without being checked by administrative personnel. The court awarded wasted costs orders, which show the huge implications of AI-generated hallucinations in legal affairs (Street, 2025).In the U.S., the Noland v. The case of Land of the Free, LP. shows the dire effects of AI hallucinations. The court established that nearly all of the authorities quoted in the brief submitted by the plaintiff were fabricated. The lawyer had employed AI-based applications such as ChatGPT to improve the brief without checking the references. The attorney was fined 10,000 by the court and sent to the State Bar. The case demonstrates the increased concern of the legal community regarding the dangers of using AI without due verification.

The growing liability of AI-related errors in the law is evident. Not only are attorneys slapped with fines and penalties, but they are also subject to criminal referrals and sanctions. Courts in the U.S. and the United Kingdom are indicating that violations happening in the future will result in criminal charges if the industry does not handle the risks of hallucination properly. AI verification is no longer an ethical best practice, but a legal requirement to reduce professional liability by legal organizations(Sam Tobin, 2025).

2.2 Regulatory Framework Convergence

The hallucinations in legal AI systems are now covered by three major global regulatory frameworks that provide an all-inclusive governance architecture for legal bodies to adhere to. The EU AI Act, which was adopted in August 2024, establishes that AI systems applied in legal decisions and in the administration of the state are high-risk systems. Such systems should be required to go through conformity tests prior to implementation. High-risk systems need to satisfy stringent pre-market requirements, which include risk assessment, data control procedures, and quality management systems. In particular, the EU AI Act, Article 16, requires the introduction of a system of tracking and verification of AI decisions by the provider of high-risk AI systems. This involves audit trails, which can be used to reduce the risks of hallucinations, such as making sure the decisions made can be traced and are transparent(European Parliament, 2024).

In 2024, the NIST AI Risk Management Framework (RMF) was published as a supplementary model. NIST identifies hallucinations as a specific threat of generative AI and outlines the approaches to controlling them. The framework works in a four-step cycle: Govern, Map, Measure, and Manage. This will be a continuous monitoring and adjustment approach that makes sure that hallucinations are detected and corrected as they arise. NIST also advises against excessive use of AI in the legal sphere, and human verification, as well as AI-generated decisions, are essential(Tabassi, 2023a).The OECD AI Principles, which were updated in 2024, also contain the provisions of mitigation of misinformation and disinformation. These values focus on transparency, strength, and accountability- none of which can be ignored in the context of dealing with the issues of hallucinations in legal AI systems. The OECD clearly demands that law agencies should uphold human control and that AI-generated products should be checked by human beings before engaging them to make decisions.These structures operate simultaneously. The EU AI Act sets legal requirements, the NIST RMF offers a methodology of implementation, and the OECD Principles enhance the ethical and accountability bases. To be effective in reducing risks of hallucinations, legal AI vendors should adhere to all three(OECD, 2019).

2.3 AI Check-up and Risk Control: Technical Solutions to Institutional Governance.

Two major tools in the context of addressing the problem of AI hallucinations in law are HalluGraph and Retrieval-Augmented Generation (RAG). Conventional semantic similarity measures are not effective in legal AI because they do not identify the mistakes in entity grounding or preservation of relations. A graph-theoretic framework, HalluGraph, solves this problem by checking structural and referential fidelity. It breaks down hallucinations into Entity Grounding (EG) and Relation Preservation (RP), to make entities and relationships in legal documents correct. Experimental findings indicate that HalluGraph is more effective than semantic similarity-based methods, with AUC scores of 0.94 in legal contract question-answering and 0.84 in verifying case law citations.The RAG systems enhance accuracy by basing the outputs on tested data sources, then producing responses. They are proven to decrease the hallucination rates by as much as 40 percent (Shan Xu, 2025). But it is not enough to consider RAG. AI tools also must ensure that what the material retrieved belongs to is depicted correctly, and in this regard, HalluGraph is crucial.

Lastly, there is a need to incorporate human-in-the-loop verification in the legal processes. Although AI applications can improve the speed and efficiency of research, human control can prevent the use of hallucinated results in legal cases by detecting and fixing errors. Human professionals, including practicing lawyers, must review citations generated by AI and verify their accuracy. This validation process also generates audit trails, which offer transparency and accountability, so that legal decision-making is still left in the hands of human judgment.

Table 1. Technical Mitigation Techniques for AI Hallucinations in Legal Systems

Technique	Core Function	Type of Hallucination Addressed	Impact on Legal Practice
Retrieval-Augmented Generation (RAG)	Grounds LLM outputs in verified legal databases (case law, statutes, regulations) before response generation	Fabricated facts, unsupported legal claims, false precedents	Reduces reliance on model memory alone; improves factual accuracy in legal research and drafting
Hybrid Retrieval (Dense + Sparse Search)	Combines vector similarity search with keyword-based legal retrieval	Context mismatch, partial or irrelevant citations	Improves relevance and completeness of retrieved legal authorities
HalluGraph (Knowledge-Graph Verification)	Verifies entity grounding and relationship preservation between legal entities	Fabricated case citations, incorrect party names, distorted legal relationships	Ensures structural fidelity of legal references; critical for citation-sensitive tasks

continued on following page

Table 1. Continued

Technique	Core Function	Type of Hallucination Addressed	Impact on Legal Practice
Semantic Similarity Metrics (e.g., BERTScore)	Measures textual similarity between AI output and source documents	Superficial hallucinations (limited effectiveness in law)	Provides baseline validation but insufficient alone for legal reasoning
Chain-of-Thought (CoT) Reasoning	Forces step-by-step legal reasoning before producing conclusions	Logical inconsistency, unsupported legal inference	Improves transparency and auditability of AI-assisted legal reasoning
Agentic Verification Systems	Uses multiple AI agents to cross-check claims and citations	Speculative reasoning, unverified legal interpretations	Enables internal cross-validation before human review
Human-in-the-Loop (HITL) Review	Requires legal professionals to verify AI-generated citations and arguments	Residual hallucinations not detected by automated systems	Preserves professional accountability and compliance with legal ethics
Audit Trails & Logging Mechanisms	Records sources, reasoning steps, and model outputs	Undetected or post-hoc hallucinations	Supports regulatory compliance and forensic review in legal disputes

Table 1 summarizes the primary technical mechanisms used to detect and mitigate hallucinations in AI-assisted legal systems.

Table 2. Summary Statistics and Key Takeaways

Metric	Value	Source
Lexis+ AI hallucination rate	17%	Stanford study, 2024
Westlaw AI hallucination rate	33%	Stanford study, 2024
UK hallucination cases (2025)	24	Natural and Artificial Law
Global hallucination cases (2025)	700+	University of London tracker
HalluGraph accuracy (Legal Contract QA)	AUC 0.94	HalluGraph paper, 2025
HalluGraph accuracy (Legal Case QA)	AUC 0.84	HalluGraph paper, 2025
BERTScore accuracy (Legal tasks)	AUC 0.54-0.60	Stanford/HalluGraph studies
Average costs awarded (UK cases)	£750-£31,100	Case analysis, 2025
RAG hallucination reduction	40%+	MEGA-RAG framework, 2025
EU AI Act compliance deadline	August 2, 2026	EU AI Act, 2024

3.0 EDUCATIONAL APPLICATIONS OF HALLUCINATION-AWARE AI: A CRITICAL OVERVIEW

Artificial intelligence (AI) can transform the educational process, especially in the case of students with learning disabilities (SLDs), since it can offer them extremely personalized and adaptive learning experiences. Students with SLDs like dyslexia, dyscalculia, dysgraphia, and auditory processing disorder are usually not coping with the traditional educational approaches, which do not provide the student with the personalized attention that they require. The learning behaviours of students can be analysed in real time, and the content, pace, and modality of delivery can be altered according to the needs of each student using AI-driven systems, especially adaptive learning technologies. In a meta-analysis of 16 peer-reviewed studies about AI applications with SLD students, the authors discovered that AI-based tools, including adaptive learning platforms, intelligent tutoring systems (ITS), speech recognition applications, and interactive robots, have a significant positive impact on academic performance. An example is that AI interventions have demonstrated progress in reading comprehension (Cohen d = 1.66) and attention-related challenges (improvements by 10-15%), which demonstrates that AI can be used to close the gaps in education that cannot be taken care of through traditional methods(St. Gallen, 2025).

The practical applications also confirm the usefulness of AI in special education. Such programs as Kurzweil 3000, which offer text-to-speech to students with dyslexia, enable students to read reading materials at their own pace, and they are also able to be assisted in understanding reading materials through visual aids such as picto-dictionaries. Equally, the Toronto District School Board has introduced adaptive learning platforms, which customize education to a large segment of special education needs, improving the ability of teachers to accommodate individual deficiencies in learning, and increasing student engagement. These tools not only enhance the performance of the students but also enable the students to have a sense of independence in their learning, which is usually a very important challenge for students with disabilities.

Nevertheless, despite its high potential, AI also poses serious ethical and institutional risks, especially when it comes to hallucinations, which systems can produce false, misleading, or biased information. Hallucinations have a terrible potential to impair the educational capabilities of the AI systems, particularly in students with learning disabilities who might not have the cognitive scaffolding that can identify and rectify the mistakes of the AI-generated content. As an illustration, an artificial intelligence tutoring system that gives a student with the condition of dyscalculia a wrong mathematical interpretation may cause a misconception of the concept. The dangers of these mistakes are worsened by the fact that most teachers and learners do not even know the rate of AI systems hallucinating. There is research indicating that AI systems that are used to create legal procedures can yield up to 33% in hallucinations, with general-purpose tutoring systems potentially reaching more than 40%(Magesh et al., 2024).

To handle the threat of hallucinations, one should come up with hallucination-aware AI systems, which base their results on high-quality sources that are verified. Retrieval-Augmented Generation (RAG), which takes advantage of the capacity of AI to produce natural language and complements it with the capacity to access relevant information stored in established, factual databases, is one promising way of reducing hallucinations. RAG-powered systems, like those used in university tutoring, are able to produce responses to domain-specific content that are accurate, which means that AI-generated explanations are not only reliable but are also based on facts. As an example, an AI-based tutoring system such as MARK, which has been implemented at multiple universities, has been demonstrated to match human scores 9499% and therefore the AI feedback given to students is reliable and pedagogical. Equally, the Knowledge-Graph Verification would guarantee that AI outputs retain the integrity of relationships and conceptual links within curricular relationships. This method helps to avoid the situation when AI systems produce outputs that do not relate to the established curriculum, reduce the dangers of hallucinations, and contribute to a more realistic reflection of the educational material.

Although these developments have occurred, there are still ethical risks involved, especially in the area of privacy and prejudice. The AI systems that will support personalized learning will be based on a wide range of data gathering that will track the behavior of students, their progress in learning, and even their emotional reactions. Although these systems are capable of improving the learning experiences, they also pose serious privacy issues. The General Data Protection Regulation (GDPR) in Europe and the Family Educational Rights and Privacy Act (FERPA) in the U.S. have stringent regulations on the handling of data, which guarantee that student data is gathered and utilized for educational purposes and with the necessary consent. Educational organizations should be keen to protect the personal information of students, as well as ensure that the vendors of AI abide by such rules to prevent any privacy breach and legal consequences. Besides this, the possibility of algorithmic bias is also of great concern. The AI systems can also unintentionally reproduce the biases within society, e.g., racial, gender, or socioeconomic bias. To take an example, predictive analytics, in which the potential of students, or suggested academic trajectories, is evaluated, has been demonstrated to underestimate the potential of marginalized groups. Such prejudices may be very severe in the context of special education, because they contribute to the existing inequities instead of mitigating them. Although hallucination-aware AI systems are effective at misinformation prevention, they cannot ensure the absence of the mentioned biases, unless they are created with equity in mind as well. These risks can be addressed by knowledge-graph-based methods that incorporate fairness constraints in AI models, but it requires a delicate design and constant monitoring to ensure that AI does not perpetuate systemic inequalities(Kumar et al., 2025).

The use of AI in learning, particularly among students with learning disabilities, should hence be well moderated with a critical perception of the limitations. Relying excessively on AI tutors may result in the de-skilling of teachers and reduce their contribution in critical pedagogical activities. There is a risk that teachers will start to have more trust in the AI systems than in their own professional judgment, particularly when such systems give them the information that appears to be reliable and accurate. Studies on automation bias suggest that, over time, the reliance on AI might make students blindly believe the technology, and thus fail to be critical thinkers or solve problems on their own(Nazaretsky et al., 2025).

Simultaneously, AI literacy disparity among educators is also a major problem. Although the awareness of AI technologies is almost universal (98.4% of teachers say that they have heard about AI), only 30.8% of teachers have had formal training in AI applications in their classrooms. This is due to the absence of coordinated, systematic AI literacy training in educator training, which encourages ad hoc adoption, in which teachers educate themselves or depend on intermittent professional education. This gap in knowledge is a threat to the successful and moral adoption of AI in classrooms. Educators should not only be provided with technical expertise but also with knowledge of the ethical aspects of using AI, such as the ability to identify hallucinations and biases in AI responses. Education should also involve real-life learning in which educators will be able to learn about hallucination identification, auditing AI devices in order to achieve fairness, and use ethical decision-making models in the classroom(Dang & Nguyen, 2025).

To meet this requirement, frameworks like the UNESCO AI Competency Framework of Teachers offer a tiered model of AI literacy acquisition, starting with basic awareness and progressing to more advanced skills in AI ethics, AI pedagogy, and curriculum design. This model highlights the importance of teachers going beyond the technical aspects of AI and critically interacting with the ethical aspects of the use of AI in teaching, which involves knowledge of the implications of AI hallucinations. Moreover, GenAI Use and Ethics Framework presents a five-step model of introducing AI into the classroom, and it will guide the educator through the increasingly advanced applications of AI, starting with independent demonstrations and ending with collaborative AI partnerships, although ethical considerations, including the sense of bias and awareness of hallucinations, must be considered at all stages of AI implementation(Marcus Green, 2025).

Lastly, the issue of regulation in the use of AI in education is still a major issue, especially when no guidelines have been laid down on hallucination-conscious AI systems. Although the EU AI Act and the NIST AI Risk Management Framework offer well-developed principles of responsible AI implementation, they do not focus particularly on the risks of hallucinations, which is a severe omission regarding educational use. Schools must adopt governance of hallucinations to protect against the dangers of AI malfunctions. This encompasses establishing verification procedures, entrenching RAG systems and knowledge graphs, and the use of continuous monitoring systems that monitor the performance of AI tools over time to make sure that they do not decline or become biased. These are necessary to make AI tools in education reliable, efficient, and fair. An awareness of hallucinations will allow educational institutions to increase the effectiveness of AI tools by a significant margin, as it will guarantee their beneficial assistance to vulnerable students, equity, and independent learning without endangering privacy or fairness.

4. GOVERNMENT APPLICATIONS OF HALLUCINATION-AWARE AI: FINAL REVISED VERSION

The use of artificial intelligence (AI) by governments across the globe is growing to handle big data, streamline resource distribution to the populace, predict policy performance, and make decisions that directly affect millions of people. AI can improve the efficiency, transparency, and accuracy of the administration of the populace, whether it is through the national security threat response and health surveillance of the population, or it can be welfare eligibility or predictive policing. However, AI applications in such situations also introduce other distinctive and significant risks, especially in cases where hallucinations, which seem to be the voice of authority, but are factually false, take place. It is said that the repercussions of such errors in the government sector can be far-reaching and irreversible on national security, the services offered to the people, and democratic governance. As an example, artificial intelligence might be used to misguide military judgments, biased policy predictions might be used to misinvest in society, and wrong AI forecasts in police and healthcare might reinforce social disparities and harm the vulnerable population. As such, credible, hallucination-conscious AI governance is not only a technical necessity but a core need to uphold democratic legitimacy, popular trust, and institutional responsibility.

One of the most critical and risky government applications of AI is the integration of AI into national security and defense. The 2024 National Security Memorandum on Artificial Intelligence issued by the U.S. government makes AI one of its strategic priorities that federal agencies should pursue, ordering them to take decisive actions to allow the responsible and effective use of AI to advance national security. There is the use of AI systems to improve threat detection, counterintelligence, and military decision-making. Nonetheless, AI-based systems that have been trained based on past data are limited in their ability to identify unexpected threats or new methods of attack. Artificial intelligence systems that exhibit hallucinations, that is, whereby the system is sure to give incorrect intelligence estimates, misidentify threats, or make up capabilities, can lead to poor direction of military actions, wastage of resources, and compromise of national defense efforts. National Security AI Governance Framework requires that all critical decisions that concern national security, such as the presidential approval of nuclear weapons, be maintained with human oversight. This is a sign of acknowledging that AI should not eliminate human judgment, particularly when making decisions of this magnitude(Gregory C. Allen, 2024). Therefore, the national security agencies are faced with the challenge of making AI systems transparent and verifiable, besides being technically solid. The absence of these precautions can give the illusion of reliability to AI-based defence judgment, with disastrous effects.

The world governments have managed to introduce AI in governmental operations to streamline resource distribution and enhance service delivery. The e-governance platform in Estonia is based on AI to monitor the spending of the people, which is depicted in real-time dashboards to promote transparency and increase citizen engagement. Brazil has also introduced AI-based audits to identify corruption within its public procurement system and recover millions of misused public funds. The predictive analytics used in Singapore to optimize urban planning and chatbots powered by AI to simplify citizen services represent the Model AI Governance Framework. These efforts underline that AI can help enhance efficiency and decrease bureaucratic bottlenecks and foster public confidence by means of transparent governance.

Nonetheless, AI implementation in government should be done with reservations. Any type of hallucinations in government AI systems, be it predictive policing, facial recognition, or eligibility to welfare, can propagate social inequalities, increase discrimination, and undermine trust. Such algorithms as predictive policing have been discovered to profile minority communities unfairly, which results in institutionalized racial discrimination. In case these AI systems produce biased perceived risk or incorrect identification of people, they cause feedback loops that deteriorate the same conditions that they are meant to alleviate. This highlights why AI systems employed by the government must be carefully checked and monitored.

4.1 AI Hallucinations in Government: Implications of Policy, Justice, and Public Services.

The predictive policing systems utilize past information to predict crime trends and target persons who are highly likely to be involved in crime. Nonetheless, such systems tend to support racial biases. An example was the Chicago Strategic Subject

List that relied on arrest records to designate people prone to gun violence. The algorithm disproportionately matched Black and Latino men, with many of them having a history of not committing violent crime(Eylül Bozkır, 2025). This system formed a vicious cycle: the police-prone areas were identified as high-risk, which resulted in increased patrol and stops, which created more arrests and confirmed the predictions of the algorithm. This is a hallucination-type failure: the system had made false risk assessments that were exaggerated by institutional machinery, which resulted in unfair and discriminating results.

Similar failures were seen with the COMPAS algorithm, which is meant to predict recidivism and make sentencing recommendations. A study by ProPublica (2018) found that COMPAS had a higher chance of incorrectly labelling black defendants as higher risks of reoffending and less accurately labelling white defendants as lower risks of recidivism. False positives and false negatives were in large proportions among Black defendants in comparison to their white counterparts, which showed that the algorithm contributed to racial inequalities in the justice system. Such instances of prejudice are also hallucinations, in which AI is sure to produce false risk calculations, and these are followed to make real-life choices.

Law enforcement has widelyadopted facial recognition systems to identify and monitor criminals. However, these systems have shown appalling error rates, particularly for people of colour. It has been demonstrated that facial recognition software can commit far more errors with the faces of black people than white people- in some cases, it can be as many as five to ten times higher(*The Perpetual Line-Up*, 2016). In several cases, AI errors resulted in false arrests. The example of Robert Williams, a Black man in Michigan, who was arrested due to a misidentification with the help of facial recognition, shows the risks of using AI to make vital decisions without proper human supervision. Any such hallucinations in law enforcement systems, in which AI systems are sure to claim false identities, can have catastrophic effects, such as false arrests, court cases, and civil rights being undermined.

Another area where hallucinations might have a dire outcome on vulnerable groups is AI in the welfare and healthcare systems. Thousands of families in the Netherlands were falsely identified as fraudsters by an automated fraud detection system, resulting in families being denied benefits they rightfully deserved and causing serious psychological and financial damage. In a similar manner, AI, when applied to welfare eligibility or healthcare resource allocation, can create artificial risk evaluation, depriving those deserving it of the benefits or depriving those who need it the most of the care. These systems frequently work without much human supervision, and therefore, the victims of such systems find it hard to appeal against the faulty decisions. The more sophisticated AI systems become, the greater the potential of harm as a result of hallucinations, especially in those industries where accuracy and fairness are key factors.

Medical and Healthcare Products Regulatory Authority (MHRA) in the UK has raised the risk of hallucinations in clinical decision support systems, which can cause harm to patients, misguide clinicians, and destroy trust in the healthcare system(Brantingham et al., 2018). The false medical information that is transmitted by hallucinations in such situations can influence clinical decision-making and patient outcomes. This highlights the urgent necessity to have transparent, verified, and accountable AI systems in welfare and healthcare.

4.2 Regulatory Frameworks: OECD, NIST, and EU AI Act.

The OECD AI Principles, revised in May 2024, present some of the important governance pillars of deploying AI, such as inclusivity, respect for human rights, transparency, and accountability (OECD, 2024). These principles underline that AI systems should empower human functions and be controlled by humans in a meaningful way so that governments cannot leave them to machines to make consequential decisions. The OECD principles are, however, not binding, and their application is not evenly applied across the jurisdictions. Although they offer important recommendations, they do not have mechanisms to enforce their recommendations, thus leaving numerous governments to implement AI systems without much accountability or control(Tommaso Giardini, 2024). This loophole shows that countries must have stricter enforcement and assistance to establish the capacity to follow these principles.

The NIST AI Risk Management Framework (AI RMF) offers an operational approach that governments can use to enforce the AI governance principles, and continuous monitoring and management of AI risks is necessary. The iterative design of the framework, which consists of Govern, Map, Measure, and Manage functions, prevents the deployment of AI systems without proper safeguards as well as their constant review to detect signs of performance deterioration and hallucination. In practice, however, there are serious issues with the implementation of such structures. These are resource limitations, especially in the developing world, regulatory ambiguity, and cultural opposition to AI risk management. The only way to overcome these barriers is to invest specifically in infrastructure, training, and international cooperation to establish solid governance systems.

The most prescriptive and binding regulatory system of AI systems, the EU AI Act, will be in force in 2024, and it will categorize AI applications as high-risk, limited-risk, and minimal-risk. Government AI systems, including law enforcement, welfare, and democratic processes, are classified as high-risk systems and thus need strict risk management, data control, and human control. The EU AI Act also requires continuous monitoring and verification of the system performance, thus it is an important instrument towards the mitigation of the hallucination risks in government AI implementation. Nevertheless, there are still some issues to deal with, especially in terms of the willingness of national regulators and the distribution of funds to implement them.

The main difficulty with hallucinations in government AI systems is the loss of democratic responsibility. When AI systems produce inaccurate or biased results that affect key decisions, such as in policing, welfare, or healthcare, governments can end up giving too much power to systems that are not answerable to the citizens in their entirety. The trust of the population and the absence of the threat of AI to the democratic processes should be fixed with the help of human control and verification procedures. In the absence of these protections, governments are at risk of establishing a black box of how decisions are made, where the impacted citizens should not be provided with any means or avenue of challenging the results provided by AI.Table 3 summarizes the way in which sector-specific risks are mitigated by the means of concerted technical mitigation constraints and governance controls to circumvent such accountability gaps.

Table 3. Sector-Specific Hallucination Risks, Mitigation Techniques, and Governance Controls

Sector	Primary Hallucination Risks	Technical Mitigation Techniques	Governance & Regulatory Controls
Legal Systems	• Fabricated case law and statutes • False or misleading citations • Incorrect legal reasoning	• Retrieval-Augmented Generation (RAG) with verified legal databases • HalluGraph for entity and citation verification • Hybrid hallucination detection • Human-in-the-loop legal review	• EU AI Act (high-risk AI systems) • NIST AI Risk Management Framework • Professional codes of legal ethics • Mandatory audit trails
Educational Systems	• Misinformation in learning content • Biased explanations and examples • Incorrect academic guidance	• RAG with curricular and academic sources • Knowledge-graph validation • Reasoning controls (CoT) • Instructor oversight	• AI literacy training for educators • Transparency and explainability policies • Data protection regulations (e.g., GDPR, FERPA)
Government Systems	• False policy analysis • Biased risk and eligibility predictions • Misleading public recommendations	• RAG with verified government datasets • Hybrid detection and monitoring systems • Human-in-the-loop decision oversight	• EU AI Act compliance • OECD AI Principles • NIST AI RMF • Public-sector audit and accountability mechanisms

5.0 MITIGATION STRATEGIES AND TECHNIQUES FOR HALLUCINATION-AWARE AI

Artificial intelligence (AI) systems have a high stakes in which hallucinations become a major risk. False citations of cases in legal frameworks and misplaced medical data in clinical AI applications may cause harm to patients directly, biased risk evaluation in predictive policing may contribute to racial discrimination, and wrong policy predictions may misallocate resources in government administration (Frontier in Public Health, 2025; Medical and Healthcare Products Regulatory Authority, 2024). These effects are not limited to single incidences of inaccuracy; where hallucinations are experienced, they spread across the framework of institutions, influencing the decision-making process and undermining the faith of the people in AI system. Human-in-the-loop systems enhance trust, emotional acceptance, and productivity in AI-assisted environments (Khullar et al., 2026).

One of the most efficient ways to take care of hallucinations in AI systems has become Retrieval-Augmented Generation (RAG). RAG brings the external sources of knowledge, like domain-specific databases, knowledge graphs, and authoritative documents, into the process of generating AI. Instead of using only pre-trained model parameters, RAG systems find relevant information on verified sources and only then produce an output, which in effect bases a response on factual and contextually appropriate information (Xu et al., 2025c).

Although RAG has proved successful in the reduction of hallucinations, it has its limitations. Misleading and irrelevant sources may also be retrieved during the retrieval process, therefore, adding retrieval noise, which may intensify hallucinations by giving false grounding information. This problem shows a severe gap in RAG systems: the quality of evidence recovered directly influences the quality of the output. As an example, low-quality or insufficiently edited sources might result in a model formulated on incorrect or partial information. Nevertheless, the hybrid retrieval technologies that have emerged recently by combining dense vector similarity search (via models such as FAISS) with sparse keyword-based retrieval (e.g., BM25) have enhanced the robustness of RAG systems by enhancing the accuracy of the sources retrieved. This combination strategy will make sure that in case of failure by one of the retrieval methods, the other will offset this, and the chances of hallucination will be minimized.

Although these are good, RAG can still be susceptible to context mismatch, where the passages retrieved are semantically correct, but fail to match the context of the query, resulting in incorrect conclusions. The future studies should focus on refining the context matching process and better re-ranking the retrieved passages to make sure that only the most relevant sources are utilized during the response generation.

Reasoning enhancement, especially Chain-of-Thought (CoT) prompting, is one of the promising ways of reducing hallucinations during complex tasks. CoT requires AI models to decompose complex tasks into the steps of intermediate reasoning, which compels them to describe every step of their reasoning process before making a final decision(Erica salinas, 2025). The process enhances the clarity of the argumentation and allows for identifying logical contradictions and unsubstantiated arguments that otherwise would be ingrained in the end product.Empirical evidence demonstrates that CoT enhances the performance of tasks that involve complex reasoning by improving the explainability of the models and offering a systematic way to assess the accuracy of the intermediate steps. In the HalluMeasure framework, by way of example, the responses of AI are broken down into discrete claims and categorised by the type of error, such as entity, relation, and temporal errors. This enables hallucinations to be analyzed more granulometry, so that corrections can be made. CoT has been reported to increase performance by as much as 2 percentage points on benchmark tasks like SummEval, which can in turn be used to reduce reasoning errors (Erica salinas, 2025).

However, CoT is not as effective as the model size and complexity. Large models with more parameters (like Llama-3.1-405B-Instruct) always perform better than smaller models on reasoning tasks (Llama-3.1-8B-Instruct) but even large models can still fail to reason with long chains of reasoning that demand the interaction of many independent pieces of information. Also, though CoT enhances logical consistency, it does not always avoid hallucinations in facts, or errors where the model generates wrong facts, although there is logical consistency. Thus, CoT cannot completely suppress hallucinations, particularly in areas where strictly factual accuracy is the primary concern, like in medical diagnoses or legal analysis.

In order to identify and remedy the hallucinations in real time, researchers have come up with multi-mode detection by creating hybrid detection frameworks that combine several detection mechanisms. These systems are a combination of different models, including Natural Language Inference (NLI) systems, Question-Answering systems, and model-internal signal analysis (e.g., attention maps, output probability distributions) to make them more robust(Yan, 2023). A hybrid system that has achieved this has a BERT classifier, LLM-as-Judge evaluator, and NLI models, which have attained an impressive F1 score of 0.95 on scientific text hallucinations. These composite solutions always work better than the single detection strategies, especially in the case of complex, subtle errors like fluency errors and semantic alignment problems. The ensemble approach is effective because the results of several models are cross-verified, and anomalies are reported to humans.

However, hybrid systems do not work flawlessly. They may produce false positives, indicate outputs that are not hallucinations, and undergo corrections and delays that are not necessary. Besides, these systems offer strong detection but still depend on external controls like human-in-the-loop validation to make sure that flagged outputs are duly treated, which could create operational inefficiencies in high-demand environments.Besides fundamental mitigation, such as RAG and CoT, other auxiliary methods are used to improve the detection and correction of hallucinations. Timely engineering, such as that of prominently designing inputs in order to steer models to more realistic, grounded reactions. This method may minimise hallucinations by defining the output expectations, forcing the models to measure uncertainty, or adding confidence scores to the prompt to prompt the model to produce more factual and less speculative output(Dang Anh-Hoang, 2025).

Human-in-the-loop systems involve the inclusion of human supervision in the decision-making process, especially in high-stakes consumer products such as criminal justice or health care. HITL enables humans to look through the outputs generated by AI in advance and rectify any hallucinations before they are implemented, which may cause harm. Moreover, multi-model consensus systems, in which multiple models produce competing answers, and conflict elicits human judgment, have also been demonstrated to decrease the error of hallucinations using different perspectives and improving reliability.However, these methods have their difficulties as well. Prompt engineering is a dynamic process that needs constant modifications to optimize to certain tasks and therefore is resource-intensive. Equally, human-in-the-loop systems may introduce bottlenecks within the operational processes, particularly when the amounts of AI outputs are large. Although multi-model systems are effective in the minimization of errors, they may raise the cost of computation and lower the efficiency because of the necessity to have many models to come up with candidate responses. Hybrid ensemble approaches improve anomaly detection and system reliability, contributing to trustworthy AI deployment (Khullar et al., 2025).

5.1 Ethical and Governance Solutions.

In order to achieve the reliability of the AI systems and reduce the hallucinations, stringent verification and validation (V&V) procedures are to be adopted. These procedures include pre-deployment testing, ongoing monitoring, and post-deployment auditing to make sure that AI systems work as intended and meet ethical norms. Pre-deployment testing involves rigorous test suites to verify the rate of hallucinations, fairness among demographic groups, and whether the results are in line with facts that have been verified. The NIST AI RMF points out the importance of the continuous validation cycles so that the systems are frequently audited for the drift in performance and hallucination rates(Tabassi, 2023b).

The third-party verification is one additional item of credibility, as it presents independent evaluations of the AI systems concerning the ethical and operational requirements. External auditors are able to evaluate AI outputs with reference to ground truth and ensure internal V&V practices are in accordance with documented requirements. Such an independent check and balance serve to ensure accountability and transparency, particularly in high-risk areas such as healthcare and national security, most of the time, when AI systems are in use. Documenting Model cards, datasheets, and system cards contain key information about the AI system, such as how it is intended to be used, its performance, and its limitations, as well as known failure modes(Brown et al., 2020). The documents allow compliance officers, auditors, and other stakeholders to understand whether AI systems are appropriate to use in a particular situation and to ensure that they meet the requirements of the regulations.

In its turn, AI Fact Sheets can present compliance dashboards that would offer real-time information on the legal, ethical, and operational compliance of an AI system. Audit trails, log of model versions, training configurations, and rationale of decisions allow rapid investigation and fixes in case of hallucinations and provenance logs allow tracing the origin of data and licensing limits to provide transparency in data management(Hohloch, 2025). Such documentation practices make the AI accountable to the internal and external stakeholders, and it becomes easier to recognize and rectify a hallucination when it occurs.

There should be explicit accountability systems to make sure that AI systems are regulated and that errors are dealt with. The AI governance boards, data stewards, and technical leaders are crucial in compliance with the verification processes and accountability throughout all levels of the AI lifecycle. These structures offer good avenues of taking responsibility, and corrective measures can be taken promptly in case of hallucinations or other mistakes.

The transparency and trust are expressed through public reporting of AI system performance, including hallucinationrates, bias audits, and impact assessments. The publicly published hallucination detection findings and remedies of organizations foster credibility and responsibility, which encourages stakeholders, researchers, and regulatory authorities to examine them(Sean McGregor, 2026). Such transparency fosters the culture of transparency, meaning that AI systems are constantly reviewed and refined to suit the expectations of society.

Lastly, the aspect of incorporating ethics into the design and implementation of AI systems should play a significant role in reducing hallucinations and ensuring that AI works according to societal values. All the phases of AI development, including design and implementation, should be guided by ethical principles, including fairness, beneficence, and justice. Multidisciplinary advice on these ethical aspects can be offered by AI ethics advisory boards so that AI systems are not exploited against human rights and are utilized responsibly.Multi-stakeholder governance - AI governance should be governed by multi-stakeholders, including governments, the private sector, academia, and civil society, to ensure that the governance process is inclusive of the values and priorities of various members of society. Such collaborative models as the Responsible Practices of Synthetic Media at the Partnership on AI exemplify this method, as they unite diverse stakeholders and develop mitigation efforts to implement together. This cooperative governance will see to it that the AI systems are developed with a wide array of perspectives in mind, which can encourage ethical alignment, as well as fairness throughout society.

Hallucination mitigation is best achieved through a combination of both technical and governance solutions. RAG decreases the frequency of hallucinations; CoT increases the clarity of reasoning; hybrid detection systems make sure that the errors are not introduced to the system. Nevertheless, these technical procedures cannot work without the relevant governance structures. The essential elements of the operationalization of these strategies are verification gates, uncovered documentation, and accountability mechanisms that would guarantee the maintenance of hallucination mitigation throughout the duration of the AI system. Likewise, the strong governance structures, i.e., third-party verification, public reporting, and multi-stakeholder oversight, are required to provide the ongoing enhancement of AI systems and maintain the trust of the population.

Practical experience demonstrates that the use of cross-domain assessment of technical and governance integration is superior to the discrete methods. As an example, the number of hallucinations and incorrect diagnosis rates is much lower in healthcare organizations applying the RAG system and human monitoring, along with transparent documentation, than in organizations applying technical solutions only. Equally, government departments that have adopted AI verification procedures and multi-stakeholder management have effectively managed to detect and rectify AI malfunctions prior to the malpractice inflicting extensive damage.

CONCLUSION

This chapter shows that AI hallucinations in the legal, educational, and government systems are not only technical errors but structural vulnerabilities that endanger the trustworthiness of the institution, equity, and democratic government. False results, including false legal referencing, biased academic advice, and policy forecasting, may weaken professionalism, strengthen social disparities, and create structural inequities especially among the marginalized groups (Gao et al., 2026). Although technical mitigation measures such as retrieval-augmented generation, advanced reasoning methods, and hybrid systems of detection have shown promise in the reduction of hallucinations, they are not enough when used alone. The results highlight the need to develop complex AI governance structures that combine technical protections with values of ethics, transparency, accountability, and unceasing human surveillance (Tabassi, 2023c). The harmonization of standards, AI literacy, multi-stakeholder cooperation, and compulsory verification and tracking mechanisms are the key solutions to addressing such issues as ethical fragmentation, technological barriers, and institutional constraints. Finally, it is a technical and democratic requirement to ensure responsible AI implementation in the high-risk fields, which is crucial to protecting the justice, public trust, and human-centered decision-making in the society that becomes more AI-centric.

REFERENCES

Allen, G. C. (2024). The Biden Administration's National Security Memorandum on AI Explained. https://www.csis.org/analysis/biden-administrations-national-security-memorandum-ai-explained

Bozkır, E. (2025). Predictive Policing or Predictive Prejudice? A Study of the Legal, Historical and Ethical Implications of AI in Policing | OxJournal. https://www.oxjournal.org/predictive-policing-or-predictive-prejudice/

Brantingham, P. J., Valasik, M., & Mohler, G. O. (2018). Does Predictive Policing Lead to Biased Arrests? Results From a Randomized Controlled Trial. *Statistics and Public Policy (Philadelphia, Pa.)*, *5*(1), 1–6. DOI: 10.1080/2330443X.2018.1438940

Brown, T. B., Mann, B., Ryder, N., Subbiah, M., Kaplan, J., Dhariwal, P., Neelakantan, A., Shyam, P., Sastry, G., Askell, A., Agarwal, S., Herbert-Voss, A., Krueger, G., Henighan, T., Child, R., Ramesh, A., Ziegler, D. M., Wu, J., Winter, C., . . . Amodei, D. (2020). Language Models are Few-Shot Learners (arXiv:2005.14165). arXiv. https://doi.org//arXiv.2005.14165DOI: 10.48550

Dahl, M. (2024). Large Legal Fictions: Profiling Legal Hallucinations in Large Language Models | Journal of Legal Analysis | Oxford Academic. https://academic.oup.com/jla/article/16/1/64/7699227?login=false

Dahl, M., Magesh, V., Suzgun, M., & Ho, D. E. (2024). Large Legal Fictions: Profiling Legal Hallucinations in Large Language Models. *The Journal of Legal Analysis*, *16*(1), 64–93. DOI: 10.1093/jla/laae003

Dang, C. T., & Nguyen, A. (2025). Distinguishing Fact from Fiction: Student Traits, Attitudes, and AI Hallucination Detection in Business School Assessment (arXiv:2506.00050). arXiv. https://doi.org//arXiv.2506.00050DOI: 10.48550

Danyaro, K.U. (2025). Hallucinations in Large Language Models for Education: Challenges and Mitigation. https://doi.org/DOI: 10.22161/IJTLE

Esquire Deposition Solutions. (2025, August 13). Federal Court Turns Up the Heat on Attorneys Using ChatGPT for Research—Esquire Deposition Solutions. https://www.esquiresolutions.com/federal-court-turns-up-the-heat-on-attorneys-using-chatgpt-for-research/

European Parliament. (2024). Regulation (EU) 2024/1689 of the European Parliament and of the Council of 13 June 2024 laying down harmonised rules on artificial intelligence and amending Regulations (EC) No 300/2008, (EU) No 167/2013, (EU) No 168/2013, (EU) 2018/858, (EU) 2018/1139 and (EU) 2019/2144 and Directives 2014/90/EU, (EU) 2016/797 and (EU) 2020/1828 (Artificial Intelligence Act)Text with EEA relevance.

Freeman, J. (2025). Student Generative AI Survey 2025.

Gallen, S. (2025). Avallain Reinforces its Commitment to Research-Driven Solutions with a Newly Commissioned GenAI Report. Avallain. https://www.avallain.com/blog/avallain-reinforces-its-commitment-to-research-driven-solutions-with-a-newly-commissioned-genai-report

Gao, Q., Chen, L., & Huang, Z. (2026). Opportunities and challenges of artificial intelligence in public health: A systematic review on technological efficacy, ethical dilemmas, and governance pathways. *Frontiers in Public Health, 13*. Advance online publication. DOI: 10.3389/fpubh.2025.1748797

Giardini, T. (2024). The 2024 update to the OECD AI Principles—Global Trade Alert. https://globaltradealert.org/reports/64

Green, M. (2025). GenAI Use and Ethics Framework: A Pedagogical Model for Responsible AI Integration in K-12 and Higher Education—Online Learning Consortium. https://onlinelearningconsortium.org/olc-insights/2025/11/genai-use-and-ethics-framework/

greggwirth. (2025, August 18). GenAI hallucinations are still pervasive in legal filings, but better lawyering is the cure. Thomson Reuters Institute. https://www.thomsonreuters.com/en-us/posts/technology/genai-hallucinations/

HalluGraph. (2025). HalluGraph: Auditable Hallucination Detection for Legal RAG Systems via Knowledge Graph Alignment. ChatPaper. https://chatpaper.com/paper/214536

Hiltzik, M. (2025, May 22). Commentary: AI 'hallucinations' are a growing problem for the legal profession. Los Angeles Times. https://www.latimes.com/business/story/2025-05-22/ai-lawyers-hallucinations-a-growing-problem-for-lawyers

Hoang, D. A. (2025). Frontiers | Survey and analysis of hallucinations in large language models: Attribution to prompting strategies or model behavior. https://www.frontiersin.org/journals/artificial-intelligence/articles/10.3389/frai.2025.1622292/full

Hohloch, S. (2025). Homoclinic Floer homology via direct limits (arXiv:2402.12345). arXiv. https://doi.org//arXiv.2402.12345DOI: 10.48550

Kumar, R., Kumar, H., & Shalini, K. (2025). Detecting and Mitigating Bias in LLMs through Knowledge Graph-Augmented Training (arXiv:2504.00310). arXiv. https://doi.org//arXiv.2504.00310DOI: 10.48550

Khullar, S., Mounika, G. R., Singh Chauhan, S., Garg, G., Priyanka, T. P., & Kaliappan, S. (2025). Advanced hybrid ensemble learning for blockchain-enabled secure voting: Leveraging random forest, XGBoost, and neural networks for robust anomaly detection and integrity assurance. In Proceedings of the 1st International Conference on Advancement in Futuristic Technologies (ICAFT) (pp. 1–7). IEEE. https://doi.org/10.1109/ICAFT66710.2025.11452780.

Khullar, S., Baghel, R. S., & Swami, P. (2026). Human-AI collaboration: Balancing trust, emotion, and productivity. In AI hallucination management in the enterprise metaverse (pp. xx–xx). IGI Global. https://doi.org/10.4018/979-8-3373-7534-2.ch003.

Khullar, S., Kate, C., Rao, A. S., Sharrif, U. H., Gupta, A., & Kaliappan, S. (2026). Explainable intelligence for ethical human-centric AI: Trust modeling using gradient boosting. Proceedings of the 5th International Conference on Innovative Practices in Technology and Management (ICIPTM). https://doi.org/10.1109/ICIPTM69057.2026.11465350.

Liu, R., & Lin, L. (2025). Addressing Generative AI Hallucinations in Business Education: A Study on Multilevel Mitigation Strategies. 294–305. https://doi.org/DOI: 10.2991/978-2-38476-462-4_33

Magesh, V. (2024). Hallucination-Free? Assessing the Reliability of Leading AI Legal Research Tools. alphaXiv. https://www.alphaxiv.org/abs/2405.20362

Magesh, V., Surani, F., Dahl, M., Suzgun, M., Manning, C. D., & Ho, D. E. (2024). Hallucination-Free? Assessing the Reliability of Leading AI Legal Research Tools (arXiv:2405.20362). arXiv. https://doi.org//arXiv.2405.20362DOI: 10.48550

Magesh, V., Surani, F., Dahl, M., Suzgun, M., Manning, C. D., & Ho, D. E. (2025). Hallucination-Free? Assessing the Reliability of Leading AI Legal Research Tools. *Journal of Empirical Legal Studies*, *22*(2), 216–242. DOI: 10.1111/jels.12413

McGregor, S. (2026). Welcome to the Artificial Intelligence Incident Database. https://incidentdatabase.ai/

Merken, S. (2025). Trouble with AI 'hallucinations' spreads to big law firms | Reuters. https://www.reuters.com/legal/government/trouble-with-ai-hallucinations-spreads-big-law-firms-2025-05-23/

Nazaretsky, T., Mejia-Domenzain, P., Swamy, V., Frej, J., & Käser, T. (2025). The critical role of trust in adopting AI-powered educational technology for learning: An instrument for measuring student perceptions. *Computers and Education: Artificial Intelligence*, *8*, 100368. DOI: 10.1016/j.caeai.2025.100368

Nishisako, S., Higashi, T., & Wakao, F. (2025). Reducing Hallucinations and Trade-Offs in Responses in Generative AI Chatbots for Cancer Information: Development and Evaluation Study. *JMIR Cancer*, *11*, e70176. DOI: 10.2196/70176

OECD. (2019). AI Principles Overview. https://oecd.ai/en/principles

Prolic, R. (2025, November 12). Tools and strategies for detecting AI case citation hallucinations in legal materials. CALL Bulletin. https://bulletin.chicagolawlib.org/2025/11/detecting-ai-hallucinations-in-legal-materials/

Rose, N. (2025, November 21). Law firm faces claim over £1.5m paid out of escrow amid AI concern. Legal Futures. https://www.legalfutures.co.uk/?p=147874

Salinas, E. (2025). Automating hallucination detection with chain-of-thought reasoning—Amazon Science. https://www.amazon.science/blog/automating-hallucination-detection-with-chain-of-thought-reasoning

Street, B. (2025). IN THE COUNTY COURT AT BIRMINGHAM.

Tabassi, E. (2023a). *Artificial Intelligence Risk Management Framework (AI RMF 1.0) (NIST AI 100-1; p. NIST AI 100-1)*. National Institute of Standards and Technology., DOI: 10.6028/NIST.AI.100-1

Tabassi, E. (2023b). *Artificial Intelligence Risk Management Framework (AI RMF 1.0) (NIST AI 100-1; p. NIST AI 100-1)*. National Institute of Standards and Technology., DOI: 10.6028/NIST.AI.100-1

Tabassi, E. (2023c). *Artificial Intelligence Risk Management Framework (AI RMF 1.0) (NIST AI 100-1; p. NIST AI 100-1)*. National Institute of Standards and Technology., DOI: 10.6028/NIST.AI.100-1

The Perpetual Line-Up. (2016). Perpetual Line Up. https://www.perpetuallineup.org/

Tobin, S. (2025). Lawyers face sanctions for citing fake cases with AI, warns UK judge | Reuters. https://www.reuters.com/world/uk/lawyers-face-sanctions-citing-fake-cases-with-ai-warns-uk-judge-2025-06-06/

Xu, S. (2025). MEGA-RAG: a retrieval-augmented generation framework with multi-evidence guided answer refinement for mitigating hallucinations of LLMs in public health—PMC. https://pmc.ncbi.nlm.nih.gov/articles/PMC12540348/

Xu, S., Yan, Z., Dai, C., & Wu, F. (2025a). MEGA-RAG: A retrieval-augmented generation framework with multi-evidence guided answer refinement for mitigating hallucinations of LLMs in public health. *Frontiers in Public Health, 13*. Advance online publication. DOI: 10.3389/fpubh.2025.1635381

Yan, E. (2023, September 3). Evaluation & Hallucination Detection for Abstractive Summaries. Eugeneyan.Com. https://eugeneyan.com/writing/abstractive/

Compilation of References

Adel, A., & Alani, H. (2024). Can generative AI reliably synthesise literature? Exploring Hallucination issues in ChatGPT. *Information Processing & Management, 61*(4), 103–118.

Adewale, B. A., Ene, V. O., Ogunbayo, B. F., & Aigbavboa, C. O. (2024). A systematic review of the applications of AI in a sustainable building's lifecycle. *Buildings (Basel, Switzerland), 14*(7), 2137. DOI: 10.3390/buildings14072137

Albrecht, M., Shanks, D., Shah, T., Hudson, T., Thompson, J., Filardi, T., Wright, K., Ator, G., & Smith, T. R. (2024). *Enhancing Clinical Documentation Workflow with Ambient Artificial Intelligence: Clinician Perspectives on Work Burden, Burnout, and Job Satisfaction*. Health Informatics. DOI: 10.1101/2024.08.12.24311883

Allen, G. C. (2024). The Biden Administration's National Security Memorandum on AI Explained. https://www.csis.org/analysis/biden-administrations-national-security-memorandum-ai-explained

Amirizaniani, M., Zhao, X., Shao, Y., Mireshghallah, F., Koyejo, S., Berg-Kirkpatrick, T., & Daumé, H., III. (2024). *Developing a framework for auditing large language models using human-in-the-loop*. arXiv.org. /arxiv.2402.09346DOI: 10.48550

Anh-Hoang, D., Tran, V., & Nguyen, L.-M. (2025). Survey and analysis of hallucinations in large language models: Attribution to prompting strategies or model behavior. *Frontiers in Artificial Intelligence, 8*, 1622292. DOI: 10.3389/frai.2025.1622292 PMID: 41098969

Aparisi-Cerdá, I., Ribó-Pérez, D., García-Melón, M., D'Este, P., & Poveda-Bautista, R. (2024). Drivers and barriers to the adoption of decentralised renewable energy technologies: A multi-criteria decision analysis. *Energy, 305*, 132264. DOI: 10.1016/j.energy.2024.132264

Aqeel, I., Khormi, I. M., Khan, S. B., Shuaib, M., Almusharraf, A., Alam, S., & Alkhaldi, N. A. (2023). Load Balancing Using Artificial Intelligence for Cloud-Enabled Internet of Everything in Healthcare Domain. *Sensors (Basel), 23*(11), 5349. DOI: 10.3390/s23115349 PMID: 37300076

Arize, A. I. (2024). *LibreEval: The open-source benchmark for RAG Hallucination detection.* https://arize.com/libreeval

Aswathy, V. K., & Kumar, S. (2025). Silent Struggles: Revealing the Mental Health Crisis Among Kattunauakan Tribal Adolescents in Kerala, South India. In Poddar, S., & Ansar, W. (Eds.), *Sustainable Development Goals (SDG) and Its Intersection With Health and Well-Being* (pp. 377–398). IGI Global., DOI: 10.4018/979-8-3693-9755-8.ch013

Azaria, A., & Mitchell, T. (2023). The internal state of an LLM knows when it's lying. In Findings of the Association for Computational Linguistics: EMNLP 2023 (pp. 967–976). Association for Computational Linguistics. DOI: 10.18653/v1/2023.findings-emnlp.68

Baker Donelson. (n.d.). *The Perils of Legal Hallucinations and the Need for AI Training for Your In-House Legal Team!* Retrieved from https://www.bakerdonelson.com/the-perils-of-legal-hallucinations-and-the-need-for-ai-training-for-your-in-house-legal-team

Bakonyi, Z. (2024). How can companies handle paradoxes to enhance trust in artificial intelligence solutions? A qualitative research. *Journal of Organizational Change Management, 37*(7), 1405–1426. Advance online publication. DOI: 10.1108/JOCM-01-2023-0026

Baldassarre, M. T., Gigante, D., Kalinowski, M., & Ragone, A. (2024). Polaris: A framework to guide the development of trustworthy AI systems. *Proceedings of the ACM/IEEE 46th International Conference on Software Engineering* (pp. 1–12). DOI: 10.1145/3644815.3644947

Bang, Y., Cahyawijaya, S., Lee, N., Dai, W., Su, D., Wilie, B., Lovenia, H., Ji, Z., Yu, T., Chung, W., Do, Q. V., Xu, Y., & Fung, P. (2023). A multitask, multilingual, multimodal evaluation of ChatGPT on reasoning, hallucination, and interactivity. In *Proceedings of the 13th International Joint Conference on Natural Language Processing and the 3rd Conference of the Asia-Pacific Chapter of the Association for Computational Linguistics* (Volume 1: Long Papers) (pp. 675–718). DOI: 10.18653/v1/2023.ijcnlp-main.45

Bang, Y., Ji, Z., Schelten, A., Hartshorn, A., Fowler, T., Zhang, C., Cancedda, N., & Fung, P. (2025). *HalluLens: LLM Hallucination Benchmark.* ACL Anthology.

Barocas, S., Hardt, M., & Narayanan, A. (2019). *Fairness and machine learning*. fairmlbook.org.

Bayoudh, K., Knani, R., Hamdaoui, F., & Mtibaa, A. (2022). A survey on deep multimodal learning for computer vision: Advances, trends, applications, and datasets. *The Visual Computer*, *38*(8), 2939–2970. DOI: 10.1007/s00371-021-02166-7 PMID: 34131356

Beam AL, Kohane IS. Big data and machine learning in health care. JAMA. 2018;319(13):1317–1318. . 4DOI: 10.1001/jama.2017.18391

Belay, S., Goedert, J., Woldesenbet, A., & Rokooei, S. (2022). AHP based multi criteria decision analysis of success factors to enhance decision making in infrastructure construction projects. *Cogent Engineering*, *9*(1), 2043996. DOI: 10.1080/23311916.2022.2043996

Bender, E. M., Gebru, T., McMillan-Major, A., & Shmitchell, S. (2024). On the dangers of stochastic parrots. In *Proceedings of the ACM Conference on Fairness, Accountability, and Transparency* (pp. 610–623).

Bertino, E. (2016). Data Security and Privacy: Concepts, Approaches, and Research Directions. *2016 IEEE 40th Annual Computer Software and Applications Conference (COMPSAC)*, 400–407. DOI: 10.1109/COMPSAC.2016.89

Biswas, A., & Talukdar, W. (2024). *Intelligent Clinical Documentation: Harnessing Generative AI for Patient-Centric Clinical Note Generation*. https://doi.org/DOI: 10.48550/ARXIV.2405.18346

Bommasani, R., et al. (2024). *Foundation models and trust calibration in generative AI systems* (Technical report). Stanford CRFM.

Bommasani, R., Hudson, D. A., Adeli, E., Altman, R., Arora, S., von Arx, S., . . . Liang, P. (2021). On the opportunities and risks of foundation models. arXiv preprint arXiv:2108.07258.

Boscardin, C. K., Gin, B., Golde, P. B., & Hauer, K. E. (2024). ChatGPT and Generative Artificial Intelligence for Medical Education: Potential Impact and Opportunity. *Academic Medicine*, *99*(1), 22–27. DOI: 10.1097/ACM.0000000000005439 PMID: 37651677

Bozkır, E. (2025). Predictive Policing or Predictive Prejudice? A Study of the Legal, Historical and Ethical Implications of AI in Policing | OxJournal. https://www.oxjournal.org/predictive-policing-or-predictive-prejudice/

Brandão, P. R. (2025). The impact of artificial intelligence on modern society. *AI*, *6*(8), 190. DOI: 10.3390/ai6080190

Brantingham, P. J., Valasik, M., & Mohler, G. O. (2018). Does Predictive Policing Lead to Biased Arrests? Results From a Randomized Controlled Trial. *Statistics and Public Policy (Philadelphia, Pa.)*, *5*(1), 1–6. DOI: 10.1080/2330443X.2018.1438940

Briganti, G., & Le Moine, O. (2020). Artificial Intelligence in Medicine: Today and Tomorrow. *Frontiers in Medicine*, *7*, 27. DOI: 10.3389/fmed.2020.00027 PMID: 32118012

Brintnall-Karabelas, J., Sung, S., Cadman, M. E., Squires, C., Whorton, K., & Pao, M. (2011). Improving Recruitment in Clinical Trials: Why Eligible Participants Decline. *Journal of Empirical Research on Human Research Ethics; JERHRE*, *6*(1), 69–74. DOI: 10.1525/jer.2011.6.1.69 PMID: 21460590

Burns, C., Ye, H., Klein, D., & Steinhardt, J. (2023). Discovering latent knowledge in language models without supervision. In The Eleventh International Conference on Learning Representations. OpenReview. DOI: 10.48550/arXiv.2212.03827

Calvert, J. (2025). Principles and framework for the operationalisation of meaningful human control over autonomous systems. *Science and Engineering Ethics*, *31*(5), 27. Advance online publication. DOI: 10.1007/s11948-025-00554-z PMID: 40991137

Cao, M., Dong, Y., & Cheung, J. C. K. (2022). Hallucinated but factual! Inspecting the factuality of hallucinations in abstractive summarization. In *Proceedings of the 60th Annual Meeting of the Association for Computational Linguistics* (Volume 1: Long Papers) (pp. 3340–3354). Association for Computational Linguistics. DOI: 10.18653/v1/2022.acl-long.236

Chen, G., Liu, C., Ooi, G. A., Tan, M., Xie, Z., Yin, J., Yip, J. W. L., Zhang, W., Zhu, J., & Ooi, B. C. (2025). *Generative AI for Healthcare: Fundamentals, Challenges, and Perspectives* (Version 1). arXiv. DOI: 10.48550/ARXIV.2510.24551

Chen, A., Liu, L., & Zhu, T. (2024). Advancing the democratization of generative artificial intelligence in healthcare: A narrative review. *Journal of Hospital Management and Health Policy*, *8*, 12–12. DOI: 10.21037/jhmhp-24-54

Choubisa, V., & Choubisa, D. (2024). Towards trustworthy AI: An analysis of the relationship between explainability and trust in AI systems. *International Journal of Science and Research Archive*, *11*(1), 2219–2226. DOI: 10.30574/ijsra.2024.11.1.0300

Christiano, P. F., Leike, J., Brown, T., Martic, M., Legg, S., & Amodei, D. (2017). Deep reinforcement learning from human preferences. arXiv preprint arXiv:1706.03741.

Chuang, Y.-S., Xie, Y., Luo, H., Kim, Y., Glass, J., & He, P. (2024). DoLa: Decoding by contrasting layers improves factuality in large language models. In The Twelfth International Conference on Learning Representations. OpenReview. DOI: 10.48550/arXiv.2309.03883

Cohen, R., Hamri, M., Geva, M., & Globerson, A. (2023). LM vs LM: Detecting factual errors via cross examination. In *Proceedings of the 2023 Conference on Empirical Methods in Natural Language Processing* (pp. 12621–12640). Association for Computational Linguistics. DOI: 10.18653/v1/2023.emnlp-main.778

Corea, F., Bertolini, A., Bolognini, L., Luciano, F., & Memorandum, V. (2022). A principle-based approach to AI: The case for European Union and Italy. *AI & Society*, *37*(4), 1397–1408. DOI: 10.1007/s00146-022-01453-8

Dagan, N., Magen, O., Leshchinsky, M., Makov-Assif, M., Lipsitch, M., Reis, B. Y., ... & Balicer, R. D. (2024). Prospective evaluation of machine learning for public health screening: identifying unknown hepatitis C carriers. NEJM AI, 1(2), AIoa2300012.

Dahl, M. (2024). Large Legal Fictions: Profiling Legal Hallucinations in Large Language Models | Journal of Legal Analysis | Oxford Academic. https://academic.oup.com/jla/article/16/1/64/7699227?login=false

Dahl, M., Magesh, V., Suzgun, M., & Ho, D. E. (2024). Large Legal Fictions: Profiling Legal Hallucinations in Large Language Models. *The Journal of Legal Analysis*, *16*(1), 64–93. DOI: 10.1093/jla/laae003

Danyaro, K.U. (2025). Hallucinations in Large Language Models for Education: Challenges and Mitigation. https://doi.org/DOI: 10.22161/IJTLE

Deloitte. (2020). Technology making health care work more meaningful [Internet]. Available from: https://www2.deloitte.com/us/en/ insights/industry/health-care/technology-making-health-care-wo rk-more-meaningful.html. Accessed May 31, 2024.

Deloitte. (n.d.). *AI doesn't lie, it hallucinates and M&A due diligence must address that.* Retrieved from https://www.deloitte.com/ch/en/services/consulting/perspectives/ai-hallucinations-new-risk-m-a.html

Dewangan, S., Kumar, S., & Tyagi, P. K. (2024). Transforming Hospitality and Tourism With AI and Innovative Technologies. In Talukder, M. B., Kumar, S., & Tyagi, P. K. (Eds.), *Advances in Hospitality, Tourism, and the Services Industry* (pp. 66–83). IGI Global., DOI: 10.4018/979-8-3693-6755-1.ch004

Di Salvatore, S., Drissi Yahyaoui, O., De Marchi, M., & Rauch, E. (2025). The integration of ethical and trustworthy AI in industrial engineering: Practical approaches. *Engineering Proceedings*, *97*(1), 42. DOI: 10.3390/engproc2025097042

Duke, A. (2023). *Human-in-the-loop*. In Interpretable machine learning with Python (pp. 145–168). Apress. DOI: 10.1007/978-1-4842-9306-5_6

Dwork, C., & Roth, A. (2014). The algorithmic foundations of differential privacy. *Foundations and Trends in Theoretical Computer Science*, *9*(3–4), 211–407. DOI: 10.1561/0400000042

Dziri, N., Kamalloo, E., Mathewson, K. W., Zaiane, O. R., & Reddy, S. (2022). On the Origin of Hallucinations in Conversational Models: Is it the Datasets or the Models? *Proceedings of the 2022 Conference on Empirical Methods in Natural Language Processing*, 527–542. DOI: 10.18653/v1/2022.naacl-main.387

Ebrahimi, E., Fathi, M. R., & Sobhani, S. M. (2023). A modification of technique for order preference by similarity to ideal solution (TOPSIS) through fuzzy similarity method (a numerical example of the personnel selection). *Journal of Applied Research on Industrial Engineering*, *10*(2), 203–217.

Emish, M., & Young, S. D. (2024). Remote Wearable Neuroimaging Devices for Health Monitoring and Neurophenotyping: A Scoping Review. *Biomimetics*, *9*(4), 237. DOI: 10.3390/biomimetics9040237 PMID: 38667247

Esquire Deposition Solutions. (2025, August 13). Federal Court Turns Up the Heat on Attorneys Using ChatGPT for Research—Esquire Deposition Solutions. https://www.esquiresolutions.com/federal-court-turns-up-the-heat-on-attorneys-using-chatgpt-for-research/

European Parliament. (2024). Regulation (EU) 2024/1689 of the European Parliament and of the Council of 13 June 2024 laying down harmonised rules on artificial intelligence and amending Regulations (EC) No 300/2008, (EU) No 167/2013, (EU) No 168/2013, (EU) 2018/858, (EU) 2018/1139 and (EU) 2019/2144 and Directives 2014/90/EU, (EU) 2016/797 and (EU) 2020/1828 (Artificial Intelligence Act)Text with EEA relevance.

European Union. (2024). *Artificial Intelligence Act*. Official Journal of the European Union.

Evans-Lacko, S., Knapp, M., McCrone, P., Thornicroft, G., & Mojtabai, R. (2013). The Mental Health Consequences of the Recession: Economic Hardship and Employment of People with Mental Health Problems in 27 European Countries. *PLoS One*, *8*(7), e69792. DOI: 10.1371/journal.pone.0069792 PMID: 23922801

Eysenbach, G. (2023). The Role of ChatGPT, Generative Language Models, and Artificial Intelligence in Medical Education: A Conversation With ChatGPT and a Call for Papers. *JMIR Medical Education*, *9*, e46885. DOI: 10.2196/46885 PMID: 36863937

Fabbri, A. R., Kryściński, W., McCann, B., Xiong, C., Socher, R., & Radev, D. (2022). QAFactEval: Improved QA-based factual consistency evaluation for summarization. In *Proceedings of the 2022 Conference of the North American Chapter of the Association for Computational Linguistics: Human Language Technologies* (pp. 2587–2601). Association for Computational Linguistics. DOI: 10.18653/v1/2022.naacl-main.187

Farquhar, S., Kossen, J., Kuhn, L., & Gal, Y. (2024). Detecting hallucinations in large language models using semantic entropy. *Nature*, *630*(8017), 625–630. DOI: 10.1038/s41586-024-07421-0 PMID: 38898292

Ferdaus, M. H., Rahman, M. M., Hossain, M. A., & Rahman, M. S. (2024). Trust in large language models: Framework for ethical oversight and transparency in sensitive domains. *Proceedings of the ACM on Human-Computer Interaction, 8*(CSCW1), Article 189. DOI: 10.1145/3644817

Ferdaus, M. M., Abdelguerfi, M., Loup, E., Niles, K. N., Pathak, K., & Sloan, S. (2026). Towards trustworthy AI: A review of ethical and robust large language models. *ACM Computing Surveys*, *58*(7), 176. Advance online publication. DOI: 10.1145/3777382

Ferrara, E. (2024). Fairness and bias in artificial intelligence: A brief survey of sources, impacts, and mitigation strategies. *Sci*, *6*(1), 3. DOI: 10.3390/sci6010003

Fierro, C., & Søgaard, A. (2022). Factual consistency of multilingual pretrained language models. In Findings of the Association for Computational Linguistics: ACL 2022 (pp. 3046–3052). Association for Computational Linguistics. DOI: 10.18653/v1/2022.findings-acl.240

Financial Stability Board. (2022). *Artificial intelligence and machine learning in financial services* (Technical report).

Freeman, J. (2025). Student Generative AI Survey 2025.

Futoma, M., Simons, M., Panch, T., Doshi-Velez, F., & Celi, L. A. (2020, September). Simons, T. Panch, F. Doshi-Velez, and L. A. Celi, "The myth of generalisability in clinical research and machine learning in health care,". *The Lancet. Digital Health*, *2*(9), e489–e492. DOI: 10.1016/S2589-7500(20)30186-2 PMID: 32864600

Gallen, S. (2025). Avallain Reinforces its Commitment to Research-Driven Solutions with a Newly Commissioned GenAI Report. Avallain. https://www.avallain.com/blog/avallain-reinforces-its-commitment-to-research-driven-solutions-with-a-newly-commissioned-genai-report

Gangavarapu, T. (2025). *Mastering AI governance*. Springer., DOI: 10.1007/978-3-031-93681-4

Gao, L., Dai, Z., Pasupat, P., Chen, A., Chaganty, A. T., Fan, Y., Zhao, V., Lao, N., Lee, H., Juan, D.-C., & Guu, K. (2023). RARR: Researching and revising what language models say, using language models. In *Proceedings of the 61st Annual Meeting of the Association for Computational Linguistics* (Volume 1: Long Papers) (pp. 16856–16872). Association for Computational Linguistics. DOI: 10.18653/v1/2023.acl-long.910

Gao, Q., Chen, L., & Huang, Z. (2026). Opportunities and challenges of artificial intelligence in public health: A systematic review on technological efficacy, ethical dilemmas, and governance pathways. *Frontiers in Public Health, 13*. Advance online publication. DOI: 10.3389/fpubh.2025.1748797

Gardas, B. B. (2022). Organizational hindrances to Healthcare 4.0 adoption: An multi-criteria decision analysis framework. *Journal of Multi-Criteria Decision Analysis, 29*(1-2), 186–195. DOI: 10.1002/mcda.1766

Garg, S. (2025). The Role of Generative AI in Personalized Medicine and Treatment Recommendations. *Clinical Medicine And Health Research Journal, 5*(02), 1214–1227. DOI: 10.18535/cmhrj.v5i02.463

Gendlin, E. T. (1962). *Experiencing and the creation of meaning*. Free Press of Glencoe.

Gerner, T.. (2025). *ORION: Grounded in context – Retrieval-based method for Hallucination detection*. arXiv. https://arxiv.org/abs/2501.00000

Ghai, S., Pan, L., & Mueller, M. (2024). Measuring trustworthiness in large language models. *IEEE Transactions on Artificial Intelligence, 5*(1), 45–58.

Ghim, J. L., & Ahn, S. (2023). Transforming clinical trials: The emerging roles of large language models. *Translational and Clinical Pharmacology, 31*(3), 131–138. DOI: 10.12793/tcp.2023.31.e16 PMID: 37810626

Gholamzadeh, M., Abtahi, H., & Safdari, R. (2023). The application of knowledge-based clinical decision support systems to enhance adherence to evidence-based medicine in chronic disease. *Journal of Healthcare Engineering, 2023*(1), 8550905. DOI: 10.1155/2023/8550905 PMID: 37284487

Giardini, T. (2024). The 2024 update to the OECD AI Principles—Global Trade Alert. https://globaltradealert.org/reports/64

Gilpin, L. H., Bau, D., Yuan, B. Z., Bajwa, A., Specter, M., & Kagal, L. (2018). Explaining explanations: An overview of interpretability of machine learning. In *Proceedings of the 2018 IEEE 5th International Conference on Data Science and Advanced Analytics (DSAA)* (pp. 80–89). IEEE. DOI: 10.1109/DSAA.2018.00018

Glaa, B., Zoghlami, N., & Taghipour, A. (2014). Outsourcing and off-shoring healthcare services: A way to cut the costs and improve quality. *2014 International Conference on Advanced Logistics and Transport (ICALT)*, 189–194. DOI: 10.1109/ICAdLT.2014.6864116

Goodfellow, I., Shlens, J., & Szegedy, C. (2015). Explaining and harnessing adversarial examples. In *Proceedings of the International Conference on Learning Representations.*

Green, M. (2025). GenAI Use and Ethics Framework: A Pedagogical Model for Responsible AI Integration in K-12 and Higher Education—Online Learning Consortium. https://onlinelearningconsortium.org/olc-insights/2025/11/genai-use-and-ethics-framework/

Green, A., & Chen, K. (2019). The principles and limits of algorithm transparency. *IEEE Security and Privacy*, *17*(6), 24–31.

greggwirth. (2025, August 18). GenAI hallucinations are still pervasive in legal filings, but better lawyering is the cure. Thomson Reuters Institute. https://www.thomsonreuters.com/en-us/posts/technology/genai-hallucinations/

Gudivaka, R.K. (2023). Transforming Business Operations: The Role of Artificial Intelligence in Robotic Process Automation. IMPACT: International Journal of Research in Business Management (IMPACT: IJRBM), 12(1).

Guerrier, C., McDonnell, C., Magoc, T., Fishe, J. N., & Harle, C. A. (2022). Understanding health care administrators' data and information needs for decision making during the COVID-19 pandemic: A qualitative study at an academic health system. *MDM Policy & Practice*, *7*(1), 23814683221089844. DOI: 10.1177/23814683221089844 PMID: 35368410

Gunasekara, L., El-Haber, N., Nagpal, S., Moraliyage, H., Issadeen, Z., Manic, M., & De Silva, D. (2025). A systematic review of responsible artificial intelligence principles and practice. *Applied System Innovation*, *8*(4), 97. DOI: 10.3390/asi8040097

Hacking, S. (2024). ChatGPT and Medicine: Together We Embrace the AI Renaissance. [Google Scholar] [CrossRef] [PubMed]. *JMIR Bioinformatics and Biotechnology*, *5*, e52700. DOI: 10.2196/52700 PMID: 38935938

HalluGraph. (2025). HalluGraph: Auditable Hallucination Detection for Legal RAG Systems via Knowledge Graph Alignment. ChatPaper. https://chatpaper.com/paper/214536

Hammerschmidt, T., Stolz, K., & Posegga, O. (2025). Bridging the gap: Inequalities that divide those who can and cannot create sustainable outcomes with AI. *Behaviour & Information Technology*, •••, 1–30. DOI: 10.1080/0144929X.2025.2500451

Hanna, M. G., Pantanowitz, L., Jackson, B., Palmer, O., Visweswaran, S., Pantanowitz, J., Deebajah, M., & Rashidi, H. H. (2025, March). Ethical and Bias Considerations in Artificial Intelligence/Machine Learning. *Modern Pathology*, *38*(3), 100686. DOI: 10.1016/j.modpat.2024.100686 PMID: 39694331

Harrath, Y., Adohinzin, O., Kaabi, J., & Saathoff, M. (2025). Bridging domains: Advances in explainable, automated, and privacy-preserving AI for computer science and cybersecurity. *Computers*, *14*(9), 374. DOI: 10.3390/computers14090374

Hasan, H. E., Jaber, D., Al Tabbah, S., Lawand, N., Habib, H. A., & Farahat, N. M. (2024). Knowledge, attitude and practice among pharmacy students and faculty members towards artificial intelligence in pharmacy practice: A multinational cross-sectional study. *PLoS One*, *19*(3), e0296884. DOI: 10.1371/journal.pone.0296884 PMID: 38427639

Hasan, S. S., Fury, M. S., Woo, J. J., Kunze, K. N., & Ramkumar, P. N. (2025). Ethical Application of Generative Artificial Intelligence in Medicine. *Arthroscopy*, *41*(4), 874–885. DOI: 10.1016/j.arthro.2024.12.011 PMID: 39689842

He, F., Lai, Q., Ma, J., Wei, G., & Li, W. (2023). Design and Application of an Early Warning and Emergency Response System in the Transboundary Area of the Taihu Lake Basin. *International Journal of Environmental Research and Public Health*, *20*(2), 1340. DOI: 10.3390/ijerph20021340 PMID: 36674094

Heidegger, M. (2010). *Being and time* (Stambaugh, J., Trans.). State University of New York Press. (Original work published 1927)

Hiltzik, M. (2025, May 22). Commentary: AI 'hallucinations' are a growing problem for the legal profession. Los Angeles Times. https://www.latimes.com/business/story/2025-05-22/ai-lawyers-hallucinations-a-growing-problem-for-lawyers

Hoang, D. A. (2025). Frontiers | Survey and analysis of hallucinations in large language models: Attribution to prompting strategies or model behavior. https://www.frontiersin.org/journals/artificial-intelligence/articles/10.3389/frai.2025.1622292/full

Ho, D. E. (2025). *Hallucination-Free? Assessing the Reliability of Leading AI Legal Research Tools*. Stanford University.

Hohma, E., & Lütge, C. (2023). From trustworthy principles to a trustworthy development process: The need and elements of trusted development of AI systems. *AI*, *4*(4), 904–925. DOI: 10.3390/ai4040046

Honovich, O., Choshen, L., Aharoni, R., Neeman, E., Szpektor, I., & Abend, O. (2021). Q^2: Evaluating factual consistency in knowledge-grounded dialogues via question generation and question answering. In *Proceedings of the 2021 Conference on Empirical Methods in Natural Language Processing* (pp. 7856–7870). Association for Computational Linguistics. DOI: 10.18653/v1/2021.emnlp-main.619

Huang, L., Yu, W., Ma, W., Zhong, W., Feng, Z., Wang, H., Chen, Q., Peng, W., Feng, X., Qin, B., & Liu, T. (2025). A survey on hallucination in large language models: Principles, taxonomy, challenges, and open questions. *ACM Transactions on Information Systems*, *43*(2), 42. Advance online publication. DOI: 10.1145/3703155

Hu, D., Guo, Y., Zhou, Y., Flores, L., & Zheng, K. (2025). A systematic review of early evidence on generative AI for drafting responses to patient messages. *Npj Health Systems*, *2*(1), 27. DOI: 10.1038/s44401-025-00032-5

Husserl, E. (1970). *The crisis of European sciences and transcendental phenomenology* (Carr, D., Trans.). Northwestern University Press. (Original work published 1936)

Husserl, E. (2001). *Ideas pertaining to a pure phenomenology and to a phenomenological philosophy, First Book* (Kersten, F., Trans.). Springer. (Original work published 1913)

IAPP. (n.d.). *Hallucinations in LLMs: Technical challenges, systemic risks and AI governance implications*. Retrieved from https://iapp.org/news/a/hallucinations-in-llms-technical-challenges-systemic-risks-and-ai-governance-implications

International Organization for Standardization. (2023). *ISO/IEC 23894: Artificial intelligence—Risk management*.

Iyenghar, P. (n.d.). *Clever Hans in the loop? A critical examination of ChatGPT in a human-in-the-loop framework for machinery functional safety risk analysis*. DOI: 10.3390/eng6020031

Ji, J., Qiu, T., Chen, B., Zhou, J., Zhang, B., Hong, D., & Gao, W. (2026). AI alignment: A contemporary survey. *ACM Computing Surveys*, *58*(5), 132. Advance online publication. DOI: 10.1145/3770749

Ji, Z., Lee, N., Frieske, R., Yu, T., Su, D., Xu, Y., Ishii, A., Bang, Y. J., Madotto, A., & Fung, P. (2023). Survey of hallucination in natural language generation. *ACM Computing Surveys*, *55*(12), 1–38. DOI: 10.1145/3571730

Jobin, A., Ienca, M., & Vayena, E. (2019). The global landscape of AI ethics guidelines. *Nature Machine Intelligence*, *1*(9), 389–399. DOI: 10.1038/s42256-019-0088-2

Johnson, K. B., Wei, W. Q., Weeraratne, D., Frisse, M. E., Misulis, K., Rhee, K., Zhao, J., & Snowdon, J. L. (2021). Precision Medicine, AI, and the Future of Personalized Health Care. *Clinical and Translational Science*, *14*(1), 86–93. DOI: 10.1111/cts.12884 PMID: 32961010

Joshi, R. (2024). Comprehensive review of AI Hallucinations: Impacts and mitigation strategies for financial and business applications. *Journal of AI Ethics*, *3*(2), 45–67.

Kamil, H., Rachmah, R., Irvanizam, I., & Wardani, E. (2020). Exploring health professionals' perceptions on Health-ID, an electronic integrated patient progress documentation system: A qualitative study in Indonesia. *Journal of Multidisciplinary Healthcare*, •••, 1649–1656.

Kamran, F., Tjandra, D., Heiler, A., Virzi, J., Singh, K., King, J. E., ... & Wiens, J. (2024). Evaluation of sepsis prediction models before onset of treatment. Nejm Ai, 1(3), AIoa2300032.

Kapoor, S., Narayanan, A., & Wallace, B. A. (2025). Evaluating trust, safety, and alignment in generative AI. *IEEE Security and Privacy*, *23*(1), 72–81.

Karim, A. (2024). Implementation of the Multi-Objective Optimization Method on the Basic of Ratio Analysis (MOORA) and Entropy Weighting in New Employee Recruitment. [JOSH]. *Journal of Information System Research*, *5*(2), 704–712. DOI: 10.47065/josh.v5i2.4859

Karpukhin, V., Oguz, B., Min, S., Lewis, P., Wu, L., Edunov, S., Chen, D., & Yih, W.-t. (2020). Dense passage retrieval for open-domain question answering. In *Proceedings of EMNLP*. DOI: 10.18653/v1/2020.emnlp-main.550

Karthikeyan, E., & Sivaneswari, S. (2025). Artificial Intelligence in Personalized Medicine for Head and Neck Cancer: Optimizing Prescriptions and Treatment Planning. *Biomedical Materials & Devices*. Advance online publication. DOI: 10.1007/s44174-025-00320-6

Kasula, B. Y. (2023). Framework Development for Artificial Intelligence Integration in Healthcare: Optimizing Patient Care and Operational Efficiency. *Transactions on Latest Trends in IoT*, *6*(6), 77–83.

Kazlaris, I., Antoniou, E., Diamantaras, K., & Bratsas, C. (2025). From Illusion to Insight: A Taxonomic Survey of Hallucination Mitigation Techniques in LLMs. *AI*, *6*(10), 260. DOI: 10.3390/ai6100260

Khairy, A., Bashier, H., Nuh, H., Ahmed, N., Ali, Y., Izzoddeen, A., Mohamed, S., Osman, M., & Khader, Y. (2024). The role of the Field Epidemiology Training Program in the public health emergency response: Sudan armed conflict 2023. *Frontiers in Public Health*, *12*, 1300084. DOI: 10.3389/fpubh.2024.1300084 PMID: 38356953

Khosravi, M., Zare, Z., Mojtabaeian, S. M., & Izadi, R. (2024). Artificial Intelligence and Decision-Making in Healthcare: A Thematic Analysis of a Systematic Review of Reviews. [CrossRef] [PubMed]. *Health Services Research and Managerial Epidemiology*, *11*, 23333928241234863. DOI: 10.1177/23333928241234863 PMID: 38449840

Khullar, S., Baghel, R. S., & Swami, P. (2026). Human-AI collaboration: Balancing trust, emotion, and productivity. In AI hallucination management in the enterprise metaverse (pp. xx–xx). IGI Global. https://doi.org/10.4018/979-8-3373-7534-2.ch003.

Khullar, S., Kate, C., Rao, A. S., Sharrif, U. H., Gupta, A., & Kaliappan, S. (2026). Explainable intelligence for ethical human-centric AI: Trust modeling using gradient boosting. Proceedings of the 5th International Conference on Innovative Practices in Technology and Management (ICIPTM). https://doi.org/10.1109/ICIPTM69057.2026.11465350.

Khullar, S., Mounika, G. R., Singh Chauhan, S., Garg, G., Priyanka, T. P., & Kaliappan, S. (2025). Advanced hybrid ensemble learning for blockchain-enabled secure voting: Leveraging random forest, XGBoost, and neural networks for robust anomaly detection and integrity assurance. In Proceedings of the 1st International Conference on Advancement in Futuristic Technologies (ICAFT) (pp. 1–7). IEEE. https://doi.org/10.1109/ICAFT66710.2025.11452780.

Kim, E., Chandrasekaran, A., & Gunning, D. (2022). Designing AI explanations for trust calibration. *IEEE Computer*, *55*(2), 40–49.

Kim, Y., Jeong, H., Chen, S., Li, S. S., Park, C., Lu, M., Alhamoud, K., Mun, J., Grau, C., Jung, M., Gameiro, R., Fan, L., Park, E., Lin, T., Yoon, J., Yoon, W., Sap, M., Tsvetkov, Y., Liang, P. P., & Breazeal, C. (2025). Medical Hallucination in Foundation Models and Their Impact on Healthcare. *medRxiv*. DOI: 10.1101/2025.02.28.25323115

Kossen, J., Farquhar, S., Gal, Y., & Rainforth, T. (2024). Semantic entropy probes: Robust and cheap hallucination detection in LLMs. In The Thirteenth International Conference on Learning Representations. OpenReview. DOI: 10.48550/arXiv.2406.15927

Krishnamoorthy, S. (2024). Enhancing responsible AGI development: Integrating human-in-the-loop approaches with blockchain-based smart contracts. *Journal of Advances in Mathematics and Computer Science*, *39*(9), 1–15. DOI: 10.9734/jamcs/2024/v39i91924

Kryscinski, W., McCann, B., Xiong, C., & Socher, R. (2020). Evaluating the factual consistency of abstractive text summarization. In *Proceedings of the 2020 Conference on Empirical Methods in Natural Language Processing* (pp. 9332–9346). Association for Computational Linguistics. DOI: 10.18653/v1/2020.emnlp-main.750

Kuhn, L., Gal, Y., & Farquhar, S. (2023). Semantic uncertainty: Linguistic invariances for uncertainty estimation in natural language generation. In The Eleventh International Conference on Learning Representations. OpenReview. DOI: 10.48550/arXiv.2302.09664

Kulkarni, P. S., Awadallah, A. S., & Srikant, R. (2020). Trustworthy human–AI collaboration. In *Proceedings of the AAAI Conference on Artificial Intelligence* (pp. 13533–13541).

Kumar, H., Aswathy, V. K., & Kumar, S. (2025). Converging Realms of Social Health, Domestic Workers, and Telemedicine Landscape: Challenges and Prospects. In Özbek, M. F., & Christiansen, B. (Eds.), *Organizational Sociology in the Digital Age* (pp. 165–180). IGI Global., DOI: 10.4018/979-8-3693-7398-9.ch010

Kumar, S. (2024). The Role of Digital Marketing on Customer Engagement in the Hospitality Industry. In Bansal, R., Ngah, A. H., Chakir, A., & Pruthi, N. (Eds.), (pp. 177–191). Advances in Business Information Systems and Analytics. IGI Global., DOI: 10.4018/979-8-3693-0815-8.ch010

Kumar, S., Talukder, M. B., & Kaiser, F. (2024). Artificial Intelligence in Business: Negative Social Impacts. In Dadwal, S., Goyal, S., Kumar, P., & Verma, R. (Eds.), (pp. 81–97). Advances in Human Resources Management and Organizational Development. IGI Global., DOI: 10.4018/979-8-3693-0724-3.ch005

Kung, T. H., Cheatham, M., Medenilla, A., Sillos, C., De Leon, L., Elepaño, C., Madriaga, M., Aggabao, R., Diaz-Candido, G., Maningo, J., & Tseng, V. (2023). Performance of ChatGPT on USMLE: Potential for AI-Assisted Medical Education Using Large Language Models. [Google Scholar] [CrossRef]. *PLOS Digital Health*, *2*(2), e0000198. DOI: 10.1371/journal.pdig.0000198 PMID: 36812645

Laban, P., Schnabel, T., Bennett, P. N., & Hearst, M. A. (2022). SummaC: Re-visiting NLI-based models for inconsistency detection in summarization. *Transactions of the Association for Computational Linguistics*, *10*, 163–177. DOI: 10.1162/tacl_a_00453

Laban, P., Schnabel, T., Bennett, P. N., & Hearst, M. A. (2023). SummEdits: Measuring LLM ability at factual reasoning through the lens of summarization. In *Proceedings of the 2023 Conference on Empirical Methods in Natural Language Processing* (pp. 9662–9676). Association for Computational Linguistics. DOI: 10.18653/v1/2023.emnlp-main.600

Lakera. (2025). *LLM Hallucinations in 2025: How to Understand and Tackle AI's....* Retrieved from https://www.lakera.ai/blog/guide-to-hallucinations-in-large-language-models

Lattimer, M., Blair, P., & Chen, I. (2023). Fast and accurate factual inconsistency detection over long documents. In *Proceedings of the 2023 Conference on Empirical Methods in Natural Language Processing* (pp. 1045–1060). Association for Computational Linguistics. DOI: 10.18653/v1/2023.emnlp-main.105

Lee, J. D., & See, K. A. (2004). Trust in automation: Designing for appropriate reliance. *Human Factors*, *46*(1), 50–80. DOI: 10.1518/hfes.46.1.50.30392

Lee, S. M., Lee, G., Kim, T. K., Le, T., Hao, J., Jung, Y. M., Park, C.-W., Park, J. S., Jun, J. K., Lee, H.-C., & Kim, D. (2022). Development and Validation of a Prediction Model for Need for Massive Transfusion During Surgery Using Intraoperative Hemodynamic Monitoring Data. *JAMA Network Open*, *5*(12), e2246637. DOI: 10.1001/jamanetworkopen.2022.46637 PMID: 36515949

Leung, F., Lau, Y. C., Law, M., & Djeng, S. K. (2022). Artificial intelligence and end user tools to develop a nurse duty roster scheduling system. *International Journal of Nursing Sciences*, *9*(3), 373–377.

Lewis, P., Perez, E., Piktus, A., Karpukhin, V., Goyal, N., Küttler, H., . . . Riedel, S. (2020). Retrieval-augmented generation for knowledge-intensive NLP. arXiv preprint arXiv:2005.11401.

Li, J., ... (2023). *HaluEval: A large-scale Hallucination evaluation benchmark for LLMs*. In *EMNLP 2023 Proceedings*.

Liang, P. P., Zadeh, A., & Morency, L. P. (2024). Foundations & trends in multimodal machine learning: Principles, challenges, and open questions. *ACM Computing Surveys*, *56*(10), 1–42. DOI: 10.1145/3656580

Liao, C. T., Tsay, S. F., & Chen, H. C. (2024). Exploring generative AI's role in alleviating nursing workload and burnout in Taiwan. *Journal of the Formosan Medical Association*, *123*(7), 736–737. Advance online publication. DOI: 10.1016/j.jfma.2024.02.003 PMID: 38368187

Li, J., Cheng, X., Zhao, X., Nie, J.-Y., & Wen, J.-R. (2023). HaluEval: A large-scale hallucination evaluation benchmark for large language models. In *Proceedings of the 2023 Conference on Empirical Methods in Natural Language Processing* (pp. 6449–6464). Association for Computational Linguistics. DOI: 10.18653/v1/2023.emnlp-main.397

Li, J., Zhou, Y., Yao, J., & Liu, X. (2021). An empirical investigation of trust in AI in a Chinese petrochemical enterprise based on institutional theory. *Scientific Reports*, *11*(1), 1–12. DOI: 10.1038/s41598-021-92904-7 PMID: 34193907

Lin, S., Hilton, J., & Evans, O. (2022). TruthfulQA: Measuring how models mimic human falsehoods. In *Proceedings of the 60th Annual Meeting of the Association for Computational Linguistics* (Volume 1: Long Papers) (pp. 3214–3252). Association for Computational Linguistics. DOI: 10.18653/v1/2022.acl-long.229

Lipton, Z. (2018). The mythos of model interpretability. *ACM Queue; Tomorrow's Computing Today*, *16*(3), 31–57. DOI: 10.1145/3236386.3241340

Liu, R., & Lin, L. (2025). Addressing Generative AI Hallucinations in Business Education: A Study on Multilevel Mitigation Strategies. 294–305. https://doi.org/DOI: 10.2991/978-2-38476-462-4_33

Liu, J., Wang, Y., & Wang, Z. (2023). Uncertainty-aware natural language generation. *IEEE Transactions on Neural Networks and Learning Systems*, *34*(5), 2341–2354.

Liu, X., Xie, L., Wang, Y., Zou, J., Xiong, J., Ying, Z., & Vasilakos, A. V. (2021). Privacy and Security Issues in Deep Learning: A Survey. *IEEE Access : Practical Innovations, Open Solutions*, *9*, 4566–4593. DOI: 10.1109/ACCESS.2020.3045078

Li, Y., & Li, J. (2024). Generative artificial intelligence in medical education: Way to solve the problems. *Postgraduate Medical Journal*, *100*(1181), 203–204. DOI: 10.1093/postmj/qgad116 PMID: 38061077

Luhmann, N. (1979). *Trust and power*. Wiley.

Lukyanenko, R., Maass, W., & Storey, V. C. (2022). Trust in artificial intelligence: From a foundational trust framework to emerging research opportunities. *Electronic Markets*, *32*, 1993–2020. DOI: 10.1007/s12525-022-00605-4

Lundberg, S., & Lee, S.-I. (2017). A unified approach to interpreting model predictions. *Advances in Neural Information Processing Systems*, *30*, 4765–4774.

Magesh, V. (2024). Hallucination-Free? Assessing the Reliability of Leading AI Legal Research Tools. alphaXiv. https://www.alphaxiv.org/abs/2405.20362

Magesh, V., Surani, F., Dahl, M., Suzgun, M., Manning, C. D., & Ho, D. E. (2025). Hallucination-Free? Assessing the Reliability of Leading AI Legal Research Tools. *Journal of Empirical Legal Studies*, *22*(2), 216–242. DOI: 10.1111/jels.12413

Manakul, P., Liusie, A., & Gales, M. J. F. (2023). SelfCheckGPT: Zero-resource black-box hallucination detection for generative large language models. In *Proceedings of the 2023 Conference on Empirical Methods in Natural Language Processing* (pp. 9004–9017). Association for Computational Linguistics. DOI: 10.18653/v1/2023.emnlp-main.557

Manickam, P., Mariappan, S. A., Murugesan, S. M., Hansda, S., Kaushik, A., Shinde, R., & Thipperudraswamy, S. P. (2022). Artificial intelligence (AI) and internet of medical things (IoMT) assisted biomedical systems for intelligent healthcare. *Biosensors (Basel)*, *12*(8), 562. DOI: 10.3390/bios12080562 PMID: 35892459

Maynez, J., Narayan, S., Bohnet, B., & McDonald, R. (2020). On faithfulness and factuality in abstractive summarization. In *Proceedings of the 58th Annual Meeting of the Association for Computational Linguistics* (pp. 1906–1919). Association for Computational Linguistics. DOI: 10.18653/v1/2020.acl-main.173

McGregor, S. (2026). Welcome to the Artificial Intelligence Incident Database. https://incidentdatabase.ai/

Merken, S. (2025). Trouble with AI 'hallucinations' spreads to big law firms | Reuters. https://www.reuters.com/legal/government/trouble-with-ai-hallucinations-spreads-big-law-firms-2025-05-23/

Merleau-Ponty, M. (2012). *Phenomenology of perception* (Landes, D. A., Trans.). Routledge. (Original work published 1945)

Miller, T. (2019, February). Explanation in artificial intelligence: Insights from the social sciences. *Artificial Intelligence*, *267*, 1–38. DOI: 10.1016/j.artint.2018.07.007

Min, S., et al. (2023). FActScore: Fine-grained Atomic Evaluation of Factual Precision in Long Form Text Generation. *NeurIPS*.

Min, S., Krishna, K., Lyu, X., Lewis, M., Yih, W., Koh, P. W., Iyyer, M., Zettlemoyer, L., & Hajishirzi, H. (2023). FActScore: Fine-grained atomic evaluation of factual precision in long form text generation. In *Proceedings of the 2023 Conference on Empirical Methods in Natural Language Processing* (pp. 12076–12100). Association for Computational Linguistics. DOI: 10.18653/v1/2023.emnlp-main.741

Mir, A. H. (2025). *The geometry of truth: Layer-wise semantic dynamics for Hallucination detection in LLMs*. arXiv. https://arxiv.org/abs/2510.00000

Mishra, A., Molnar, P., & Rüdiger, S. (2025). Robustness and reliability metrics for generative AI models. *ACM Computing Surveys*, *57*(2), 1–38.

Mitchell, E., ... (2024). Quantifying hallucination and faithfulness in large language models. *arXiv preprint arXiv:2402.09723*.

Mittelstadt, B., Russell, C., & Wachter, S. (2019). Explaining explanations in AI. In *Proceedings of the ACM Conference on Fairness, Accountability, and Transparency* (pp. 279–288). DOI: 10.1145/3287560.3287574

Monti, A., Bourgeois-Republique, C., Benfenati, E., & Paini, A. (2025). *The second life of hallucinations: A neurosymbolic framework for transforming errors into insights through human–AI collaboration*. Frontiers in Artificial Intelligence and Applications. DOI: 10.3233/FAIA250685

Morley, M., Floridi, L., Kinsey, L., & Elhalal, A. (2020). From what to how: An initial review of publicly available AI ethics tools, methods and research. *Science and Engineering Ethics*, *26*(4), 2141–2168. DOI: 10.1007/s11948-019-00165-5

Moulaei, K., Yadegari, A., Baharestani, M., Farzanbakhsh, S., Sabet, B., & Reza Afrash, M. (2024). Generative artificial intelligence in healthcare: A scoping review on benefits, challenges and applications. *International Journal of Medical Informatics*, *188*, 105474. DOI: 10.1016/j.ijmedinf.2024.105474 PMID: 38733640

Mozannar, H., Bansal, G., Fourney, A., & Horvitz, E. (2025). *Magentic-UI: Towards human-in-the-loop agentic systems*. Microsoft Research.

Mündler, N., He, J., Jenko, S., & Vechev, M. (2024). Self-contradictory hallucinations of large language models: Evaluation, detection and mitigation. In The Twelfth International Conference on Learning Representations. OpenReview. DOI: 10.48550/arXiv.2305.15852

Nana, V. K., & Marshall, M. T. (2025). Generative Artificial Intelligence in Healthcare: A Bibliometric Analysis and Review of Potential Applications and Challenges. *AI*, *6*(11), 278. DOI: 10.3390/ai6110278

Nastoska, A., Jancheska, B., Rizinski, M., & Trajanov, D. (2025). Evaluating trustworthiness in AI: Risks, metrics, and applications across industries. *Electronics (Basel), 14*(13), 2717. DOI: 10.3390/electronics14132717

National Institute of Standards and Technology. (2024). *Towards a standard for measuring trust in generative AI: NIST AI Risk Management Framework – Generative AI Profile*.

Nazaretsky, T., Mejia-Domenzain, P., Swamy, V., Frej, J., & Käser, T. (2025). The critical role of trust in adopting AI-powered educational technology for learning: An instrument for measuring student perceptions. *Computers and Education: Artificial Intelligence, 8*, 100368. DOI: 10.1016/j.caeai.2025.100368

Nishisako, S., Higashi, T., & Wakao, F. (2025). Reducing Hallucinations and Trade-Offs in Responses in Generative AI Chatbots for Cancer Information: Development and Evaluation Study. *JMIR Cancer, 11*, e70176. DOI: 10.2196/70176

OECD. (2019). AI Principles Overview. https://oecd.ai/en/principles

Okolo, C. T. (2025). Governance of AI-based algorithms. In Xu, W. (Ed.), *Handbook of human-centered artificial intelligence*. Springer., DOI: 10.1007/978-981-97-8440-0_84-1

Okonji, O. R., Yunusov, K., & Gordon, B. (2024). *Applications of Generative AI in Healthcare: Algorithmic, ethical, legal and societal considerations. Preprints*. DOI: 10.36227/techrxiv.171527587.75649430/v1

Open, A. I. (2025). *Why language models hallucinate*. OpenAI Blog. https://openai.com/research

Organisation for Economic Co-operation and Development. (2019). *Recommendation of the Council on Artificial Intelligence* (OECD/LEGAL/0449).

Ouyang, L., Wu, J., Jiang, X., Almeida, D., Wainwright, C., Mishkin, P., . . . Amodei, D. (2022). Training language models to follow instructions with human feedback. arXiv preprint arXiv:2203.02155.

Pagnoni, A., Balachandran, V., & Tsvetkov, Y. (2021). Understanding factuality in abstractive summarization with FRANK: A benchmark for factuality metrics. In *Proceedings of the 2021 Conference of the North American Chapter of the Association for Computational Linguistics: Human Language Technologies* (pp. 4812–4829). Association for Computational Linguistics. DOI: 10.18653/v1/2021.naacl-main.383

Pahune, S., Akhtar, Z., Mandapati, V., & Siddique, K. (2025). The importance of AI data governance in large language models. *Big Data and Cognitive Computing*, *9*(6), 147. DOI: 10.3390/bdcc9060147

Palaniappan, K., Lin, E. Y. T., & Vogel, S. (2024). Global regulatory frameworks for the use of artificial intelligence (AI) in the healthcare services sector. *Health Care*, *12*(5), 562. DOI: 10.3390/healthcare12050562

Palo Alto Networks. (n.d.). *What Are AI Hallucinations? [+ Protection Tips].* Retrieved from https://www.paloaltonetworks.com/cyberpedia/what-are-ai-hallucinations

Pan, X., ... (2025). *Towards reliable large language models: A survey on Hallucination detection.* In *ICIC 2025 Proceedings*. DOI: 10.1007/978-981-95-0014-7_37

Pan, L., Saxon, M., Xu, W., Nathani, D., Wang, X., & Wang, W. Y. (2023). Automatically correcting large language models: Surveying the landscape of diverse automated correction strategies. *Transactions of the Association for Computational Linguistics*, *12*, 484–506. DOI: 10.1162/tacl_a_00660

Papernot, N., McDaniel, P., Sinha, A., & Wellman, M. (2018). SoK: Security and privacy in machine learning. In *Proceedings of the IEEE European Symposium on Security and Privacy* (pp. 399–414). DOI: 10.1109/EuroSP.2018.00035

Patel, A., & Arasanipalai, A. (2021). Applied Natural Language Processing in the Enterprise: Teaching Machines to Read, Write, and Understand. O'Reilly Media., Available online https://www.oreilly.com/library/view/ applied-natural-language/9781492062561/ch01.html, Retrieved May 11, 2021, from.

Patel, V. L., Kaufman, D. R., & Kannampallil, T. G. (2013). Diagnostic Reasoning and Decision Making in the Context of Health Information Technology. *Review of Human Factors and Ergonomics*, *8*(1), 149–190. DOI: 10.1177/1557234X13492978

Peng, B., Narayanan, S., & Papadimitriou, C. (2024). On Limitations of the Transformer Architecture. *arXiv preprint arXiv:2402.08164.*

Phukan, A., ... (2025). *Beyond logit lens: Contextual embeddings for robust Hallucination detection & grounding in VLMs.* In *NAACL 2025 Proceedings*. DOI: 10.18653/v1/2025.naacl-long.488

Pinecone. (n.d.). *Understanding Hallucinations in AI: A Comprehensive Guide.* Retrieved from https://www.pinecone.io/learn/ai-hallucinations/

Preiksaitis, C., & Rose, C. (2023). Opportunities, Challenges, and Future Directions of Generative Artificial Intelligence in Medical Education: Scoping Review. *JMIR Medical Education*, *9*, e48785. DOI: 10.2196/48785 PMID: 37862079

Prolic, R. (2025, November 12). Tools and strategies for detecting AI case citation hallucinations in legal materials. CALL Bulletin. https://bulletin.chicagolawlib.org/2025/11/detecting-ai-hallucinations-in-legal-materials/

Purves, D., Sturm, S., & Madock, J. (2024). What to trust when we trust artificial intelligence (extended abstract). *Proceedings of the AAAI/ACM Conference on AI, Ethics, and Society, 7*(1), 1–5. DOI: 10.1609/aies.v7i1.31713

Pushadapu, N. (2023). Artificial Intelligence for Standardized Data Flow in Healthcare: Techniques, Protocols, and Real-World Case Studies. *Journal of AI-Assisted Scientific Discovery*, *3*(1), 435–474.

Qazi, M. A., Nadeem, M., & Yaqub, M. (2025). *Beyond Generative AI: World Models for Clinical Prediction, Counterfactuals, and Planning* (Version 1). arXiv. DOI: 10.48550/ARXIV.2511.16333

Rabbani, S. A., El-Tanani, M., Sharma, S., Rabbani, S. S., El-Tanani, Y., Kumar, R., & Saini, M. (2025). Generative Artificial Intelligence in Healthcare: Applications, Implementation Challenges, and Future Directions. *BioMedInformatics*, *5*(3), 37. DOI: 10.3390/biomedinformatics5030037

Rahwan, I. (2017). Society-in-the-loop: Programming the algorithmic social contract. *Ethics and Information Technology*, *20*(1), 5–14. DOI: 10.1007/s10676-017-9430-8

Raji, A.. (2020). Closing the AI accountability gap. In *Proceedings of the ACM Conference on Fairness, Accountability, and Transparency* (pp. 33–44).

Raju, T. P. (2024, May). Artificial Intelligence: From Theory to Application and Ethical Considerations. *International Journal for Research in Applied Science and Engineering Technology*, *12*(5), 639–641. DOI: 10.22214/ijraset.2024.59463

Rasheed, K., Qayyum, A., Ghaly, M., Al-Fuqaha, A., Razi, A., & Qadir, J. (2022). Explainable, trustworthy, and ethical machine learning for healthcare: A survey. *Computers in Biology and Medicine*, *149*(Oct), 106043. DOI: 10.1016/j.compbiomed.2022.106043 PMID: 36115302

Raunak, V., Menezes, A., & Junczys-Dowmunt, M. (2021). The Curious Case of Hallucinations in Neural Machine Translation. *Findings of the Association for Computational Linguistics: EMNLP*, *2021*, 1226–1241. DOI: 10.18653/v1/2021.naacl-main.92

Ravichander, A., Ghela, S., Wadden, D., & Choi, Y. (2025). THE HALOGEN BENCHMARK: FANTASTIC LLM HALLUCINATIONS AND WHERE TO FIND THEM. *OpenReview*.

Ribeiro, L. F. R., Liu, M., Gurevych, I., Dreyer, M., & Bansal, M. (2022). FactGraph: Evaluating factuality in summarization with semantic graph representations. In *Proceedings of the 2022 Conference of the North American Chapter of the Association for Computational Linguistics: Human Language Technologies* (pp. 3238–3253). Association for Computational Linguistics. DOI: 10.18653/v1/2022.naacl-main.236

Ribeiro, M. T., Singh, S., & Guestrin, C. (2016). "Why should I trust you?" In *Proceedings of the ACM SIGKDD International Conference* (pp. 1135–1144).

Roberts, L., & Candi, M. (2024, August). Artificial intelligence and innovation management: Charting the evolving landscape. *Technovation*, *136*, 103081. DOI: 10.1016/j.technovation.2024.103081

Rose, N. (2025, November 21). Law firm faces claim over £1.5m paid out of escrow amid AI concern. Legal Futures. https://www.legalfutures.co.uk/?p=147874

Russell, S. (2019). *Human compatible: Artificial intelligence and the problem of control*. Viking.

Rydzewski, N. R., Dinakaran, D., Zhao, S. G., Ruppin, E., Turkbey, B., Citrin, D. E., & Patel, K. R. (2024). Comparative evaluation of LLMs in clinical oncology. Nejm ai, 1(5), AIoa2300151.

Sachan, S., Alsamhi, S. H., Hawbani, A., Shvetsov, A. V., Shvetsova, S. V., & Gupta, S. K. (2025). *Responsible LLM deployment for high-stake decisions by decentralized technologies and human–AI interactions*. In *2025 International Conference on Human-Machine Systems (ICHMS)* (pp. 1–6). IEEE. DOI: 10.1109/ICHMS65439.2025.11154208

Sadeghi R, K., Ojha, D., Kaur, P., Mahto, R. V., & Dhir, A.K. Sadeghi R. (2024, May). D. Ojha, P. Kaur, R. V. Mahto, and A. Dhir, "Explainable artificial intelligence and agile decision-making in supply chain cyber resilience,". *Decision Support Systems*, *180*, 114194. DOI: 10.1016/j.dss.2024.114194

Sahoo, S.. (2024). *A comprehensive survey of Hallucination in large language, image, video and audio foundation models*. arXiv. https://arxiv.org/abs/2410.00000 DOI: 10.18653/v1/2024.findings-emnlp.685

Salehi, P., Ba, Y., Kim, N., Mosallanezhad, A., Pan, A., Cohen, M. C., Wang, Y., Zhao, J., Bhatti, S., Sung, J., Blasch, E., Mancenido, M. V., & Chiou, E. K. (2024). Towards trustworthy AI-enabled decision support systems: Validation of the multisource AI scorecard table (MAST). *Journal of Artificial Intelligence Research*, *80*, 1311–1341. DOI: 10.1613/jair.1.14990

Salinas, E. (2025). Automating hallucination detection with chain-of-thought reasoning—Amazon Science. https://www.amazon.science/blog/automating-hallucination-detection-with-chain-of-thought-reasoning

Sallam, M. (2023). ChatGPT utility in healthcare education, research, and practice: Systematic review on the promising perspectives and valid concerns. *Health Care*, *11*, 887. PMID: 36981544

Sarnaik, T., Shah, M., & Hegde, R. (2025). PROPEX-RAG: Enhanced GraphRAG using Prompt-Driven Prompt Execution. arXiv preprint arXiv:2511.01802.

Saxena, A., & Bhattacharyya, P. (2024). *Hallucination detection in machine generated text: A survey*. arXiv. https://arxiv.org/abs/2401.00000

Seangpraw, K., & Ong-Artborirak, P. (2020). Knowledge and behaviors toward health care for elderly patients with hypertension, and quality of life among informal caregivers in Northern Thailand. *Journal of Multidisciplinary Healthcare*, •••, 1771–1780.

Selvam, P. K., Surendran, R., & Ramkumar, M. (2025). *Human-in-the-loop models for ethical AI grading: Combining AI speed with human ethical oversight*. Salud, Ciencia y Tecnología – Serie de Conferencias, 4, 413. DOI: 10.56294/ai2025413

Sharkey, T., & Sharkey, N. (2012). Granny and the robots: Ethical issues in robot care for the elderly. *Ethics and Information Technology*, *14*(1), 27–40. DOI: 10.1007/s10676-010-9234-6

Shi, W., Han, X., Lewis, M., Tsvetkov, Y., Zettlemoyer, L., & Yih, S. (2024). Trusting your evidence: Hallucinate less with context-aware decoding. In *Proceedings of the 2024 Conference of the North American Chapter of the Association for Computational Linguistics: Human Language Technologies* (Volume 2: Short Papers) (pp. 783–791). Association for Computational Linguistics. DOI: 10.18653/v1/2024.naacl-short.69

Shumba, A. T., Montanaro, T., Sergi, I., Fachechi, L., De Vittorio, M., & Patrono, L. (2022). Leveraging IoT-aware technologies and AI techniques for real-time critical healthcare applications. *Sensors (Basel)*, *22*(19), 7675. DOI: 10.3390/s22197675 PMID: 36236773

Shuster, K., Poff, S., Chen, M., Kiela, D., & Weston, J. (2021). Retrieval augmentation reduces hallucination in conversation. In Findings of the Association for Computational Linguistics: EMNLP 2021 (pp. 3784–3803). Association for Computational Linguistics. DOI: 10.18653/v1/2021.findings-emnlp.320

Shuster, K., Xu, J., Komeili, M., Roller, S., Ju, D., Smith, E. M., . . . Weston, J. (2022). BlenderBot 3: a deployed conversational agent that continually learns to responsibly engage. arXiv preprint arXiv:2208.03188.

Sitaraman, S. R. (2022). Anonymized AI: Safeguarding IoT Services in Edge Computing – A Comprehensive Survey. *Journal of Current Science*, *10*(4).

Skitka, M., Mosier, K., & Burdick, M. (1999). Does automation bias decision-making? *Human Factors*, *41*(1), 50–60.

Song, P., Ojo, A., & Curry, E. (2026). Trustworthy requirements for foundation models—A comprehensive survey and roadmap. *Engineering Applications of Artificial Intelligence*, *163*(Part 6), 113111. DOI: 10.1016/j.engappai.2025.113111

Song, R., Li, X., Zhao, X., Liu, M., Zhou, J., & Wang, F. Y. (2023). Identifying critical test scenarios for lane keeping assistance system using analytic hierarchy process and hierarchical clustering. *IEEE Transactions on Intelligent Vehicles*, *8*(10), 4370–4380. DOI: 10.1109/TIV.2023.3297592

Street, B. (2025). IN THE COUNTY COURT AT BIRMINGHAM.

Sun, L.. (2024). *ReDeEP: Detecting Hallucination in retrieval-augmented generation via mechanistic interpretability*. arXiv. https://arxiv.org/abs/2412.00000

Tabassi, E. (2023a). *Artificial Intelligence Risk Management Framework (AI RMF 1.0) (NIST AI 100-1; p. NIST AI 100-1)*. National Institute of Standards and Technology., DOI: 10.6028/NIST.AI.100-1

Talukder, M. B., Huda, M. N., Kumar, S., & Hasan, Md. M. (2025). Metaverse Future of Digital Medical Tourism: In V. I. Hassan, A. Singh, A. S. Jaboob, & A. Sorayyaei Azar (Eds.), *Advances in Healthcare Information Systems and Administration* (pp. 173–198). IGI Global. DOI: 10.4018/979-8-3693-7888-5.ch007

Talukder, M. B., Kumar, S., & Das, I. R. (2024). Mindfulness of Digital Detoxification: Healthy Lifestyle in Tourism. In Kankaew, K., Chaudhary, S., & Widtayakornbundit, S. (Eds.), (pp. 56–71). Advances in Logistics, Operations, and Management Science. IGI Global., DOI: 10.4018/979-8-3693-1273-5.ch004

Talukder, M. B., Swarna, D. A., Kumar, S., & Kabir, F. (2025). Leveraging Technology for Employee Wellness in Hospitality: Smart Solutions for a Vibrant Service Culture. In Baez, M. D. (Ed.), (pp. 221–246). Advances in Logistics, Operations, and Management Science. IGI Global., DOI: 10.4018/979-8-3373-1687-1.ch008

Tam, W., Huynh, T., Tang, A., Luong, S., Khatri, Y., & Zhou, W. (2023). Nursing education in the age of artificial intelligence powered Chatbots (AI-Chatbots): Are we ready yet? *Nurse Education Today*, *129*, 105917. DOI: 10.1016/j.nedt.2023.105917 PMID: 37506622

Tang, L., Goyal, T., Fabbri, A. R., Laban, P., Xu, J., Mehta, S., Chang, B., Hakkani-Tur, D., & Durrett, G. (2023). Understanding factual errors in summarization: Errors, summarizers, datasets, error detectors. In *Proceedings of the 61st Annual Meeting of the Association for Computational Linguistics* (Volume 1: Long Papers) (pp. 11626–11644). Association for Computational Linguistics. DOI: 10.18653/v1/2023.acl-long.650

Te'eni, D., Schwarz, A., & Newman, M. (2025). What it takes to control AI by design: Human learning. *AI & Society*. Advance online publication. DOI: 10.1007/s00146-025-02401-y

Teo, Z. L., Thirunavukarasu, A. J., Elangovan, K., Cheng, H., Moova, P., Soetikno, B., Nielsen, C., Pollreisz, A., Ting, D. S. J., Morris, R. J. T., Shah, N. H., Langlotz, C. P., & Ting, D. S. W. (2025). Generative artificial intelligence in medicine. *Nature Medicine*, *31*(10), 3270–3282. DOI: 10.1038/s41591-025-03983-2 PMID: 41053447

Terzi, D. S., Terzi, R., & Sagiroglu, S. (2015). A survey on security and privacy issues in big data. *2015 10th International Conference for Internet Technology and Secured Transactions (ICITST)*, 202–207. DOI: 10.1109/ICITST.2015.7412089

The Perpetual Line-Up. (2016). Perpetual Line Up. https://www.perpetuallineup.org/

Thoppilan, R., De Freitas, D., Hall, J., Shazeer, N., Kulshreshtha, A., Cheng, H. T., . . . Le, Q. V. (2022). LaMDA: Language Models for Dialog Applications. arXiv preprint arXiv:2201.08239.

Thorne, J., Vlachos, A., Christodoulopoulos, C., & Mittal, A. (2018). FEVER: a large-scale dataset for fact extraction and VERification. In *Proceedings of NAACL-HLT*. DOI: 10.18653/v1/N18-1074

Tobin, S. (2025). Lawyers face sanctions for citing fake cases with AI, warns UK judge | Reuters. https://www.reuters.com/world/uk/lawyers-face-sanctions-citing-fake-cases-with-ai-warns-uk-judge-2025-06-06/

Topol, E. (2019). *Deep medicine: How artificial intelligence can make healthcare human again*. Basic Books.

UNESCO. (2023). *Guidance on generative AI in education and research.*

University of Oxford. (2024). *Major research into 'hallucinating' generative models advances reliability*. Oxford News. https://www.ox.ac.uk/news

Uppal, S., Bhagat, S., Hazarika, D., Majumder, N., Poria, S., Zimmermann, R., & Zadeh, A. (2022). Multimodal research in vision and language: A review of current and emerging trends. *Information Fusion*, *77*, 149–171. DOI: 10.1016/j.inffus.2021.07.009

van Breugel, B., Liu, T., Oglic, D., & van der Schaar, M. (2024, October). Synthetic data in biomedicine via generative artificial intelligence. *Nature Reviews Bioengineering*, *2*(12), 991–1004. DOI: 10.1038/s44222-024-00245-7

Veale, M., & Borgesius, F. Z. (2021). Demystifying the draft EU Artificial Intelligence Act. *Computer Law Review International*, *22*(4), 97–112. DOI: 10.9785/cri-2021-220402

Viergever, R. F., & Li, K. (2015). Trends in global clinical trial registration: An analysis of numbers of registered clinical trials in different parts of the world from 2004 to 2013. *BMJ Open*, *5*(9), e008932. DOI: 10.1136/bmjopen-2015-008932 PMID: 26408831

Vrdoljak, J., Boban, Z., Vilovic, M., Kumric, M., & Bozic, J. (2025). A Review of Large Language Models in Medical Education, Clinical Decision Support, and Healthcare Administration. *Health Care*, *13*, 603. PMID: 40150453

Wachter, S., Mittelstadt, B., & Russell, C. (2018). Counterfactual explanations without opening the black box. *Harvard Journal of Law & Technology*, *31*(2), 841–887.

Walter, Y. (2024). Managing the race to the moon: Global policy and governance in artificial intelligence regulation—A contemporary overview and an analysis of socioeconomic consequences. *Discover Artificial Intelligence*, *4*, 14. Advance online publication. DOI: 10.1007/s44163-024-00109-4

Wang, X., Wei, J., Schuurmans, D., Le, Q., Chi, E., Narang, S., Chowdhery, A., & Zhou, D. (2023). Self-consistency improves chain of thought reasoning in language models. In The Eleventh International Conference on Learning Representations. OpenReview. DOI: 10.48550/arXiv.2203.11171

Wang, Y., ... (2023). *Hallucination detection for generative large language models by Bayesian sequential estimation*. In *EMNLP 2023 Proceedings*. DOI: 10.18653/v1/2023.emnlp-main.949

Wang, Z.. (2025). *Joint evaluation of answer and reasoning consistency for Hallucination detection in large reasoning models (RACE)*. arXiv. https://arxiv.org/abs/2502.00000

Westover, M. (n.d.). *Human–AI handovers: A dynamic authority reversal framework for trust calibration and transitional accountability*. Manuscript in preparation.

Więckowski, J., Kizielewicz, B., Paradowski, B., Shekhovtsov, A., & Sałabun, W. (2023). Application of multi-criteria decision analysis to identify global and local importance weights of decision criteria. *International Journal of Information Technology & Decision Making*, *22*(06), 1867–1892. DOI: 10.1142/S0219622022500948

Williamson, S. M., & Prybutok, V. (2024). The era of artificial intelligence deception: Unraveling the complexities of false realities and emerging threats of misinformation. *Information (Basel)*, *15*(6), 299. DOI: 10.3390/info15060299

Wong, M. O., & Lee, S. (2023). Indoor navigation and information sharing for collaborative fire emergency response with BIM and multi-user networking. *Automation in Construction*, *148*, 104781. DOI: 10.1016/j.autcon.2023.104781

Wünn, T., Sent, D., Peute, L. W. P., & Leijnen, S. (2023). Trust in artificial intelligence: Exploring the influence of model presentation and model interaction on trust in a medical setting. *Communications in Computer and Information Science*, *1917*, 76–86. DOI: 10.1007/978-3-031-50485-3_6

Wu, Y., Feng, X., Gong, M., Han, J., Jiao, Y., Li, S., Li, T., Shen, C., Wang, H.-Y., Yu, X., Zhang, Z., Zhang, Z., Zhao, Y., Zhou, P., Wang, H., & Zhang, Z. (2023, June). Evolution and major changes of the diagnosis and treatment protocol for COVID-19 patients in China 2020–2023. *Health Care Science*, *2*(3), 135–152. DOI: 10.1002/hcs2.45 PMID: 38939112

Xenoss. (n.d.). *How to prevent AI hallucinations in production*. Retrieved from https://xenoss.io/blog/how-to-avoid-ai-hallucinations-in-production

Xie, Y., Zhou, K., & Ma, X. (2023). Defending ChatGPT against jailbreak attack via self-reminders. *Nature Machine Intelligence*, *5*(12), 1486–1496. DOI: 10.1038/s42256-023-00765-8

Xiong, M., Hu, Z., Lu, X., Liu, Y., Liu, T., Zhang, D., & Hooi, B. (2024). Can LLMs express their uncertainty? An empirical evaluation of confidence elicitation in large language models. In The Twelfth International Conference on Learning Representations. OpenReview. DOI: 10.48550/arXiv.2306.13063

Xu, S. (2025). MEGA-RAG: a retrieval-augmented generation framework with multi-evidence guided answer refinement for mitigating hallucinations of LLMs in public health—PMC. https://pmc.ncbi.nlm.nih.gov/articles/PMC12540348/

Xue, V. W., Lei, P., & Cho, W. C. (2023). The potential impact of ChatGPT in clinical and translational medicine. *Clinical and Translational Medicine*, *13*(3), e1216. DOI: 10.1002/ctm2.1216 PMID: 36856370

Xu, S., Yan, Z., Dai, C., & Wu, F. (2025a). MEGA-RAG: A retrieval-augmented generation framework with multi-evidence guided answer refinement for mitigating hallucinations of LLMs in public health. *Frontiers in Public Health*, *13*. Advance online publication. DOI: 10.3389/fpubh.2025.1635381

Xu, Y., Huang, Y., Wang, J., & Zhou, D. (2024). How do employees form initial trust in artificial intelligence: Hard to explain but leaders help. *Asia Pacific Journal of Human Resources*, *62*(3), 1–18. DOI: 10.1111/1744-7941.12402

Yampolskiy, R. V. (2025). On monitorability of AI. *AI and Ethics*, *5*, 689–707. DOI: 10.1007/s43681-024-00420-x

Yan, E. (2023, September 3). Evaluation & Hallucination Detection for Abstractive Summaries. Eugeneyan.Com. https://eugeneyan.com/writing/abstractive/

Yang, X., Jia, J., Zhou, X., & Wang, S. (2024). The future of artificial intelligence: Time to embrace more international collaboration. *The Innovation*, *5*(6), 100703. DOI: 10.1016/j.xinn.2024.100703

Yu, L., & Zhai, X. (2024). Ethical and Regulatory Challenges of Generative Artificial Intelligence in Healthcare: A Chinese Perspective. *Journal of Clinical Nursing*, jocn.17493. DOI: 10.1111/jocn.17493

Zafar, A., Parthasarathy, V. B., Van, C. L., Shahid, S. M., Khan, A. H., & Shahid, A. (2023). Building trust in conversational AI: Integrating LLMs and knowledge graphs. *Proceedings of the 28th International Conference on Intelligent User Interfaces* (pp. 1–13). DOI: 10.1145/3581641.3584078

Zahid, N., Sodhro, A. H., Kamboh, U. R., Alkhayyat, A., & Wang, L. (2022). AI-driven adaptive reliable and sustainable approach for internet of things enabled healthcare system. *Mathematical Biosciences and Engineering*, *19*(4), 3953–3971. DOI: 10.3934/mbe.2022182 PMID: 35341282

Zanotti, G., Petrolo, M., Chiffi, D., & Schiaffonati, V. (2023). Keep trusting! A plea for the notion of trustworthy AI. *AI & Society*. Advance online publication. DOI: 10.1007/s00146-023-01789-9

Zhang, T., Roller, S., Goyal, N., Artetxe, M., Chen, M., Chen, S., . . . Dinan, E. (2022). OPT: Open Pre-trained Transformer Language Models. arXiv preprint arXiv:2205.01068.

Zhang, K., Meng, X., Yan, X., Ji, J., Liu, J., Xu, H., Zhang, H., Liu, D., Wang, J., Wang, X., Gao, J., Wang, Y., Shao, C., Wang, W., Li, J., Zheng, M.-Q., Yang, Y., & Tang, Y.-D. (2025). Revolutionizing Health Care: The Transformative Impact of Large Language Models in Medicine. [Google Scholar] [CrossRef] [PubMed]. *Journal of Medical Internet Research, 27*, e59069. DOI: 10.2196/59069 PMID: 39773666

Zhang, P., & Kamel Boulos, M. N. (2023). Generative AI in Medicine and Healthcare: Promises, Opportunities and Challenges. *Future Internet, 15*(9), 286. DOI: 10.3390/fi15090286

Zhang, R., Li, H.-W., Qian, X.-Y., Jiang, W.-B., & Chen, H.-X. (2025). On large language models safety, security, and privacy: A survey. *Journal of Electronic Science and Technology, 23*(1), 100301. DOI: 10.1016/j.jnlest.2025.100301

Zhang, Y.. (2024). *Enhancing Hallucination detection through perturbation-based synthetic data generation*. In *Findings of ACL 2024*. Kalai, A., et al. (2025). *Why language models hallucinate*. arXiv. https://arxiv.org/abs/2509.00000

Zhang, Y., Li, J., & Varshney, K. R. (2024). Fairness metrics for generative AI systems. In *Proceedings of the AAAI Conference on Artificial Intelligence* (pp. 13421–13429).

Zhang, Y., Li, Y., Cui, L., Cai, D., Liu, L., Fu, T., Huang, X., Zhao, E., Zhang, Y., Chen, Y., Wang, L., Luu, A. T., Bi, W., Shi, F., & Shi, S. (2024). Siren's song in the AI ocean: A survey on hallucination in large language models. *Computational Linguistics, 50*(4). Advance online publication. DOI: 10.1162/COLI.a.16

Zha, Y., Yang, Y., Li, R., & Hu, Z. (2023). AlignScore: Evaluating factual consistency with a unified alignment function. In *Proceedings of the 61st Annual Meeting of the Association for Computational Linguistics* (Volume 1: Long Papers) (pp. 11328–11348). Association for Computational Linguistics. DOI: 10.18653/v1/2023.acl-long.634

Zhou, J., ... (2025). *HaDeMiF: Hallucination detection and mitigation in large language models*. In *ICLR 2025 Proceedings*

Zhou, T., & Lu, H. (2024). The effect of trust on user adoption of AI-generated content. *The Electronic Library*. Advance online publication. DOI: 10.1108/EL-08-2024-0244

About the Contributors

Baisakhi Das is a Professor in the Department of Information Technology at the Institute of Engineering & Management, Kolkata, India. She earned her Ph.D. (Engineering) and M.Tech degrees from the Indian Institute of Engineering Science and Technology (IIEST), Shibpur, and holds a B.Tech from the West Bengal University of Technology, India. With over 19 years of academic experience, Dr. Das has established herself as a committed educator and researcher. Her primary research interests include Blockchain, Artificial Intelligence, and Cellular Automata. She has published extensively in international journals, conferences, and edited book volumes. Dr. Das has actively contributed to the academic community through her roles as a Technical Program Committee (TPC) member at various international conferences and as a reviewer/editorial board member for several international journals. She has also served as organizing chair, co-convener, and committee member for multiple international conferences. She is a senior member of IEEE, reflecting her dedication to advancing research and collaboration in emerging technologies.

Thinagaran Perumal was awarded the 2014 Early Career Award by the IEEE Consumer Electronics Society for his pioneering contributions to the field of consumer technologies. He obtained his PhD from Universiti Putra Malaysia, specializing in smart technology and robotics. Currently, he is an Associate Professor and serves as the Head of the Department of Computer Science at the Faculty of Computer Science and Information Technology, University Putra Malaysia. Additionally, he holds the position of Chair of the IEEE Consumer Technology Society Malaysia Chapter. Dr. Thinagaran's research focuses on Interoperability in Smart Homes and the Internet of Things (IoT), wearable computing, and cyber-physical systems. His notable contributions include the development of proactive IoT architectures, cognitive and semantic IoT frameworks for smart homes, and wearable technology for rehabilitation purposes. Since 2018, he has been leading the

National Committee on Standardization for IoT (IEC/ISO TC/G/16) as Chairman. He is also actively involved in the IEEE Consumer Technology Society and its Future Directions Committee on IoT, contributing to the advancement of emerging technologies. Dr. Thinagaran has been invited to deliver keynote speeches and plenary talks on IoT at various international institutions and organizations. He has received four Best Paper Awards, delivered over 20 keynote speeches, and participated in five panel discussions at renowned global conferences.

Satyajit Chakrabarti, is a Professor, Technologist, Software Developer, Content Creator, Author, Serial Entrepreneur and Venture Capitalist. He obtained his PhD in Nanotechnology from the National Institute of Technology and Masters in Computer Science from the University of British Columbia. Prof. Chakrabarti manages companies in the field of Technology, Healthcare and Education. He is an avid philanthropist and social Entrepreneur and runs non profits and two educational Universities and five colleges in India in the fields of Engineering, Management, Hospitality, Law, Healthcare with over 10,000 students and over 100,000 alumni. His Technology companies work with big multinational companies to deliver products and services in the fields of Artificial Intelligence, Internet of Things, Virtual and Augmented Reality, Cybersecurity and Web Development. Prof. Chakrabarti is a passionate researcher with over 100 publications in the fields of Artificial Intelligence, IOT and Data Science and over 20 patents filed in various fields of Technology. Prof. Chakrabarti is an avid investor in early stage startups and a mentor and teacher to thousands of students across the globe. Prof. Satyajit Chakrabarti is very passionate about technology, Innovation, entrepreneurship, clean energy, nature and sustainability, renewable energy, learning technologies and education, media, design, arts and culture. His special expertise includes Angel Investment, Venture Capital and Private Equity, Investments, Management Consulting, Strategic Management, Technology Applications, Problem Solving using innovation and innovative technologies.

Kouichi is engaged in research and development on cryptography and information security at the Computer and Information Systems Laboratory at Mitsubishi Electric Corporation from 1988 to 1994. From 1994, Joined to work for the Dept. of Computer Science of Kyushu University in the capacity of associate professor, and became a full professor there in 2002. Also worked with the Institute of Systems & Information Technologies and Nanotechnologies as the chief of the Information Security Laboratory, aiming to foster collaboration between industry, academia, and government under the theme "Enhancing IT Security in Social Systems." From 2005 to 2006, he successfully led a Cooperative International Research Project supported by the National Institute of Information and Communications Technology

(NICT), facilitating cooperation on security technologies between Japan, China, and Korea. Furthermore, in March 2006, he initiated a groundbreaking partnership in information security by signing a Memorandum of Understanding with Professor Bimal Kumar Roy, marking Japan's first collaboration with the Cryptology Research Society of India (CRSI). Was a member of JST-DST SICORP " SECURITY IN THE INTERNET OF THINGS SPACE" with IIT Delhi (2016-2022). Also he was working with MOFA as a part of Memorandum of Cooperation between the Ministry of Human Resource Development of India and the Ministry of Foreign Affairs of Japan concerning Indian Institute of Information Technology, Jabalpur, visit to give Intensive lectures three times (2017, 2018, 2019). This collaboration evolved into the JSPS Japan-India Bilateral Joint Research Project " Investigation of power of Deep Neural Networks against various adversarial attacks and their applications to Cybersecurity " (Kyushu Univ and IIIT-dmj, 2022-2023)."

George A. Papakostas received the Diploma, M.Sc., and Ph.D. degrees in electrical and computer engineering from the Democritus University of Thrace (DUTH), Greece, in 1999, 2002, and 2007, respectively. He has 15 years of experience in large-scale systems design as a Senior Software Engineer and a Technical Manager. He is the Head of the Machine Learning and Vision (MLV) Research Group. He is a tenured Full Professor with the Department of Informatics, Democritus University of Thrace, Greece. He has (co)authored more than 240 publications in indexed journals, international conferences, book chapters, one book (in Greek), two edited books, and six journal special issues. His publications have over 4500 citations with an H-index of 36 (Google Scholar). His research interests include machine learning, computer/machine vision, pattern recognition, and computational intelligence. Prof. Papakostas is a member of the ACM, IAENG, MIR Laboratories, EUCogIII, and the Technical Chamber of Greece (TEE). He is a reviewer in numerous journals and conferences.

***

Hilda Afeku-Amenyo is a PhD researcher at Montclair State University. She develops applied AI solutions for climate resilience and sustainable finance, creating data pipelines and risk analytics tools that translate environmental and financial complexity into transparent, equitable decision-support systems for community-centered investment.

Sapana Agicha is a Postdoctoral Research Fellow in the Department of English at Shri Govind Guru University, Godhra. Her research explores the intersection of New Materialism and Post-Humanism, especially in Contemporary American

Fiction. She is currently investigating the cli-fi genre in Indian Contemporary Novels. Her work has been published in journals such as Glocal Publications and Langlit.

Emmanuel I. Archibong is a Senior Faculty member, Lecturer and Researcher in the Department of Philosophy, University of Uyo, Nigeria. He specialises in Philosophy of Science with foundation in Metaphysics. His area of research interests span across Climate Issues, Biomedical Issues, Developmental Studies as well as Gender Studies. He has several published articles in reputable journals indexed in Scopus and Web of science.

Firoj Kabir is a researcher, Lecturer of the Department of "Tourism and Hospitality Management" at the Daffodil International University, Dhaka, Bangladesh, with a solid academic background in BBA and MBA majoring in Tourism and Hospitality Management from the University of Dhaka. His passion lies in exploring the intersection of travel and culture. His diverse areas of interest include archaeological tourism, sustainable tourism, and the unique characteristics of Generation Z travelers. Through extensive research and insightful writing, he sheds light on the intricate connections between historical sites, responsible tourism, and the evolving preferences of the next generation of travelers. His work not only enriches the field of tourism but also inspires readers to engage with the world around them in meaningful and responsible ways.

Shikha Khullar is an academic researcher and author with expertise in artificial intelligence, emerging technologies, and their applications across interdisciplinary domains. Her research interests include AI governance, ethical AI, intelligent systems, and technology-driven societal transformation. She has contributed scholarly work to international journals, edited volumes, and conferences, focusing on responsible and high-impact applications of AI.

Sanjeev Kumar Is a Professor in Lovely Professional University Punjab India. He received Undergraduate in Hotel Management from Osmania University, Postgraduate in Tourism Management from Madurai Kamaraj University. He completed Doctor of Philosophy in Hospitality Management in 2019 from Amity University Jaipur India. His research areas lies in food Service Industry, his research focuses on Alcoholic beverages, Event management and Sustainable Management Practices, Metaverse, AI Machine Learning and Artificial Intelligence. He published more than 80 research papers, articles and chapters in Scopus Indexed, UGC Approved and peer reviewed Journals and books. Dr. Sanjeev Kumar participated and acted as resource person in various National and International conferences, seminars, session chair, research workshops and industry talks and his work has been widely cited. Dr. Sanjeev also edited more than 20 books with various International

Publishers such as IGI Global, Cambridge Scholars, Emerald, CABI, Bentham Science, Taylor & Francis. Dr Sanjeev is an active researcher and has published numerous research articles in prestigious National and International journals and books.

Nguyen Le My Kim earned her Master's degree in Law from Southwest University of Political Science and Law in Chongqing, China, from 2018 to 2020. She is currently a lecturer in the Law Department at the University of Economics and Law, part of Vietnam National University in Ho Chi Minh City. Her research interests include human rights, environmental law, and feminism, among others.

Bekzod Madaminov serves in the Department of General Professional Sciences at Mamun University, Khiva, Uzbekistan. His academic and professional pursuits focus on enhancing the quality of higher education through innovative pedagogical practices and interdisciplinary approaches. With a strong commitment to fostering academic excellence, he actively contributes to curriculum development, student mentorship, and research in applied sciences and education. His scholarly interests encompass modern educational methodologies, sustainable academic frameworks, and skill-oriented learning models that align with the evolving demands of contemporary academia. Through his teaching and research endeavors, Mr. Madaminov continues to play a vital role in promoting intellectual growth and professional competence among students and colleagues alike.

Anirban Mitra (Ph.D. in Science & Technology—Computer Science) is currently associated with the School of Computing and Information Technology, Eastern International University (Ho Chi Minh City, Vietnam). He previously served as a Professor of Computer Science and Engineering in the School of Engineering and Technology at Amity University Kolkata, India. He is a Senior Member of IEEE and a Member of ACM. His academic and professional interests include data-driven systems, social network analysis, and knowledge graph applications. He is actively engaged in teaching, mentoring student research, and developing industry-relevant curricula. He also contributes to the scholarly community through research publications, peer review, and academic collaboration.

Musam venkata siva kumar graduated in Information Technology from JNTU in the year 2006. I have started my career as a QA analyst in 2008 from nisum technologies and learned the QA concepts and applied those in the work. I have learned more about web applications and their functionality and architecture to perform the QA role.

Nagendra Kumar Musham has Bachelor's Degree in Electrical and Electronic Engineer from Acharya Nagarjuna University (2005). Currently working as Senior Software Developer at Celer Systems Inc.

Subrata Paul is currently working as Assistant Professor and Departmental Examination Coordinator of Department of CSE-AI, School of Engineering at Brainware University and is also a PhD scholar under MAKAUT. He had completed his B.E(CSE) from VTU – Belgaum, Karnataka in 2010 and M.Tech (CS) from Berhampur University in the year 2013. His research area includes Social Network Analysis, Computational Intelligence and Cloud Computing. He has authored 10 books that were published by national and International Publishers. He has 53 publications at national and international levels, both in journals, conferences and book chapters. He is also a reviewer of few referred Journals. He is a member of several Professional Associations like ACM, ICSES, SDIWC etc. He had an experience of nearly 14 years in teaching undergraduate courses and 4 year in handling post graduate classes.

Amitava Podder is an Assistant Professor with expertise in Artificial Intelligence, Image Processing, Computer Networking, and the Internet of Medical Things (IoMT), possessing extensive academic and industry experience. Holds Bachelor's and Master's degrees in Computer Science and Engineering and is pursuing a Ph.D. Authored scholarly books, published extensively in reputed venues, and holds patents in smart devices and IoT-based innovations, demonstrating a steadfast commitment to research and innovation.

Namita Rath, MA (PMIR), MBA (HR), MPhil, PhD, is an Associate Professor in Organizational Behavior & Human Resource Management at the Sri Sri University, Cuttack, India. She did her PhD in Personnel Management Industrial Relations from Utkal University. She has teaching experience of over 20 years in business schools with bachelor's and master's programmes. She has published 33 papers in Scopus, ABDC, UGC Listed and peer reviewed indexed journals, and 12 book chapters along with 3 books to her credits. She presented papers at different National and International Conferences. Her research interests include Organizational Behavior, Industrial Relations and Talent Management. She is currently guiding three doctoral candidates.

Piyal Roy is an accomplished academician in the field of Computer Science & Engineering. He has completed his BSc in Computer Science, MSc in Computer Science and MTech in Computer Science & Engineering. Currently, he is working as an Assistant Professor at Computer Science & Engineering department at Brainware University, India.

Alok Kumar Sahai, is a graduate of Indian Institute of Management Bangalore and obtained his PhD in Behavioural Finance from the National Law University Jodhpur. Presently, he is an associate professor in the Faculty of Management at Sri Sri University, Cuttack. His research interests include Behavioural Finance, Psychology of Commodity Markets and Consumer Behaviour.

S. P. Santhoshkumar received the Bachelor's Degree in Electronics and Communication Engineering from Anna University, Chennai in 2006, the Master's Degree in Software Engineering from Anna University of Technology, Coimbatore in 2011, and the Philosophy of Doctorate degree in Information and Communication Engineering from Anna University, Chennai in 2024, respectively. He is currently working as an Assistant Professor (SG) at the Department of Computer Science and Engineering, School of Computing, Vel Tech Rangarajan Dr. Sagunthala R&D Institute of Science and Technology, Avadi, Chennai. His research areas include Machine Learning, Cloud Computing, Deep Learning, Software Engineering and Web Development. He has quality of publications to his credit, including Journal Articles, Conference Publications, Patents, Books and Book Chapters. Also, he received best faculty awards in national level.

Poonam Sharma, Professor of Information Technology with 21+ years of academic experience. My research areas include AI and Data Science, with over 20 research publications and 6 book contributions. I have actively contributed to the academic community through conferences, seminars, and research-oriented activities.

Swati Sood is a graduate of IGNOU, Bhopal and is pursuing a Ph.D in Management/ IT from Pacific University, Rajasthan. Presently, she is working as faculty in BIITM, Bhubaneswar, and is associated with various institutes as visiting faculty. Her research interest includes Information Technology, Artificial Intelligence and General Management.

Vishal Sood, is a graduate of IMS, DAVV, Indore and obtained a Ph.D in Finance from DAVV, Indore. Presently, he is a Professor in the Faculty of Management Studies at Sri Sri University, Cuttack. His research interests include Behavioral Finance, Commodity & Stock Markets, General Management and Human Resource Management.

Mohammad Badruddoza Talukder is an Associate Professor & Chairman at the College of Tourism and Hospitality Management at the International University of Business Agriculture and Technology (IUBAT) in Dhaka, Bangladesh. Holding a PhD from Lovely Professional University, India, he is renowned for his innovative integration of cutting-edge technologies such as Artificial Intelligence (AI), the Internet of Things (IoT), and Blockchain into tourism and hospitality management. His research explores the transformative impact of these technologies on smart tourism, cloud kitchens, and the broader industry landscape. As a prolific author, Dr. Talukder has published numerous scholarly articles and books, with forthcoming titles that address AI innovations in hospitality, the evolution of cloud kitchens, and the enhancement of digital literacy within hospitality education. His work shapes contemporary tourism and hospitality practices, skillfully marrying technological advancements with practical industry applications. Since 2008, Dr. Talukder has imparted his knowledge through a diverse array of courses in tourism and hospitality across various universities in Bangladesh.

Somesh Varandani is a dynamic communication professional with a strong foundation in journalism, mass communication, event management, and organizational operations. He holds a Master's degree in Journalism and Mass Communication, along with a Post-Graduate Diploma in the same field from Indira Gandhi National Open University. Additionally, he completed a PGDEM in Event Management and PR from the National Academy of Event Management & Development, Jaipur, reflecting his diverse academic background and keen interest in media and events. Somesh has built a multifaceted career across education, banking, media, and event industries. He is currently serving as an Admission & Outreach Associate at Poornima University, Jaipur, where he specializes in admissions counseling, outreach coordination, student engagement, and promotional communication. Previously, he worked as a Training & Placement Officer at Poornima Group, handling placement coordination, student interactions, reporting, and academic activity management. Before joining the education sector, Somesh gained significant experience in the banking industry as a Branch Digital Officer and Branch Money Officer with AU Small Finance

Kirti Varandani is a visionary architect and academician based in Jaipur, Rajasthan, whose work reflects a deep commitment to sustainable design and innovative urban development. With over eight years of combined experience in architecture, interior design, and academia, she has established herself as a thoughtful designer and educator dedicated to creating spaces that blend functionality, aesthetics, and environmental responsibility. Kirti completed her Master of Design (M.Des.) in Sustainable Design from Vivekananda Global University, Jaipur (2019–2021), where she specialized in sustainable architectural practices and green building concepts. She also holds a Post-Graduate Diploma in Urban Planning and Development from Indira Gandhi National Open University (IGNOU) and a Bachelor of Architecture (B.Arch.) from Jagannath University, Jaipur (2009–2014).

Her academic foundation has been enriched through various professional training programs, workshops, and certifications focused on sustainable architecture, daylight optimization, and green building standards. Currently, Kirti serves as an Assistant Professor (Guest Faculty) at the Faculty of Design, Banasthali Vidyapith, where she teaches design subjects in the Interior Design Department. Previously, she held faculty positions at Vivekananda Global University (VGU), Jaipur, and the Apex Group of Institutions, Jaipur, where she taught architecture and interior design. Her teaching philosophy centers on encouraging students to approach design as a social, cultural, and ecological process—aimed at improving human well-being and environmental health. Before entering academia, Kirti gained substantial professional experience in architectural practice. She worked as an Architect with SNG Group, Jaipur, where she was responsible for preparing architectural and landscape drawings, designing internal services, and overseeing large residential projects such as Samriddhi, Krishnangan, Shree Enclave, Shivangan, and Dusad Garden. She also worked as a Trainee Architect at Sanidhya Design Consultancy Pvt. Ltd., Jaipur, collaborating on residential and commercial projects for prominent developers such as Dhanuka Group, Anukampa Group, and Pink City Consortium. Her earlier professional experiences at Design Core Consultancy and Khilnani Associates helped her refine her technical proficiency and design sensibility. Kirti's portfolio includes a wide range of architectural and interior projects—residences, educational institutions, offices, and hospitality spaces. Some notable works include the Residence cum Hospital at Jaipur, Boys' Hostel at MPUAT Bhilwara, Dev Group of Colleges at Jaipur, and Landscape proposals for farmhouses and resorts across Rajasthan. Her commitment to sustainable architecture is evident in her research publications, including papers in the EPRA Journal (2021) on Optimization of Daylight in Museums and Art Galleries and Impact of Green Roofs on Heating and Cooling in Different Climatic Zones of India. An active learner and researcher, Kirti has participated in numerous professional development programs, including workshops on Griha Rating and Certification, Affordable Housing, and Daylighting Simulation by ECBC. She was also recognized with the Built Today Architectural Journalism Award (2010) for her contribution to architectural writing. Beyond her professional achievements, Kirti finds inspiration in teaching, continuous learning, and sustainable innovation. Her vision is to contribute to the development of eco-conscious design education and to inspire the next generation of architects to create spaces that harmonize human needs with environmental balance.

Rushil Varma obtained an MA in Psychology and an MBA from Lucknow University and is presently working BBD University and completed his Doctoral degree at Amity University, Lucknow. He has research interest in Psychological contracts, High-performance works systems and Job Crafting.

Index

A

C

D

E

www.ingramcontent.com/pod-product-compliance
Lightning Source LLC
LaVergne TN
LVHW062324300926
849161LV00007B/1566